Fingers crossed

Britain Alone!

European Monograph Series

VOLUME 96

Editor

Prof. Andrea Biondi is Professor of European Law and Director of the Centre of European Law at King's College London

Introduction & Contents/Subjects

As the process of European integration assumes an increasingly complex character, the EU legal system continues to undergo sweeping changes. The European Monographs series offers a voice to thoughtful, knowledgeable, cutting edge legal commentary on the now unlimited field of European law. Its emphasis on focal and topical issues makes the series an invaluable tool for scholars, practitioners, and policymakers specializing or simply interested in EU law.

Objective

The aim is to publish innovative work appealing to academics and practitioners alike. The result is an original and ongoing library of detailed analyses, theories, commentaries, practical guides, and proposals, each of which furthers the cause of meaningful European integration. Cumulatively, the series may be regarded as a 'work in progress' engaged in building a sharply defined representation of law in Europe.

Readership

Academics and practitioners dealing with EU law.

The titles published in this series are listed at the end of this volume.

Britain Alone!

The Implications and Consequences of United Kingdom Exit from the EU

Edited by

Patrick J. Birkinshaw
Andrea Biondi

Wolters Kluwer

Published by:
Kluwer Law International B.V.
PO Box 316
2400 AH Alphen aan den Rijn
The Netherlands
Website: www.wklawbusiness.com

Sold and distributed in North, Central and South America by:
Wolters Kluwer Legal & Regulatory U.S.
7201 McKinney Circle
Frederick, MD 21704
United States of America
Email: customer.service@wolterskluwer.com

Sold and distributed in all other countries by:
Turpin Distribution Services Ltd
Stratton Business Park
Pegasus Drive, Biggleswade
Bedfordshire SG18 8TQ
United Kingdom
Email: kluwerlaw@turpin-distribution.com

Printed on acid-free paper.

ISBN 978-90-411-5832-1

Printed in the United Kingdom.

Editors

Andrea Biondi is Professor of European Union Law and the Director of the Centre of European Law at King's College London. Prof. Biondi is also Visiting Professor at the College of Europe in Warsaw and at Bocconi University in Milan.

Patrick J. Birkinshaw is Professor of Public Law and Director of the Institute of European Public Law, Hull University and Editor of *European Public Law*.

Table of Contents

Foreword

This book contains a fascinating collection of contributions on the possible withdrawal of the United Kingdom from the European Union.

As is made clear, the issue of withdrawal, even for the most impartial observer, may have profound constitutional implications for the United Kingdom itself: possibly for its very survival as a United Kingdom, since doubts may arise about Scotland, Wales and Northern Ireland; and in any event for its internal constitutional arrangements.

And across many fields of law and policy where the Member States of the European Union are now part of an interwoven fabric, difficult questions will arise.

The decision, if it is for withdrawal, will be only the starting point. Indeed, the contributions to this book bring home one of the essentials: that withdrawal from the EU, if it occurs, will raise a great variety of important issues – social, economic, political, constitutional, legal – which will still need to be resolved.

Moreover, many of these are vital issues which may need to be resolved, after the decision, by negotiation with the EU and its Member States of the terms of withdrawal – and above all, by agreement on the extent of re-engagement with the EU. To take just three examples, it can be assumed that the issues will include continued access, on some basis, to the European internal market; the role of UK financial services, as the key element in the UK's economy, in relation to the Eurozone and to European capital markets; and cooperation and interaction on the environment, a subject of possibly even more fundamental importance for the future of us all.

The choice offered in the referendum between 'remaining in the EU' and 'leaving the EU' is therefore perhaps misleading. Although there is no relevant precedent, to leave the EU, as has been said elsewhere, is not exactly like leaving a golf club.

A further, more fundamental question might have been whether a referendum is the appropriate method of taking such a decision. It is still a rather novel method of decision-making in the UK, and insofar as it might be hoped that it would resolve the issue definitively, the recent example of the Scottish referendum is not reassuring.

In any event, all will, it is hoped, agree that the decision should be based on informed debate. This book therefore serves a potentially very valuable service, with expert contributions on a wide range of crucial issues.

Francis G. Jacobs
Professor of Law at King's College, London and
Jean Monnet Professor

Introduction

Patrick J. Birkinshaw & Andrea Biondi

By the end of the current United Kingdom Parliament in May 2020, that Parliament and the people of the United Kingdom will have addressed some of the most momentous constitutional issues facing our society in fifty years, possibly a century. These questions will involve an In/Out referendum on the EU, the British (United Kingdom) bill of rights and the future of the European Convention on Human Rights, further devolution, and the question of English-only MPs voting for English laws. Unlike Blair's government which enjoyed huge majorities in the House of Commons and which presided over major constitutional changes in the UK the present Conservative Government has a modest Commons' majority of twelve in the new Parliament, and is likely to face considerable difficulties in the House of Lords, especially in its European measures. One only has to recall the difficulties faced by John Major with a Commons majority of twenty-one in 1992, gradually whittled away by 1997 and his Parliamentary battles over Europe. We expect interesting times. They began immediately after the Queen's Speech in May 2015.

In terms of the UK's global position, the most important question is our membership, or otherwise, of the European Union. The UK has been a member of that Union and its predecessors, the EEC and EC, since 1973. This book examines the implications of withdrawal from the EU. Also up for scrutiny could be our membership of the European Convention on Human Rights. The UK was one of the founding members of the Council of Europe, which produced the ECHR. The Council has as its core mission the promotion of human rights, democracy and the rule of law through the continent. The UK ratified the ECHR in 1951 and accepted individual petition to the Court of Human Rights in 1966. The attack on the ECHR, and particularly the European Court of Human Rights as well as the UK Human Rights Act 1998 which implemented much of the ECHR, has been as sustained as those on the EU. This theme is referred to in several contributions but the focus in this book is on withdrawal from the EU.

While our relationship with the Union has often been a strained one, several factors have combined to curdle domestic perspectives on the UK's relationship with Europe. Sovereignty, or rather loss of sovereignty, has been a persistent complaint.

Loss of power, over regulation and bureaucratic expansionism have been other long-standing gripes. Being different, never really trusting European initiatives or initiatives in Europe and harping back to halcyon days of a self-sufficient Commonwealth were often repeated. Complaints grew of loss of commercial freedom and enterprise, loss of autonomy in international trade negotiations and loss of resources such as fisheries. The UK opted out of Union policies, in particular those of monetary union and the Schengen Agreement on abolition of internal border controls, and the non-Union financial stability measures although it was not alone in these opt outs. The pre-Lisbon Justice and Home Affairs provisions on criminal law were opted out off only for the more important measures to be opted back into.

To these were added complaints of a Union that somehow transmuted from an economic union and a common market to a fully fledged political union claiming not just political sovereignty but also legal sovereignty including sovereignty over national constitutions. These latter themes are unravelling in the top courts of Member States as we write. There is no doubt, however, that the Union absorbed more and more characteristics of a multi-nation state so that federalism was often used to describe the relationship between the members and the union. These developments were accompanied by, what some saw as, increasingly interventionist social and employment policies including Union citizenship and human rights protection as well as a Union criminal law to protect an area of freedom, security and justice. While some saw these as the necessary corollaries of societies working more closely together and consequential residence rights based on free movement, others deeply resented what they chose to view as globalised alienation.

As so often in the UK's past, immigration came to be seen as a cause of deep felt discontent and a subject on which it is easy to foment nationalist fears. Now the threat was not from the new Commonwealth but from the new members of the EU, especially Eastern Europe. These fears were fanned by political parties. Both Labour and Conservative parties had significant anti-EU elements but the emergence of a populist and anti immigration party UKIP (United Kingdom Independence Party) initially appeared to eat into the Conservative vote. It subsequently became a threat to Labour. There is no need to recount the well-known UKIP onslaught on Europe. UKIP spoke on behalf of the frustrations of swathes of English voters who felt threatened by globalisation and accompanying immigration with effects on employment, wage restraint, public services and housing. The ideological anxieties of UKIP were echoed by Conservative Party politicians who were fearful of UKIP inroads into Conservative constituencies.

In January 2013, David Cameron outlined his ideas for EU treaty reform which he then hoped to negotiate successfully with EU partners before putting the results to an in/out referendum vote for the British people.[1] In his speech, Cameron argued for a

1. https://www.gov.uk/government/speeches/eu-speech-at-bloomberg. The European Union Act 2011 had already made a referendum a requirement before the UK could agree to an amendment of the Treaty on European Union or of the Treaty on the Functioning of the European Union; or before the UK could agree to certain decisions already provided for by TEU and TFEU transferring power to the EU.

Union of greater competition, flexibility, choice, openness, diversity, repatriation of powers, democratic accountability and fairness. 'I have no illusions of the scale of the task ahead.'

Subsequently, the most publicised change was in freedom of movement of EU workers[2] and a desire as expressed in some quarters to 'reclaim our borders'. By 2015, the Conservative Party manifesto for the general election contained the following proposals for restrictions on EU freedom of movement: EU workers would have to earn for 'a number of years' in the UK before receiving benefits such as tax credits which top up low wages and child benefit; there would be no job-seeking benefits for EU job seekers; there would be residency requirements for social housing; restrictions on unemployment benefit; return of EU workers after six months if unemployed; restrictions on child benefit and child tax credits where children are living abroad; stronger powers facilitating deportation and preventing re-entry will be introduced – although one should note Eurosceptic opposition to the European Arrest Warrant making extradition easier! There will be tougher penalties for those abusing free movement provisions. Non-EU spouses will face restrictions on joining EU spouses with income thresholds and language tests. Free movement rights will not apply to new Member States until their economies have converged more closely with 'existing Member States'. Generally, immigration law and enforcement will be strengthened.

Most of those proposals are unlikely to be welcomed by the other EU partners. The governing provisions on Union citizenship and free movement are well-established principles that guarantee to confer lawfully on EU migrant citizens the right to equal treatment with nationals in the host state.[3] If the UK negotiated a change in EU law to legitimise any proposed reforms to free movement, changes in secondary law would be subject to scrutiny by the ECJ. If the objective was a reform agreed with all other Member States by a change in the treaty this would be likely to meet with overwhelming opposition. If the UK left the EU then preservation of free movement and residence rights – EU citizenship would no longer apply under Article 20 TFEU – would depend upon the arrangements with the other members of the EU that the UK could successfully negotiate. If a status quo ante were to be sought to protect the rights of UK citizens then it is difficult to see what advantage the UK would gain from Brexit unless it only applied to existing arrangements and did not cover future arrangements.[4]

2. See David Cameron's JCB Staffordshire Speech November 2014. https://www.gov.uk/government/speeches/jcb-staffordshire-prime-ministers-speech.
3. Although both secondary legislation and recent case law of the Court (Case C-333/13 *Dano*, ECLI:EU:C:2014:2358 leave some degree of discretion to Member States as far as access to public benefits and welfare support are concerned. See also Case C-67/14 *Alimanovic* [2015] EUECJ (15/09/15). See also on prisoners' voting rights *Thierry Delvigne v. Commune de Lesparre-Médoc etc* [2015] EUECJ C-650/13 (6 Oct 2015).
4. If the EU has not irreversibly vested the nationals of the Union with a legal heritage of rights including free movement and residence [see J Herbst *German Law Journal* (6:2005) 1755 and *Leaving the EU* Research Paper 13/42 (July 2013) House of Commons Library] then the UK and EU would have to negotiate a transitional period to protect vested rights such as free movement and residence. Art. 50 TEU exists for the purpose of 'taking account of the framework for [a state's] future relationship with the Union' (see chapter six). This occurred when Greenland left the EEC in 1975. In the absence of such an agreement, Greenland retained the 'substance' of free

The refugee crisis in the summer of 2015 showed David Cameron's resistance to EU based solutions to an international problem. Cameron insisted on a distinctly British approach to the crisis. The ongoing crisis is testing European solidarity to its limits. It is a catastrophe together with terrorism threatening the continuation of the Schengen agreement itself. The scheme to deal with quotas allocating refugees to Member States announced by the President of the EU Commission in September 2015 seemed unlikely to apply to the UK.

Along with the above manifesto promises on free movement came calls for a 'red card' policy for national Parliaments or perhaps groups of Parliaments to veto EU legislation; exemption from the 'ever closer Union' Treaty provision; but in the latter case the point was suggested that exempting the UK from such a treaty provision might be accompanied by loss of a veto power in the Council; preserving our trade negotiating rights at the international level irrespective of an EU competence; boosting competiveness and reducing 'red tape': guaranteed protection for the UK and its access to the common market and non-discrimination against the UK for its non-membership of the Eurozone. In October 2015, the EU state leaders requested the desired reforms be put in writing. Cameron's letter to the President of the EU Council in November 2015 seemed modest. Nevertheless, it met with a hostile reaction from members of his own party.

With Brexit becoming the largest single issue to affect the United Kingdom's place in the world, the Centre of European Law, King's College University of London and the Institute of European Public Law of the University of Hull organised a Conference in May 2014 at Senate House University of London. The conference theme was 'Britain Alone! The Implications and Consequences of United Kingdom Exit from the European Union.' The theme became the title for our jointly edited book. We are grateful to Lisa Zoltowska and Kluwer Law International for their generous support and encouragement for this conference.

Many of the presentations of that day are updated and have been included in this edited volume. Several new contributions have also been added. Brexit was becoming the biggest issue in the oncoming election – although it was somewhat muted in the

---

movement rights for workers from the EEC in Greenland but as the Commons paper explains '[the Commission] did not say whether the rest of the EU should retain these rights for workers from Greenland.' (p 15). Future membership of the EEA and EFTA and the implications for free movement agreements are examined in chapter twelve.

In the absence of any transitional or special treaty arrangements then under international law, withdrawal from a treaty releases the parties from any future obligations to each other 'but does not affect any rights or obligations acquired under it before withdrawal': see *Leaving the EU* above and citations. In other words vested or acquired rights are retained.

In terms of non-EU, EEA and Swiss nationals the UK has not signed up to the Schengen arrangements on visas and border controls and it is not 'automatically bound by EU legislation on border controls, non-EU immigration and asylum': *Leaving the EU* above p. 67. The UK has not opted into the recast directives on asylum but is bound by the legislation adopted in the first phase of 2000–2005. The UK has opted into the revised Dublin regulations on preventing asylum shopping and which establish hierarchically which state should have responsibility for processing a claim.

In the case of non-EU/EEA/Swiss entrants to the UK the existing legal restrictions on entry and immigration would still apply. See Piris Chapter 6 *infra*.

immediate months before the run-up to the election in 2015. Indeed, polls suggested an increasing support for European membership among UK voters after the 2015 election.[5] Polls, however, had not had a good election.

The May 2015 election led to a Conservative majority of twelve in the House of Commons. In the event, only one UKIP MP was elected to Parliament despite 3,881,099 (12.6 pc of the total) UK votes. The election result meant that a referendum on membership of the European Union would take place by 2017 – pressure immediately grew for such a referendum to take place within 2016. The European Union Referendum Bill was introduced in the House of Commons and faced its second reading on 9 June 2015. The Committee stage, as a committee of the whole House, took place on 16 June.

The question initially proposed to be put to those entitled to vote in the referendum (the electorate is that of a UK Parliamentary general election with modifications allowing peers to vote as well as Commonwealth and Irish Republic citizens in Gibraltar) will be: 'Should the United Kingdom remain a member of the European Union?' Following a recommendation from the statutory Electoral Commission it was agreed to change the wording to one which did not, the Commission believed, favour a vote in favour of the status quo. The Commission recommendation was: 'Should the United Kingdom remain a member of the European Union or leave the European Union?'

Factors that could well arise on possible amendments include the following. Should there be a fixed majority in favour of 'No' to take effect? Should there be majorities in favour of leaving in all UK countries, and what of Gibraltar? Should the age of voting be reduced for the referendum to 17 or 16? An immediate question was whether Government ministers should abide by a collective decision in favour of voting 'Yes' – David Cameron's stated preference – or whether they would be allowed a free vote. Would the government refrain from campaigning for a 'Yes' vote which would involve deployment of the resources of the state in the month before the referendum? Confusion and attempted clarification and the prospect of dramatic divisions over amendments inevitably arose. A government proposal to relax the so-called 'purdah' rules before the EU referendum was defeated in the Commons.[6] The rules provide for restrictions on government publicity and publicly funded communications favouring one position for up to twenty-eight days before polling day (see p. 10). There were thirty-seven Conservative MPs who helped defeat the government. There should be little doubt that many politicians and citizens will see the ensuing months as a battle to the death over Europe. We have only been able to trace events until January 2016. A development in September saw the largest British trade union, Unite, warn that any negotiated settlement between David Cameron and EU partners leaving a reduction in employment rights would be opposed by the Union. This outcome could influence its members to vote against continuing EU membership it warned.

5. *Financial Times* 3 June 2015, p. 6. By September 2015 polls suggested a tiny minority in favour of leaving the EU.
6. HC Debs Col 78 et seq (7 September 2015). The restriction is contained in s. 125 Political Parties, Elections and Referendums Act 2000. Section 125(3) contains exceptions.

The attack on Europe was not aimed solely at the EU. The ECHR had also been subjected to vitriolic criticism. Should the UK be unable to persuade our partners in the Council of Europe of changes in the ECHR to satisfy the UK government, then not only would membership of the ECHR be brought to termination; our membership of the Council of Europe would also be placed in doubt. In June 2015, the Foreign Secretary stated that leaving the ECHR was not an option. The Prime Minister's Press Office memorandum on the Queen's Speech of May 2015 spoke of bringing 'forward proposals for a Bill of Rights to replace the Human Rights Act' restoring 'common sense' to human rights laws while protecting existing rights 'which are an essential part of a modern, democratic society' and which would give better protection against abuse. With the prospect of widespread opposition to repeal of the HRA, proposals will be subject to yet further consultation.

One has to acknowledge that the pro-European initiative has been waning. The efforts and vision required to bring Europe back from catastrophe post-1945 are now consigned to history. So too are the memories of more recent European dictatorships and Soviet hegemony in Member States. Events in the Ukraine have rekindled memories of the latter. The EEC and its successors have produced peace in western Europe for sixty years and assisted in the transformation of thirteen former dictatorships to EU members since 1980. But the craving for European peace and security that impelled economic integration over sixty years ago seems no longer there. It is too early to assess the effects of terrorist outrages on European unity or disunity. European disunity is no response to global dilemmas.

The Eurozone crisis has been a sickening blow to economic prosperity as well as the reputation of the EU; although the proverbial green-shoots may be emerging in some member states, in others crisis management appears endemic. The Commission and European Central Bank together with Germany and the International Monetary Fund have been associated with austerity measures that have been accused of bringing the European ideal to its knees and overriding national democratic will. Where lies the balance between supranationalism and national democratic will? The refugee crisis outlined above has stretched solidarity to breaking point.

What, however, are the benefits of the Union? 'What, in other words, has Europe done for us?'[7] Not much, argued one commentator, apart from providing 57% of our trade, structural funding to areas hit by industrial decline, clean beaches and rivers, cleaner air, lead free petrol, restrictions on landfill dumping, cheaper mobile charges, cheaper air travel, improved consumer protection and food labelling, a ban on growth hormones and other harmful food additives, better product safety, single market competition bringing quality improvements and better industrial performance, break up of monopolies, Europe-wide patent and copyright protection, no paper work or customs throughout the Union, price transparency and removal of commission on currency exchanges throughout the Eurozone, freedom to travel, work and live across the Union, funded opportunities for young people to undertake placements abroad, access to European health services, labour protection and enhanced social welfare,

7. The following is from Simon Sweeney *Letters The Guardian* 12 January 2013.

smoke-free work places, equal pay legislation, holiday entitlement, the right not to work more than a 48-hour week without overtime, the strongest wild-life protection in the world, improved animal welfare in food production, EU funded research and industrial collaboration, EU representation in international forums, bloc EEA negotiation at the World Trade Organization, Freedom, Security and Justice measures necessary for security and safety, support for democracy and human rights and anti-trafficking across Europe and beyond and contributing to better living standards and educational, social and cultural capital.

The EU has provided a platform on which the UK can make its contribution to the resolution of global problems that can only be successfully tackled collectively. The editors view the benefits of these achievements positively. Counter arguments will be advanced in the ensuing debate and referendum.

David Cameron was not alone in suggesting that a referendum on European membership would be necessary. The then Labour leader Ed Miliband qualified his assurance on a referendum stating this would occur if there were a further transfer of powers to the Union. The Liberal Democrats came to support a Union referendum despite their avowed support for the European Union. Above all the rhetoric there was a sense that the argument had to be addressed that the people of the United Kingdom had not agreed in the 1975 EEC referendum to the European Union of 2015 and that the narrative was no longer the same. The changes required approval by plebiscite. We do not know whether all the contributors to this book agree with such a plebiscite or not. We believe, however, that all would agree that now that it is to take place the people should vote on full, impartial and undistorted information on the pros and cons of continuing membership. The debate was supposed to be informed by the Coalition Government's Balance of Competencies' Review between the EU and Member States. This was hailed by the government as the most extensive analysis ever undertaken of the UK's relationship with the EU. The House of Lords Select Committee on the EU described the thirty-two reports as 'ambitious' and 'unprecedented' and 'for the most part' 'fair and neutral assessments'. But the reports had not been well publicised and contained, the committee reported, omissions and displayed over-emphasis of the government position.[8]

It is not only on the global level that we face enormous uncertainty. The future of the UK as an integrated union of four countries has also been brought into question.

8. Below *Twelfth Report* paras 25–28. These points are developed in chapter five. The coalition government's 'balance of competencies' review, announced in July 2012, on EU and national competencies was significantly downplayed by the government. Such a response from the government was heavily criticised by the House of Lords EU Select Committee (HL 140 (2014-15 *Twelfth Report*)). If the review was intended to inform public debate '[T]his seems an unrealistic aim, as long as the public are unaware of the Review's existence.' [Para 57] 'The lack of balance in the Single Market: Free Movement of Persons, Animal Health and Welfare and Food Safety and Fisheries reports, and the undue weight given to evidence reflecting the Government's own position, is a disappointing blemish on the Review as a whole.' [Para 28] The Treaty of Lisbon (TEU and TFEU), for the first time in an EEC/EC/EU treaty, listed the 'exclusive' competencies conferred on the EU by member states together with competences shared with member states, coordinated economic policies and supporting, coordinating or supplementing competences: TFEU Arts 2-6. Member states retain competences not conferred upon the Union: TEU Art. 4.

The Scottish independence referendum question, like that of Europe, has not disappeared. The response to a Scottish decision not to secede from the Union in September 2014 was greeted with a call in some quarters for the promotion of England as a devolved country in its own right with its specific devolved powers including an English Parliament making English legislation. David Cameron's response advocated English only MPs in the Commons voting on English bills (English votes for English laws), or English and Welsh MPs only [E & W] voting on English and Welsh only subjects. Such a reform presumes that the entity of an 'English only bill' or 'English and Welsh only bill' can be readily identified.

Would such a measure passed into law benefit from the constitutional principle of Parliamentary sovereignty around which so much of Brexit enthusiasts rally? The concept of 'English' is a limiting one which cuts across sovereignty. It is inherently confined. The press release accompanying the Queen's Speech referred to a change being brought about by Standing Orders of the House of Commons, not legislation. Opposition to such a change in Standing Orders appeared intially to grow among government supporters. Such a method may be seen as an attempt to avoid litigation. This is far removed from the question before the Appellate Committee of the House of Lords in *Attorney General v. Jackson.*[9] Here the House of Lords Appellate Committee had to rule on the legality of the Parliament Act 1949, and legislation passed thereunder, which enhanced the position of the House of Commons in the legislative process while reducing that of the House of Lords by restricting the duration of the latter's veto powers.

Why in principle should bills for England alone [or E & W], passing through selective procedures, differ from those of the devolved legislatures? The latter bills have to be within legislative competence and not contrary to EU or ECHR law. They may be prevented from being submitted for Royal Consent where they contain, inter alia, provisions which are incompatible with international obligations. It should be noted that E or E & W bills have to be certified by the Speaker as being 'within devolved legislative competence'. This is a justiciable term of art and invites legal challenge. Unlike Parliament Act Bills, or indeed all other public bills, English [or E & W] bills will not be put to the whole Commons in *all* stages of the bill procedure but only to a part of that chamber. Here we would argue that a part of the chamber cannot replace the whole. Earlier models involving English-only MPs [or E & W] would have confirmed our view. However, the model set out in the Conservative Party Manifesto does not use an exclusively English-only [or E & W] procedure.[10] English-only [or E & W] MPs will

9. [2005] UKHL 56. See Lord Thomas in *Recovery of Costs for Asbestos Diseases (Wales) Bill* [2015] UKSC 3 esp paras 119–126.
10. *The Conservative Party Manifesto 2015*, p. 70. https://s3-eu-west-1.amazonaws.com/manifesto2015/ConservativeManifesto2015.pdf.
The Commons Procedure Committee raised the subject of English votes for English laws in 1999: HC 814 (1998-99) paras 7–10. The use of standing orders to bring about E or E&W votes is not a new proposal. It is also perceived as an antidote to the long identified 'West Lothian Question' whereby Scottish, Northern Irish or Welsh MPs in Westminster may vote on purely English matters whereas English MPs in Westminster cannot vote on devolved issues in devolved Parliaments. The Commons Procedure Committee reported in July 2015 'The Committee is satisfied that certification by the Speaker in pursuit of Standing Orders of the House

sit at various stages, i.e., at the Committee stage to examine bills in detail after second reading and at a Grand Committee after report at which a consent to legislate motion will be put. Thereafter it will go to a third reading of all the House for a vote and to the Lords. This combination of procedures appears to have been crafted in the hope of avoiding questions of sovereignty being raised in the courts. The Order addresses the procedure for Bills commencing in the Lords and statutory instruments.

As we write the UK Supreme Court has joined its EU counterparts in asserting a domestic constitutional space or identity for 'UK constitutional questions'. The judgments of two recent domestic cases argue for a national primacy in constitutional litigation involving domestic constitutional interpretation of questions containing an EU element.[11] The UK government and Parliament have every reason to be cautious of judicial intervention in matters constitutional . This involves questions of whether a 'statute' is law, as in *Jackson,* or whether legislation is to all intents inviolable. Interesting questions remain to be addressed and resolved in domestic and EU jurisprudence (see Chapter 1).

The chapters which follow address the major concerns and uncertainties associated with Brexit. We commence with the impact that our European Union experience has had on the UK constitution. The subject of Brexit is then examined from a Scottish, Northern Irish and Welsh perspective. The constitutional questions and implications of a referendum are analysed. In Part II concerned with 'managing alone?' the question 'Why Leave?' is posed and examined. The implications for environmental law and the complications associated with negotiating treaties are explored. The chapters from then on cover Brexit and opting out in the areas of judicial protection, EU criminal law, immigration, equality, labour rights and the EU Charter of Fundamental Rights. The final chapters in Part II cover aspects of financial and economic governance: state aids and the single supervisory mechanism and banking regulation.

We are delighted with the quality of the contributions and the level of argument and detail that the authors have brought to this discussion. We are grateful to all of them. We cannot claim comprehensive coverage of all issues and possibilities involved in a departure from the European Union. Indeed, the enormity of those issues and possibilities makes the prospect of Brexit daunting.

The editors wish to record their gratitude and appreciation for the assistance in this project of Maria Kendrick who is also one of the contributing authors. We are also grateful once again to Liza Zoltowska for her patience and unstinting support in helping us realise and bring to fruition this project together with the support of Christine Robben and Kluwer Law International.

should not be subject to any form of review in the courts. Since it is for the courts to determine the application of Article IX Bill of Rights ... the Committee cannot rule out the possibility that a determined challenger to a certification might be granted leave to apply for judicial review or succeed in the application.' Procedure Committee *English Votes for English Laws Standing Orders: Interim Report* Summary HC 410 (2015-16). See Hansard HC Debs 22 October 2015, cols 1159 et seq. See Cabinet Office *English Votes for English Laws* July 2015 https://www.gov.uk/government/uploads/system/uploads/attachment_data/file/441848/English_votes_for_English_laws_explanatory_guide.pdf.

11. Chapter 1 pp. 21-27.

We have been able to track developments until 17 December 2015. By mid-December, the EU Referendum Bill had passed all Parliamentary stages. An attempt to lower the voting age to include 16 and 17 year olds failed. The government re-introduced powers to relax the 'Purdah' rules (above p. 5) allowing ministers to make press and media statements on routine EU business in the run-up to the referendum. Lords' amendments placing a duty on the government to report on the outcome of negotiations with member states on the UK's concerns regarding EU membership, as well as the government's opinion on what was agreed, were accepted. Also accepted was a duty on the government to publish a report on rights and obligations arising from EU membership and arrangements agreed with non-EU member states by the EU. The reports have to be published at least ten weeks before the date of the referendum. The outcome of discussions at the EU summit on 17–18 December 2015 is outlined in a postscript to Chapter 6 (Jean Claude Piris). At proof stage we were able to add that David Cameron allowed a ministerial free vote on in or out of the EU despite the government policy of negotiating terms supporting an in vote. The freedom to campaign against collective government policy arises after the terms of renegotiation are agreed.

Part I Constitutional Issues

CHAPTER 1

Britain Alone Constitutionally: Brexit and *Restitutio in Integrum*

Patrick J. Birkinshaw & Mike Varney

§1.01 INTRODUCTION

In this first chapter, we set out to examine the lasting legacy of UK membership of the European Union (EU), and to a lesser extent the European Convention on Human Rights (ECHR), on the UK's constitution and public law. Suffice to say forty three years ago there was very little that was *judicial* in our constitutional law. The common law of judicial review was in a comparative adolescence despite a three hundred year, and sometimes proud,[1] heritage. Law in context courses adopted the view that to concentrate on the courts in UK constitutional law would be to give a completely inaccurate view of our constitution. 'It has been a particular weakness of public law in the United Kingdom in the past that this is exactly what has happened.'[2] The fact that government could do what any other individual could do, and infinitely more besides under statutory and prerogative powers, did not encourage judicial examination of governmental legitimacy. If we were to leave the Union, and for good measure the Council of Europe,[3] what lasting constitutional and legal legacies would the European experience leave us?

We will set out briefly how, and to what extent, the constitution has become judicialised and how legality (dare one say legitimacy?) has become a key principle.

1. On the sometimes proud heritage *see*: S. Sedley, *The Sound of Silence: Constitutional Law without a Constitution*, in *Ashes and Sparks* Ch. 7 (2011) and S. Sedley *Lions Under the Throne: Essays on the History of English Public Law* (2015); P. Craig *UK, EU and Global Administrative Law* (2015).
2. G. Wilson p. V *Cases and Materials on Constitutional and Administrative Law* (2nd ed. 1976).
3. *See European Human Rights – A Force for Good or a Threat to Democracy?* Lord Phillips Centre of European Law, King's College London 17 Jun. 2014. *See* S. Boyron (2016) 1 *European Public Law* 149 on analysis of judicial speeches and judgments on 'Europe' by UK judges.

How sovereignty and our constitution have changed and how our public law has been enriched by European influence. Let us start with three positions on Community and Union law.

§1.02 THREE POSITIONS

> 'Community law has little direct effect on the ordinary life of private citizens. In so far as it imposes obligations, it does so mostly in relation to industrial and commercial activities and does not touch citizens in their private capacities. Our basic legal system and legal methods will remain unchanged.' [OFFICIAL REPORT, House of Lords, 8th May, 1967; Vol. 282, c. 1203, Lord Gardiner, Lord Chancellor.]

> 'In future, in transactions which cross the frontiers, we must no longer think of English law as something on its own. ... This means a great effort for the lawyers. We have to learn a new system.' Lord Denning *Bulmer v. Bollinger* [1974] 2 All ER 1226 at 1232 b

> 'My views on matters European are well known. British justice is the envy of the world, and I will not countenance any attempt to replace it with a pan-European justice system. It would be entirely wrong for Britain to hand over control of Justice and Home Affairs entirely to the European Union or its Court of Justice and, under this Government, that is not going to happen ...' [7 April 2014 Column 87]

> '... I am clear that I do not want, and will not tolerate, the idea of us becoming part of a Europeanised justice system.' [Ibid, Column 93] Justice Secretary Grayling.[4]

It is a movement from complacency and misunderstanding, to endeavour and to contempt. Is the next phase in our relationship with Europe to be determined by uncertainty and prevarication? If the UK voted to leave the EU it would present this country with a position of unprecedented complexity in relation to unravelling laws, rights and privileges emerging from well over forty years of supranational engagement and partnership.

§1.03 THE CONSTITUTIONAL CHANGES

> Jacob Rees-Mogg: 'My right hon. Friend is fully aware that Parliament can overrule any court in this country by an Act of Parliament. That is how our constitution works; it is the absolute essence of our constitution and our democracy.' [HC debs 7 April 2014 Column 64]

> 'If it is not our judges – who are subject to our democratic control – who make decisions, we will not be able to run our own affairs.' [Column 66]

However, in a separate passage Rees-Mogg invested our judges in our courts with the ability to interpret international treaties replacing the EU treaties – a denial of dualism he so fervently espouses elsewhere![5]

Our first thesis is that sovereignty has changed under European influence. This is at the heart of political populist outrage against the EU. But sovereignty is often used in

4. http://www.publications.parliament.uk/pa/cm201314/cmhansrd/cm140407/debtext/140407-0001.htm#14040711000001.
5. *See ibid.* Column 65. On the changing focus of sovereignty arguments on Europe, *see* G. Gee & A.L. Young (2016) 1 *European Public Law* 131.

a simplistic sense. It may mean the most powerful or hierarchically most superior. It may relate to territorial integrity, the definition of nation or nationality, the conditions for the existence of an independent state and citizens of that state, or the power to conduct international negotiations on behalf of the state. Much of the Eurosceptic UK focus has been upon the legislative omnipotence of the Crown in Parliament and the inability of anyone else to overrule or set aside that legislation. Sovereignty of one class of laws over another does not entail *overall* sovereignty (below). The UK, it is argued, gave away sovereignty without the people or Parliament being properly informed and without an opportunity prior to 1973 to vote through a referendum on the transfer. Will ending membership of the EU return sovereignty back to the UK and, if so, return sovereignty [what kind?] to whom?

It is clear that our presence in Europe has led to a qualification of legislative sovereignty. Several judges have also spoken of a 'twin sovereignty' of the Crown in Parliament and the Crown it its courts.[6] Sir John Laws, echoing Professor Hart,[7] wrote twenty years ago that sovereignty resides in the *conditions* under which the exercise of governmental powers operate (including we add government control of Parliament) and not in the exercise of those powers.[8] The implications have to be made explicit, he wrote, 'as a framework of fundamental constitutional principles'. This, it appeared, was the task for a common law constitution. The implications of this statement are addressed in this chapter.

Limitation (transfer) of sovereign rights or 'supremacy' was effected under the terms of the 1972 European Communities Act (ECA), which incorporated the jurisprudence of the European Court of Justice (ECJ) including its famous case law on supremacy and direct effect.[9] That was legal supremacy within the competences of the then European Economic Community (EEC) and successive treaties. In Declaration No. 17 Treaty of Lisbon supremacy is now styled 'primacy'. The change in word as well as the detail in drafting, especially from the EU Constitutional Treaty, is not without significance. In the field occupied by EU law, national law must cede pride of place. In the UK, we have arrived at a position where constitutional principles and laws cannot be displaced in the way that legislation, regulations or case law may be. We discuss this below.

The UK's 2011 European Union Act (an Act to reassert sovereignty?) states that any directly applicable or effective EU law was effected via an act of Parliament (section 18). What Parliament gives Parliament may take back. The 2011 Act, it has been argued, itself establishes a new form of self-embracing sovereignty in so far as Parliament has bound its future action on many Union initiatives to a popular referendum. Bogdanor has argued that the people are now a constituent part of Parliament.[10] Taking treaty changes, for instance, section 2(1) provides that a treaty

6. Lord Bridge in *X v. Morgan-Grampian* [1990] 2 All ER 1 at 13 (HL), Nolan LJ in *M v. Home Office* [1992] 4 All ER 98 at 146 (CA), Lord Mustill in *R v. Secretary of State for the Home Department ex p Fire Brigades' Union* [1995] 2 All ER 244, 267-68 (HL).
7. *The Concept of Law* (1961).
8. Sir John Laws (1995) *Public Law* 72 at 92.
9. Case 6/64 *Costa v. ENEL* [1964] ECR 545 and Case 26/62 *van Gend en Loos* [1963] ECR 1.
10. V Bogdanor (2012) 32 OJLS 179.

amending or replacing the TEU or TFEU is not to be ratified until a statement has been laid before Parliament in accordance with section 5, Parliament has approved the treaty and the referendum or exemption condition is satisfied.[11] Under section 2(2), the referendum condition is that:

> (a) the Act providing for the approval of the treaty provides that the provision approving the treaty is not to come into force until a referendum about whether the treaty should be ratified has been held throughout the United Kingdom or, where the treaty also affects Gibraltar, throughout the United Kingdom and Gibraltar;
> (b) the referendum has been held, and
> (c) the majority of those voting in the referendum are in favour of the ratification of the treaty.

If the go-ahead for an exit referendum is given by 2017 and Parliament proceeds to an Act authorising exit we will see assertions of the proof of the continuing sovereignty of Parliament. But is Parliament 'sovereign' in the way it was in 1972. Has that sovereignty been changed, changed utterly, and taken a new embodiment?

§1.04 DID THE UK LOSE SOVEREIGNTY?

It still appears remarkable that in 1972 Parliament seemed unaware of the extent of the principles of sovereignty, or supremacy, and direct effect of the ECJ's jurisprudence. It was not really until *Factortame No. 2* (1990) (and the *EOC* case (1994)) that the penny dropped.[12] But even *Factortame* recognised a new reality that the UK had through its executive and Parliament willingly agreed to. Not only must domestic courts disapply domestic legislation, or parts of it, which contravene EU law, but courts had to fashion the application of remedies against the Crown, or correctly officers of the Crown in their official capacity, which the House of Lords had only recently rejected (wrongly as it subsequently transpired under domestic law).[13]

We remain of the view that this was 'revolutionary' – a reflection of a state of affairs 'voluntarily' taken on board. Was it simply the adaptation of the rule of recognition of ultimate legal validity by judicial development or was it a belated recognition of something completely new? The latter seems more appropriate. However, that 'newness' of *Factortame* is approaching its quarter centenary since the judgment. And it has developed. *Factortame* sparked the original debate; but the debate has continued, shifted and excavated more deeply as we describe. Even if Parliament is still sovereign, it is not sovereign in the manner in which it was in 1972.

We are not aware of *cases* prior to our recent past which have actually put questions to the *nature* of Parliamentary sovereignty. Medieval philosophy that had made no fine distinction between law and morality and which had placed the King

11. Sections 3–10 cover other revisions, decisions, etc. requiring Parliamentary approval and possible referendum. Exemption conditions are contained in section 4(4).
12. Case C 213/89 *R v. Secretary of State for Transport ex p Factortame Ltd (No. 2)* [1991] 1 All ER 70 (CJEC & HL); *Equal Opportunities Commission v. Secretary of State for Employment* [1994] 1 All ER 910 (HL).
13. *M v. Home Office* [1993] 3 All ER 537 (HL).

under the law, but with no means of human enforcement of that subordination short of murder, would not do in an age requiring certainty and stability through Parliament – a *Leviathan*.[14] Coke's utterances against acts of Parliament repugnant to nature[15] gave way to Dicey's strictures on the interpretation of statutes in accordance with private and international morality. But no judge could refuse to obey the clear words of a statute.

So the decision by Sir John Laws in the Metric Martyrs case on the unlawful sale by imperial weights (under EU – then EC – requirements) of market produce is a landmark. It put questions to sovereignty. Parliament was sovereign because the common law said so. In saying so, it put limits on what Parliament could do. EU law could not become entrenched because Parliament could not entrench laws. The common law placed limits on implied repeal of 'constitutional statutes' but not express or unequivocal repeal:

> Parliament cannot bind its successors by stipulating against repeal, wholly or partly, of the ECA. It cannot stipulate as to the manner and form of any subsequent legislation. It cannot stipulate against implied repeal any more than it can stipulate against express repeal. Thus there is nothing in the ECA which allows the Court of Justice, or any other institutions of the EU, to touch or qualify the conditions of Parliament's legislative supremacy in the United Kingdom. Not because the legislature chose not to allow it; because by our law it could not allow it. That being so, the legislative and judicial institutions of the EU cannot intrude upon those conditions. The British Parliament has not the authority to authorise any such thing. Being sovereign, it cannot abandon its sovereignty. Accordingly there are no circumstances in which the jurisprudence of the Court of Justice can elevate Community law to a status within the corpus of English domestic law to which it could not aspire by any route of English law itself. This is, of course, the traditional doctrine of sovereignty. If it is to be modified, it certainly cannot be done by the incorporation of external texts. The conditions of Parliament's legislative supremacy in the United Kingdom necessarily remain in the United Kingdom's hands. But the traditional doctrine has in my judgment been modified. It has been done by the common law, wholly consistently with constitutional principle.[16]

Laws LJ's famous dicta conceal as much as they reveal (below). The dicta in *Thoburn* (paragraphs 58–70) were re-visited and cited with approval in the highly significant *HS2* case, discussed below.

And in *Jackson*, the House of Lords decision on the powers of the Parliament Acts, the European dimension to our constitution, it was stated, had placed limits on Parliamentary sovereignty and the common law constitution would not allow fundamental interference with those limitations. The interference would of course be by a Parliamentary chamber dominated by the executive. The dominance of the representative chamber should not be an excuse for *unbridled* executive domination. Limits on

14. *See* J.W. Gough, *Fundamental Law in English Constitutional History* OUP (1955).
15. *See* Gough at pp. 35–36 on *Bonham's* case.
16. *Thoburn v. Sunderland City Council* [2002] 4 All ER 156 paragraph 59. *See HS2* below and *H v. Lord Advocate* [2012] UKSC 24 per Lord Hope on support for 'constitutional' statutes.

such a use have been explained in several cases following *Jackson* such as *AXA Insurance*, in the latter in relation to a non-sovereign Scottish Parliament.[17]

AXA is important in setting out the common law limits on a legislative body where fundamental rights and the rule of law are abused. The ratio, to repeat, is about a devolved parliament. Why should anything Lords Reed and Hope say on such a legislative assembly not apply rationally to Westminster? What today, we ask, gives a democratic legislative body, voting through a majority of its members, power deliberately to abuse human rights and the rule of law? A doctrine developed historically to provide certainty and stability in troubled domestic politics should not be allowed to authorise breaches of internationally and widely agreed norms of human rights and access to justice. The court in *AXA* ruled there could be no judicial common law review of Scottish primary legislation on grounds of irrationality or unreasonableness. Courts were not to be surrogate legislators.

In an extra-judicial capacity, Lord Bingham (who gave a conventional judgment in *Jackson*) wrote in support of a traditional doctrine of Parliamentary sovereignty:

> The British people have not repelled the extraneous power of the papacy in spiritual matters and the pretensions of royal power in temporal in order to subject themselves to the unchallengeable rulings of unelected judges. A constitution should reflect the will of a clear majority of the people, and a constitutional change of the kind here contemplated [judicial control of legislation] should be made in accordance with that will or not at all. As was put by a MP in 1621: 'the judges are judges of the law, not of Parliament. God forbid the state of the kingdom should ever come under the sentence of a judge.[18]

Lord Hope has observed that the fact that Parliament may legislate on any subject does not mean that the judges will accept whatever is enacted. In a chapter in a recent book[19] entitled 'Is the Rule of Law now the Sovereign Principle' he writes:

> The absence of a general power to strike down legislation which [Parliament] has enacted does not mean that the courts could never fashion a remedy for use in an exceptional case when the survival of the rule of law itself was threatened because their role as the ultimate guardians of [the rule of law] was being removed from them. (p. 97).

What does the common law of sovereignty consist of? Is it simply what a judge or judges think are the appropriate limits on executive/legislative action? How does it function in specific detail? What are the consequences of refusing to enforce a provision in legislation which is repugnant to the rule of law, if that is what Lord Hope

17. *AXA General Insurance v. Lord Advocate* [2011] UKSC 46; though *see* Lord Hope at paragraphs 42–50 and Lord Reed at paragraphs 140–153. *See* J. Jowell 'Parliamentary Sovereignty under the New Constitutional Hypothesis', (2006) *Public Law* 562.
18. T. Bingham, *The Rule of Law* (2010) at p. 168 citing J. Goldsworthy, *The Sovereignty of Parliament* (1999) at p. 103. Lord Hope in R. Rawlings, P. Leyland & A. Young eds, *Sovereignty and the Law* (2013) Chapter 6 p. 97. *See* Lord Neuberger, *Who is the Master Now?* April 2011 https://www.judiciary.gov.uk/Resources/JCO/Documents/Speeches/mr-speech-weedon-lecture-110406.pdf – but *see* Neuberger (2014) at http://supremecourt.uk/docs/speech-141010.pdf.
19. *Sovereignty and the Law* above.

has in mind? Where stands the official who acts under the provision and who seeks to invoke the measure to protect him or herself from legal actions? What limits are placed on judges? Can they really defy the clearest of Parliamentary formulations in statute? Is it restricted to interference by the executive through Parliament of the rule of law and fundamental right as *AXA* suggests?

The Common law constitution from which Laws LJ received his inspiration is an uncertain beast. It reminds us of that constant resort to 'fundamentalism and fundamental right' in the ancient constitution of England of which we were recently reminded when it was recalled how a matter remained a 'constitutional right' even though no law embraced it. Someone, somewhere, felt an immanent sense of rightness.[20] Fine in sentiment but devil and detail?

§1.05 COMMON LAW CONSTITUTIONALISM

'Common law' takes various meanings. It might be argued that the common law constitution represents that system of rule and governance imposed by the Normans on England and which adapted, developed and centralised the governing techniques and legal methodology of the Anglo Saxons. Lacking incorporation in any one document, it is fluid and dynamic. It represents(ed) the accepted system of rule and law in England and later was extended to other territories. At its origins are a relationship between the King (Sovereign), his Council and the sovereign's means of doing justice through his judges and courts. The King has to rule through his Council and administer justice via his judges. This is what makes the King sovereign. But he is not alone. Institutional complexity characterises the process of governance and eventually we see the three estates in institutionally representative bodies together with the Crown. Together they, and what they produce officially, represent the 'State' – that *locus* of official power.

Institutional complexity inevitably leads to tensions between competing claims to sovereignty. Even assuming that sovereignty is an indivisible concept, the common law emerged in a context in which sovereignty was qualified. The Church and Canon law made their claims to sovereignty which made the Church very unpopular with political elites from the twelfth century onwards. The sovereign power of the King is confined in a series of Charters, initially unsuccessfully so. The most important clashes occur between the Crown as sovereign and Parliament, especially the Commons. What emerges ultimately, and what is given judicial endorsement, is the sovereignty of the Crown in Parliament and the legislative sovereignty and omnipotence of that entity. Just as with its precursors, the doctrine that dominated our constitutional landscape arose from the common law. It built on, but did not remove, those foundations.

The fact that this outcome, sovereignty and omnipotence, has been accepted for several hundred years by the judges legally does not mean that it represents the end of the common law journey. Nor should it be overlooked that sovereignty was heavily qualified in the common law system as outlined above. The king was below the law but

20. J. Goldsworthy, *Parliamentary Sovereignty: Contemporary Debates* (2010) p. 315. *See* Gough *supra* n. 14.

was not susceptible to the jurisdiction of those courts which reflected his own sovereignty.

We argue that a source of contemporary confusion rests in a failure by Goldsworthy and others, including Laws whom he criticises, to identify precisely what they mean by the 'common law'.[21] Our reference would be to that system of governance and rule outlined above. What Goldsworthy seems to have in mind is that process of making decisions by a common law system i.e., precedent, *stare decisis* and so on. This is but one of several uses of 'common law'. Others include the common law system as opposed to equity, now only of historical relevance since their fusion. It also includes the system of common law in which all were equally under the common law save the *fons et origo* of law the King and in which particular procedures were adopted such as the jury. A 'common law' system prevented the emergence of a public and civil division in our law. It may also refer to the distinction between common law and statutory law.

These are but examples of that bigger concept of sovereignty within the common law as outlined in this paper which denotes a system of law and governance and which forms the constitutional basis of law and governance today.

The message from judicial opinion seems to be, and not all judges would agree with this, there are things 'up with which they will not put'. As Lord Hope expressed it 'The Rule of Law is now sovereign in our constitution'. Not a rule of law framed in private law relationships as Dicey believed but one which takes legality and human rights seriously in the face of arbitrary power. The rule of law *not* the rule of *the* law.[22] This viewpoint, we believe, is a legacy of European influence. It is durable. It was EU law that catalysed the current debate on sovereignty. The seeds of that debate pre-exist that influence. It is a debate that has led to an examination of the changing contours of domestic sovereignty today.

§1.06 THE RULE OF LAW

This chapter considers only briefly the rule of law - one of the esteemed British values of which we have heard so much recently. But that epithet was also served by thin gruel in 1972. It has been reinforced beyond recognition by the EU, now with the Charter of Fundamental Rights and the ECHR and the Human Rights Act.[23]

Section 1 of the Constitutional Reform Act 2005 may cause considerable unease:

> This Act does not adversely affect –
>
> (a) the existing constitutional principle of the rule of law, or
> (b) the Lord Chancellor's existing constitutional role in relation to that principle.

---

21. J. Goldsworthy (1999) Chapters 9 and 10, (2010) Chapter 2. *See* T.R.S. Allan, *Law, Liberty and Justice: The Legal Foundations of British Constitutionalism* (1993) and *The Sovereignty of Law: Freedom, Constitution and Common Law* (2013).
22. J. Goldsworthy (2010) *ibid*. Chapter 3 p. 75.
23. P. Birkinshaw, *Like Canute: Pushing Back the Waters of the Incoming Tide. Prospects for Repatriating UK Constitutionalism*, in *The EU and National Constitutional Law* (P. Huber ed., 2012).

If the rule of law is constitutionally axiological does it need statutory expression and confirmation? Does that not deprive it of its significance as something that pre-exists and informs statutes? Section 17 establishes an oath of office for the Lord Chancellor by which s/he promises to respect the rule of law and defend the independence of the judges. S/he is no longer required to take the judicial oath because s/he will no longer sit as a judge. For centuries the office of Lord Chancellor was placed in the hands of a lawyer (who as a member of the Cabinet sat on the bench of the Lords Appellate Committee). The 2005 Act gave the position to a joint Lord Chancellor/ Secretary of State for Justice. Former Secretary of State Grayling's outbursts against 'European justice' were outlined above. As a politician, he was responsible for the most drastic attack on judicial review and legal aid ever witnessed. We are not party to exchanges between the Lord Chief Justice and Secretary Grayling but one wonders what a constitutional court under a national constitution would have made of these political attacks on vital elements on the rule of law and access to justice?[24] Despite anti-European rhetoric, provision is made for the availability of legal aid in respect of certain of the rights granted by EU law and the ECHR, although the coverage is not absolute.[25] The reforms to civil legal aid in public law cases have been criticised by a Parliamentary Select Committee[26] and an endeavour on the part of the government to introduce a requirement that recipients of civil legal aid meet a residency test through secondary legislation has been declared unlawful by the High Court.[27] Significant questions may remain as to the compatibility of certain of these reforms with both EU Law and the ECHR.[28]

§1.07 JUDICIAL ATTACKS ON EUROPE

In short, the pristine sense of Parliamentary legal sovereignty has been qualified and changed under European influence. But we now bear witness to judicial scepticism of matters European, both judicially and extra-judicially. Lord Sumption has attacked the

24. Case C-279/09 *DEB Deutsche Energiehandels etc* and *Airey v. Ireland* 9 Oct. 1979 (Eur. Court H.R., Series A, No 32, p. 11) and *Steel and Morris v. UK*, judgment of 15 Feb. 2005 [thanks to correspondence with A Mowbray].
25. *See* sections 8–12 of the Legal Aid, Sentencing and Punishment of Offenders Act 2012, along with Schedule 1. It still remains possible to obtain civil legal aid for judicial review claims, but subject to considerable exceptions. In particular, claims for damages for breach of a Convention right under the Human Rights Act 1998 are specifically excluded by paragraph 12 of Part 2 of Schedule 1.
26. Joint Committee on Human Rights, *The Implications for Access to Justice of the Government's Proposals to Reform Legal Aid* (2013–2014), HC 766, HL 100. *See* now Criminal Justice and Courts Act 2015 Pt 4 and amendments to the Civil Procedure Rules Part 54.
27. *R (Public Law Project) v. Secretary of State for Justice* [2014] EWHC 2365 (Admin) although the decision was reversed by the Court of Appeal: *Public Law Project v. The Lord Chancellor* [2015] EWCA Civ 1193. *See also R (Gudanaviciene), etc v. Director of Legal Aid Casework* [2014] EWCA Civ 1662; *IS v. Director of Legal Aid Casework & Lord Chancellor* [2015] EWHC 1965 (Admin).
28. *See ibid.* [51]–[88] and Joint Committee on Human Rights, *supra* n. 26, where a detailed analysis of the implications in relation to Convention Rights is considered.

enervating influence of the Court of Human Rights on our democratic process,[29] an approach to some degree echoed by Lord Neuberger, although with acknowledgement that the Court of Human Rights has sometimes been willing to interpret Convention law in light of the peculiarly British approach to certain issues.[30] Laws speaks against the EU's attack on the Catholicity of the common law – has not that Catholicity (meaning eclecticism) actually inspired the common law rather than straight-jacketed it?[31] Neuberger has seen an anti-Catholic sentiment in anti-Europeanism?[32]

A whole raft of cases have shown judges to be less inclined to refer matters to the ECJ – even where the case raised important and unresolved points of EU law.[33] There has been strong judicial support not to accept a breach of EU law to require a mandatory remedy in *Walton* (incidentally a generous decision on *locus standi*) even though apparently the point was not argued:

> Where the court is satisfied that the applicant has been able in practice to enjoy the rights conferred by the European legislation, and where a procedural challenge would fail under domestic law because the breach has caused no substantial prejudice, I see nothing in principle or authority to require the courts to adopt a different approach merely because the procedural requirement arises from a European rather than a domestic source.[34]

HS2 brings many of these points together.[35] The case concerned the high speed rail link between London, the midlands and the north. It amounts to the most important development affecting national interests since the construction of the Channel tunnel. The central questions were: to what extent did the Command Paper (CP) on HS2 *constrain* the decisions in Parliament for development consent through a

29. Lord Sumption 'The Limits of Law' (2013) http://supremecourt.uk/docs/speech-131120.pdf. *See* Boyron *supra* n. 3. *See also* Sir P. Sales 'Law and Democracy in a Human Rights Framework' in D. Feldman (ed.), *Law in Politics, Politics in Law* (2013) ch. 15.
30. Lord Neuberger, *The British and Europe* (Cambridge Freshfields Annual Law Lecture 2014, Cambridge, 12 Feb. 2014) http://www.supremecourt.uk/docs/speech-140212.pdf paragraph 36 (accessed 21 Oct. 2014). The specific case law examples to which he refers are *R v. Horncastle* [2010] 2 AC 373 and *Al-Khawaja and Tahery v. United Kingdom* [2011] ECHR 2127, [2012] Crim LR 375. *See also Hutchinson v. UK* 57592/08 – Chamber Judgment Fourth Section [2015] ECHR 111 (03 Feb. 2015) and *R v. Newell* [2014] EWCA Crim 188 where the CHR explained an earlier decision of the Grand Chamber (*Vintner & Ors v. UK* 66069/09) and held life sentences in England and Wales compliant with Article 3 ECHR because of residuary discretionary review.
31. Sir John Laws http://www.judiciary.gov.uk/wp-content/uploads/JCO/Documents/Speeches/laws-lj-speech-hamlyn-lecture-2013.pdf.
32. UKSC site http://supremecourt.uk/docs/speech-140212.pdf.
33. *HS2* [2014] below, *Walton* [2012] UKSC 44; *X v. Mid Sussex CAB* [2012] UKSC 59 – no reference; *HMRC v. Aimia Coalition* [2013] UKSC 15 – no reference; *Home Office v. Tariq* [2011] UKSC 35 – no reference; Cf *R (Client Earth) v. Secretary of State for the Environment etc* [2013] UKSC 25 – reference made and *see* [2015] UKSC 28; *R (Chester) v. Secretary of State for Justice* [2013] UKSC 63 and *Test Claimants* [2012] UKSC 19; *Cooper v. Att General* [2010] EWCA Civ 464 and judicial liability under *Köbler* – no reference; *Stott v. Thomas Cook* [2014] UKSC 15 – no reference.
34. Lord Carnwath in *Walton* [139] *see* Lord Hope paragraph 155 in agreement. See Case C-72/12 *Gemeinde Altrip* [2014] 12 PTSR 311 discussed in *R (Champion) v North Norfolk DC* [2015] UKSC 52 paras 54-61, Lord Carnwath.
35. *R (HS2 Action Alliance Ltd) etc v. Secretary of State for Transport* [2014] UKSC 3. *See* P. Craig (2014) *Public Law* 374. Disclosure of information under the Freedom of Information Act on HS2 was the occasion for the seventh veto from a Cabinet Minister under section 53 of that Act early in 2014.

hybrid bill procedure?[36] Or did the CP merely *influence* decisions? Was it a plan or procedure setting the framework of development required by legislative, regulatory or administrative provisions? If so, it was subject to a requirement of a Structural Environmental Assessment (SEA) under EU law.[37] An SEA had not occurred. The Supreme Court determined that the CP was not within SEA requirements. But the matter was not referred under Article 267 TFEU despite an apparent disagreement between the Advocate General and Fourth Chamber of the ECJ.[38]

An attack was also launched on the Environmental Impact Assessment (EIA) to be conducted through the hybrid procedure in Parliament. An EIA, it was argued, would not consider alternatives in the same detail as a SEA. The allegation was that the Parliamentary procedure would be heavily compromised politically and opportunities for proper scrutiny and wider public involvement would not be undertaken. There would not be an examination of the significant environmental effects of the proposal based on 'appropriate information' as required under EU law.[39]

The appellants' case is set out in detail by Lord Reed.[40] In effect, the Government they argued intended to seek development consent for HS2 through the hybrid bill procedure in Parliament, without going through all the procedures required by the EIA Directive. The Government relied on the exemption granted by Article 1(4) of the EIA Directive which exempted 'projects the details of which are adopted by a specific act of national legislation, since the objectives of this Directive, including that of supplying information, are achieved through the legislative process'.

The argument was, based upon the opinions of Advocates General in the EU litigation, that the ECJ had required there to be a full and complete review of the environmental impact and provision of relevant information to Parliament.[41] The ECJ ruled there had to be a review that was 'substantive' not merely 'formal' by national legislatures. The appellants also relied on arguments expressed by the Advocates General that national courts had to investigate that procedures within Parliament satisfied these tests. The word 'since' in Article 1(4) above had been interpreted to mean 'provided that'. This would confront the difficulty under Article 9 Bill of Rights that proceedings in Parliament shall not be called into question by the courts. National courts were required to ensure such a review had occurred allowing 'early and effective public participation' by Article 6(4) of the Directive, it was argued. This would include information provided by the appellants capable of influencing the outcome including their proposal for the 'optimised alternative' and 'Members of Parliament must be able to consider it and to be influenced by it' [para 68].[42] The appellants argued this was not possible under the hybrid bill procedure.

36. *High Speed Rail: Investing in Britain's Future – Decisions and Next Steps* Cm 8247 (2012).
37. Directive 2001/42/EC.
38. *HS2* paragraphs 187–188 and Case C-567/10 *Inter Environnement Bruxelles Asbl.*
39. Directive 2011/92/EU.
40. *HS2* paragraphs 67–76.
41. *Bexus v. Regionie Wallon* C-128/09 [2011] ECR I-9711 at [84] and *Nomarchiaki AA Ypourgos Perivallontos etc* C-43/10 CJEU 11/09/12 [136]-[137].
42. Paragraph 68.

According to Lord Reed:

> 69. The Government has already taken the critical decision to accept the economic case for HS2 and to reject the optimised alternative. The bill for Phase 1 will reflect that decision. Parliament will be asked to approve the principle of the bill at second reading. It will have available to it an environmental statement prepared on behalf of the Secretary of State. It will also have available to it the comments on the environmental statement and the assessor's summary of those comments. The Secretary of State has however confirmed in correspondence that the vote at the conclusion of the debate will be subject to the whip. Ministers will face the alternatives of resignation or dismissal from office if they vote against the bill. Backbenchers will risk disciplinary sanctions.

The subsequent examination of the bill by a select committee will not, it was argued by the challengers, involve any consideration of the principle behind the bill, and therefore will not involve consideration of alternatives to HS2 or of the economic case for the project. Any argument that the environmental impact as set out in the environmental statement should outweigh the need for HS2 will not be considered by the select committee. The final vote on the bill at third reading will again be subject to the whip and collective ministerial responsibility preventing full and proper scrutiny and rendering public participation ineffective contrary to Article 6(4) of the Directive.

Lord Reed, with whom all justices agreed, accepted that the court had jurisdiction to rule on the claim before the commencement of Parliamentary proceedings. He assessed ECJ case law and, in the light of that case law, saw no reason why the Parliamentary procedure would be legally inadequate.[43] Parliament's review was substantive and was based on copious information. In addition, the policy and political context of a decision such as this had to be considered by the court and formed a vital component of the overall public interest.

Although the interpretation of the EIA Directive is a matter of EU law, the constitutional context for the operation of the EIA [involving, if the appellants were correct, a clash between Article 9 Bill of Rights and EU law by virtue of the 1972 Act] is a matter of national law. 'EU law nevertheless draws inspiration from the constitutional traditions of the Member States; and the observations in these decisions reflect constitutional principles which apply in other Member States besides the United Kingdom.'[44] A decision of the Court of Justice should not be read by a national court in a way that places in question the identity of the national constitutional order.[45] The ECJ had made it clear it expects national courts to apply principles from ECJ judgments 'in the context of their own national systems'.[46] That court could not expect a national

43. Paragraphs 98–117.
44. *HS2* paragraph 105.
45. Paragraph 111 citing the German Federal Constitutional Court: 'There is in addition much to be said for the view, advanced by the German Federal Constitutional Court in its judgment of 24 Apr. 2013 on the Counter-Terrorism Database Act, 1 BvR 1215/07, paragraph 91, that as part of a co-operative relationship, a decision of the Court of Justice should not be read by a national court in a way that places in question the identity of the national constitutional order.'
46. Paragraph 117.

court to engage in 'a qualitative assessment of the legislature's actual consideration of the proposal'.[47]

'*Factortame*' said Lords Neuberger and Mance, with whom all justices agreed, was 'a significant development' recognising the special status of the 1972 Act and the commitment of loyalty to EU law:[48]

> But it is difficult to see how an English court could fully comply with the approach suggested by the two Advocates General without addressing its apparent conflict with other principles hitherto also regarded as fundamental and enshrined in the Bill of Rights. Scrutiny of the workings of Parliament and whether they satisfy externally imposed criteria clearly involves questioning and potentially impeaching (i.e., condemning) Parliament's internal proceedings, and would go a considerable step further than any United Kingdom court has ever gone.
>
> The United Kingdom has no written constitution, but we have a number of constitutional instruments. They include Magna Carta, the Petition of Right 1628, the Bill of Rights and (in Scotland) the Claim of Rights Act 1689, the Act of Settlement 1701 and the Act of Union 1707. The European Communities Act 1972, the Human Rights Act 1998 and the Constitutional Reform Act 2005 ... The common law itself also recognises certain principles as fundamental to the rule of law. It is, putting the point at its lowest, certainly arguable (and it is for United Kingdom law and courts to determine) that there may be fundamental principles, whether contained in other constitutional instruments or recognised at common law, of which Parliament when it enacted the European Communities Act 1972 did not either contemplate or authorise the abrogation.
>
> We are not expressing any view on whether or how far Article 9 of the Bill of Rights would count among these, but the point is too important to pass without mention. ... Important insights into potential issues in this area are to be found in their penetrating discussion by Laws LJ in the Divisional Court in *Thoburn v. Sunderland City Council* [2002] EWHC 195 (Admin), [2003] QB 151, especially paras 58-70, although the focus there was the possibility of conflict between an earlier 'constitutional' and later 'ordinary' statute, rather than, as here, between two constitutional instruments, which raises yet further considerations.

The constitution is now in the interpretation of the courts. It is arguable, they say, that there are fundamental principles of the common law that the 1972 legislation did not override.

As Lord Mance continued in *Pham,* a case dealing with national citizenship which 'identifies the constitution's participants'[49] 'this court in [*HS2]* recognised the potential which exists for jurisdictional limits on the extent to which [sections 2 and 3 ECA 1972] confer competence on the Court of Justice over fundamental features of the British constitution. Questions as to the meaning and effect of Treaty provisions are in principle capable of being distinguished from questions going to the jurisdiction conferred on the European Union and its court under the treaties'. The Treaty on European Union (TEU) Articles 4 and 5 deal with conferral of powers by Member States including subsidiarity, proportionality and acting within the limits of conferred competences. Article 4(2) proclaims that the Union shall respect the equality of Member

47. Paragraphs 111–112.
48. Paragraphs 206–208.
49. *R (GI) v. Secretary of State for the Home Department* [2013] QB 1008 paragraph 43 Laws LJ.

States 'inherent in their fundamental structures, political and constitutional'.[50] He omits reference to sincere cooperation in Article 4(3). Subsequently Mance does refer to mutual respect and caution when engaging in interpretation of Member States' constitutional identity reflecting 'the spirit of co-operation of which both the *Bundesverfassungsgericht* and this court [UK Supreme Court] have previously spoken' (paragraph 91).

Unless the power to determine national constitutional measures by the Court of Justice is unlimited under domestic law 'a domestic court must ultimately decide for itself what is consistent with its own domestic constitutional arrangements, including in the case of the 1972 Act what jurisdictional limits exist under the European Treaties and upon the competence conferred on the European institutions including the Court of Justice' (paragraph 90)

Our questions are: if this power exists in domestic courts over the internal workings of Parliament and nationality what other constitutional issues may be brought within domestic judicial control? How can other parties to an international agreement place complete reliance on what has been agreed to if domestic courts establish a constitutional no-go area for EU law? At what point would the Union cease to be a *union*? Does 'respect' for national constitutions mean they override the Union framework? The rule of recognition, Mance continues, must view 'the United Kingdom as independent, Parliament as sovereign and European law as part of domestic law because Parliament has so willed' (paragraph 80). Or so the judges say. The constitutional points made by Mance in this part of his judgment, as those made in the judgments in *Thoburn* and *HS2*, are pure *obiter*.

Scepticism has been expressed by several 'top' courts around the EU, most particularly by the German Federal Constitutional Court on the ECJ's initial non-commitment to human rights' protection, to national democracy and national constitutional integrity and the ECJ's expansive jurisdiction.[51] The UK Supreme Court is now joining the list.

It is almost as if our courts feel they have grown up, matured constitutionally and can now act as a corrective to Luxembourg and Strasbourg. They *have* grown up. The

50. *Pham v. Secretary of State for the Home Department* [2015] UKSC 19 paragraph 82 Lords Neuberger, Wilson and Lady Hale concurring. *See* Mance's reference to Cruz Villalón AG's Opinion in Case C-62/14 *Gauweiler v. Deutscher Bundestag* 14 Jan. 2015 at paragraphs 78–79 on a reference from the German Federal Constitutional Court concerning purchase by the European Central Bank of bonds issued by Member States. *See* Cruz Villalón's Opinion paragraphs 30–69 on the subjection of EU law to the 'unalterable core content of national constitutional law' and the application of ultra vires tests by national courts to EU institutions. The AG's hopeful prediction for convergence in constitutional identity between the Union and its members (paragraph 61) in 'the medium and long term' is questioned by Mance at paragraph 79. The ECJ upheld the legality of the ECB's decisions, [2015] EUECJ C-62/14 16 Jun. 2015, simply noting that Article 267 was built on judicial 'direct cooperation' (paragraph 15) and judgments on preliminary rulings are 'binding on the national court, as regards the interpretation or the validity of the acts of the EU institutions' (paragraph 16) and possess 'definitive consequences as regards the resolution of the main proceedings' (paragraph 14).

51. Case C-144/04 *Mangold*; Case C-617/10 *Fransson*; Case C-396/11 *Radu* (29/01/13); Case C-399/11 *Melloni* (26/02/13); Case C-279/09 *DEB Deutsche Energiehandels-und BeratungsGmbH;* Case C-236/09 *Assoc Belge*: Lord Mance, 'The Interface between National and European Law' (2013) *Eur LR* 437.

Government knows this and resents this. Witness the Ministry of Justice papers on judicial review reform.[52] But our belief is the UK courts would not be where they are today without the EU and ECHR inspiration. That debt should be acknowledged. It has been but now there is a reflective taking of stock. Furthermore, we wonder to what extent our courts are saying 'We have matured; we take legality seriously. But the inspiration is not European. It is domestic. It is based in *our* constitution which is preserved to us and which is interpreted by our judges.' And we can protect human rights domestically.

§1.08 COMMON LAW OF HUMAN RIGHTS

The common law of human rights flows from the common law constitution. It has, we believe, been reinforced by European influence. One of the most dramatic instances of invocation of such common law rights came in the *Ahmed v. HM Treasury* decisions.[53] The government reaction illustrated the pristine sense of Rees Mogg's constitutionalism when Parliament reversed by interim legislation the effects of the two Supreme Court decisions pending legislation to implement necessary judicial protection concerning anti-terrorist financial measures. The common law of human rights was invoked by the Court because it was believed, incorrectly it transpired, that the ECHR did not apply.

From the 1980s courts had built on traditions of statutory construction so that only clear precise words could defeat what today we would refer to as human rights although examples pre-date that period.[54] Its clearest enunciation came in *Simms*.[55] What has happened since is an unfolding of specific rights under the common law: sustenance, right to life, access to justice – strikingly illustrated by the effect of Article 6 on judicial protection under EEC law,[56] protection of property and most recently transparency following on from the earlier case law[57] on freedom of speech and open justice. The common law, said Lord Cooke, 'goes so deep'.[58]

The case of *Kennedy v. Charity Commission* is a remarkable illustration of a home grown fundamental right and one that would not fit easily within a human rights catalogue: transparency.[59] There has been a striking development of common law human rights and a common law provenance for general principles of law.[60] *Kennedy*

52. *Judicial Review – Proposals for Further Reform* Cm 8703 (2013) Ministry of Justice following Cm 8515 (2012) and Criminal Justice and Courts Bill 2014-15 Part 4. *See* now Criminal Justice and Courts Act, *supra* n. 26.
53. [2010] UKSC 2 & 5.
54. *Anisminic v. FCC* [1969] 2 AC 147. The origins of modern judicial review go back to the seventeenth century.
55. *R v. Secretary of State for the Home Department ex p Simms* [1999] 3 All ER 400 (HL).
56. Case 222/84 *Johnstone v. CC RUC* [1986] ECR 1651.
57. *AG v. Guardian Newspapers* [1988] 3 All ER 545 (QBD, CA, HL) and *R (Guardian News Ltd) v. City of Westminster Magistrates' Court* [2012] EWCA Civ 420.
58. *Daly v. Secretary of State for the Home Department* [2001] UKHL 26 paragraph 31.
59. [2014] UKSC 20.
60. *Bank Mellat v. HM Treasury No 2* [2013] UKSC 39; *R (Bourgass) v Secretary of State for Justice* [2015] UKSC 54.

is significant because it seems to us to herald an ambitious attempt to patriate human rights arguments. The case involved a refusal to disclose papers possessed by the Charity Commission involving inquiries into a charity organised by George Galloway MP. ECHR case law 'travelling in one direction' was not followed to read section 32 Freedom of Information Act FOIA (giving an absolute exemption to a tribunal's papers) down under Article 10 ECHR although there was strong dissent. It is really not that long ago that Lord Wilberforce and Lord Keith stated 'it is not for courts to act as advocates for open government' or to establish a freedom of information act.[61] There was no general common law right to openness and access. It was context specific. Lord Mance supporting an earlier judgment by Toulson LJ in 2012[62] stated that Convention rights have 'common law homologues'.[63] The court on a request for information could place itself in the position of a public authority and make a merits review on disclosure with the benefit of full inspection bearing in mind the statutory duties, functions and objectives of the statute and 'the nature and importance of the duties involved'.[64] 'Only in that way could it undertake any review to ascertain whether the relevant interests had been properly balanced. The interests involved and the balancing exercise would be of a nature with which the court is familiar and accustomed to evaluate and undertake.' 'I therefore doubt whether there could or would be any real difference in the outcome of any judicial review of a Charity Commission refusal to disclose information, whether this was conducted under Article 10, ..., or not.'[65]

Lord Toulson spells out the approach to judicial review of the Charity Commission's refusal which is concerned with 'transparency' and not a decision on an enquiry subject to a limited form of review:

> The reason for the High Court deciding itself whether the open justice principle requires disclosure of the relevant information is linked to the reason for the principle. It is in the interests of public confidence that the higher court should exercise its own judgment in the matter and that information which it considers ought to be disclosed is disclosed [132].
>
> The analysis set out above is based on common law principles and not on Article 10, which in my view adds nothing to the common law in the present context. This is not surprising. What we now term human rights law and public law has developed through our common law over a long period of time. The process has quickened since the end of World War II in response to the growth of bureaucratic powers on the part of the state and the creation of multitudinous administrative agencies affecting many aspects of the citizen's daily life. The growth of the state has presented the courts with new challenges to which they have responded by a process of gradual adaption and development of the common law to meet current needs. This has always been the way of the common law and it has not ceased on the enactment of the Human Rights Act 1998, although since then there has sometimes been a baleful and unnecessary tendency to overlook the common law.

61. *Burmah Oil v. Bank of England (Governor and Company)* [1980] AC 1090 per Lords Wilberforce and Keith.
62. *Guardian News and Media Ltd above.*
63. *Kennedy* paragraphs 45–47.
64. Paragraph 56.
65. *Ibid.*

> It needs to be emphasised that it was not the purpose of the Human Rights Act that the common law should become an ossuary [133].

Kennedy is resolutely domestic law.[66] A graphic illustration of EU law and Article 6 ECHR (Articles 47 and 52 CFR) and influence in transparency came in the Court of Appeal in *Evans v. Attorney General.*[67] *Evans* involved the FOIA and the EU based Environmental Information Regulations (EIR). The case is of real constitutional significance involving refusals to disclose information held by government departments about Prince Charles' correspondence. The correspondence would now be protected by an absolute exemption not one qualified, as in *Evans*, by a public interest test. The law was changed.[68] Disclosure had been ordered by the Upper Tribunal but a veto was issued under section 53 FOIA. Lord Dyson's judgment in the Court of Appeal is a very brave one. Under EU law, as well as domestic law, the Attorney General's case in issuing a veto fell apart, he believed. Arguments under EU law centred upon Article 6 of the EI Directive: non-compliance with Articles 47 CFR and 52 (equivalent to ECHR Article 6 right to judicial protection). Lord Dyson's reasons in relation to the EIR implementing the Directive were:

(i) the focus of judicial review is wrong as an appropriate remedy he believed – the Attorney General, not a public authority who made the decision, was the target of a judicial review;
(ii) a section 53 veto wrongly overrides judicial appeal procedure under statute/regulations – i.e., the judicial decision is not 'final and binding' and judicial review may not occur. If it does and succeeds it is only against the Attorney General (point (i) above);
(iii) there was an absence of legal certainty and equality of arms - a tribunal decision can be set at nought by an 'accountable person' provided only that he has on reasonable grounds formed the opinion that there was no failure falling within section 53(1)(b). There is, of course, no corresponding right in a person who has requested information to set aside a tribunal decision that is adverse to him if he has on reasonable grounds formed the opinion that there has been a failure to comply with section 1(1)(a) or (b) of the FOIA (paragraph 66).

The Supreme Court upheld the Court of Appeal under both domestic and EU grounds but the majority did not address arguments on the EU Charter of Fundamental Rights.[69] Under FOIA the prospects for the executive successfully invoking the veto power seem remote and under the EIR the veto clashes with Article 6 of the Directive making it incompatible with EU law because the veto could prevent a judicial determination on the merits. The more sustained arguments centred around the FOIA

66. *See also* the comments of Lady Hale 'UK Constitutionalism on the March?' (Keynote Address to the Constitutional and Administrative Law Bar Association Conference 2014, 12 Jul. 2014) http://www.supremecourt.uk/docs/speech-140712.pdf (accessed 21 Oct. 2014).
67. [2014] EWCA Civ 254 and [2015] UKSC 21.
68. Constitutional Reform and Governance Act 2010 section 46 and Schedule 7.
69. *R (Evans) v. HM Attorney General* [2015] UKSC 21.

and domestic constitutional inhibitions preventing a veto denying access to a judicial body for a final determination of one's rights.

There are other dramatic statements about the common law basis of fair procedures and open justice having an existence independent of the Convention. Lord Reed has stated:[70]

> Properly understood, Convention rights do not form a discrete body of domestic law derived from the judgments of the European court. As Lord Justice-General Rodger once observed, 'it would be wrong ... to see the rights under the European Convention as somehow forming a wholly separate stream in our law; in truth they soak through and permeate the areas of our law in which they apply.[71]

§1.09 EU CHARTER OF FUNDAMENTAL RIGHTS

Withdrawal from the ECHR is enthusiastically promoted by members of the Conservative Party and by UKIP. The 2015 Conservative Party manifesto spoke of replacement of the HRA by a British Bill of Rights which will remain faithful to the basic principles of human rights in the Convention and sever the link between the Strasbourg court and UK courts. The UK Supreme Court will become the 'ultimate arbiter' of human rights law. Judgments of the Strasbourg court are binding on the UK government under the Convention and international law, not the courts. The Human Rights Act does not make Strasbourg judgments binding on our domestic courts.

Leaving the EU would obviously entail non-incorporation and non-applicability of the EU Charter of Fundamental Rights (see Beale ch 14). The Charter is legally binding on domestic courts and can be directly effective. The Charter has now become an ogre according to Eurosceptics:

> '...[W]hat the last Government said about the charter of fundamental rights was simply an untruth. There are many quotes in which they clearly talked about an opt-out from the charter, but that opt-out does not exist. We on the Government Benches have our differences on aspects of human rights law, but there is unity across the coalition on the role and presence of the charter of fundamental rights. None of us wishes to see it become part of UK law [it is!], and none of us wishes the ambitions of some in Brussels who talk about it being extended into national law come to pass. We will resist that absolutely...' [Justice Secretary 7 April 2014 Column 89]. 'We share the aspiration, aim and absolute clear goal that the Charter will not become part of national law in this country.' [Column 91]

Hear the words of shock horror in the judgment of Mostyn J concerning the CFR in *AB*:

---

70. In *Osborn v. The Parole Board* [2013] UKSC 61 on the common law of access to fairness and oral procedure in parole hearings for prisoners and the same judge in *A v. BBC* [2014] UKSC 25 – but cf *R (T) v. Secretary of State for the Home Department* [2014] UKSC 35 where the ECHR Article 8 was the basis of protection under the Rehabilitation of Offenders Act 1974 and related orders and the Police Act 1997. *See R (Bourgass) v. Secretary of State for Justice* [2015] UKSC 54.
71. Citing *HM Advocate v Montgomery* 2000 JC 111, 117 at para 63 *Osborne*.

> The constitutional significance of [*NS* – in which the ECJ ruled there was no UK opt-out from the Charter although Article 1(2) was not in issue] can hardly be overstated. The Human Rights Act 1998 incorporated into our domestic law large parts, but by no means all, of the European Convention on Human Rights. Some parts were deliberately missed out by Parliament. The Charter of Fundamental Rights of the European Union contains, I believe, all of those missing parts and a great deal more. Notwithstanding the endeavours of our political representatives at Lisbon it would seem that the much wider Charter of Rights is now part of our domestic law. Moreover, that much wider Charter of Rights would remain part of our domestic law even if the Human Rights Act were repealed.[72]

The Commons European Scrutiny Committee has recommended an Act to exclude the Charter from the UK.[73] Why the fear? Because of its European origins and its uncontrollable potential, as witness the *Digital Rights, Google Spain* and *Schrems* cases of the ECJ[74] and the emergency legislation by the UK government to avoid EU legal regulation in retention of data communications.[75] But what we have witnessed above is a patriation of human rights jurisprudence whose origins, it is argued, lie in common law and whose future scope is pregnant with possibility. But for government that possibility will be seen as a threat.

§1.10 THE GENERAL PRINCIPLES

We spoke earlier about the absence at the time of accession to the EEC of 'judicial' in our constitutional law and the elementary condition of judicial review through the first sixty years or so of the twentieth century, despite its long and proud heritage. The

72. *R (AB) v. Secretary of State for the Home Department* [2013] EWHC 3452 (Admin) para 14. *See NS v. SSHD* [2010] EWCA Civ 990 paragraphs 7–7 Lord Neuberger. *UK Ass of Fish Producer Orgs v. Secretary of State for the Environment* [2013] EWHC 1959 (Admin), *Benkharbouche etc v. Embassy of Sudan etc* [2015] EWCA Civ 33, *Google Inc v. J Vidal-Hall* [2015] EWCA Civ 311 and *D Davis MP infra* n. 75 on important domestic use of the Charter.
73. HC 979 (2013-14).
74. *Digital Rights* [2014] EUECJ C-293/12 (8 Apr. 2014) http://www.bailii.org/eu/cases/EUECJ/2014/C29312.html. *Google Spain AEPD* [2014] EUECJ C-131/12 (13 May 2014) http://www.bailii.org/eu/cases/EUECJ/2014/C13112.html. Case C-3 62/14 *Schrems v Data Protection Commissioner* (6 Oct. 2015).
75. Data Retention and Investigatory Powers Act 2014. This Act faces repeal on 31 Dec. 2016. In *D Davis MP et al v. Secretary of State for the Home Department* [2015] EWHC 2092 (Admin) the Administrative Court ruled section 1 of the Act and regulations made thereunder in breach of the CFR Articles 7 and 8 ('EU law') and issued a prospective and deferred order disapplying section 1. The Court of Appeal referred the case to the ECJ and cast some doubts on whether *Digital Rights* set mandatory EU requirements for national legislation and whether in addition aspects of the national law were outwith the EU legal framework: *Secretary of State for the Home Department v D, Davis* [2015] EWCA Civ 1185. *See* the Investigatory Powers Tribunal's rulings of legality under the HRA for the legal regime and surveillance practices under the Regulation of Investigatory Powers Act 2000 in *Liberty et al v. General Communications HQ et al* [2014] UKIPTrib 13-77-H (5/12/2014) and [2015] UKIPTrib 13-77-H (6/02/15). Also [2015] UKIPTrib13_132H *A H Belhaj et al v. Security Service et al. See* D. Anderson's Recommendations for Review of UK Surveillance Laws: *A Question of Trust* (June 2015) *https://terrorismlegislationreviewer.independent.gov.uk/wp-content/uploads/2015/06/IPR-Report-Print-Version.pdf.* See Investigatory Powers Bill 2015 https://www.gov.uk/government/uploads/system/uploads/attachment_data/file/473770/Draft_Investigatory_Powers_Bill.pdf.

advent and influence of general principles of review from an EU provenance are well known. But like the constitution, something strange is happening. Take proportionality – again a common law heritage is claimed. The outcome of use of proportionality and unreasonableness in review may often be the same but a far more focused form of review emerged from the influence of general principles including proportionality. The adoption of the general principles by domestic courts will not disappear on Brexit. Legal certainty was actually used as a means of critique of EU law-making in *HS2*.[76]

Rugby FU v. CIS Ltd[77] shows that flexibility in approach not only in absorbing general principles and adapting them but in setting a broad context for the qualification 'in implementing Union law ...'. We agree with the points made by Lord Reed above on how the general principles – arguably in the common law but undeveloped – have blended with domestic law. We would say not unlike the confluence of common law and equity.

Note, however, recent local colour in the use of proportionality. Lord Reed in *Bank Mellat No. 2* has provided a detailed appraisal.[78] After observations linking proportionality to 'margin of appreciation', a formulation which is formally to become a part of the ECHR under reforms,[79] and explaining why national approaches cannot 'simply mirror' Strasbourg ones, Reed explains how proportionality under the HRA has developed from a common law heritage.[80] Although this produced a three-fold test 'bearing some affinity' with Strasbourg case law, viz sufficiently important legislative objectives, rational connection and means that are 'necessary' to accomplish the objective, Canadian case law (*Oakes*) added a further requirement to those in *De Freitas*. This is 'the need to balance the interests of society with those of individuals and groups'.[81] This approach has been upheld in *Huang*[82] and *Quila*.[83] 'The judgment of Dickson CJ in *Oakes* provides the clearest and most influential judicial analysis of proportionality within the common law tradition of legal reasoning'.[84] Subsequent judgments of the UK Supreme Court have confirmed the vitality of proportionality in purely domestic legal contexts.[85]

76. Paragraphs 165–174. On EU general principles and domestic legislation: *Commissioners for HMR&C v. Pendragon plc et al* [2015] UKSC 37.
77. [2012] UKSC 55. See *Davis* above note 75 [2015] EWCA Civ 1185.
78. *Bank Mellat v. HM Treasury No 2* [2013] UKSC 39 paragraphs 71–74 and agreed by Lord Sumption for the majority paragraph 20, and at paragraph 21 'the making of government and legislative policy cannot be turned into a judicial process.' *See also R (Lord Carlisle) v. Secretary of State for the Home Department* [2014] UKSC 60. In *R (Robinson et al) v. Secretary of State for Justice* [2014] UKSC 66 the Supreme Court refused to follow *James v. UK* [2012] EHRR 399 in respect of the CHR rulings in relation to Article 5(1) ECHR.
79. Protocol 15 ECHR (awaiting ratification) http://www.echr.coe.int/Documents/Protocol_15_ENG.pdf.
80. *De Freitas* [1999] per Lord Clyde and Dickson, Canadian CJ, in *R v. Oakes* [1986].
81. Paragraph 73.
82. [2007] UKHL 11.
83. [2011] UKSC 45.
84. *Bank Mellat* Paragraph 74.
85. *Pham v. Secretary of State for the Home Department* [2015] UKSC 19 and *Akerman-Livingstone v. Aster Communities Ltd* [2015] UKSC 15. See the qualifications in *Keyu v Secretary of State for Foreign etc Affairs* [2015] UKSC 69 at paragraphs 131–134 Lord Neuberger, paragraphs 271–283 Lord Kerr, paragraphs 302–313 Baroness Hale.

From *Kennedy* examined above emphasising common law review of fact and law and the appropriateness of a remedy via that route rather than an ECHR inspired one, Lord Mance advanced the suitability of domestic judicial review as a means of providing an appropriate remedy as opposed to the ECHR route.[86] Judicial review is now an appropriate remedy to cover issues of fact (a French provenance) as well as law. Both reasonableness review and proportionality involve 'weight and balance, with the intensity of the scrutiny and the weight to be given to any primary decision-maker's view depending on the context'. The terminology of proportionality adds 'structure' to considerations involving suitability, necessity and balance or imbalance of benefits or disadvantages. 'There seems no reason why such factors should not be relevant in judicial review even outside the scope of Convention and EU law.' The factors are context specific and while in fundamental rights case law the level of review is more intense, English courts have recognised that proportionality is not always associated with an intense review. In some cases it may be limited to a *Wednesbury* level of review.[87] Proportionality, like human rights and legal sovereignty, has been domesticised and belongs to the common law.

§1.11 THE SEPARATION OF POWERS

Like the EU, the UK has no developed strict system of separation of powers although judicial independence is proclaimed. In 1972, the UK judiciary was fiercely independent but limited. Judges had a small, self-denying role within the constitution. There was little constitutional jurisprudence. And judges were criticised for their unarticulated political prejudices.[88] Because of the influence of Article 6 ECHR the UK moved its top court from the Legislature to premises across the road in the new Supreme Court.[89] As the court has become more independent institutionally it so happens that its constitutional docket has grown but it inherited a developing docket from the Appellate Committee of the House of Lords. Its devolved constitutional jurisprudence was inherited from the Privy Council. Article 6 ECHR brought institutional integrity to our top court. One of the reasons cited by Lord Reed in *HS2* for not judicially examining the adequacy of the operation of Parliamentary procedures was to avoid a breach of the separation of powers via Article 9 Bill of Rights. But the challenge was examined by the court *before* Parliamentary proceedings began. In the litigation concerning assisted suicide the Supreme Court ruled that although it had power to issue a declaration of incompatibility under the Human Rights Act, it would give Parliament the opportunity to legislate on a divisive issue which Parliament is better qualified to assess.[90] In other

86. *Kennedy* Paragraph 54.
87. *See R v. Chief Constable Sussex Police ex p ITF Ltd* [1999] 2 AC 418.
88. JAG Griffith *The Politics of the Judiciary* (5th ed 1997).
89. *See McGonnell v. UK* (2000) 30 EHRR 289; *R (Barclay) v. Lord Chancellor etc* [2008] EWCA Civ 1319, [2010] 1 AC 464.
90. *R (Nicklinson) v. Ministry of Justice* [2014] UKSC 38 and section 2 Suicide Act 1961 and Article 8 ECHR. Nicklinson's appeal to the Court of Human Rights was rejected as inadmissible: *Nicklinson & Lamb v. United Kingdom* 2478/15 [2015] ECHR 709. In September 2015, the UK House of Commons overwhelmingly voted against reforming assisted suicide laws. *See also*

case law, the Supreme Court has reviewed delegated legislative powers on the most exacting of scrutiny where the separation of powers had not been respected by the executive.[91]

§1.12 REMAINING QUESTIONS

If we are correct in our argument that our constitution has changed, that the European influence has been the crucial feature in this change, and that Parliamentary sovereignty is not today recognised in the manner in which it was in 1972, we need to address several concluding questions.

First of all, there are questions of devil and detail. Where is the case or ratio that supports the argument for a change to sovereignty? It is not there yet. The dicta and comments of several judges do not add up to a new constitution. In any event, as Goldsworthy claims, judges retire and are replaced. New judges may think more conservatively. Our belief is that when an occasion may arise in which there is an egregious abuse of a fundamental right or an abuse of the rule of law threatening that principle's very survival, the words of Lord Hope cited earlier should act as an inspiration to fashion a remedy to prevent such abuse. If we leave the ECHR then there would likely be no Human Rights Act. There could be no provision for a declaration of incompatibly. We would have to wait and see what the HRA's replacement might provide although the Queen's Speech opening Parliament in May 2015 indicated that repeal would be deferred pending further consultation. The former Commons Political and Constitutional Reform Committee in discussing the role of the judiciary under a *written* UK constitution floated the idea of a declaration of unconstitutionality.[92] Could this be such a remedy in the case of such an abuse? Unconstitutionality under the common law? Furthermore, would senior judges refuse to enforce such legislative provisions? This would not amount to *Marbury v. Maddison* review. It would be a declaration and non-enforcement.

Secondly, Martin Loughlin in his recent book on the British constitution has asked are these the lawyers (Supreme Court justices from commercial law backgrounds) to act as our public conscience in the common law constitution – do they display 'solidarity and common citizenship'?[93] May we add, do they have that panorama of experience and catholicity required not simply to be grand interpreters of the pattern of politics but perhaps to act as the shapers of collective conscience? Our own view is that this is not an improper question given the way that constitutional jurisprudence has developed and, if we are right, with an altered sovereignty. We are,

---

R (Chester) v. Secretary of State for Justice [2013] UKSC 63 on prisoners' voting rights – the matter was before Parliament and Parliament should be given the opportunity to amend the law. See *Thierry Delvigne v. Commune de Lesparre Médoc etc* [2015] EUECJ C-650/13 (6 Oct. 2015).

91. *Ahmed v. HM Treasury* [2010] UKSC 3 & 5, *Alvi* [2012] UKSC 33, *Walumba Lumba v. Secretary of State for the Home Department* [2011] UKSC 12, *R (Reilly) v. Secretary of State for Work and Pensions* [2013] UKSC 68.
92. Commons Political and Constitutional Reform Committee *Constitutional Role of the Judiciary if there were a Codified Constitution* Chapter 4 HC 802 (2013-14).
93. *The British Constitution: A Very Short Introduction* (2013).

however, very sceptical of trying to produce a 'fit' for such a role. Numerous cases from 2000 have also shown judicial reluctance to step over boldly into the area of policy choice – a limitation is set by respect for the separation of powers.[94]

Thirdly, what of the transient qualities of the common law? It flows and ebbs to borrow from Denning's famous fluvial EEC metaphor. It may be mighty today, mouse-like alone, without European inspiration, tomorrow. We do not know.

Fourthly, as well as loss of sovereignty and fears of immigration floods, a major point in the debate over Europe concerns the precise quantity of our laws made in Europe. Whatever the percentage[95] there is hardly an aspect of our law that is not influenced, or indeed completely occupied, by EU law. Will we repeal our laws on data protection, public procurement, environmental information and protection, competition, state aids, public service and utilities, consumer protection, discrimination, corporate law and so on? Some of these points are addressed in subsequent chapters. A complex web of regulatory law, regulatory agencies and regulatory networks would have to be unpicked from realms as disparate as competition law to aviation safety. Could we re-nationalise public service providers giving them special terms which would otherwise breach EU case law.[96]

Last of all, if there were an exit from the EU and also the ECHR/Council of Europe, would this foment pressure for the creation of a written constitution? Would a heightened sense of legality, constitutionalism and human rights actually prompt developments on a written constitution?[97] We have, we suggest, under European influence, juridified our constitution. But the ultimate safeguard of legality, the *guaranteed* supremacy of law over combined executive and legislative authority, is not a part of our constitution as Lord Bingham recognised.[98] There is still a point at which constitutional convention and legal right are not coeval.[99] We do not have that 'somewhat fundamental' as Cromwell expressed the point in 1654. The judges have taken great strength from European influence, an influence that would survive upheaval of our membership of Europe we maintain. What lies behind Laws LJ's judgment in *Thoburn* is that happy compromise, as Laws sees it, of a 'balanced constitution' reinforced by common law constitutionalism. Would we have arrived there without EU influence? We doubt it. How long would common law fundamentalism survive without that influence? We in the UK have placed a special focus on the ECHR unlike other countries because human rights protection is in their written constitutions, but not with us. A Prime Ministerial Commission examined the case for

94. *Rehman* [2003] 1 AC 153, *Gentle* [2008] UKHL 20, *Nicklinson supra* n. 90, *HS2 supra* n. 35.
95. *See* House of Commons Research Paper 10/62 *How Much Legislation Comes from Europe?* V. Miller (2010) http://www.echr.coe.int/Documents/Protocol_15_ENG.pdf.
96. In April 2014, the ECJ ruled that the legal status of the French mail company, La Poste, is contrary to EU law. Financial guarantee against bankruptcy constitutes state aid http://curia.europa.eu/juris/document/document.jsf?text=&docid=150285&pageIndex=0&doclang=EN&mode=lst&dir=&occ=first&part=1&cid=103101.
97. Political and Constitutional Reform Committee *A New Magna Carta?* HC 463 (2014-15).
98. T. Bingham, *supra* n. 18, at 169–170 and Neuberger *supra* n. 18.
99. J. Goldsworthy (2010) *supra* n. 20, at 315.

a UK Bill of Rights in 2012.[100] The subject has been deferred for yet further consultation in the Queen's Speech in May 2015. To what extent could the rule of law and the separation of powers be meaningfully achieved without a written constitution? The latter is something that the devolved nations now arguably have in the devolution legislation. But what are the arching guiding principles of union and devolution?[101]

If we may return to Laws LJ in *Thoburn* (at paragraph 64) it seems clear the inspiration behind his new formulation of a balanced constitution is the EU factor. How long would that balance remain without the EU? If a balance were seen as under threat, would that re-focus attention on a UK written constitution to replace our self-referential one?

> This development of the common law regarding constitutional rights, and as I would say constitutional statutes, is highly beneficial. It gives us most of the benefits of a written constitution, in which fundamental rights are accorded special respect. But it preserves the sovereignty of the legislature and the flexibility of our uncodified constitution. It accepts the relation between legislative supremacy and fundamental rights is not fixed or brittle: rather the courts (in interpreting statutes, and now, applying the HRA) will pay more or less deference to the legislature, or other public decision-maker, according to the subject in hand. Nothing is plainer than that this benign development involves, as I have said, the recognition of the ECA as a constitutional statute.
>
> The 'limitation of sovereignty' to which Lord Bridge in *Factortame* referred arises only in the context of Community law's substantive provisions. It has no application where the question is, what is the legal foundation within which those substantive provisions enjoy their primacy, and by which the relation between the law and institutions of the EU law and the British State ultimately rests. The foundation is English [*sic* we add] law. [66]
>
> The fundamental legal basis of the United Kingdom's relationship with the EU rests with the domestic, not the European, legal powers. In the event, which no doubt would never happen in the real world, that a European measure was seen to be repugnant to a fundamental or constitutional right guaranteed by the law of England, a question would arise whether the general words of the ECA were sufficient to incorporate the measure and give it overriding effect in domestic law. But that is very far from this case. [Para 69]

What, we add, of a statutory provision 'repugnant to a fundamental or constitutional right guaranteed by the [common] law of England' and, we also add, Wales and Scotland and Northern Ireland?

---

100. http://www.bailii.org/eu/cases/EUECJ/2014/C13112.html The Prime Minister spoke originally of a *British* Bill of Rights. *See* the Conservative Party *Protecting Human Rights in the UK* (2014) http://www.theguardian.com/politics/interactive/2014/oct/03/conservatives-human-rights-act-full-document advocating severance of the 'link' between the CHR and the UK courts and a limitation of human rights, and the lecture by former Attorney General and Conservative MP Dominic Grieve supporting continuing membership of the ECHR 'Why Human Rights Should Matter to Conservatives.' http://www.ucl.ac.uk/constitution-unit/constitution-unit-news/031214a.
101. *See* the Bingham Centre's proposals for principles of a fair and durable settlement within the Union in a Charter of the Union: *A Constitutional Crossroads: Ways Forward for the United Kingdom* (2015) http://www.biicl.org/documents/595_a_constitutional_crossroads.pdf.

In short our European experience has made us think differently about the constitution and legality. This is what the Europeans have given us. They have helped bring out the catholicity of the common law. Leaving the EU and repealing the Human Rights Act will not remove this influence, we believe.

CHAPTER 2

A Tale of Two Referendums: Scotland, the UK and Europe

Stephen Tierney & Katie Boyle

§2.01 INTRODUCTION

On 18 September 2014, Scots were asked the question: 'Should Scotland be an independent country?' Fifty-five per cent said 'No' on a turnout of 84%. The referendum on Scottish independence produced much debate concerning how an independent Scotland would come to membership of the European Union. In this chapter we will reflect upon this debate since it is of on-going significance for a number of reasons. The first is the way in which it opened up discussion about membership of the EU for sub-state territories, a debate which has resonance beyond the borders of the UK, most obviously in Spain. Secondly, the Scottish independence debate is unlikely to go away and may well be revived by Scottish nationalists in the medium term, reviving the whole debate about how a region of Europe can join the EU from within. Thirdly, the referendum has led to a process to devolve more and more powers, particularly fiscal responsibility to the Scottish Parliament,[1] which may well see Scotland seeking to develop specific, bilateral economic ties with its European partners as it seeks to use these powers to develop a distinctive economic trajectory. And fourthly and most dramatically, the plans by the Conservative Government to stage an in/out referendum[2] could well reawaken the issue of Scotland's place in Europe, particularly if Scots are faced with withdrawal from the European Union.

We will now look at how the issue of EU membership became so central to the Scottish independence debate, exploring the issue of whether and if so how Scotland would have achieved membership of the EU. In Part III we will turn to the question of

1. Scotland Bill (HC) 2015–16.
2. European Union (Referendum) Bill (HC) 2015–16.

how the current debate over the UK's membership of the EU has a territorial dimension within the UK, and the potential scenarios that might follow respectively a Yes or No outcome in a referendum on whether or not the UK ought to exit the European Union.

§2.02 THE IMPACT OF EU ISSUES UPON THE SCOTTISH INDEPENDENCE DEBATE

[A] Background: The Status of EU Law in Scots Law

The law of the European Union has effect in Scotland. The European Communities Act 1972 provides that all rights, powers, liabilities, obligations and restrictions created by or arising under EU treaties will be recognisable and given effect to in UK law.[3] The Act also ensures that courts in the UK are bound by decisions of the Court of Justice of the European Union (CJEU).[4] The primacy of EU law, in areas of EU competence, is further reinforced by section 2(4) of the Act which provides that any legislation passed after the entry into force of the Act should be construed and given effect to in accordance with EU law. This hierarchical relationship reflects the doctrine of the supremacy of EU law as developed by the CJEU.[5] The domestic jurisprudence of the UK courts has also evolved in light of the Strasbourg case law, to the point where national courts are prepared to disapply primary legislation of the UK Parliament which is inconsistent with EU law.[6] The jurisprudence of the CJEU also affords individuals the right to rely on EU law in national courts under the principle of direct effect.[7]

In Scotland, which has its own legal system, the jurisprudence of the *Factortame* and related cases has been fully accepted.[8] Furthermore, EU law is accorded specific primacy in relation to the executive and legislative organs of Scottish government by the devolution settlement of 1998.[9]

---

3. European Communities Act 1972, section 2(1).
4. European Communities Act 1972, section 3.
5. *See Van Gend en Loos v. Nederlandse Administratie der Belastingen* (1963) Case 26/62 where the Court of Justice held that EC law constitutes a discrete system of law which operates with direct effect in Member States, and *Costa v. Enel* (1964) Case 6/64 where the Court held that EC law supersedes national law including the constitutional law of Member States in cases of incompatibility between the two legal systems.
6. *Factortame (No. 1)* [1990] 2 AC 85; *Factortame (No. 2)* [1991] 1 AC 603 and *R v. Secretary of State for Transport, ex p. Equal Opportunities Commission* [1995] 1 AC 1.
7. *Van Gend en Loos v. Nederlandse Administratie der Belastingen* (1963) Case 26/62.
8. *R. (on the application of Chester) v. Secretary of State for Justice* [2013] UKSC 63; *Somerville v. Scottish Ministers* [2007] UKHL 44, as per Lord Hope, paragraph 17 and Lord Mance paragraph 180.
9. The Scotland Act 1998 (section 29) provides that any provision of an Act of the Scottish Parliament is *ultra vires* if it is incompatible with EU law, and (section 57) that Ministers of the Scottish Government have no power to act incompatibly with EU law.

[B] How Would an Independent Scotland Have Negotiated Membership?

It was the intention of the Scottish Government[10] that, following a 'Yes' vote on 18 September 2014, negotiations would begin to bring about an agreement with the UK Government as to the terms of Scottish independence, leading to a declaration of independence in March 2016.[11] The Scottish Government intended that negotiations would also take place with the European Union during this interim period to bring about Scottish membership of the EU on the same date as independence from the UK is achieved.[12]

A crucial issue during the referendum campaign was how steps would be taken, concurrently with these domestic negotiations, to secure Scotland's membership of the European Union. This issue was of considerable significance for the UK as a whole, given the commitment of the Conservative Party to hold a referendum on EU membership, provisionally scheduled for 2017. This chapter is concerned principally with Scotland's membership of the EU, but the uncertainty relating to the UK's commitment to the EU could well have been a factor in negotiations both between the two governments and in Scotland's discussions with the EU itself, and, as the UK continues to question the terms of its own membership of the EU, may well keep the independence debate alive.

[C] Parties to Negotiation

In the period immediately following a Yes vote Scotland would not have been an independent state of course and, therefore, if negotiations were to commence in relation to Scotland becoming an independent member of the EU, it was unclear who would take part in such negotiations or how they would be conducted.

The situation was unprecedented. No territory has ever joined the European Union from the inside as it were, seceding from an existing Member State.[13] Two main options presented themselves. The first was a bilateral process conducted by the UK on Scotland's behalf with the institutions of the EU. In these negotiations Scottish representatives could attend on behalf of the UK. In our view a more likely scenario was that the Scottish Government would itself have been represented in these talks.

10. The Scottish Government, 'Scotland's Future', 26 Nov. 2013, Part 4 'Transition', p. 338, also pp. 51–52. Hereafter '*Scotland's Future*'.
11. *Scotland's Future*, pp. 20, 51, 338.
12. 'In the period between a vote for independence on 18 September 2014 and independence day on 24 March 2016 agreements will be reached with the rest of the UK, represented by the Westminster Government, and with the EU and other international partners and organisations'. *Scotland's Future*, p. 338, *See also*: 'The UK and Scottish Governments, along with the EU institutions and Member States, will have a shared interest in working together to conclude these negotiations to transfer Scotland's EU membership from membership as part of the UK to membership as an independent Member State.' *Scotland's Future*, p. 53.
13. The Scottish situation must be distinguished from cases where territories in effect were withdrawn from the jurisdiction of the European Communities, as were Algeria and Greenland: Stephen Tierney, *Legal Issues Surrounding the Referendum on Independence for Scotland*, Eur. Const. L. Rev. 359–390, p. 382.

Another issue was whether negotiations with the EU would involve only the Scottish Government negotiating for Scottish membership and EU officials, or whether they would include representatives of the United Kingdom whose membership would inevitably be affected by the transition. A tripartite process was the more likely scenario, particularly as it would have been necessary at some point to adjust the UK's level of representation within European institutions.

[D] The United Kingdom's Position

One argument was that it would not have been in the UK's interests to help negotiate Scotland's accession to the European Union. And in the course of the referendum campaign, the UK Government certainly set out to accentuate the potential difficulties Scotland would face in seeking to join the EU.[14] But we need to distinguish positions adopted during a referendum campaign from those likely to be taken following a 'Yes' vote. While it was clearly not in the interests of the UK Government prior to the referendum to suggest that the process towards Scotland's EU membership would be smooth (indeed accentuating uncertainty over Scotland's EU position was a key strategy of the Better Together campaign), following a 'Yes' vote the UK Government would most likely have considered it to be in the UK's interests to have its close neighbour inside rather than outside the EU, particularly if the two countries continued to share matters of vital interest.

The current devolution arrangements governing relations between the UK government and the devolved governments provide for a spirit of cooperation.[15] The Scottish and UK administrations have tended to cooperate well over relations with the EU, even when the parties in office in Edinburgh and London have been ideologically very different. This may have changed following a 'Yes' vote since the principles of cooperation were based upon common interests within one state. Nonetheless, there are strong reasons to believe that an independent Scotland and the rest of the UK would have continued to share many common interests in relation to the EU, not least a

14. In a policy paper the UK Government argued that Scotland's negotiations to join the EU 'could be complex and long, and the outcome could prove less advantageous than the status quo'. It contended that Scotland will face difficulties in negotiating membership of the EU, in particular in any attempt to secure similar terms to the existing membership arrangements which the UK enjoys as a Member State. The UK Government argued that Scotland would not be able to secure the same terms in relation to monetary union, Schengen, the budgetary rebate, and would no longer have the guaranteed support of the rest of the UK in relation to matters of common interest such as fisheries policy. 'Scotland Analysis: EU and International Issues', (HM Government, January 2014), p. 55.
15. Memorandum of Understanding and Supplementary Agreements between the United Kingdom Government, the Scottish Ministers, the Welsh Ministers, and the Northern Ireland Executive Committee', 2000, as updated in September 2012. This Memorandum also informs the approach underpinning the Edinburgh Agreement by which the UK and Scottish Governments agreed terms for the holding of the referendum: 'Agreement between the United Kingdom Government and the Scottish Government on a referendum on independence for Scotland', 15 Oct. 2012.

resistance to monetary union through the Euro and a common approach to border controls.[16]

This leads also to the Edinburgh Agreement, the terms of which provided that the two governments would work together in the best interests of the people of Scotland and of the rest of the UK following the referendum.[17] This did not expressly commit the UK Government to help facilitate Scotland's membership, but it was widely viewed that the mutual interests of both peoples would have been best served by Scotland's membership of the EU.

[E] Attitude of the European Union

The position of the EU institutions was not entirely clear. Former President of the European Commission, Jose Manuel Barroso, said it would be 'extremely difficult, if not impossible' for an independent Scotland to join the European Union.[18] This view was heavily criticised by observers,[19] and was neither substantiated nor elaborated upon by Mr Barroso. On the other hand, Jean-Claude Juncker, elected on 15 July 2014 to succeed Mr Barroso as the new President of the Commission (his appointment as President took effect from 1 November 2014), was reportedly 'sympathetic' to an independent Scotland joining the EU.[20] Although Mr Juncker took the general view that there should be no further enlargement until 2019, clarification from EU officials indicated that this 'ban' on further enlargement did not apply to an application for membership by a newly independent Scotland which would be treated as a 'special and separate case' as it already meets 'core-EU requirements'.[21] One of Scotland's MEPs, David Martin, also suggested that the EU Commission would recommend membership for an independent Scotland and that this process towards accession could begin on an informal basis before independence.[22]

16. We should also note of course that the currency union issue was contentious and that there could be have been other pressure points. For example, if the Scottish Government sought to charge UK students tuition fees higher than those charged to other EU citizens. *See* Niamh Nic Shuibhne, 'University Fees and rUK Students – the EU Legal Framework', *Scottish Constitutional Futures Forum Blog*, 18 Dec. 2013. http://www.scottishconstitutionalfutures.org/OpinionandAnalysis/ViewBlogPost/tabid/1767/articleType/ArticleView/articleId/2759/Niamh-Nic-Shuibhne-University-Fees-and-rUK-Students--the-EU-Legal-Framework.aspx.
17. 'Agreement between the United Kingdom Government and the Scottish Government on a referendum on independence for Scotland', 15 Oct. 2012, paragraph 30.
18. *Scottish Independence: Barroso says joining EU would be difficult*, 16 Feb. 2014, available at http://www.bbc.com/news/uk-scotland-scotland-politics-26215963.
19. Neil Walker, 'Hijacking the Debate', *The Future of the United Kingdom and Scotland (ESRC) Blog*, 21 Feb. 2014 http://www.futureukandscotland.ac.uk/blog/hijacking-debate.
20. Scot MacNab, *Junker bans any new EU member for 5 years,* The Scotsman, 15 Jul. 2014, available at http://www.scotsman.com/news/politics/top-stories/independence-juncker-sympathetic-to-scots-eu-bid-1-3482266.
21. Scot MacNab *ibid. See also* Andrew Whitaker, 'Independence: Juncker "sympathetic" to Scotland EU bid', 20 Jul. 2014, available at http://www.scotsman.com/news/politics/top-stories/row-as-juncker-bars-any-new-eu-members-for-5-years-1-3477066.
22. Angus Roxburgh, 'Labour MEP: "independence no barrier to EU membership"', Sunday Herald, 18 May 2014, http://www.heraldscotland.com/politics/referendum-news/labour-mep-independence-no-barrier-to-eu-membership.24250593.

[F] Treaties and Admission

It was always highly likely that in the event of independence the rest of the UK would have continued in membership of the European Union,[23] although there would also have been a need for treaty amendments to accommodate a smaller UK in a proportionate way within European institutions.[24] But how would Scotland have been admitted to membership? The European treaties do not provide for the situation of a territory joining from the inside as it were.

In light of the uniqueness of the Scottish situation we saw a debate among commentators concerning whether Articles 48 or 49 of the Treaty on European Union respectively would offer the more appropriate route. Article 49 provides the process for new applicant States, joining the EU from the outside (hereafter 'formal accession'). By this provision a new State needs to apply for EU membership leading to an accession agreement that would require to be sanctioned unanimously and ratified by all Member States. There are a number of criteria laid down in Article 49 and if these are met then accession is effected by the unanimous decision of the Council, a majority decision of the European Parliament, and subsequent ratification of the accession treaty by the Member States in accordance with their own respective constitutions. It was argued by some that this was the only feasible route by which Scotland could accede to the EU.[25] Another possibility was that accession could be arrived at by way of treaty amendments, deploying Article 48 in a process which would be, on the face of things, less cumbersome.

It would appear that both Articles 48 and 49 offer plausible routes to membership for sub-state territories seeking to join the EU from within, with the Article 48 route endorsed as a possibility by, for example, David Edward.[26] Both of these routes were discussed at some length by Tierney in an earlier paper.[27] It seems that in the end Article 49 may, however, be the more plausible route for membership for a sub-state

---

23. Tierney 2013. And *see* Case 148/77, *Hansen v. Hauptzollamt Flensburg* [1978] ECR 1787 which suggests that the limits of the territory of a Member State is for the State to define. Cited by James Crawford and Alan Boyle, 'Referendum on the Independence of Scotland – International Law Aspects'. Opinion published in annex to the UK Government's 'Report on "Devolution and the Implications of Scottish Independence"', UK Government, Cm 8554, February 2013, paragraph 159, hereafter 'Crawford and Boyle'.
24. Crawford and Boyle, paragraph 150.
25. Jean-Claude Piris, unpublished paper presented at European University Institute, 2 Jul. 2014 (on file with the authors).
26. David Edward. 'Scotland and the European Union', Scottish Constitutional Futures Forum blog, 17 Dec. 2012 http://www.scottishconstitutionalfutures.org/OpinionandAnalysis/ViewBlogPost/tabid/1767/articleType/ArticleView/articleId/852/David-Edward-Scotland-and-the-European-Union.aspx.

    See also Bruno de Witte, 'Seamless Transition? Scottish Membership of the EU by Means of Treaty Revision. Rather than Accession', unpublished paper presented at European University Institute, 2 Jul. 2014 (on file with the authors), who also considered the Article 48 route to be feasible, as did Sionaidh Douglas-Scott, 'Why the EU Should Welcome and Independent Scotland', *Scottish Constitutional Futures Forum blog*: http://www.scottishconstitutionalfutures.org/OpinionandAnalysis/ViewBlogPost/tabid/1767/articleType/ArticleView/articleId/4041/Sionaidh-Douglas-Scott-Why-the-EU-Should-Welcome-an-Independent-Scotland.aspx.
27. Tierney 2013.

territory moving to independent statehood. Herman Van Rompuy, President of the European Council, took this view.[28] Another reason is that the case law of the CJEU establishes that specific articles have preference over general ones. While Article 48 provides a general route to membership, Article 49 is the only article which specifically deals with accession and admission of a State as a member of the EU. And on this basis it would seem to be the default route.

We see the expression of this view in advice to the Scottish Parliament by Jean-Claude Piris, the former Legal Counsel of the European Council and of the EU Council and Director General of the Legal Service of the EU Council (1988–2010):

> On a formal legal point of view, the case law of the Court of Justice of the EU establishes that one cannot choose freely an article of the EU Treaties to adopt an act or make a decision. The Court refers to '*the aim and content*' of an act or decision as being the only way to determine the correct choice of its legal base. It also stresses that specific articles have priority upon general ones. Article 49 is the only article in the EU Treaties which provides the specific procedure to be followed for the admission of a State as a member of the EU. Article 49 specifically mentions that adjustments to the Treaties will be entailed by the admission procedure, and that they will be dealt with at the same time and in the same international agreement which will contain the conditions of admission. The sole aim and content of the decisions to be made in the present case would be the admission of Scotland in the EU. Article 48 does not deal with the issue of the admission of a State as a member of the EU but, in general, with possible amendments to the EU Treaties. I will thus conclude that, from a formal legal point of view, Article 49, which deals specifically with admission, must be followed in any case of admission...[29]

This is of course the position as Piris sees it from a 'formal legal point of view', and it is open to the EU to adopt a different process if it sees fit, applying Article 48 if this is preferred.[30] This could be the case if the process were not to be treated as one of formal accession for example, but as a way of realigning the treaties to admit Scotland and perhaps at the same time adjusting the UK's representation within EU institutions. But in such processes it seems wise not to assume that formal legality will hamstring political decision-making. As Michael Keating has noted: 'European leaders do not normally look to law to tell them what to do. They decided what they want to do politically and then find a legal means.'[31]

So while Article 49 looks the more plausible route, Article 48 remains a feasible alternative for sub-state admission. Regardless of whether Article 48 or 49 is used, a

28. 'Remarks by President of the European Council, Herman Van Rompuy, on Catalonia', 12 Dec. 2013, http://www.consilium.europa.eu/uedocs/cms_Data/docs/pressdata/en/ec/140072.pdf.
29. Written Evidence from Jean-Claude Piris to the European and External Affairs Committee of the Scottish Parliament, 23 Jan. 2014, pp.28–29.
30. *See* de Witte *supra* n. 26.
31. M. Keating, 'Would an Independent Scotland be in the European Union, in 'Scotland Decides' Jeffery and Perman eds (David Hume Institute, 2014), 47, http://www.futureukandscotland.ac.uk/papers/scotlands-decision-16-questions-think-about-referendum-18-september. *See also* Graham Avery: 'If Scotland votes for independence, the decision on how to proceed will not be taken by lawyers, but by the EU's leaders in the European Council, and they will decide on the basis of practical and political considerations.' Graham Avery, 'Could an independent Scotland join the European Union?' European Policy Centre, Policy Brief, 28 May 2014.

crucial factor is that the ratification of all Member States would still be needed either for a new accession treaty or for treaty amendments.

[G] Period of Negotiation and Process of Membership

As noted, it was the Scottish Government's intention that negotiations with the EU, as well as ratification of any treaty or treaty amendments, would be concluded within eighteen months in order to achieve Scotland's full membership of the EU at the same time as independence from the UK.

A number of commentators were sceptical of this time frame, although they tended also to point out that EU rights and obligations in relation to Scotland could be protected by way of interim measures. For example, Nick Barber argued that the proposed timescale of eighteen months was 'unrealistically tight, and likely to harm Scotland in a number of ways' as Scotland would be negotiating from a place of 'comparative weakness' within a restrictive timeframe with both the UK and the EU. Barber predicted that Scotland would be more likely to be able to negotiate EU membership by 2020 with an international agreement in place to preserve Scotland's legal position in the interim period:

> Whilst the timeframe of Scotland's Future is unrealistic, it is highly likely that Scotland would be able to join the EU before 2020. It is in no-one's interest to exclude Scotland from the Union. If, as is almost certainly the case, Scotland cannot complete the Article 48 process before the 2016 deadline, it is conceivable that some sort of international agreement could be reached between Scotland and the EU to preserve Scotland's legal position. Perhaps Scotland would then be treated a little like Norway: possessing many of the privileges and duties of EU membership, but not able to return MEPs to the European Parliament or appoint Commissioners.'[32]

A similar view was expressed by Kenneth Armstrong. He argued that accession could not occur until after independence and suggested that eighteen months was unrealistic. Although again, like Barber, he considered it conceivable that core substantive aspects of the accession treaty could be agreed as having provisional effect pending formal ratification through an interim international agreement under Article 218(5) TFEU.[33] Again, David Martin MEP, who dismissed the suggested period of eighteen months as 'nonsensical' (bearing in mind his membership of the Labour Party which is opposed to Scottish independence), conceded that 'temporary solutions could be found to smooth the transition.'[34]

---

32. 'Nick Barber, 'After the Vote', *Scottish Constitutional Futures Forum blog*, 14 Jan. 2014 http://www.scottishconstitutionalfutures.org/OpinionandAnalysis/ViewBlogPost/tabid/1767/articleType/ArticleView/articleId/4004/Nick-Barber-After-the-Vote-the-Citizenship-Question.aspx.
33. Written Evidence from Professor Kenneth Armstrong, House of Commons, European and External Affairs Committee, 23 Jan. 2014, paragraphs 38–39.
34. As quoted by Angus Roxburgh, 'Labour MEP: "independence no barrier to EU membership"', Sunday Herald, 18 May 2014, http://www.heraldscotland.com/politics/referendum-news/labour-mep-independence-no-barrier-to-eu-membership.24250593.

On the other hand James Crawford, co-author of a report for the UK government setting out the constitutional and international implications of Scottish independence,[35] expressed the view in a Radio 4 interview that the 'Scottish estimate is about eighteen months, and that seems realistic'.[36]

In the end of course it is now impossible to guess how quickly negotiations might have been concluded. But for Scotland as for any other sub-state territory seeking independent membership of the Union there would have been a number of initial steps in setting up negotiations:

- a request to the EU to open negotiations;
- planning how these would proceed, and establishing terms;
- working out relations between the territory and the Member State vis-à-vis these negotiations, how each would be represented, etc.
- formulating negotiating teams on all sides; establishing mandates for each, etc.

As noted above, the UK Government clearly had an interest in emphasising that negotiations could be difficult and stated that Scotland's negotiations to join the EU 'could be complex and long, and the outcome could prove less advantageous than the status quo'.[37] To some extent this was of course campaign posturing but it is also the case that Scotland would have faced significant challenges in seeking opt outs from the single currency and in relation to the Schengen agreement. There was also the question of the budgetary rebate which the UK currently enjoys but which is due for review in 2020.[38]

Finally, there would have been a need to secure the ratification of all Member States to any accession treaty or treaty amendment. Some have argued that certain states might have opposed Scottish membership and if so they might have tried to use the ratification process either to delay their consent or to refuse it altogether. Spain is an obvious case since it would not want to set a precedent for its own sub-state nations, in particular Catalonia, which has a strong 'independence in Europe' movement. Michael Keating observed however that Spanish Ministers when invited to do so declined to state that Spain would veto Scottish accession, and instead distinguished the Scottish case from that in Spain, where, in the central government's view, the constitution does not permit either acts of secession or referendums on secession.[39] Graham Avery also cites Spain's Foreign Minister García-Margallo who stated: 'the attitude of the United Kingdom would be the determining factor at the time of deciding our vote'.[40] Avery observes: 'That is logical, for Spain wants its own voice to be

35. Crawford and Boyle.
36. Professor James Crawford, *Today Programme*, Radio 4, 11 Feb. 2013.
37. 'Scotland Analysis: EU and International Issues', (HM Government, January 2014), available at https://www.gov.uk/government/uploads/system/uploads/attachment_data/file/271794/2901475_HMG_Scotland_EUandInternational_acc2.pdf, p.55.
38. The Scottish Government's aspirations in respect of each of these issues are set out in *Scotland's Future, see* e.g., p. 223.
39. M. Keating, 'Would an Independent Scotland be in the European Union', in Jeffery and Perman eds., *Scotland Decides* (David Hume Institute, 2014), p. 47.
40. Avery *supra* n. 31, at 3.

determinant in the case of Catalonia.'[41] A veto by any Member State in the end seemed highly unlikely. If the UK Government was prepared to recognise an independent Scotland and work towards its membership of the EU with the cooperation of the EU institutions and the overwhelming majority of other Member States, then it was simply unimaginable that this would be vetoed by an individual Member State.

That does not mean of course that the ratification process would have been concluded quickly. It could have been done in a short period of time but it is also useful to consider the situation where either negotiations were not concluded or ratification of all Member States had not been achieved by the date of Scottish independence.

[H] Scotland outside of the European Union?

In the event that the negotiation or ratification processes were not complete by March 2016, what would have happened? One option would have been for Scotland to delay a declaration of independence. This would seem to be unlikely. The Scottish Government was keen for formal independence to be declared before the Scottish Parliament elections scheduled for May 2016. Any proposed delay could also have faced the opposition of the UK Government which may well have taken the view that if the decision had been taken by Scotland to go then it was in the best interests of the UK if this was done as quickly as possible to end the period of constitutional limbo.

In this event would Scotland, in declaring independence, have found itself outside of the European Union? For a number of reasons this seems an unlikely scenario. Scotland is already part of the EU, it is of economic, strategic and territorial importance to the EU, it is integrated into its institutions, its territory is subject to EU law, and residents of Scotland enjoy the rights of EU citizenship. For these reasons it seems that it would have been in the interests of the EU to ensure that the jurisdiction of EU law and the rights and responsibilities of citizenship continued to apply to Scotland in any intervening period between independence and full EU membership rather than try to deal with the administrative upheaval which the removal of Scotland from the writ of EU law would have brought.

The whole debate also took place at a time of uncertainty for the European Union in light of the economic crisis and problems in Ukraine. As Keating puts it: 'It is difficult to see why either the European institutions or the Member States would want to add to their troubles by seeking to exclude Scotland, disrupting the internal market and discrediting an eminently democratic means of resolving a self-determination dispute.'[42]

As we discussed in relation to the period for negotiations, a more likely prospect was an interim arrangement which would secure rights and privileges of European citizens in relation to Scotland, but would have delayed formal membership by Scotland until negotiations and/or the ratification process were concluded. Armstrong suggested this as a possible interim solution:

41. *Ibid.*
42. M. Keating, *Would an Independent Scotland be in the European Union*, 48.

> [C]ore substantive aspects of the accession treaty could be agreed as having provisional effect pending formal ratification. This could be written into the treaty itself and include important aspects of EU law relating to the Single Market. While there is no direct precedent for this in the context of accession – Austria, Sweden and Finland had the continuing benefit of their EFTA membership of the EEA pending their formal EU accession – it is far from being an implausible legal strategy to avoid certain disruptions in Scotland- EU relations. Moreover, there is specific provision in Article 218(5) TFEU for international agreements between the EU and third counties or international organisations to have provisional application pending the entry into force of the agreement. By analogy this might also apply in an accession context.[43]

Jean-Claude Piris, whom we have seen is strongly of the view that an Article 49 process would be needed to bring about accession, seemed also to consider that an interim arrangement would preserve Scotland's position in relation to the EU:

> the duty of the EU and of its Member States would be to try and reach a swift agreement with the new State, in order to avoid complex legal situations and negative economic effects, as well as disrupting the lives of many individuals. The delay between the date of the political decision on independence and its entry into force could be used in order to try and reach such an agreement, at least on provisional arrangements during a period of transition.[44]

See also Graham Avery:

> From a practical point of view, no Member State has a material interest in Scotland remaining outside the EU, even for a short time. This would deprive the EU of the benefits of Scotland's membership (budgetary contribution, fisheries resources, etc.). Scotland outside the EU, and not applying EU rules, would be a legal nightmare for EU Member States, whose citizens and enterprises would lose their rights in Scotland. No Member State, particularly not the rest of the UK, would have an interest in creating such an anomaly.[45]

In the end these various positions were not tested. But the notion that Scotland would have been able to accede to membership of the Union and also that there would be little likelihood of any period of membership limbo both remain very pertinent points as we consider both that the independence issue is unlikely to go away,

---

43. Kenneth Armstrong, Written Evidence from Kenneth Armstrong to the European and External Affairs Committee of the Scottish Parliament, January 2014 paragraph 39.
44. Piris *supra* n. 29, p. 6.
45. Avery *supra* n. 31, p. 2. *See* again the blog by David Edward *supra* in which he discusses what he sees as the absurdity of the following situation: 'Until the moment of separation, Scotland would remain an integral part of the EU; the Scottish people and all EU citizens living in Scotland would enjoy all the rights of citizenship and free movement; and the same would apply, correspondingly, to all other EU citizens and companies in their relations with Scotland. Then, at the midnight hour, all these relationships would come abruptly to an end.

    The logical consequence in law would be that the acquis communautaire would no longer, as such, be part of the law of Scotland. Scotland would cease to be constrained in relation to the rates of VAT and corporation tax. Erasmus students studying in Scotland would become 'foreign students' liable to pay full third country fees, as would students from England, Wales and Northern Ireland. Non-Scottish fishermen would be excluded from Scottish waters. And all the waters between Scotland and Norway would cease to be within the jurisdiction of the EU – an important security consideration quite apart from fishery rights.'

particularly giving the Scottish National Party's astonishing success (winning fifty-six of fifty-nine seats in Scotland) in the General Election of May 2015, and that it may in fact be revived depending upon the result and consequences of the planned referendum at UK level on EU membership.

§2.03 SCOTLAND AFTER THE REFERENDUM: THE DEBATE OVER UK MEMBERSHIP OF THE EU

[A] A Referendum on UK Membership: The 'No Vote' Scenario

In the event that a majority vote 'No' in the referendum on UK membership[46] it would seem at first glance that everything will stay the same, but will it? One thing which may be relevant is a breakdown in the vote from region to region within the UK. If polls were to show that a majority of Scots voted 'No' to exit from the European Union and that this was decisive to an overall result, given a majority vote within the rest of the UK to leaving the EU, this would surely stoke resentment particularly among pro-exit voters in England.

Of course an obvious response would be that the UK is one country and the result must be accepted at a pan-UK level. But the notion that this disjuncture between English and Scottish voting outcomes would simply have to be accepted by English people sharing the UK state may in fact be undermined by the Scottish referendum itself. A political argument could emerge that Scots have shown themselves no longer to be fully committed to the British project both by holding a referendum on independence and by the closeness of the result in that referendum, not to mention the 2015 election. If Scots are indeed seen as semi-detached from the UK then the idea that they should exercise an effective veto on England's EU membership will not, to say the least, sit very comfortably. We also know from recent attitudes data that those identifying as exclusively or primarily English not British are also much more likely to favour the independence from Europe movement.[47] It seems very possible that English nationalist sentiment could well be intensified if people sense they are being forced to remain within the EU by a part of the UK that appears to be so disengaged from the British project. This sentiment may be further compounded by the fact the electorate on the Scottish independence referendum was restricted to those living in Scotland meaning there was no English voice or English determination of the future of England's union with Scotland.

Another issue is the moving constitutional landscape of the UK itself following a 'No' vote in the independence referendum. The Better Together campaign in Scotland towards the end of the process promised extensive constitutional change and this led to the establishment of the Smith Commission.[48] This body was created by the UK

46. The proposed question is: 'Do you think that the United Kingdom should be a member of the European Union?'. European Union (Referendum) Bill 2015-16, clause 1(4).
47. Wyn Jones, R. et al, 'England and its Two Unions', 2013, http://www.ippr.org/publications/england-and-its-two-unions-the-anatomy-of-a-nation-and-its-discontents.
48. https://www.smith-commission.scot/.

Government and given the task of convening cross-party talks to produce, by 30 November 2014 recommendations for further devolution of powers to the Scottish Parliament. On 27 November the Smith Commission published its report proposing radical new powers for the Scottish Parliament, in particular tax powers including control over income tax in Scotland and responsibility for certain important welfare powers.[49] The remit of this body was to focus only upon more powers that might be ceded to the Scottish Parliament. Since the 2015 election these proposals have been taken forward by the UK Government. The draft Scotland Bill published in June 2015 will realign significantly the balance of competences currently set out in the Scotland Acts of 1998 and 2012. However, one question is whether giving significantly more powers, particularly tax powers, to the Scottish Parliament might have implications for Scotland's relationship with Europe. When the Scotland Bill is passed, Scotland will indeed acquire far more fiscal responsibility, making it possibly the most fiscally devolved territory within Europe. If so, this will involve the Scottish Government in setting its own economic policies, and to this end it is likely that it will seek input to Brussels decision-making and also to bilateral trade relations with EU states and regions.

This may be a particular issue if Scotland is left to generate its own wealth through new fiscal autonomy. In other words, if tax revenue falls and Scotland finds itself with reduced funding and the Barnett formula on grant distribution to Scotland from the UK is no longer there to top up any shortfall. This would put pressure on Scotland to maximise trade development, use of capital investment, infrastructure investment, etc. to advance Scotland's interests. Indeed such a proposal has already been made; only one month after the referendum the SNP was already calling for direct representation for Scotland within the EU.[50] In its submission to the Smith Commission the Scottish Government also states: 'Scotland should be able to act directly in the European Union on fisheries, marine environment and food and drink exports, given their importance within the Scottish economy and the distinctive policy positions in Scotland. In areas such as fisheries, where Scotland has the predominant interest within the UK, Scotland should have the lead role at Council, where appropriate.'[51] The Smith Commission did make certain modest recommendations about giving Scotland a stronger role in UK representation in Brussels,[52] but it seems that the aspirations of the Scottish Government could well outstrip these proposals.

In addition to seeking representation within the European Union, further fiscal devolution may well see the devolved institutions of Scotland linking Scotland directly to state and private European partners where possible, building direct relationships with public bodies and with corporations in attempts to attract trade and investment. The lure of specific tax policies may be used in this way. Now that there has been a 'No' vote in the Scottish referendum the reality is that devolution is here to stay for the time

49. https://www.smith-commission.scot/about/.
50. 'Scotland "needs direct EU representation" – Hyslop', The Scotsman, 15 Oct. 2014.
51. The Scottish Government, 'More Powers for the Scottish Parliament, Scottish Government Proposals', Edinburgh 2014, available at http://www.scotland.gov.uk/Resource/0046/00460563.pdf, p. 20.
52. Smith Commission report, paragraph 31.

being (although when the SNP might try to hold a second referendum we do not know). Will Scottish institutions do better in developing a regional presence, accessing the informal networks within European decision-making than other regions do? There are regions in Europe that are much better networked than sub-state territories in the UK and it may be that stronger efforts will be made to learn from these. This may be particularly the case in light of the devolution of more powers.

Such efforts at 'paradiplomacy' could well face opposition not only within the UK which will not be keen to see radically different tax regimes across the state, but also because of the institutional disposition of the EU itself. There will be specific issues about state aid which will need to be analysed carefully, but beyond this there is the bigger picture within which regions in Europe struggle for meaningful representation. The reality for sub-state territories within Europe is that states are the only serious actors at the political level, at least at the level of formal representation. All sorts of imaginative scenarios in constitutional design are possible within states as a way of managing plural territorial identities, but this reality has not been replicated at the EU level where the Committees of the Regions initiative has not offered much to sub-state territories. This no doubt lies behind the Scottish Government's new goal of better representation within Europe, but the reality is that hopes for such a change are slim. The European order has not yet caught up with the development and emergence of regional powers in what has been termed a 'post-independence' era.[53] Regional territories are emerging as 'dynamic, networked, territorial configurations embedded in their referential nation-states and driven by a wide range of diverse, transformative promotional policies'.[54] Without a coherent infrastructure to recognise the formation of regional powers, nation-states, the EU and the regional powers themselves face uncertainty.[55]

The European Union works on the basis of the Union on the one hand, with its own state-like aspirations, and Member States on the other, with no real scope for regions to play a meaningful role in European deliberations. This arguably goes against one of the founding principles of the EU project, the principle of subsidiarity – i.e., that decisions be made as close to the citizen as possible. Whilst the EU may well be committed to this principle of subsidiarity at a regional level through consultation with the Committee of the Regions,[56] the infrastructure for supporting regional mechanisms remains weak. In addition to this, the reaction to the very idea of such a region leaving its existing state to become an independent Member State was met with something

53. Igor Calzada, 'Europe is witnessing a new regional order, built on territories such as Scotland, Catalonia and the Basque Country', London School of Economics European Politics and Policy Blog (EUROPP), 22 Oct. 2014, available at http://blogs.lse.ac.uk/europpblog/2014/10/22/europe-is-witnessing-the-establishment-of-a-new-regional-order-built-on-territories-such-as-scotland-catalonia-and-the-basque-country/.

54. *Ibid.*

55. *Ibid.*

56. *See* for example the consultative rights the Committee of the Regions has under the Lisbon Treaty and the ability to bring judicial action in relation to consultative rights under Article 8 of the Protocol on the Application of the Principles of Subsidiarity and Proportionality, Treaty of Lisbon Amending the Treaty on European Union and the Treaty Establishing the European Community, 13 Dec. 2007, 2007/C 306/01.

approaching open hostility. We see this in the attitude of senior EU actors to the prospect of Scottish independence. We cited above the intervention by European Commission President Jose Manuel Barroso, reiterating a strongly statist position in arguing that Scotland would find negotiating entry to the EU to be difficult. The hostility which the Scottish independence movement faced shows that in many quarters no account is taken of the very reality of national pluralism within states. This is an ironic conclusion to draw given that the EU itself embodies national pluralism and has been fashioned upon the need to manage this both institutionally politically and constitutionally. In many ways the EU establishment, for all the talk among academics about constitutional pluralism, remains quite old-fashioned on the issue of state powers and territorial integrity. The world remains a binary one of states and international institutions.

Paradoxically, this lack of representation for regions may well be stoking the kind of secessionism which the EU dislikes. During the referendum campaign the Scottish nationalists were able to argue that the only way to achieve meaningful representation in the EU for Scotland was through independence. In the end it was difficult to develop this argument too far because the Yes campaign remained on the back foot since it also had to defend its claim that EU membership would be straightforward and the terms of entry would be favourable. In other words, the 'Yes' campaign found it hard to move the debate on to discussing the advantages of independent membership. But this is an argument that continues to be made not only in Scotland but also currently in the Catalan independence debate.

[B] What If the UK Votes to Leave the EU?

The second scenario is a referendum outcome where a majority of UK voters vote to leave the EU but voting data shows that a majority of Scots voted to remain. This would potentially re-open the entire constitutional debate in Scotland. It would be argued that many would not have voted against independence in 2014 if it had been known that the UK was destined to leave the EU a few years later. Such an argument is made more plausible by the way in which the Scottish Government made EU membership such a central plank of its campaign for a newly independent Scotland.

It is widely expected that the independence referendum has settled the issue for the foreseeable future. But EU exit by the UK could cause this to be re-opened. The SNP has argued that the EU referendum should in fact require the support of all four 'nations' of the UK, Scotland, Wales, England and Northern Ireland, before an exit vote could be deemed to be valid, in effect providing Scotland with a veto over the decision.[57] Faced with the prospect of EU exit, Scottish nationalists would no doubt see this as a mandate to ask Scots separately to choose the UK or the EU in a new Scottish

57. 'SNP's Sturgeon says UK withdrawal from EU "must have" four nation backing', BBC News 29 Oct. 2014, http://www.bbc.co.uk/news/uk-scotland-scotland-politics-29805045.

referendum.[58] And perhaps many who would not describe themselves as nationalists would take the view that this was indeed legitimate. For some the issue would simply be one of choice. The Scottish people should be allowed to decide on independence again before the country exits the EU; for others it may be an issue of substantive choice, with some who did not vote 'Yes' in the 2014 referendum deciding that they would prefer to live in an independent Scotland within the EU than a United Kingdom outside of the common market.

And what of the EU itself? Let's not forget that a vote to leave the EU by the UK need not be the end of the matter. There is after all Article 50 TEU. By this provision the withdrawal of a State from the EU requires negotiation of the terms of this act, and withdrawal will take effect only on the date agreed or two years after notification. This period of negotiations could well lead to a new agreement on UK membership, or could provide an opportunity for the Scottish government to open negotiations on succeeding to UK membership, with a referendum planned on this.

§2.04 CONCLUSION

This is a highly volatile period. The UK has passed through one of the most dramatic constitutional events in centuries when the threat of the break-up of the country seemed very real indeed. The Scottish referendum outcome of 55% to 45% was in the end quite narrow, and the polls towards the end suggesting that the result was too close to call in the final two weeks of campaigning. The UK is still taking stock of this result and has also to digest a General Election result in which the Conservatives were very successful in England and the SNP almost swept all seats in Scotland. The consequence is a potentially very unstable period for the Anglo-Scottish union.[59] However, at the same time it is rushing into further constitutional change, on a path that will devolve extensive tax powers to Scotland in the current Scotland Bill.

This is the unsettled backdrop to the possibility of a referendum on membership of the EU. The Conservative Government is now in earnest in seeking to achieve a repatriation of significant powers from Brussels. There are indeed many ifs and buts, and the prospect of the UK actually withdrawing from the EU remains highly unlikely. Still, the very debate highlights that across the UK attitudes towards the EU are diverging. There was in fact similar levels of Euroscepticism in Scotland and England until recently, but the independence debate in Scotland has coincided with a divergence and a more positive attitude to Europe within Scotland at the same time as the rise of the United Kingdom Independence Party (UKIP) denotes a growing scepticism towards the EU within England, particularly over the issue of immigration. This could have significant implications for internal UK relations in the longer term regardless of the outcome of any in/out referendum.

58. 'Sturgeon warns of second referendum over EU exit', The Scotsman, 2 Jun. 2015 http://www.scotsman.com/news/politics/top-stories/sturgeon-warns-of-second-referendum-over-eu-exit-1-3790044.
59. S. Tierney, *Can the Union Survive the Election?* U.K. Const. L. Blog (9th May 2015) (available at http://ukconstitutionallaw.org).

The Scottish referendum campaign is significant because it opened up the debate about how an independent Scotland would be able to join the EU. Most commentators came to the conclusion that this would be achievable, the only real disagreement being over how long this would take and the terms of entry. In the event of a vote by the UK people to leave the EU the question of Scottish independence will no doubt be re-opened, particularly if there is evidence that a majority in Scotland voted to remain in Europe. In this sense the Scottish referendum will have taken on more significance and the pressure to repeat the exercise will be strong.

Even without such a scenario we are now living in a period of increased devolution and there is already an attempt by the Scottish Government to secure more powers with which Scotland can become a more active player within Europe. This could in turn lead to tensions both within the EU itself and within the UK. The future is unclear but what is certain is that the issue of Europe and the UK's position within it is set to remain a central feature of territorial politics within the UK itself.

CHAPTER 3

'Britain Alone': A View from Northern Ireland

Gordon Anthony[*]

§3.01 INTRODUCTION

Northern Ireland is often said to be different from the rest of the United Kingdom not just because of its geographical detachment from Britain ('alone'?), but also because of its historical and contemporary systems of devolved government.[1] In terms of possible UK withdrawal from the European Union, its contemporary system of government – which is premised upon a particular form of consociationalism[2] – presents something of a paradox. On the one hand, the fact that the devolved institutions in Northern Ireland have worked within policy areas that have been heavily conditioned by EU law might be expected to provide an opportunity for reinvigorated local decision-making in the event of EU withdrawal,[3] particularly as the UK moves towards a form of

* I wish to thank a number of friends and colleagues for their comments on earlier versions of this chapter: Pat Birkinshaw; Leanne Cochrane; Brice Dickson; John Morison; Thomas Muinzer; and Alex Schwartz. All opinions and errors are mine.

1. On the historical systems see B. Hadfield, *The Constitution of Northern Ireland* (SLS Legal Publications, Belfast, 1989) and J. Morison & S. Livingstone, *Reshaping Public Power: Northern Ireland and the British Constitutional Crisis* (Sweet and Maxwell 1995). For current structures *see* C Knox, *Devolution and Governance in Northern Ireland* (Manchester U. Press, 2010).
2. *See* J. McGarry & B. O'Leary, *Constitutional Theory, Northern Ireland's Conflict, and its Agreement. Part I: What Consociationalists Can Learn From Northern Ireland* 41 Govt. & Opposition 43 (2006).
3. For an insight into the extent of overlap between EU policy and NI competence *see*, *Report on Assembly Committee Priorities for European Scrutiny in 2014*, NIA 159/11-15, Committee of the Office of the First Minister and Deputy First Minister, available at http://www.niassembly.gov.uk/Assembly-Business/Committees/Office-of-the-First-Minister-and-deputy-First-Minister/Reports/.

'devo-max' in the light of the Scottish referendum of 18 September 2014.[4] However, even leaving aside the obvious question of how far Northern Ireland's interests would truly become distinct from those of the EU in the event of withdrawal, its governmental structures may well frustrate the potential within any new political settlement. This is because the devolved institutions function on the basis of compulsory power-sharing between the major political parties in the Northern Ireland Assembly and within constitutional rules that allow Northern Ireland's main ethno-national groups to block initiatives in the Assembly and in the Northern Ireland Executive Committee.[5] Such structures can inevitably have a limiting influence on the development of policy, and there have been a number of high-profile disputes in areas that have included planning law and, most recently, welfare reform.[6] EU withdrawal might therefore give rise to a notionally enhanced democratic context, but it may well prove to be one that is neither efficient nor effective.

The possibility of withdrawal also has implications for at least two other important aspects of governance in Northern Ireland. The first of these is, of course, relations between Northern Ireland and the Republic of Ireland, which are set within the broader framework of relations between the UK and Irish states. At the level of inter-state cooperation, UK withdrawal would have the immediate effect of placing a land border between Northern Ireland and an EU Member State, where some commentaries have already noted that problems may arise in relation to matters of policing and criminal justice.[7] However, it is at the level of North/South inter-governmental relations that the impact of withdrawal could be expected to be at its most pronounced. Those relations entered a new period of formalised cooperation after the Belfast (or Good Friday) Agreement of 1998, which provided for the creation of a North-South Ministerial Council and a range of 'implementation' bodies in areas of mutual interest.[8] Cooperation within that framework has since been largely positive,[9] although much of

4. *See*, at the time of writing, the report of the 'Smith Commission' on devolution in Scotland at https://www.smith-commission.scot/wp-content/uploads/2014/11/The_Smith_Commission_Report-1.pdf and the Scotland Bill 2015 at https://www.gov.uk/government/publications/scotland-bill-2015-legislation-and-explanatory-notes; the Wales Act 2014, available at http://www.legislation.gov.uk/ukpga/2014/29/contents/enacted; and the 'Stormont House Agreement' of 23 Dec. 2014, https://www.gov.uk/government/uploads/system/uploads/attachment_data/file/390672/Stormont_House_Agreement.pdf, as read with 'A Fresh Start – the Stormont Agreement and Implementation Plan', 2015, at https://www.gov.uk/government/news/a-fresh-start-for-northern-ireland.
5. Northern Ireland Act 1998, Part III, esp section 28B; and section 42. Some slight changes to the workings of the rules are, however, imminent: *see* the 'Stormont House Agreement', *supra* n. 4, paragraphs 57-58, as read with 'A Fresh Start', *supra* n. 4, Appendix F3.
6. *See*, as regards planning law, A. Schwartz, 'Petitions of Concern', Northern Ireland Assembly Knowledge Exchange Seminar Series, 20 Mar. 2014, at p. 4. On welfare *see* http://www.bbc.co.uk/news/uk-northern-ireland-32894371, as now read in the light of *A Fresh Start*, n 4 supra.
7. 'Leaving the EU', House of Commons Library, Research Paper 13/42, at pp 98–99 (available at http://www.parliament.uk/business/publications/research/briefing-papers/RP13-42/leaving-the-eu).
8. J. Coakley, *The Belfast Agreement and the Republic of Ireland* in *Aspects of the Belfast Agreement* Chapter 12 (R. Wilford ed., Oxford U. Press 2001).
9. But *see Re De Brun and McGuinness' Application* [2001] NI 442; and Northern Ireland Act 1998, section 52A, as inserted by the Northern Ireland (St Andrews Agreement) Act 2006, section 12.

it has occurred under the influence of EU law and, in some instances, with direct EU funding. Withdrawal might on that basis be expected to complicate North/South relations and to raise questions about how cross-border initiatives might find support from within Northern Ireland's consociational institutions.

The other aspect of governance concerns equality and human rights law, where the prospect of EU withdrawal must be assessed alongside related debates about the possible repeal of the Human Rights Act 1998 and the introduction of a British Bill of Rights. Although there is no necessary cause and effect between EU membership and the Human Rights Act 1998, Euro-scepticism in the UK has increasingly included criticisms of the European Court of Human Rights (ECtHR), and it led the Conservative Party to commit itself to repeal the Human Rights Act 1998 in the (subsequently realised) event that it won the 2015 general election.[10] For Northern Ireland, a 'withdrawal and repeal' package may well present very significant challenges, particularly given the role that equality and human rights law have played before, during, and after the Belfast Agreement of 1998. For instance, one immediate question would concern the future jurisprudential basis for some aspects of equality law in Northern Ireland, where EU legislation and decisions of the Court of Justice of the European Union (CJEU) have been central to some of the Northern Ireland case law. However, even more fundamental is the matter of how human rights (beyond those associated with non-discrimination) might be protected in the event of withdrawal and repeal. This is essentially a point about Part 6 of the Belfast Agreement, which envisaged that rights would receive enhanced protection in Northern Ireland and that related initiatives would be developed in the Republic of Ireland and on an all-Ireland basis.[11] While it might be doubted how far an integrated approach to the protection of rights has actually been achieved (or, indeed, is achievable),[12] the European Convention on Human Rights (ECHR) and the Charter of Fundamental Rights of the European Union (the EU Charter) are sources of law both in Northern Ireland and in the Republic of Ireland.[13] UK withdrawal would of course immediately change that position in respect of the EU Charter, while repeal of the Human Rights Act 1998 would mean that the very European rights standards that have (arguably) aided Northern Ireland's transition from conflict would no longer be directly enforceable in court.[14] Repeal of the Human Rights Act 1998 might also be expected to place the UK government in breach of its commitments under the Belfast Agreement, notably to:

> complete incorporation into Northern Ireland law of the European Convention on Human Rights, with direct access to the courts, and remedies for breach of the

10. http://www.bbc.co.uk/news/uk-politics-21726612: 'Theresa May: Tories to Consider Leaving the European Convention on Human Rights'; and T. Lock, 'Legal Implications of Human Rights Reform in the UK' UK Const L Blog (15 May 2015), available at http://ukconstitutionallaw.org.
11. *See* P. Mageean & M. O'Brien, *From the Margins to the Mainstream: Human Rights and the Good Friday Agreement* 22 Fordham Intl L. J. 1499 (1998).
12. For some issues see S. Egan & R. Murray, *A Charter of Rights for the Island of Ireland: An Unknown Quantity in the Good Friday/Belfast Agreement*, 56 Intl & Comp. L. Q. 797 (2007).
13. See, in the Republic of Ireland, the European Convention on Human Rights Act, 2003; and Art 29 of the Constitution of Ireland, 1937, and the European Communities Act, 1972.
14. On the role of European standards see, e.g., B. Dickson, *The European Convention on Human Rights and the Conflict in Northern Ireland* (Oxford University Press 2010).

Convention, including power for the courts to overrule Assembly legislation on grounds of inconsistency.[15]

In developing these points, this chapter starts with a short section that addresses the question whether UK withdrawal would result in increased power in the context of devolution, and whether that would be beneficial for the Northern Ireland institutions. It thereafter divides into three sections on the 'problem' of consociationalism; North/South intergovernmental relations; and equality and rights. The section on equality and rights also touches upon broader issues of constitutional reform in the UK post- the Scottish referendum of 18 September 2014, and considers whether the devolved legislatures might themselves choose to give 'local' domestic effect to the ECHR. The conclusion offers some more general comments about Northern Ireland's place within the UK's contemporary constitutional structures.

§3.02 EU MEMBERSHIP AND NORTHERN IRELAND: BETTER IN, OR BETTER OUT?

The question whether EU membership is a positive or a negative in the context of devolution is one that has been touched upon in much of the extant literature on regionalism in the EU.[16] Although that literature does not provide an agreed answer to the question – preferences about membership and regionalism inevitably have a subjective element – it draws attention to a number of constitutional and political factors that determine how devolved power is to be accommodated within the EU's institutional framework. Perhaps the best known of these is the rule whereby the internal constitutional arrangements of a Member State are not to be affected by EU law, at least insofar as EU law neither requires the devolution of power nor prescribes minimum levels of power where devolution occurs.[17] In historical terms, this state-centric focus is consistent with the international law origins of the (now supranational) EU legal order, and it still takes form in, among other things, Article 258 TFEU. That Article famously provides the legal basis for the European Commission to initiate infraction proceedings against Member States, including in those circumstances where the infraction has been caused by the actions or inactions of a regional, or devolved, authority.[18] In such circumstances, the Member State government will be the named respondent in the proceedings and, should the infraction be proven, it is the Member State government that will potentially be subject to any fines that may be imposed under Article 260 TFEU. To guard against the financial imbalance that this might cause within the UK where, for instance, the Northern Ireland institutions breach EU law, the

15. Paragraph 2 of Part 6 of the Agreement.
16. See, e.g., A. Cygan, *Regional Governance, Subsidiarity and Accountability within the EU's Multi-level Polity*. 19 Eur. Pub. L. 161 (2013) and references therein.
17. See further G. Anthony & A. Evans, *Northern Ireland, Devolution, and the European Union*, in *Human Rights, Equality and Democratic Renewal in Northern Ireland* 53 (C Harvey ed., Hart Publishing 2001).
18. See, e.g., Case C-103/01, *Commission v. Germany* [2003] ECR I-5369.

'concordats of the constitution' provide that the Northern Ireland institutions will be responsible for the costs of proceedings.[19]

The concordats of the constitution also provide for devolved participation in EU decision-making, where there is some overlap with EU Treaty guarantees on subsidiarity and regional input into the EU process.[20] Of course, this is where the 'in/out' debate has most resonance for Northern Ireland, as a democratic critique of the EU that starts with a state perspective may become even more compelling when developed at the sub-state level. That said, such critiques often presuppose the validity of a state based model of democracy, and it has been said that that model does not offer a suitable means for assessing the legitimacy of the EU.[21] The point here is that the EU is now one actor among many in a much wider network of governance that engages institutions found at the state, sub-state, European and global levels.[22] While there is some disagreement about the constitutional theory that best explains the nature of that engagement,[23] most commentators would accept that there are inextricable links between the various sites of government and that devolved authorities should be engaged in policy formation as equal partners where their interests overlap with those of others.[24] On this reading, withdrawal from the EU would be folly because it would complicate the links that the UK would continue to have with other sites of authority and also deny the Northern Ireland and other devolved institutions the power to project their interests through, for instance, 'national' offices that are maintained in Brussels.[25]

The above analysis can, however, be criticised insofar as it presupposes that the interests of the UK, including those of Northern Ireland, can only be protected from within the EU rather than alongside it. This is certainly the essence of the political argument that has been made in favour of withdrawal, which appeals to the imagery of repatriating political power in a way that would allow the UK to take greater control of its relations with the EU and the world at large.[26] Whether this comports with current constitutional realities is the remaining doubt about such an argument, but, if it is true that power can be meaningfully repatriated, this could have far-reaching implications for the Northern Ireland institutions. As was mentioned above, the competence of those institutions is heavily conditioned by EU law and withdrawal may, in that sense,

19. 'Devolution: Memorandum of Understanding and Supplementary Agreements', B4.25, available at http://www.ofmdfmni.gov.uk/memorandum_of_understanding_and_concordate_on_co-ordination_of_eu_issues_-_march_2010.pdf. And see R. Rawlings, *Concordats of the Constitution*, 116 L. Q. Rev. 257 (2000).
20. Article 5 TEU; Prot 2 TEU; Articles 305–307 TFEU.
21. A. Moravcsik, *Is There a 'Democratic Deficit' in World Politics? A Framework for Analysis*, 39 Govt & Opposition 336 (2004).
22. N. Walker, *The Idea of Constitutional Pluralism* 65 Modern L. Rev. 317 (2002).
23. M. Loughlin, *Constitutional Pluralism: An Oxymoron?* 3 Global Constitutionalism 9 (2014).
24. G. Marks, L. Hooghe & K. Blank, *European Integration from the 1980s: State Centric v. Multi-Level Governance* 34 *Journal of Common Market Studies* 341. But compare G. della Cananea, 'Is European Constitutionalism Really Multilevel?' ZaöRV 70 (2010), 283–317, available at http://www.zaoerv.de/70_2010/70_2010_2_a_283_318.pdf.
25. For the office of the Northern Ireland Executive *see* http://www.ofmdfmni.gov.uk/index/promoting-ni/onieb.htm.
26. *See*, e.g., I Milne/The Bruges Group, *The Single Market and British Withdrawal*, 2011, available at https://www.gov.uk/government/uploads/system/uploads/attachment_data/file/278491/Bruges_Group_SingleMarketAndWithdrawal.pdf.

'free up' localised policy initiatives under the Northern Ireland Act 1998.[27] Indeed, while it is axiomatic that the terms of the Northern Ireland Act 1998 would need to be amended in the event of withdrawal, any new settlement would surely mean the devolution of more power, not less. This is particularly so given the political commitments that were made in the run-up to the Scottish independence referendum of 18 September 2014, which amounted to a virtual promise to implement 'devo-max'.[28] While it remains to be seen quite how that increase in devolved Scottish power will take form, centrifugal pressures within the UK constitution may well mean that Northern Ireland (and Wales) might acquire more power as part of a broader settlement driven by the Scottish experience.[29] On this alternative reading, EU withdrawal would dovetail with internal constitutional realignment to broaden significantly the competences of the Northern Ireland institutions.

§3.03 THE 'PROBLEM' OF CONSOCIATIONALISM

The corresponding 'problem' that is presented by Northern Ireland's consociational structures starts with their emphasis on preventing the abuse of political power in a society that is largely comprised of two ethno-national groupings. Northern Ireland's historical experience was one in which the majority British Unionist community enjoyed hegemony over the minority Irish Nationalist community at levels that included political representation, economic opportunity, and the workings of the criminal justice system.[30] The Belfast Agreement of 1998 then marked a fundamental move away from that position by emphasising the principle of political equality that now informs, among other things, the blocking mechanisms that are contained in the Northern Ireland Act 1998.[31] Those mechanisms are intended to ensure that one ethno-national grouping cannot force a measure upon the other grouping where that latter grouping's core interests would be affected by the measure. This inevitably begs the question of what constitutes an ethno-national interest, and Schwartz has suggested that they cluster around the three themes of culture, the legacy of the Northern Ireland conflict, and the core elements of the Belfast Agreement itself.[32] However, while the blocking mechanisms place strong controls at the heart of the Northern Ireland Act 1998 in respect of those interests, it is apparent that the mechanisms can also be used to limit socio-economic measures that may not easily (or at all) be linked to ethno-national concerns. Against that backdrop, more power for the Northern Ireland institutions may ultimately mean more vetoes.

27. *See supra* n. 3.
28. A. McHarg, 'The Vow: Vote No for More Devo' at http://ukconstitutionallaw.org/2014/09/17/aileen-mcharg-the-vow-vote-no-for-more-devo/.
29. For proposals for Scotland, Wales and Northern Ireland at the time of writing *see supra* n. 4.
30. Views on the extent of the hegemony vary. For a balanced account *see* M. Mulholland, *Northern Ireland: A Very Short Introduction* (OUP 2003).
31. Although compare the much earlier – and unsuccessful – 'Sunningdale Agreement': *see* B. Hadfield *supra* n. 1, at 110 ff.
32. *Supra* n. 6, at 3–4.

The principal blocking mechanism is the 'Petition of Concern' that is provided for by section 42 of the Northern Ireland Act 1998. According to that section, thirty members may petition the Assembly with their concerns about a measure that is to be voted on by the Assembly, with the result that the measure can be passed only with 'cross-community support'. 'Cross-community support' is here linked to designation rules that require members to register themselves as 'Unionist', 'Nationalist' or 'Other' when they are elected to the Assembly, and it essentially means that an impugned measure will be carried only where it attracts the support of a majority of both Nationalist and Unionist members.[33] While existing statistics on the mechanism do not suggest that it has been used to frustrate a majority of the Assembly's wider legislative programme, there is clear evidence that it has been used to block discrete initiatives that have affected ethno-national interests as well as some measures that have escaped ethno-national association. Reform of planning law, noted above, is one example of a measure that escaped such association; amendment of the law on abortion is another.[34]

Blocking mechanisms also exist in relation to exercises of Ministerial power, where departmental portfolios are for the most part allocated on the basis of party political strength in the Assembly and with reference to the so-called d'Hondt formula.[35] For instance, under section 28B of the Northern Ireland Act 1998, thirty members may again petition the Assembly to express a concern that a Ministerial decision would contravene the Ministerial Code of Conduct (which is statutory in form[36]) or that it relates to a matter of 'public importance'. Where such a petition is brought, the decision in question is to be referred to the Executive Committee for oversight, subject only to the Presiding Officer certifying, where appropriate and after having consulted the political parties, that there is a matter of 'public importance'.[37] Moreover, under the Ministerial Code of Conduct itself, powers of decision can be constrained in two further ways.[38] The first is through the requirement that Ministers bring to the attention of the Executive Committee decisions that, among other things, cross-cut departmental interests, require agreement on prioritisation, require the adoption of a common position, have implications for the Programme for Government,

33. Northern Ireland Act 1998, section 4(5)–5(A); and Order 3(7) of the Standing Orders of the Assembly. Section 4(5) defines 'cross-community support' as (a) the support of a majority of members voting, a majority of the designated Nationalists voting and a majority of the designated Unionists voting; or (b) the support of 60% of the members voting, 40% of the designated Nationalists voting and 40% of the designated Unionists voting'.
34. Schwartz, *supra* n. 6, at p. 4.
35. Northern Ireland Act 1998, section 18. But for the appointment of the First and Deputy First Ministers *see* section 16A; and for the position in relation to the Minister of Justice *see* section 21A(3A), as read with the Department of Justice Act (NI) 2010, section 2.
36. Northern Ireland Act 1998, section 28A and, e.g., *Re Solinas' Application* [2009] NIQB 43.
37. There are other procedural safeguards too: references must be made within seven days of the decision being taken or, where appropriate, notified to the Assembly; and a decision may be referred to the Executive Committee only once.
38. The text of the Code is available at http://www.northernireland.gov.uk/index/your-executive/ministerial-code.htm.

or are significant or controversial.[39] The second way is through section 28A(8)(c) of the Northern Ireland Act 1998, which requires that the Code provide:

> if any three members of the Executive Committee require the vote on a particular matter which is to be voted on by the Executive Committee to require cross-community support, any vote on that matter in the Executive Committee shall require cross-community support in the Executive Committee.[40]

It is important not to overstate the significance of such mechanisms, as government in Northern Ireland has functioned almost without interruption since 2007 and statistics on legislative productivity have been said to compare favourably to those in Scotland.[41] Nevertheless, it is also true that the blocking mechanisms can be used to considerable effect and that, where there is a more general lack of political trust between the various parties, government can enter a period of stasis. This was certainly the case during the later months of 2014 when political disputes about issues ranging from welfare reform through to the problem of dealing with Northern Ireland's violent past threatened to cancel one another out and create very real resource pressures within the Northern Ireland departments. While the disputes were apparently resolved by political agreements that were reached in December 2014 and November 2015 – these envisage use of the petition of concern mechanism only in exceptional circumstances and where there is a statement to explain why it is being used – they still reveal how the blocking mechanisms can almost undermine the very democratic purposes of the Northern Ireland institutions themselves.[42] If EU withdrawal were to entail additional competence, the promised reform of the petition of concern mechanism may therefore become a matter of very real practical need.

§3.04 NORTH/SOUTH INTERGOVERNMENTAL RELATIONS

The North/South inter-governmental relations that were noted in the introduction centre upon the North-South Ministerial Council (NSMC) and six 'implementation bodies' that work in areas of 'mutual interest': Waterways Ireland; the Food Safety Promotion Board; the Trade and Business Development Body; the Special European Union Programmes Body; the Language Body; and the Foyle, Carlingford and Irish Lights Commission. In formal terms, the NSMC and implementation bodies are creatures of international law, as they have their origins in the UK and Irish governments' commitments under the Belfast Agreement 1998 and British Irish Agreement

39. *See* paragraph 2.4 of the Code and, e.g., *Re Central Craigavon Ltd's Application* [2011] NICA 17, paragraphs 16–19.
40. In addition, see paragraph 2.12 of the Code.
41. Schwartz, *supra* n. 6 at p. 4. For details about a short period of interruption see http://www.bbc.co.uk/news/uk-northern-ireland-34426811.
42. See the 'Stormont House Agreement' 2014 and 'A Fresh Start', at *supra* n. 4. The Stormont House Agreement's provisions on the petition of concern are at paragraphs 57–58; the relevant part of 'A Fresh Start' is Appendix F3.

1999, as subsequently implemented in domestic law.[43] However, in political terms, the NSMC and implementation bodies are best understood with reference to an Irish Nationalist view of the Belfast Agreement insofar as they embody an all-Ireland dimension to the governance of Northern Ireland (an East-West dimension, preferred by Unionists, is provided for by the British-Irish Council[44]). While the NSMC does not have executive power, it has assumed a prominent political role that is at its most evident when the First Minister and Deputy First Minister and the Taoiseach convene 'plenary' meetings.[45] Otherwise, the great majority of the meetings are 'sectoral' and held to consider the work of the implementation bodies and to discuss, though not to decide, matters of policy in areas that include agriculture, education, the environment, and tourism.[46] Such sectoral meetings are (typically) to be attended by the Northern Ireland Minister and Junior Minister with responsibility for the sector in question – Ministers who will often reflect the ethno-national balance in the Assembly – and they are under a statutory duty to participate in the work of the meeting insofar as relates to their area of responsibility.[47] Where the agenda for a meeting contains an item that is 'significant or controversial', it may also be attended by the First Minister and Deputy First Minister even if the item in question does not fall within the responsibility of their office.[48]

It is not difficult to envisage how UK withdrawal would complicate the work of the NSMC and the implementation bodies. At a minimum, it would have implications for cooperation in EU influenced policy areas such as agriculture and the environment, as the Republic of Ireland would remain tied to EU policies and Northern Ireland would not. While the extent of any differences between the two jurisdictions would, again, depend upon the precise terms of UK withdrawal, the dynamics of cooperation would inevitably change precisely because there would no longer be any mutual bind to EU law. Indeed, those changed dynamics may become all the more remarkable if it were to be perceived that post-withdrawal cooperation within the framework of the NSMC was being used to foster policies that aligned Northern Ireland more closely to Irish interests rather than those in the rest of the United Kingdom. This is essentially a political point about the reservations that Unionists may have about increased cooperation on an all-Ireland basis, where recourse could again be had to the blocking mechanisms in the Northern Ireland Act 1998. In that instance, there may well be a debate about whether use of the ethno-national veto would be undermining the spirit of the Belfast Agreement or safeguarding one set of the ethno-national interests that are at the Agreement's very heart.

---

43. *See*, in the UK, Northern Ireland Act 1998, sections 52A–55, and the North/South Co-operation (Implementation Bodies) (NI) Order, 1999, SI 1998/859; and *see*, in the Republic of Ireland, the British-Irish Agreement Act, 1999.
44. Belfast Agreement, Part 5; and Northern Ireland Act 1998, section 52A. *See* V. Bogdanor, *The British-Irish Council and Devolution* 34 Govt. & Opposition 287 (1999).
45. On the various formats for meetings *see* D. Birrell, *Intergovernmental Relations and Political Parties in Northern Ireland* 14 Brit. J. Pol. & Intl Rel. 270, 277–278 (2012).
46. Belfast Agreement, Part 4.
47. Northern Ireland Act 1998, sections 52A–52B. *See also* Part 3 of the Ministerial Code of Conduct, available at http://www.northernireland.gov.uk/index/your-executive/ministerial-code.htm.
48. Northern Ireland Act 1998, section 52(A)(8), as read with section 20(3)-(4).

Withdrawal would also have financial implications because it would, among other things, end EU funding for the Special European Union Programmes Body. That body has supported a large number of initiatives including those concerned with cross-community reconciliation, and replacement funding would be needed if such initiatives were to receive post-withdrawal support. That said, there would be the potential for blocking mechanisms to be used here too if, for instance, a Northern Ireland Ministerial decision to grant funding for a project were to attract controversy. The point can be seen in relation to the earlier case of *Re Solinas' Application,*[49] which involved a challenge to a Ministerial decision to withdraw government funding from a community project in a Loyalist area of Belfast. The decision was taken because the Minister – a member of the (Nationalist) Social Democratic and Labour Party – was of the view that there was on-going paramilitary activity in the community and that that activity was in breach of the conditions under which the money had been granted. However, on an application for judicial review, the court found that the Minister had acted unlawfully in making her decision as she had failed to adhere to a number of procedural requirements that had earlier been laid down by the Executive Committee. The court thus held that the Minister had breached the Ministerial Code and quashed her decision.

§3.05 EQUALITY AND HUMAN RIGHTS LAW

The remaining matter to be addressed is that concerned with equality and human rights law. As indicated in the introduction, these are areas of law that have played an important role in reshaping Northern Ireland society, where their influence can be traced to before the signing of the Belfast Agreement of 1998.[50] In terms of equality law, the historical imperative has very much been the need to address the socio-economic imbalances that were associated with Unionist hegemony, and section 75 of the Northern Ireland Act 1998 addresses religious and political discrimination as well as that associated with race, marital status, sexual orientation, gender, disability, and the status of those with and without dependants.[51] Section 75 is not, however, a stand-alone provision in the context of addressing discrimination, as religious and political discrimination is also governed by the Fair Employment and Treatment (Northern Ireland) Order 1998 (which replaced the Fair Employment [Northern Ireland] Act 1989), while the other categories noted in section 75 overlap with a range of EU Treaty

49. [2009] NIQB 43.
50. On equality law *see* C. McCrudden, *Equality*, in *Human Rights, Equality, and Democratic Renewal in Northern Ireland* 75 (C. Harvey eds, Hart Publishing 2001); and on human rights *see* Mageean and O'Brien, *supra* n. 11.
51. Section 75(1) reads: "A public authority shall in carrying out its functions relating to Northern Ireland have due regard to the need to promote equality of opportunity – (a) between persons of different religious belief, political opinion, racial group, age, marital status or sexual orientation; (b) between men and women generally; (c) between persons with a disability and persons without; and (d) between persons with dependants and persons without".

Articles and Directives that have been implemented in domestic law.[52] That having been said, there are some important points of difference between the various statutory provisions, notably in relation to their reaches and effects. For instance, section 75, which is to be read with Schedule 9 to the Northern Ireland 1998, applies only to public bodies within the terms of the Act and is subject to an enforcement regime that centres upon the powers of the Equality Commission for Northern Ireland rather than judicial remedies[53] (albeit that judicial review can play a residual role in some cases; damages are also available where a public authority discriminates or aids or incites another person to discriminate on the ground of religious belief or political opinion).[54] This 'vertical' approach can then be contrasted with that which applies in relation to the Fair Employment and Treatment (Northern Ireland) Order 1998, which has 'vertical' and 'horizontal' dimensions and which fastens upon judicial remedies.[55] The range of related measures that have their origins in EU law likewise enjoy vertical and horizontal effect, where access to judicial remedies is underpinned by EU law's principle of the effective protection of EU law rights.[56]

The starting point in terms of human rights law is the Belfast Agreement's emphasis on the need to safeguard rights at all levels of government in Northern Ireland and in society more generally.[57] That objective was subsequently given legislative form both in the Human Rights Act 1998 – the passage of which coincided with the Belfast Agreement – and the Northern Ireland Act 1998. Of course, section 6 the Human Rights Act 1998 famously makes it unlawful for public authorities to act in a manner that is incompatible with the provisions of the ECHR that have effect under Schedule 1 to the Act, where public authorities are read as including the Northern Ireland Assembly and Northern Ireland government departments.[58] However, it is the Northern Ireland Act 1998 that reflects more fully the requirements of the Belfast Agreement, as it embeds additional constraints on legislative and executive power at the devolved level. While it is true that the Act includes an interpretive obligation whereby the courts must try to read Acts of the Assembly as within its competence[59] – challenges to Ministerial decisions may also attract judicial restraint where that is deemed appropriate[60] – it is a commonplace that exercises of power may be constrained on the basis of European human rights norms. The legislative competence of

52. For example, the Employment Equality (Sexual Orientation) Regulations (Northern Ireland) 2003, SR 2003/497, as read with Directive 2000/78/EC. *See* further chapters 12-18 of *Human Rights in Northern Ireland: The CAJ Handbook* (B Dickson and B Gormally ed, Hart Publishing, 2015).
53. *Re Neill's Application* [2006] NICA 5, [2006] NI 278.
54. On judicial review *see Re JR1's Application* [2011] NIQB 5; and on damages *see* Northern Ireland Act 1998, section 76.
55. *Re Kirkpatrick's Application* [2004] NIJB 15.
56. *See*, most famously, Case 222/84, *Johnston v. Chief Constable of the RUC* [1986] 3 CMLR 240.
57. Part 6, available at https://www.gov.uk/government/publications/the-belfast-agreement.
58. Sections 6 & 21.
59. Northern Ireland Act 1998, section 83, as read in the light of *Att-Gen v. National Assembly for Wales Commission* [2012] UKSC 53, [2012] 3 WLR 1294; *Imperial Tobacco Ltd v. Lord Advocate* [2012] UKSC 61, [2013] SLT 2; and *Re Agricultural Sector (Wales) Bill* [2014] UKSC 43, [2014] 1 WLR 2622.
60. *Department for Social Development v. MacGeagh* [2006] NI 125, 136-8.

the Northern Ireland Assembly is thus limited with reference to the ECHR/Schedule 1 to the Human Rights Act 1998 and by EU law (which includes the EU Charter);[61] while exercises of executive power are subject to related ECHR and EU law limitations.[62]

How, then, would a 'withdrawal and repeal' package of the kind that was noted in the introduction affect Northern Ireland? Taking first the field of equality law, it could be expected that any impact would be mixed, as various aspects of equality law, most notably section 75 of the Northern Ireland Act 1998 and the Fair Employment and Treatment (Northern Ireland) Order 1998, would remain in force. Moreover, to the extent that elements of the wider body of anti-discrimination law are sourced in EU law, there is no reason in principle why the relevant domestic law measures could not be kept in force and given a 'domestic' interpretation as cases arise in the future. This is certainly the logic that underpins 'transitional' or 'savings' provisions in legislation and, while repeal of the European Communities Act 1972 would obviously present challenges on a larger scale, any Act that effects its repeal could easily include Schedules of 'saved' secondary legislation. That said, there would inevitably also be an element of fiction to any such arrangement, as the legislation that would be saved would have been moulded by the case law of the CJEU, which would continue to give (what would be) non-binding rulings about the EU measures that first underpinned the 'domestic' legislation. This would thus mean that the Northern Ireland courts would be faced with the option of either ignoring the relevant rulings of the CJEU – which may often include consideration of the Equality Chapter of the EU Charter – or affording them the value of persuasive precedents. In the event that they (even occasionally) adopt the latter approach, this would strengthen the well-established argument that legal systems cannot fully close themselves off from one another in the modern global polity and that they should not seek to do so.[63]

The repeal of the Human Rights Act 1998 would of course end any direct role for Article 14 ECHR in domestic proceedings, as well as for all of the Articles within whose ambit Article 14 ECHR must fall in order to be actionable. In a UK-wide sense, this is a prospect that should perhaps now be viewed against the backdrop of an increased judicial emphasis on the role that the common law can play in protecting rights, where the clear implication is that repeal may not lead to reduced levels of rights protection but rather to a different means of achieving protection (there is also the fact that the Human Rights Act 1998 may be replaced by a British Bill of Rights).[64] However, in the specific context of Northern Ireland, repeal may carry with it a very different consequence given the UK government's commitments under the Belfast Agreement 1998. As was noted in the introduction, Part 6 of the Belfast Agreement requires the UK government to incorporate the ECHR into Northern Ireland law and to provide for a system of judicial remedies that includes the power to strike-down Assembly legislation. UK-wide repeal of the Human Rights Act 1998 without more would therefore not

61. Northern Ireland Act 1998, sections 6, 79–81, 83, 98.
62. Northern Ireland Act 1998, sections 24, 98.
63. M. Hunt, *Using Human Rights Law in English Courts* Chapters 1–3 (Hart Publishing 1997).
64. On the common law *see*, e.g., *R (Osborn) v. Parole Board* [2013] UKSC 61, [2014] AC 1115; and Birkinshaw, Chapter one, this volume.

only place the UK government in apparent breach of its commitments under the Belfast Agreement but would also have a complicating effect on the scheme of guarantees that are presently contained in the Northern Ireland Act 1998. In a practical sense – and perhaps the most worrying sense of all – it would further mean that individuals would no longer be able to rely upon European human rights standards in litigation arising from state (in)action during the Northern Ireland conflict,[65] albeit that there would remain the option of petitioning the Strasbourg Court itself.[66]

It might be thought that there would be some way around such difficulties in relation to human rights protection. For instance, on the assumption that the UK government would remain as a contracting party to the ECHR notwithstanding the repeal of the Human Rights Act 1998, its international law obligations might still be given specific territorial effect in Northern Ireland (something that might also discharge a narrow reading of the UK government's obligations under the Belfast Agreement). However, a matter of very real importance to any such territorially limited scheme would be the meaning that would be given to 'public authority' within what would become the statutory equivalent of section 6 of the Human Rights Act 1998. While almost all human rights cases in Northern Ireland would still be concerned with the actions and inactions of public authorities that are seated in Northern Ireland (the Police Service of Northern Ireland, local councils, etc), issues may also arise in relation to decisions taken by central UK government departments. The most obvious area in which this might cause concern is the investigation of conflict-related deaths that involved members of the British Army, as the Ministry of Defence would be a party to any potential proceedings. While it is presently accepted that Article 2 ECHR applies to such cases even though the facts at issue pre-date the coming into force of the Human Rights Act 1998,[67] a statutory scheme that did not apply to central government departments would end that possibility and may greatly complicate efforts to deal with Northern Ireland's past.[68] Indeed, it is not hard to envisage that cases that may have involved the police and the Army working in concert may result in only greater uncertainty about what the state may have done: while the actions of the police would be governed by the exacting standards of Article 2 ECHR, those of the Army would not.

The other possibility would be for the Northern Ireland Assembly itself to seek to enact legislation to give effect to the ECHR. This is certainly something that the Assembly might come to consider in tandem with the other devolved legislatures, as the expected increase in devolved powers post-September 2014 may lead the Scottish and Welsh legislatures to re-evaluate core civic values, including openness to European influences. For instance, one model that might be adopted is that which has already been used by the National Assembly for Wales in relation to the UN Convention on the Rights of the Child, where the Rights of Children and Young Persons (Wales) Measure

65. As in, e.g., *Re Finucane's Application* [2013] NIQB 45.
66. For a recent conflict related application *see McCaughey v. UK* (2014) 58 EHRR 13.
67. *Re McCaughey and Quinn* [2011] UKSC 20, [2011] 2 WLR 1279. But compare *R (Keyu) v. Secretary of State for Foreign and Commonwealth Affairs* [2014] EWCA Civ 312, [2015] QB 57, on appeal to the UKSC at the time of writing.
68. On which efforts *see* G. Anthony & L. Moffett, 'Law, Politics, and the "Problem of the Past"' (2014) 20 *EPL* 395.

2011 imposes a duty on Welsh Ministers to have 'due regard' to the UN Convention when exercising their functions.[69] However, even leaving aside the question of how far such duties would be meaningfully enforceable in practice – it may be that Ministerial decisions would be open to challenge only on grounds of failure to take relevant considerations into account and/or *Wednesbury* unreasonableness[70] – the constitutional setting in Northern Ireland may ultimately frustrate attempts to give local legislative effect to the ECHR. The point here is not just that consociationalism may again problematise the passage of any Assembly Bill – the Unionist ethno-national bloc tends to be less inclined towards the mobilisation of human rights arguments than the nationalist bloc, at least where those arguments relate to Northern Ireland's past[71] – but also that any clauses touching upon national security/anti-terrorism measures would fall out-with the competence of the Assembly.[72] In that scenario, it may well be that the UK government's failure to fulfil its obligations under the Belfast Agreement 1998 would be made only even more apparent by the Northern Ireland Assembly's inability to impose those obligations by proxy.

§3.06 CONCLUSION

This chapter began by observing that UK withdrawal from the EU might present something of a paradox in the context of Northern Ireland. Certainly, the idea that withdrawal might free up localised policy initiatives has been seen to be complicated by a form of consociationalism that can frustrate responsive government as much as it can facilitate it. In constitutional terms, this is perhaps an unavoidable consequence of Northern Ireland's history, where any increase in devolved power post-withdrawal would have to be reconciled with the need to constrain competing ethno-national preferences. Indeed, while it has been seen that the consociational system is (arguably) open to abuse under the Northern Ireland Act 1998, it remains as one of the most rudimentary features of the Belfast Agreement and is, in that sense, something of a constitutional fundamental.[73] Any increase in power – whether prompted by EU withdrawal and/or a move towards 'devo-max' – would therefore have to face the reality that democracy in Northern Ireland can sometimes be about nothing more constructive than stopping things from being done.

Of course, such comments assume that EU withdrawal would result in a meaningful repatriation of power at the UK level and that any internal reconfiguration of the domestic constitution would have a centrifugal dynamic. While a centrifugal dynamic would seem to be guaranteed given the experience of the Scottish referendum

69. Section 1.
70. On *Wednesbury* in the context of other due regard duties *see*, e.g., *Re JR1's Application* [2011] NIQB 5 (Chief Constable of the PSNI's approach to his due regard duties under section 75 of the Northern Ireland Act 1998 not unreasonable).
71. *See generally* C. Lawther, *Truth, Denial and Transition: Northern Ireland the Contested Past* (Routledge 2014).
72. Northern Ireland Act 1998, Schedule 2, paragraph 17.
73. On the constitutional link between the Belfast Agreement and the Northern Ireland Act 1998 *see Robinson v. Secretary of State for Northern Ireland* [2002] UKHL 32, [2002] NI 390.

(and irrespective of EU withdrawal), the repatriation argument is one that is much less convincing. As was noted in the earlier part of this chapter, it is almost axiomatic that there are irreversible linkages between the various sites of government in contemporary society and that states cannot realistically close themselves off as sovereign legal orders.[74] This raises the very real possibility that EU withdrawal would ultimately become nothing other than the pursuit of a false sovereignty, and, for Northern Ireland, the most worrying implication would be at the level of equality and human rights. Such norms have long helped to define much of Northern Ireland's transition from a difficult and violent past, and they have become established as (admittedly contested) markers of civil and societal values. Should they become diminished as part of some more general UK retreat from Europe, it is not only Britain that would be 'alone' but the very idea that common values can work to the benefit of all of society.

74. *See generally* R. Rawlings, P. Leyland & A. Young (eds), *Sovereignty and the Law: Domestic, European and International Perspectives* (Oxford U. Press 2013).

CHAPTER 4

'Brexit' and Welsh Devolution: The Likely Impact

Mike Varney

§4.01 INTRODUCTION

At the time of the 1998 legislation that devolved powers to Scotland, Northern Ireland and Wales, Welsh devolution was seen to be an 'ambiguous'[1] scheme, with fewer devolved powers and with a Welsh Assembly that did not enjoy the power to legislate. The Government of Wales Act 1998 devolved relatively few powers to the Welsh Assembly and the Welsh Assembly government proved less active in its endeavours to participate in European matters than the governments in Scotland and Northern Ireland.[2] Since then, Wales has enjoyed further devolution of power from Westminster, with the Government of Wales Act 2006 granting power to the Welsh Assembly to make law, or to modify Westminster statures insofar as they apply to Wales in specific areas of competence, subject to the agreement of the Westminster Parliament. Since a vote in favour of further devolution by the Welsh public in 2011 the Assembly has seen a devolution settlement closer to that enjoyed by Scotland and Northern Ireland. Legislation passed by the Welsh Assembly is now described as 'Acts' of the Assembly[3] and the Assembly can legislate on any issue that is included in Part 1 of Schedule 7 of the Government of Wales Act 2006. Of the twenty areas where the Welsh Assembly can make law, many of these areas see considerable influence from European Law. It is difficult to quantify with any precision the exact scope of competences that are impacted by EU law, but it is clear that European law and policy significantly affect

1. N. Burrows *Devolution* 186 (Sweet and Maxwell 2000).
2. *See* M. Varney, *Devolution and European Representation in the United Kingdom*, in *The Role of the Regions in EU Governance* (C. Panara & A. De Becker eds., Springer 2010).
3. The framework for the legislative powers of the Welsh Assembly is to be found in Part 4 of the Government of Wales Act 2006.

competences in areas such as agriculture and aquaculture, planning, the environment and food.

Wales is unusual in the sense that it is a net recipient of European Union funds. A paper for the UK Parliament suggests that Wales received funding estimated to be worth around EUR 5 billion in the period 2007–2013. This funding was drawn from the Common Agricultural Policy, European Structural Funds and a number of other European Union funding streams, including those for research and development.[4] Jane Hutt, the Welsh Minister for Finance has acknowledged in an interview that if the UK withdraws from the European Union, funding from the Westminster government is unlikely to replace that received from the European Union.[5] As such, the impact of EU withdrawal could be highly significant for the finances of the Welsh government. It is also suggested that Welsh businesses engage in GPB 5 billion per annum in trade with other EU Member States and also is host to 450 firms from other Member States, which employ around 50,000 people.[6] The impact of EU membership on the Welsh economy is clearly very significant and is most likely considerably greater than the impact on the economy in other parts of the United Kingdom.

The Welsh government has expressed a desire to remain as a part of the European Union.[7] Its European Strategy, published in 2012,[8] outlines the main areas of focus for Welsh European policy in the period to 2020. Objectives include the enhancement of funding streams from the Common Agricultural and Fisheries Policies, the maximisation of support from the European Structural Funds and engagement with European transport, telecommunications and energy networks. It is evident that the Welsh government has no desire for the United Kingdom to withdraw from the European Union and it is no doubt the case that the Welsh government is enhancing, rather than reducing, its endeavours to influence and engage with the European Union.[9]

An exit from the European Union by the United Kingdom would bring about a number of profound consequences for Wales. The economic impact could significantly damage the process[10] of Welsh devolution – if the Welsh government and the Welsh economy lose considerable income from the European Union which the UK government is unable or unwilling to replace, this would likely increase the reliance of Wales on the UK government and reduce the freedom of action that the Welsh government enjoys. To some extent, the austerity cuts that have already been imposed by the UK

4. House of Commons Library Research Paper 13/42 *Leaving the EU* (House of Commons, 2013) p. 94.
5. *See* J. Lindsell, *Softening the Blow: Who Gains from the EU and How they Can Survive Brexit* 37–39 (Civitas 2014).
6. Speech by Carwyn Jones (First Minister of Wales) on 9 May 2013. Available at: http://wefo.wales.gov.uk/news/latest/130510eumembership/?skip = 1&lang = en (accessed 4 Apr. 2015).
7. Speech by Jane Hutt on 13 Mar. 2014. Available at: http://gov.wales/newsroom/international/2014/140313euspeech/?lang = en (accessed 4 Apr. 2015).
8. Welsh Government *Wales and the European Union: The Welsh Government's EU Strategy* (Welsh Government, 2012).
9. Contrast the position in 2010, outlined by the author's earlier work cited in footnote 2, where the Welsh government had not produced a European strategy, with the development of the strategy noted.
10. For an outline of Welsh devolution as a 'process' *see* R. Rawlings, *Hastening Slowly: the Next Phase of Welsh Devolution*' Pub. L. 824 (2005).

government have limited the freedom of action of the Welsh government in a number of respects[11] and further reductions in income, whether from the UK government or from the European Union would exacerbate this further. The Wales Act 2014 devolves powers to set the rate of stamp duty on property transactions and landfill tax to the Welsh Assembly, along with some other taxes. There is also the potential for a separate rate of income tax in Wales, to be set by the Welsh Assembly, should the Welsh public approve the transfer of such powers in a referendum. These new powers are significant and suggest a maturing of the devolution settlement – greater devolution of legislative powers would seem to necessitate a degree of fiscal autonomy on the part of a devolved government.[12] However, if the withdrawal of the United Kingdom from the European Union were significantly to damage the Welsh economy and if free trade between Wales and the EU were to be significantly affected by the withdrawal, it may be that the freedom of action offered by powers of taxation would be extremely limited.

A withdrawal from the European Union would also open up some difficult questions for the Union between Wales and the remainder of the United Kingdom. It was noted above that the Welsh government is of the view that the United Kingdom should remain a part of the EU. If withdrawal from the EU comes about, this may increase pressure for Wales to seek independence and to seek entry into the European Union as a separate state. It is clear that the likelihood of this is much lower for Wales than for Scotland, as the Welsh public has never demonstrated the same level of enthusiasm for devolution as the Scots. In the referendum which preceded the Government of Wales Act 1998, only 50.3% of those voting supported devolution.[13] Support for devolution has ostensibly increased, with 63.5% of those voting in the 2011 referendum which led to increased powers for the Welsh Assembly voting in favour,[14] albeit on a reduced turnout from the 1998 referendum. The absence of a strong nationalist movement in Wales with broad political support makes a move towards Welsh independence much less likely than in Scotland. It has been argued that the Welsh electorate still retains focus on UK-wide political issues, whereas the Scottish electorate tend to be more focused on issues pertaining to Scotland[15] and that '... the institutional and identity context within which sub-state elections occur also matters. The extent of autonomy enjoyed, and the degree to which any 'regions' possesses a sense of national distinctiveness also appears to be important for shaping how vote choice occurs'.[16] As things stand, it does not appear that there has been a significant growth in support for the nationalist party in Wales in the 2015 general election, though it may be that the results of the next election for the Welsh Assembly will offer a better indication of the appetite of the Welsh people for a move towards greater devolution

11. M. Drakeford, *Wales in the Age of Austerity* 32 Critical Soc. Policy 455, 456–458 (2012).
12. This view appears to be endorsed in Independent Commission on Funding and Finance for Wales *Fairness and Accountability: A New Funding Settlement for Wales* (Independent Commission on Funding and Finance for Wales, 2010), Chapter 2.
13. Burrows, *supra* n. 1, at 18.
14. Electoral Commission *Report on the referendum on the law-making powers of the National Assembly for Wales* (Electoral Commission, 2011), p. 3.
15. R. Scully, *More Scottish than Welsh? Understanding the 2011 Devolved Elections in Scotland and Wales* Reg. & Fed. Stud. 591 (2013).
16. *Ibid.* at 607.

than has been offered by the current framework offered by the existing devolution settlement for Wales.

It may be that over time, if further powers are devolved to Wales, a movement towards independence could grow, much as it has in Scotland. However, it may be that the smaller population of Wales and the fact that the Welsh economy is not supported to some extent by a strong natural resource industry may deter such a move. Ultimately, if the United Kingdom seeks to withdraw from the European Union and the Welsh people are in favour of retaining EU membership, this could place considerable strain on the Union.

The economic loss to Wales has the potential to undermine the devolution process to some extent. If the Welsh economy is significantly diminished by a United Kingdom exit from the European Union, regardless of the scope of formal powers devolved, it is extremely likely that Wales will require fiscal support from the remainder of the United Kingdom. This is acknowledged by the Silk Report on Welsh devolution, which recommends that the block grant be retained, with the Welsh Assembly generating some of its finance from devolved powers of taxation.[17] While this is the case, the Welsh government would remain dependent on the Westminster government for the provision of a significant proportion of its funding.

The remainder of this chapter will seek to focus in more detail on the likely impact of a British withdrawal from the European Union on the system of Welsh devolution. Much turns on the precise nature of the withdrawal. If the United Kingdom seeks to remain a member of the European Economic Area, then legislation pertaining to the 'four freedoms', along with many of the 'horizontal' policies on issues such as consumer protection will remain in place. If, however, the United Kingdom seeks a complete withdrawal and then endeavours to negotiate bilateral treaties with the European Union, the precise obligations that might be owed to the European Union are much less clear.

§4.02 THE IMPACT ON DEVOLVED POWERS TO MAKE LEGISLATION

It was noted above that Wales presently enjoys devolution of powers in twenty areas. Withdrawal from the EU would not directly affect this devolution in the sense that the legislative competences would remain the same, albeit that the present constraints on the competences imposed by section 108(6)(c) of the Government of Wales Act 2006, which renders the provisions of any Assembly Measure contrary to EU law ineffective. The precise scope of the additional freedom that this would offer is uncertain and dependent on the relationship that the UK would have with the EU subsequent to any withdrawal. If the UK seeks to become a member of the European Free Trade Assocation (EFTA) and also the European Economic Area (EEA), then the limitations on many of the competences will remain much the same.

17. Commission on Devolution in Wales *Empowerment and Responsibility: Financial Powers to Strengthen Wales* (Commission on Devolution in Wales, 2012), Recommendation 1.

Any increased legislative freedom granted to the Assembly by withdrawal from the EU must also be considered carefully in light of the other restrictions on legislative competence in section 108 of the Government of Wales Act 2006. Section 108(6)(c) imposes an identical restriction in relation to provisions passed in contravention of Convention rights. Evidently, if a future government also seeks to repeal the Human Rights Act 1998, presumably the requirement to legislate in compliance with Convention rights would be removed from the devolution statutes, subject to the agreement of the Scottish, Welsh and Northern Irish legislatures. If this is the case, then the precise scope of additional legislative freedom that would be offered is open to debate. It is likely that if the Human Rights Act 1998 is to be repealed, it would be replaced with an alternative 'British Bill of Rights', as the Conservative promised in their 2015 manifesto. It was noted in the Introduction how plans for legislation on this matter have been deferred pending further consultation.[18] However, it may be that the limitation on the devolved governments' ability to legislate in contravention of human rights may be removed in its entirety in such circumstances, as the Conservative proposals place greater emphasis on the issue of Parliamentary sovereignty where human rights issues are at stake, including removing the duty of interpretation which presently exists in section 3 of the Human Rights Act 1998 and also removing the duty in section 2 of the Human Rights Act 1998 for domestic courts to take account of the European Convention when determining cases.[19] If this is the situation for the Westminster Parliament, which retains its sovereignty and faces no limitations on its competence, there may be some argument that the strict requirement of Convention compliance should be lifted from the devolved legislatures.

If the limitation on competence imposed by section 108(6)(c) of the Government of Wales Act 2006 is lifted, the additional freedom that would be offered is not likely to be significant. Political realities would suggest that no Welsh Assembly government would seek to regularly legislate in contravention of the rights contained in the Convention and it is likely that some limitation on competence could be imposed as a result of the passing of legislation to implement the 'British Bill of Rights', which is likely to mirror the rights contained in the Convention.[20]

If the requirement to legislate in compliance with the Convention is removed, there may be a further question of whether such a limitation may be imposed by the common law. In the *AXA*[21] case, the Supreme Court rejected a claim brought by AXA which argued that the Scottish Parliament had exceeded the scope of its legislative competence in passing a statute to allow claims by employees for pleural plaques where employers had allowed employees to be exposed to asbestos in a negligent manner. The claim was brought on two grounds. First, it was argued that the legislation

18. Conservative Party Protecting Human Rights in the UK: The Conservatives' Proposals for Changing Britain's Human Rights Laws (Conservative Party, n.d.) Available at: https://www.conservatives.com/~/media/files/downloadable%20Files/human_rights.pdf.
19. *Ibid.* at 6–7.
20. *Ibid.*
21. *AXA General Insurance Ltd and Others v. HM Advocate and Others* [2011] UKSC 46; [2012] 1 A.C. 868.

was contrary to Article 1 of the First Protocol of the European Convention on Human Rights (ECHR). The Supreme Court unanimously rejected this claim. The second ground of the claim was that the legislation was irrational or unreasonable and thus, as a statute of a devolved Parliament, could be subject to judicial review on grounds of irrationality. This claim was also rejected, with Lord Hope DPSC arguing in his judgment that:

> ...Acts of the Scottish Parliament are not subject to judicial review at common law on the grounds of irrationality, unreasonableness or arbitrariness. This is not needed, as there is already a statutory limit on the Parliament's legislative competence if a provision is incompatible with any of the Convention rights: section 29(2)(d) of the Scotland Act 1998. But it would also be quite wrong for the judges to substitute their views on these issues for the considered judgment of a democratically elected legislature unless authorised to do so, as is the case of the Convention rights, by the constitutional framework laid down by the Westminster Parliament.[22]

If the requirement to legislate in conformity with Convention rights was removed, the courts may feel emboldened to introduce common law constraints on the legislative competence of the devolved legislatures. Lord Hope DPSC argued in *AXA* that the Scottish Parliament was not sovereign and thus ''... the rule of law does not have to compete with the principle of sovereignty'.[23] It was argued that such judicial intervention would likely be limited due to the nature of the devolved legislatures, with Lord Hope arguing:

> A sovereign Parliament is, according to the traditional view, immune from judicial scrutiny because it is protected by the principle of sovereignty. But it shares with the devolved legislatures, which are not sovereign, the advantages that flow from the depth and width of the experience of its elected members and the mandate that has been given to them by the electorate.[24]

Lord Mance JSC would adopt an approach to common law review of the legislation which has the potential to be more interventionist than that which is proposed by Lord Hope, arguing that:

> There can be decisions – to take a familiar extreme example, a blatantly discriminatory decision directed at red-headed people – where, irrespective of any limitation on the purposes for which the decision-maker might act, a court would regard what has been done as irrational, because of the way in which the decision operated. If a devolved Parliament or Assembly were ever to enact such a measure, I would have thought it capable of challenge, if not under the Human Rights Convention, then as offending against fundamental rights or the rule of law, at the very core of which are principles of equality of treatment.[25]

Lord Reed also expressed the view that the common law may intervene in circumstances where devolved legislatures might act to 'abrogate fundamental rights

22. *Ibid.* at [52].
23. *AXA, supra* n. 21 at [51].
24. *Ibid.* at [49].
25. *Ibid.* at [97].

or to violate the rule of law', but in the circumstances of the *AXA* case, held that this was not the case and thus there could be no common law review of the legislation.[26]

The legislative measures of the Welsh Assembly are now described in the same terms as those of the Scottish Parliament, so the courts will likely adopt the same approach to challenges to Welsh legislation. A recent case has found that proposed legislation of the Welsh Assembly designed to recover expenditure made by the Welsh NHS on those who have suffered asbestos related injuries and have recovered compensation from a party whose negligence led to the exposure of the claimant to asbestos from the negligent party or their insurers was contrary to Article 1 of the First Protocol ECHR and was thus outside of the Assembly's competence.[27] In this case, the common law powers of the court to exercise judicial review of the legislation on grounds of rationality was not at issue, but in light of the judgments of the Supreme Court justices in the *AXA* case outlined above, it is likely that, in the absence of legislative protection of fundamental rights, common law protection would have been invoked.

Should the UK seek to withdraw from the EU, the legislative freedom of the Welsh Assembly might also be constrained by international agreements to which the United Kingdom is a party. As an example, the UK has ratified the Aarhus Convention and would retain the need to maintain legislation similar to that provided for by EU law[28] should the UK withdraw from the European Union. Similar constraints will be imposed in relation to a number of other matters, including the regulation of fisheries.[29] Section 114(1)(d) of the Government of Wales Act 2006 permits the UK Secretary of State to issue an order prohibiting the Clerk of the Welsh Assembly from passing a Bill for royal assent if he has reasonable grounds to believe that 'would be incompatible with any international obligation or the interests of defence or national security'. There is a further power to require the Welsh Ministers to desist from taking action which is incompatible with the UK's international obligations.[30] In many areas, although obligations contained in EU law would be lifted should the UK withdraw from the EU, much legislation presently designed to deliver compliance with the requirements of EU law would have to remain in identical or similar form to meet the requirements of the UK's international obligations and the needs of its business community. This reality would be imposed and be ever present on the legislative powers of the Welsh Assembly.

26. *Ibid.* at [153]–[154].
27. *In re Medical Costs for Asbestos Diseases (Wales) Bill* [2015] UKSC 3; [2015] 2 W.L.R. 481. Lord Mance (with whom Lords Neuberger and Hodge agreed) held that the retroactive nature of the provision was not justified by an overriding objective of public policy and was thus contrary to Article 1 Protocol 1 ECHR. It is also important to note that the majority would also have found that the Assembly did not enjoy the competence to pass the legislation in any case.
28. *See*, in particular, Directive 2003/4/EC of the European Parliament and of the Council of 28 Jan. 2003 on public access to environmental information [2003] OJ L 41/26 and Directive 2003/35/EC of the European Parliament and of the Council of 26 May 2003 providing for public participation in respect of the drawing up of certain plans and programmes relating to the environment [2003] OJ L 156/17.
29. As acknowledged in V. Miller *Leaving the EU* House of Commons Library Research Paper 13/42 (House of Commons, 2013), p. 57.
30. Government of Wales Act 2006, section 82.

This section of the paper has demonstrated that while prima facie, the Welsh Assembly would gain additional legislative freedom from a UK withdrawal from the European Union, an examination of the situation suggests that the increase in legislative competence would not be significant. International obligations, the practical realities of the need for regulation in areas presently covered by EU law (and, indeed, the potential risks of modifying extant regimes) plus the potential for the UK to join EFTA and the European Economic Area all serve as likely constraints on legislative freedom. Insofar as 'Brexit' might also include a repeal of the Human Rights Act 1998 and a reconsideration of the role of the European Convention in UK law, it seems evident that the common law would likely deliver similar constraints to those presently imposed by the Convention should there be any endeavour to change the formal limits on the legislative competence of the devolved legislatures in respect of fundamental rights.

§4.03 THE IMPACT ON THE POWERS OF THE WELSH MINISTERS

The impact of a British exit from the European Union on the powers of the Welsh Ministers is perhaps more difficult to assess. As things stand, the Welsh Ministers may be designated (for the purposes of section 2(2) of the European Communities Act 1972) powers to implement EU law within the area of competence of the Welsh Government by UK Ministers.[31] This is done by statutory instrument and a number of designation orders have been made. If the UK withdraws from the EU and does not become a member of EFTA or the EEA, then such designations will no longer be necessary as such European Law will no longer be binding. This should extend the policy discretion of the Welsh Ministers in these areas of competence, although it is likely that a number of policy areas will then need legislation of the Welsh Assembly to set down a framework for the exercise of the obligations previously imposed by EU law. The Welsh Ministers would also be relieved of the obligations in section 80 of the Government of Wales Act 2006 to use their powers to implement EU law insofar as such implementation is within the sphere of competence of the Welsh Ministers. The limitation on competence in section 80(8) under which the Welsh Ministers have no power to make subordinate legislation that is contrary to EU law obligations will also need to be removed. This will likely grant enhanced scope for the Welsh Ministers to exercise their powers in the areas of competence that are most affected by EU law.

The question of just how significant any such increased freedom to act remains appears to turn on two questions. The first, as noted above in relation to the legislative freedom of the Welsh Assembly, is whether or not the UK chooses to remain in the EEA or EFTA. If this is the case, then the Welsh Ministers are likely to see many of the constraints presently imposed upon their powers by EU law remain. If the UK is not a part of the EEA or EFTA, then there will be the significant question of the extent to which the UK enters into international treaties with the EU or its individual Member States and the impact of these on the areas of competence that the Welsh Ministers

31. The power to do this can be found in section 59 of the Government of Wales Act 2006.

enjoy. Section 82(1) of the Act permits a UK Secretary of State to direct by order that the Welsh Ministers desist from any action that could be said to be incompatible with an international obligation, or under section 82(2), may require Welsh Ministers to implement measures in order to comply with the UK's international obligations. It is important to emphasise that section 82 is not a direct restriction on the competence of the Welsh Ministers in the same way as section 80 provides that it is out with the competence of the Welsh Ministers to act or create delegated legislation contrary to EU law. Up to January 2012 this power had not been used and there is no evidence that it has been used since.[32] This clearly has the potential to change if the UK becomes involved in a greater number of international agreements as a result of its withdrawal from the EU, particularly as these agreements are likely to overlap with core areas of competence presently governed by EU law. In some respects, one might argue that this will create a situation where the devolved administration could find itself in a position of certainty regarding its competence in relation to EU law obligations – it does not have the competence to act in a manner that is contrary to EU law, to one of uncertainty, where the devolved administration may enjoy greater competence as the UK Secretary of State may choose not to intervene in legislation that is contrary to international obligations. This will be addressed on the merits of each individual action taken by the Welsh Ministers and each piece of delegated legislation made.

Section 81(1) of the Government of Wales Act 2006 provides that the Welsh Ministers have no power to 'make, confirm or approve any subordinate legislation' or 'do any other act' that is incompatible with Convention Rights as defined by the Human Rights Act 1998. This position was previously brought about by section 107 of the Government of Wales Act 1998. The Welsh Ministers have seen remarkably few challenges to the exercise of their powers via this route,[33] so any removal or modification of the requirement of Convention compliance is not likely to make a significant difference to the Ministers' powers or freedom to act. It appears unlikely that the Welsh government would welcome any attempt to remove the human rights protections presently in place, with the Commission on the Bill of Rights noting:

> In Wales, the great majority of respondents and those we met expressed satisfaction with the Human Rights Act and the European Convention system, and either opposed the creation of a UK Bill of Rights or did not consider it to be necessary or desirable. Even those who supported the creation of additional rights generally wished to preserve the rights conferred by the Human Rights Act and did not express any opposition to the Human Rights Act. The First Minister said that 'it was not clear what [a UK Bill of Rights] would add to the HRA', and others echoed his suggestion that the motivation for a UK Bill of Rights emanated from England and did not extend to Wales. In their response to our Consultation Paper the

32. Wales Office *Memorandum to Welsh Affairs Committee Post-Legislative Assessment of the Government of Wales Act 2006* (Cm 8256, 2012) p. 9.
33. The only case of particular note which discusses the application of section 107 briefly appears to be *Heesom v. Public Services Ombudsman for Wales* [2014] EWHC 1504 (Admin); [2014] 4 All ER 269, with an acknowledgement of the effect of section 81 at [31].

> Counsel General and the First Minister on behalf of the Welsh Government said: 'the Welsh Government finds it difficult to see the benefits in a UK Bill of Rights'.[34]

The Welsh Government has also expressed some desire to be able to fashion a Welsh system of human rights protection, with the Silk Commission ultimately concluding on the issue of human rights and equality obligations that '... we support the principle that general rights should apply throughout the United Kingdom, the Welsh government should have powers over rights in devolved areas of policy...'.[35] This is an area where any effort by the UK government to bring about a UK Bill of Rights, or to withdraw from the European Convention as the Prime Minister has recently refused to rule out,[36] may cause considerable tension between the Welsh and United Kingdom governments. The Welsh Assembly and Government are unlikely to seek total devolution of human rights protection, not least because the Welsh Government has indicated that it would not like to see devolution of all equalities matters because:

> ...If equality were not reserved, it would require the Welsh Government and the National Assembly to take over the full range of responsibilities currently carried out at the UK level, including implementing all developments in EU equality legislation into law in Wales. This is impractical in resourcing terms.[37]

The challenge of resources, both for the Welsh Assembly and the Welsh Government may make more substantial devolution of power in relation to human rights and equality more challenging than in Scotland or Northern Ireland, particularly given the relative lack of political will for such enhanced devolution. To the extent that a 'British Bill of Rights' would most likely broadly mirror the major rights in the European Convention, it would seem unlikely that changes in the landscape of protection of human rights will have a significant impact on the scope of power enjoyed by the Welsh Ministers.

§4.04 THE WELSH POWER TO RESIST WITHDRAWAL FROM THE EU OR CHANGES TO HUMAN RIGHTS PROTECTION

An interesting question to consider is the extent to which the Welsh Ministers may be able to prevent the withdrawal from the EU, or removal of the existing system of human rights protection as it applies to the competence of the Welsh Assembly and the powers of the Welsh Ministers. The Sewel Convention, which requires the consent of the Scottish Parliament before the UK Parliament legislates for the whole of the UK on a devolved matter, may be engaged by any endeavour to alter the human rights

34. Commission on a Bill of Rights *A UK Bill of Rights? The Choice Before Us* (Vol. 1, London, 2012) at paragraph 9.22.
35. Commission on Devolution in Wales *Empowerment and Responsibility: Legislative Powers to Strengthen Wales* (Commission on Devolution in Wales, 2014) paragraph 12.6.11 (Silk Report).
36. Nicholas Watt, *Cameron Refuses to Rule Out Leaving European Convention on Human Rights, The Guardian* (London, 3 Jun. 2015) http://www.theguardian.com/law/2015/jun/03/cameron-refuses-to-rule-out-leaving-european-convention-on-human-rights (accessed 6 Jun. 2015).
37. Commission on Devolution in Wales, *supra* n. 35, Box 12.5.

framework governing the devolution settlement. Devolution Guidance Note 9,[38] sets out an identical requirement for any legislation affecting devolved matters in Wales.[39] Paragraph 49 of the Guidance note states:

> Provisions in parliamentary Bills may impose or confer new functions on the Welsh Ministers, or modify or remove their functions. The UK Government would not normally legislate in these ways, or in a way which significantly affects Welsh Ministers' executive functions, without at least the consent of the Welsh Ministers.

It is clear that the Government of Wales Act 2006 does not directly devolve the issues of EU law and membership or human rights protection to the Welsh Assembly and Welsh Ministers. As noted above, the Welsh Assembly and Ministers both have express limitations on their competence to prevent any action in breach of EU law or the Convention. Douglas-Scott has argued that any effort to modify the devolution legislation to give effect to withdrawal from the EU or the repeal of the Human Rights Act 1998 would require the consent of the devolved legislatures.[40] Elliott has argued that repeal of the Human Rights Act 1998 alone would not engage the Sewel Convention, provided that the repeal left in place the definition of 'Convention Rights' by the Human Rights Act 1998 and relied upon in section 158 of the Government of Wales Act 2006.[41]

In terms of withdrawal from the EU, it would seem impossible that the necessary changes to bring this about would not require the consent of the devolved legislatures, as although matters of negotiation with the EU are not devolved, withdrawal from the EU would without doubt create a significant change in the devolution settlement and would impact considerably, both directly and indirectly, on the powers of the devolved legislatures and the devolved executives. As such, the consent of both would need to be sought under the Sewel convention and associated guidance. As it has been emphasised, the Sewel Convention is precisely that – a constitutional convention rather than binding law.[42] However, any effort to ignore the Convention would provoke a political and constitutional crisis, not least because the evidence outlined above suggests that neither the Welsh Assembly nor the Welsh government would be in favour of withdrawal from the EU, a sentiment that is likely to be reflected by the Welsh people.

---

38. Cabinet Office (2011) *Devolution Guidance Note 9: Parliamentary and Assembly Primary Legislation Affecting Wales* London: Cabinet Office. https://www.gov.uk/government/uploads/system/uploads/attachment_data/file/186954/Parliamentary_and_Assembly_Primary_Legislation_Affecting_Wales.pdf (accessed 6 Jun. 2015).
39. *Ibid.* at paragraph 36.
40. Sionaidh Douglas-Scott 'British withdrawal from the EU: an existential threat to the United Kingdom?' (Centre on Constitutional Change Blog, 20 Oct. 2014) http://www.centreonconstitutionalchange.ac.uk/blog/british-withdrawal-eu-existential-threat-united-kingdom (accessed 6 Jun. 2015).
41. Mark Elliott 'Could the devolved nations block repeal of the Human Rights Act and the enactment of a new Bill of Rights?' (Public Law for Everyone, 12 May 2015) http://publiclawforeveryone.com/2015/05/12/could-the-devolved-nations-block-repeal-of-the-human-rights-act-and-the-enactment-of-a-new-bill-of-rights/ (accessed 6 Jun. 2015).
42. *Ibid.*

In the case of repeal of the Human Rights Act 1998, it is clear from the perspective of the Welsh government that this is not something that is desired. One possibility that is open is for the UK government to repeal the Human Rights Act 1998 and replace it with a British Bill of Rights in England and for all non-devolved matters, but to leave the current restrictions on the competence of the devolved legislatures and governments in place. This would not prima facie engage the Sewel Convention so the Welsh Assembly would not have the opportunity to prevent such a move. However, this would create a situation where the British Bill of Rights would not have effect throughout all parts of the United Kingdom in relation to all matters of government, which may create considerable uncertainty. The Commission on a Bill of Rights expressly acknowledged the possibility that there could be differing systems of human rights protection in the various parts of the United Kingdom, although the precise implications of this remain to be explored.[43] There is one particularly interesting problem that would arise if the UK were to withdraw from the European Convention on Human Rights but leave the current settlement in place for the devolved governments. International relations is a matter reserved to the Westminster government, so it would seem likely that the devolved governments would remain bound by the requirements of the Convention, yet would have no route to participate formally in the Council of Europe without changes to the devolution legislation. Even if such changes were brought about, it is unlikely that the Welsh government would find it easy to participate effectively in such international affairs given the scarce resources that it has available to put into such endeavours.[44]

§4.05 WELSH INFLUENCE ON EUROPEAN AND INTERNATIONAL POLICYMAKING

It is commonly argued that the different levels or tiers of government in the UK and at the EU level are part of a system of multi-level governance.[45] Such multi-level governance requires interactions between the various levels of government. In the system of Welsh devolution there is no devolution of international relations, so there is no formal legal basis for Wales' interactions with the EU or any other international organisation. However, there are clear channels through which the Welsh Ministers may make representations at the EU level on devolved matters, set out in a Memorandum of Understanding between the UK government and the Welsh Ministers.[46] In

43. *See* the individual paper by Anthony Speaight QC in the report cited *supra* n. 34, commencing at p. 247.
44. *See* Richard Wyn Jones & Elin Royles 'Wales in the World: Intergovernmental Relations and Sub-State Diplomacy' 14 Brit. J. Pol. & Intl Rel. 250, esp. pp. 256–259 (2012).
45. *See* e.g., L. Hooghe & G. Marks, *Unravelling the Central State, but How? Types of Multi-Level Governance* 97 Am. Pol. Sci. Rev. 233 (2003), T. Entwistle, et al. *The Multi-Level Governance of Wales: Layer Cake or Marble Cake?* 16 Brit. J. Pol. & Intl Rel. 310 (2014).
46. *See* Part B2 of the Memorandum of Understanding and Supplementary Agreements between the United Kingdom Government, the Scottish Ministers, the Welsh Ministers and the Northern Ireland Executive Committee (March 2013). https://www.gov.uk/government/uploads/system/uploads/attachment_data/file/316157/MoU_between_the_UK_and_the_Devolved_Administrations.pdf (accessed 6 Jun. 2015).

addition, there is a range of other mechanisms, both formal and informal, through which the Welsh government can make representations on EU policymaking and lawmaking. The Memorandum addresses a number of issues, including communication and consultation between the governments, the provision of information and statistics and the arrangement of Parliamentary proceedings. Paragraph 18 of the Memorandum of Understanding deals with international relations and relations with the European Union, where it states:

> As a matter of law, international relations and relations with the European Union remain the responsibility of the United Kingdom Government and the UK Parliament. However, the UK Government recognises that the devolved administrations will have an interest in international and European policy making in relation to devolved matters, notably where implementing action by the devolved administrations may be required. They will have a particular interest in those many aspects of European Union business which affect devolved areas, and a significant role to play in them.

This is complemented by paragraph 20 of the Memorandum, which provides:

> The UK Government will involve the devolved administrations as fully as possible in discussions about the formulation of the UK's policy position on all EU and international issues which touch on devolved matters. This must, obviously, be subject to mutual respect for the confidentiality of those discussions and adherence to the resultant UK line, without which it would be impossible to maintain such close working relationships.

There is then a specific concordat to the Memorandum of Understanding that provides for co-ordination mechanism that has the objective of allowing the Welsh Ministers and officials to be involved in the policy formulation process at EU level on issues that relate to devolved powers.[47] The Common Annex then sets out a set of clear mechanisms for the involvement of the devolved governments in EU policymaking and the implementation of EU law where the subject matter of EU legislation pertains to devolved matters.[48]

In addition to this formal mechanism for Welsh involvement in EU policymaking, the Welsh government also participates in a number of informal mechanisms to exert influence.[49] The Welsh government has established a representative office in Brussels and also participates in a number of groupings of sub-national authorities in the EU, including RegLeg.[50] The regional office and membership of these political networks allows the Welsh government to have a role in EU policymaking beyond that provided for in the formal Memorandum of Understanding and allows for the development of common positions with sub-national authorities sharing similar concerns. This framework, though informal and operating at the political level, may allow Wales to exert stronger influence than would be possible solely through formal channels not only in

47. *Ibid.* paragraph B2.6.
48. For further detail on this issue, *See* Varney, *supra* n. 2.
49. The right to engage in such mechanisms and particularly the opening of a representative office is acknowledged in paragraph B4.28 of the Memorandum of Understanding.
50. *See* http://www.regleg.eu/ (accessed 5 Jun. 2015).

matters of EU law and policymaking, but also in relation to broader international relations. It seems likely that if sub-national authorities can reach a common position on matters of international relations where the EU might exert an influence, the influence via the EU may be more effective than representations made by individual national channels.

If the UK were to withdraw from the EU, evidently the role of the Welsh government in EU policymaking would be removed. One might argue that this would leave the Welsh Assembly and Welsh government with a greater freedom of action; in the sense that the constraints imposed by EU law would no longer be present. However, in many matters withdrawal from the EU is likely to leave Welsh influence diminished, much as one might argue that the UK's position in many matters of international relations would be diminished. EU frameworks and the system of multi-level governance in place in the EU allow sub-national authorities to have a voice and pool their resources in a way that would be more difficult outside of the EU.[51] This would seem to be particularly important for a relatively small sub-national authority like Wales because a lack of resources might otherwise hinder effective participation in international policymaking processes.

If the UK were to withdraw from the EU, Wales would still retain the right to participate on negotiations over international agreements that impact on devolved powers, subject to the caveat that such participation must be consistent with the UK position.[52] Similarly, the Welsh government may negotiate with other foreign national or sub-national governments or international organisations on devolved matters, if the negotiations do not seek to bind the UK in international law.[53] The Memorandum also provides that the Welsh government may open representative offices within the framework of devolved responsibility.[54] The Welsh government has already opened such offices in a number of countries, some of which are part of the UK's consular mission.[55] If the UK were to withdraw from the European Union, such withdrawal would provoke the need for an enormous expansion of bilateral and multilateral treaty negotiations both with EU Member States or the EU and third countries, which would require significant additional resources for the UK Foreign and Commonwealth Office. If the European channels outlined above are lost to Wales, then a similar increase in resources will be required at the devolved level at a time when Wales may see a significant loss of income from EU funding streams.

As Wyn Jones and Royles have argued in their recent article, 'Our case studies have confirmed the centrality of asymmetry in shaping [intergovernmental relations]: asymmetry both in terms of resources and constitutional status.'[56] It is clear that the Welsh government were generally heavily reliant on the much better resourced UK

51. For an interesting theoretical and legal perspective on these issues *See* C. Panara *The Sub-national Dimension of the EU A Legal Study of Multilevel Governance* (Springer, 2014).
52. Memorandum of Understanding, *supra* n. 46, paragraph D4.5.
53. *Ibid.* paragraph D4.6.
54. *Ibid.* paragraph D4.15.
55. *See* the details at http://www.wales.com/en/content/cms/English/Business/Overseas_Offices/Overseas_Offices.aspx (accessed 15 Jun. 2016).
56. Wyn Jones & Royles, *supra* n. 44, at 265.

representation to support its activities. Furthermore, it was noted that 'In the international realm, at least, the central state is guarding its prerogatives jealously'.[57] In such circumstances, an exit from the EU, which provides a more structured and coherent framework for sub-national authorities to influence policymaking is likely to diminish the ability of the Welsh government to carry out an effective international policy.

§4.06 CONCLUSION

This chapter has sought to consider the impact of a UK exit from the EU on Welsh devolution. It has argued that while ostensibly some additional legislative and executive freedom might be granted to the Welsh Assembly and Welsh government through the lifting of EU obligations and the removal of the competence limitations that flow from EU law and adherence to Convention rights, this is unlikely to be significant. There are a multiplicity of reasons for this conclusion.

In terms of exit from the EU, one challenge would be that many obligations which are presently imposed by EU law would likely be imposed by other international agreements even if the UK were to exit the EU, particularly if the UK remained a member of EFTA or the EEA. In such circumstances, the influence of the Welsh government in these policy areas may be reduced because rather than seeking to exert influence through the various mechanisms in the EU policymaking process, Wales would need to focus resources on expanding its international relations activities. This is likely to be difficult because of a lack of resources and, indeed, the absence of any legal right to be involved in negotiations. Although one might argue that the Welsh government's ability to make formal representations at the EU level are only guaranteed by the soft law mechanism of the Memorandum of Understanding, there are clearer structures through which such representations might be made. In addition to this, there are a variety of groupings of EU sub-national authorities and other groups with common interests at the EU level that are not so strongly present in the broader international realm.

Another impact of a UK withdrawal from the EU would be a significant loss of EU funding for Wales, which would likely stretch the resources of the Welsh government considerably. As noted above, the Silk Commission Report of 2012 in addressing financial powers in Wales acknowledges that the block grant from Westminster will remain a significant part of the resources of the Welsh government.[58] Any loss of EU funding would likely leave the Welsh government in a negotiation with the UK government should it wish to seek additional funding from the block grant to make up a shortfall. Withdrawal from the EU may make it possible for Wales to gain some additional freedoms in relation to taxes such as corporation tax and VAT, although the Silk report expressed little enthusiasm for devolution of either of these to Wales even if it were possible.[59]

57. *Ibid.* at 266.
58. Silk Report, *supra* n. 35.
59. *Ibid.* R.12 (p. 84) and R. 14 (p. 87).

The possible repeal of the Human Rights Act 1998 and withdrawal from the European Convention on Human Rights raises further challenges that are outlined above. In particular, it is important to emphasise that there is little appetite for such changes in Wales – the Welsh government has made clear its support for the Convention and the Human Rights Act 1998. It was argued above that any endeavour on the part of the UK government to remove the current human rights framework as provided for in the devolution settlement would engage the Sewel Convention and would thus requires the consent of the devolved governments. There is also the issue of the common law's approach to removal of human rights limitations on devolved governments after the *AXA* case, which suggests that the common law may be willing to put limitations on the legislative freedom of devolved legislatures should none exist in legislation.

Ultimately, for Wales, the UK's continuing membership of the EU and the current human rights arrangements are what the Welsh government has suggested it would like to see maintained. Any efforts to change these arrangements are likely to create considerable tension between the UK and Welsh governments and may create constitutional crisis given the fact that the Sewel Convention provides that the devolved governments should agree before any such changes to the current settlement are made.

CHAPTER 5

Responsibility, Voice and Exit: Britain Alone?

Paul Craig

§5.01 INTRODUCTION

It became clear following the Conservative victory in the 2015 election that a referendum on UK membership of the EU would be held. The European Union Referendum Bill 2015 mandates that a referendum must be held before 31 December 2017, but does not preclude it being held earlier. It stipulates that the question to be posed is whether the UK should remain a member of the European Union or leave the European Union. The outcome, whatsoever it might be, will be of major significance for the UK going forward. If the vote is for the status quo it is likely to resolve the matter for a generation, notwithstanding the desires of the United Kingdom Independence Party (UKIP) and some Eurosceptics to the contrary. If the vote is for exit, it will signal the beginning of a lengthy unravelling exercise, and the structuring of some new relationship between the UK and the EU. It could also lead to a new Scottish referendum on independence, if the majority of Scots vote in favour of staying in the EU.[1]

The classic motif of voice and exit is particularly apposite in this context,[2] notwithstanding that it was fashioned primarily with a focus on the individual rather than the state. Renegotiation is the classic forum for 'voice' exercised by the state that feels some measure of discontent with its international obligations. Withdrawal from the EU is by the same token the classic modality of 'exit', if the terms of the renegotiation do not suffice to win approval from the people in a subsequent referendum. This leaves the concept of 'responsibility'. It reflects the theme of this chapter,

1. S. Douglas-Scott, *A UK Exit from the EU: The End of the United Kingdom or a New Constitutional Dawn?* Oxford University, Legal Research Paper Series, March 2015.
2. A. Hirschman, *Exit, Voice and Loyalty: Responses to Decline in Firms, Organizations and States* (Harvard U. Press 1970).

which is that conceptions of national constitutional responsibility are central to the discourse about voice and exit. They have been ignored in the debate concerning the EU, which is a serious failing.

The discussion begins with the status quo, connoting in this respect the present ordering of the EU. It is dissatisfaction with the status quo, combined with assumptions as to responsibility for any malaise real or apparent, that shape the call for renegotiation plus subsequent referendum. The assumption commonly made is that responsibility for these problems resides with the EU itself. This hypothesis is at the very least unbalanced. The EU institutions make mistakes like those in any other polity, but the assumption nonetheless ignores the responsibility of Member States for the status quo, judged in terms of the EU institutional architecture, the framing of key substantive Treaty provisions and the way in which we think of states when they partake in the making of EU legislation.

The focus then shifts to renegotiation, through which the state exercises constitutional voice. This necessarily requires choice as to what to take to the bargaining table, an issue on which David Cameron, the Prime Minister, was not forthcoming in the speech in which he promised a referendum, or in the period thereafter. It only became clear after the Prime Minister's speech in November 2015. This section considers the dilemmas facing the government in deciding what to renegotiate, where it has sought to steer a course that would satisfy the Eurosceptics within the Conservative Party, and keep UKIP at bay, while at the same time taking something to the bargaining table that other Member States might accept. The discussion highlights the importance of constitutional responsibility in this context, the impact that it should properly have on the subject matter for renegotiation and the way in which the matter is presented to the public.

This is then followed by discussion of the referendum itself. There is, as will be seen, a potential Catch 22 in the holding of the referendum, which flows from the fact that even if a deal is forthcoming between the UK and the other Member States, this will not be formally binding until it is agreed in accord with the constitutional requirements of each Member State. It is therefore perfectly possible for the UK to conduct a referendum on the basis of an agreement between national governments that is not later ratified by all Member States.

The chapter concludes with a hard look at the consequences of a no vote, and the UK's ensuing exit from the EU. The nature of the UK's subsequent relationship with the EU is considered. It is relatively clear what types of relationship have been rejected by the Prime Minister and the Eurosceptics. It is much less clear how they conceive of that relationship, and the possible options are canvassed in the ensuing discussion. It will be argued that the conception of government responsibility is also relevant in this context, most notably in the duty to make clear to the people the extent to which they will remain bound by EU regulatory initiatives under any conceivable relationship with the EU post exit, and that we will have no voice in the content of such measures.

§5.02 CONSTITUTIONAL RESPONSIBILITY: THE STATUS QUO

The discourse concerning the UK referendum is conducted explicitly against the status quo, and implicitly against assumptions concerning ascription of responsibility for the existing schema. The framing of the issue results from the elision of both dimensions. Thus the ills of the EU, whatsoever they might currently be, are conceived to be the responsibility of the EU, conceived in this respect primarily to be the Commission, together with other 'powers' in Brussels. It follows that it is the bounden duty of national governments to renegotiate the Treaty if possible to remove the malaise thus created. It's a great story, save for the fact that it bears little relation to reality. The central flaw resides in the implicit assumption that grounds the argument, which is like many such assumptions a good deal less secure than might initially be thought.

What is missing is considered discourse concerning the constitutional responsibility of the Member States for the status quo. I am not referring here to such responsibility insofar as it concerns national representatives in the Council, or that of heads of state within the European Council, on which there is indeed considerable discussion. I am referring rather to the way in which we think more generally about the responsibility of Member States as contracting parties to the EU. It is the very nature of the constitutional and political obligations that flow from the legal maxim *pacta sunt servanda* that are of interest here. The response might well be that there are no distinct obligations that can be cast in terms of Member State constitutional responsibility, over and beyond the narrow legal dimension of *pacta sunt servanda* that exhausts the meaning of this precept. This does not withstand examination, and reflects the very fact that consideration of national constitutional responsibility is under-theorised. Consider three applications of such responsibility.

[A] Political Responsibility, Member States and Inter-institutional Division of Power

Consider first the inter-institutional division of power within the EU. The discourse on this issue commonly includes that of democracy deficit and its implications for EU political accountability. The financial crisis unsurprisingly brought back to the fore concerns about the very design of the EU's institutional structure and issues of democracy deficit,[3] on which there is already an extensive literature.[4] There is no intent to traverse the arguments concerning democracy deficit in detail again here. Suffice it

3. *See*, e.g., D. Chalmers, 'Democratic Self-Government in Europe, Domestic Solutions to the EU Legitimacy Crisis', Policy Network Paper, May 2013; K. Nicolaïdis, *European Demoicracy and Its Crisis* 51 JCMS 351 (2013); O. Cramme & S. Hobolt (eds), *Democratic Politics in a European Union under Stress* (Oxford U. Press 2014); S. Piattoni (ed.), *The European Union: Institutional Architectures and Democratic Principles in Times of Crisis* (Oxford U. Press 2015).
4. *See*, just in terms of books, S. Garcia (ed.), *European Identity and the Search for Legitimacy* (Pinter 1993); J. Hayward (ed), *The Crisis of Representation in Europe* (Frank Cass, 1995); A. Rosas & E. Antola (eds), *A Citizens' Europe, In Search of a New Order* (Sage 1995); R. Bellamy, V. Bufacchi & D. Castiglione (eds), *Democracy and Constitutional Culture in the Union of Europe* (Lothian Foundation Press 1995); S. Andersen & K. Eliassen (eds), *The European Union: How*

to say that the disjunction between power and electoral accountability is the most potent aspect of the democracy deficit argument.[5]

There is however a dearth of literature concerning constitutional responsibility of Member States for the status quo. Consideration of the causal influences underpinning Treaty reform has not been matched by attendant analysis of what this should be taken to connote in terms of the constitutional responsibility of Member States for the resultant institutional architecture. This is a serious failing. It is standard fare that the democracy deficit critique is presented as a critique of the EU. It is the EU qua real and reified entity that suffers from this infirmity, the corollary being that blame is cast on it. The EU is of course not blameless in this respect, but nor are the Member States, viewed collectively and individually.

The present disposition of EU institutional power is the result of successive Treaties in which the principal players have been the Member States. There may well be debate as to the relative degree of power wielded by Member States and the EU institutions in the shaping and application of EU legislation, but there is greater consensus on the fact that Member States dominate at times of Treaty reform.[6] The

Democratic Is It? (Sage 1996); R. Bellamy & D. Castiglione (eds), *Constitutionalism in Transformation: European and Theoretical Perspectives* (Blackwell 1996); R. Bellamy (ed.), *Constitutionalism, Democracy and Sovereignty: American and European Perspectives* (Avebury 1996); F. Snyder (ed.), *Constitutional Dimensions of European Economic Integration* (Kluwer 1996); R. Dehousse (ed.), *Europe: The Impossible Status Quo* (Macmillan 1997); D. Curtin, *Postnational Democracy, The European Union in Search of a Political Philosophy* (Kluwer 1997); P. Craig & C. Harlow (eds), *Lawmaking in the European Union* (Kluwer 1998); J. Weiler, *The Constitution of Europe* (Cambridge U. Press 1999); C. Hoskyns & M. Newman (eds), *Democratizing the European Union* (Manchester University Press 2000); B. Laffan, R. O'Donnell & M. Smith, *Europe's Experimental Union: Rethinking Integration* (Routledge 2000); F. Mancini, *Democracy and Constitutionalism in the European Union* (Hart 2000); K. Neunreither & A. Wiener (eds), *European Integration after Amsterdam, Institutional Dynamics and Prospects for Democracy* (OUP 2000); R. Prodi, *Europe As I See It* (Polity 2000); K. Nicolaidis & R. Howse (eds), *The Federal Vision, Legitimacy and Levels of Governance in the United States and the European Union* (Oxford U. Press 2001); W. van Gerven, *The European Union, A Polity of States and Peoples* (Hart 2005).

5. J. Weiler, U. Haltern & F. Mayer, *European Democracy and its Critique*, in *The Crisis of Representation in Europe* 4 (J. Hayward ed., Frank Cass 1995); A. Follesdal & S. Hix, *Why There is a Democratic Deficit in the EU: A Response to Majone and Moravcsik* 44 JCMS 533 (2006); K. Nicolaïdis, *The Idea of European Demoicracy*, in *Philosophical Foundations of EU Law* (J. Dickson & P. Eleftheriadis eds, Oxford U. Press 2012); K. Nicolaïdis, *Our European Demoi-cracy: Is this Constitution a Third Way for Europe?* in *Whose Europe? National Models and the Constitution of the European Union* (K. Nicolaïdis & S. Weatherill eds, Oxford U. Press 2003).
6. G. Marks, L. Hooghe & K. Blank, *European Integration from the 1980s: State-Centric v. Multiple-Level Governance* 34 JCMS 341, 342 (1996); T. Risse-Kappen, *Exploring the Nature of the Beast: International Relations Theory and Comparative policy Analysis Meet the European Union* 34 JCMS 53 (1996); J. Golub, *State Power and Institutional Influence in European Integration: Lessons from the Packaging Waste Directive* 34 JCMS 313 (1996); J. Caporaso, *The European Union and Forms of State: Westphalian, Regulatory or Post-Modern* 34 JCMS 29, 44–48 (1996); F. Scharpf, *The Problem Solving Capacity of Multi-Level Governance* 4 JEPP 520 (1997); G. Marks, F. Scharpf, P. Schmitter & W. Streeck, *Governance in the European Union* (Sage 1996); A. Moravcsik, *Preferences and Power in the European Community: A Liberal Intergovernmentalist Approach* 31 JCMS 473 (1993); A. Moravcsik, *National Preference Formation and Interstate Bargaining in the European Community, 1955-86* (Harvard U. Press 1992); A. Moravcsik, *Negotiating the Single European Act: National Interests and Conventional Statecraft in the European Community* 45 Intl Org. 19 (1991); M. Pollack, 'International Relations Theory and European Integration' EUI Working Papers, RSC 2000/55.

inter-institutional distribution of power is the result of hard fought battles, the results of which are embodied in Treaty amendment. Thus insofar as the present arrangements divide EU policymaking de facto and de jure between the Commission, Council, European Parliament and European Council, this is reflective of power balances that the Member States were willing to accept. This is readily apparent when considering the initial Rome Treaty and any of the five major Treaty reforms since then. It is powerfully exemplified by the debates concerning institutional reforms in the Constitutional Treaty, which were then taken over into the Lisbon Treaty.[7] It was evident most notably in the battle as to whether the EU should have a single President who would be located in the Commission, or whether a reinforced European Council should also have a long-term President.[8] It was apparent in the debates as to Council configurations, and who would chair them. It was the frame within which the discourse took place concerning the number of Commissioners and the method of choosing them.[9]

It would be possible in theory to have a regime in which the people voted directly for two constituent parts of the legislature, the European Parliament and Council, and for the President of the Commission and the President of the European Council. It would be possible in theory to have the previous package, but only a single elected President for the EU as whole. The political reality is that radical change of this kind has not happened because the Member States were unwilling to accept such a disposition of power. It is true that the choice between two Presidents and a single President for the EU was debated during the negotiations leading to the Constitutional Treaty. It is equally true that discourse concerning the election of the Commission President began in the 1980s. It should nonetheless be recognised that the broader reforms set out above were not on the political agenda during the extensive negotiations concerning institutional power in 2003–2004 that led to the Constitutional Treaty, nor in the subsequent discussions that culminated in the Lisbon Treaty. Even if the broader package of reforms were adopted it could not ensure that the people would exercise electoral control over the direction of EU policy, since the European Council would still be populated by Heads of State, who would continue to have a marked influence over the policy agenda, and members of the Commission, with diverse political views, would still be chosen by the Member States.

There is moreover a constitutional paradox lurking here. The diminution of state power in the Council and European Council that would be entailed by change of the kind mooted above would probably not be constitutionally tolerated in some countries and would lead to the charge that the EU was truly becoming a super-state. Thus while the German Federal Constitutional Court has repeatedly chided the EU in relation to its democratic credentials, it would likely be one of the national constitutional courts to decide that an institutional configuration of the kind set out above that addressed the democratic deficit as presently understood would not be compatible with German

7. P. Norman, *The Accidental Constitution, The Making of Europe's Constitutional Treaty* (EuroComment, 2nd edn, 2005).
8. P. Craig, *The Lisbon Treaty, Law, Politics and Treaty Reform* Chapter 3 (Oxford U. Press 2010).
9. *Ibid.* Chapters 2 and 3.

constitutional law. This was because such a change would mean that the EU was moving closer to a federal state, with the consequence that the Member States could no longer be regarded as the Masters of the Treaty in the manner hitherto. The same sentiment would likely be voiced by some within the UK, albeit from a more overtly political perspective. Thus while the House of Commons European Scrutiny Committee has oft-criticised the EU for its democratic shortcomings, it would not view with equanimity institutional architecture of the kind adumbrated in the preceding paragraph, since it would be regarded as increasing the EU's legitimacy at the expense, *inter alia*, of national parliaments.

[B] Political Accountability, Member States and Substantive Treaty Provisions

Member State constitutional responsibility is also relevant in relation to substantive Treaty provisions. This can be exemplified by the financial crisis and the consequential ascription of responsibility. There is little doubt that the EU bears some responsibility in this regard, but so too do the Member States, both collectively and individually. The Treaty provisions on economic and monetary union were crafted in the Maastricht Treaty. Insofar as there was an asymmetry between EU powers over monetary as opposed to economic union, this reflected what Member States were willing to accept. This is readily apparent when one considers the architecture of the Treaty provisions on Economic and Monetary Union (EMU) and the Stability and Growth Pact.[10]

Monetary union was all about the single currency and the Treaty articles were powerfully influenced by German ordo-liberal economic thought, which demanded independence of the European Central Bank, governance by experts and the primacy of price stability. These foundational precepts were embodied in the primary Treaty articles.[11] It was integral to the Maastricht settlement that monetary policy was Europeanised. This was reinforced by the Lisbon Treaty provisions on competence, which stated that monetary policy for those countries that subscribed to the euro was within the exclusive competence of the EU.[12] This was further strengthened by mandatory Treaty provisions precluding instructions or interference from any outside party, whether that was a nation state or another EU institution.[13]

The Maastricht settlement in relation to economic policy was markedly different. It was built on two related assumptions, preservation of national authority and preservation of national liability. The former was reflected in the fact that Member States retained fiscal authority for national budgets, subject to limited oversight and coordination from the EU designed to persuade Member States, with the ultimate possibility of sanctions, to balance their budgets and not run excessive deficits. The

10. Council Regulation (EC) 1466/97 of 7 July 1997 on the strengthening of the surveillance of budgetary positions and the surveillance and coordination of economic policies [1997] OJ L209/1; Council Regulation (EC) 1467/97 of 7 July 1997 on speeding up and clarifying the implementation of the excessive deficit procedure [1997] OJ L209/6.
11. Articles 127, 130, 282(3) TFEU.
12. Articles 2(1), 3 TFEU.
13. Article 130 TFEU.

latter, preservation of national liability, was the quid pro quo for the former, which found its most powerful expression in the no bail-out provision.[14] While there was some limited qualification to this precept[15] the message was nonetheless that national governments retained authority over national economic policy, subject to the Treaty rules designed to persuade them to balance their budgets, the corollary being that if they did not do so then the consequential liabilities would remain at the door of the nation state.

Oversight of national economic policy was weakened in subsequent years through Member State unwillingness to abide by the rules, which led to their modification, the effect of which was to weaken centralised EU control.[16] The Maastricht 'deal' was nonetheless left largely unaltered in the Lisbon Treaty. The Member States recognised the proximate connection between economic and monetary policy. They understood that the economic health of individual Member State economies could have a marked impact on the valuation of the euro, hence the need for some oversight and coordination of national economic policy. They were, however, mindful of the policy decisions made in and through national budgets, including those of a redistributive nature, and were unwilling to accord the EU too much control over such determinations. It was only when the financial crisis hit the EU that the Member States were willing to accept that greater control over national economic policy was a necessary condition for monetary union. This led to the plethora of measures enacted to tighten centralised control over national budgets and national banks. While the EU should properly be held accountable for the way in which it dealt with the financial crisis, the Member States cannot escape constitutional responsibility in this regard either. They had a major role in shaping the Maastricht architecture on EMU and determined how it was applied in the years thereafter.

[C] Political Accountability, Member States and EU Legislation

It is also interesting to reflect on what Member State responsibility connotes when we think of the shaping of, and compliance with, EU legislation. It may be helpful to contrast two possible positions, while being mindful that there may well be more nuanced variations.

Member State responsibility might be regarded as coterminous with legal accountability. Thus on this view it is legitimate for Member States to behave as 'rational actors' when EU legislation is made, in the sense that resources will be deployed to ensure that the legislation best meets the needs of that particular state. The same

14. Article 125(1) TFEU.
15. Article 122(2) TFEU.
16. Case C-27/04 *Commission v. Council* [2004] ECR I-6649; I. Maher, *Economic Policy Co-ordination and the European Court: Excessive Deficits and ECOFIN Discretion*, 29 ELRev 831 (2004); Council Regulation (EC) 1055/2005 of 27 June 2005 amending Regulation 1466/97 [2005] OJ L174/1; Council Regulation (EC) 1056/2005 of 27 June 2005 amending Regulation 1467/97 [2005] OJ L174/5.

approach will shape attitudes to compliance. The state accepts the consequences of non-compliance with EU legislation, whether cast in terms of state liability in damages, Commission action for breach of EU law, or direct effect of directives. This is however conceived for what it is, legal accountability when one breaks the rules. It does not undermine the foundational precept that the state will act as a rational actor seeking to maximise the returns and minimise the costs of EU membership. It is integral to this approach that the state will regard it as politically 'natural' and normatively 'uncontroversial' to offload blame for failures to the EU itself, rather than accept that the states individually or collectively bear responsibility in this regard. The rational state actor as thus conceived describes not only how states behave in relation to the EU, but also sets the normative boundaries for their politically accountability.

Member State responsibility might, alternatively, be conceptualised more broadly, to include, but also go beyond the limits of legal accountability. The principle of sincere cooperation, whereby it is incumbent on the EU and Member States in full mutual respect to assist each other in carrying out tasks that flow from the Treaties, is central to this alternative vision.[17] So too is the remainder of this Treaty provision, which enjoins the Member States to take any appropriate measure to ensure fulfilment of the obligations arising out of the Treaties, or resulting from acts of the EU institutions, and requires Member States to facilitate achievement of the EU's tasks and refrain from any measure which could jeopardise the attainment of the EU's objectives.[18] This Treaty obligation can be used as part of the foundation for more discrete legal obligations, as exemplified by its deployment in the jurisprudence on state liability in damages.[19] It is, however, integral to this second vision that Member State responsibility is not exhausted by the legal dimension to the principle of sincere cooperation. It also has a distinctly political dimension that is expressive most fundamentally of the positive side of the maxim *pacta sunt servanda*, irrespective of whether it is capable of being embodied in a legally enforceable norm.[20] Thus the principle of sincere cooperation could provide the basis for an obligation of political good faith engagement by Member States in ensuring that Treaty obligations are fulfilled efficaciously; the injunction on Member States to take any appropriate measure to ensure fulfilment of Treaty obligations could generate a political obligation on states to be proactive in thinking about the best way to achieve Treaty imperatives; and the duty to refrain from behaviour that could jeopardise attainment of EU objectives could provide the foundation for a political obligation not to offload blame to the EU when this is unwarranted.

17. Article 4(3) TEU.
18. Article 4(3) TEU.
19. Cases C-6 & 9/90 *Francovich and Bonifaci v. Italy* [1991] ECR I-5357.
20. What has been termed here the positive side of *pacta sunt servanda* may have legal implications. The point being made here is that even if this is not so there may still be the foundations for constitutional responsibility.

§5.03 CONSTITUTIONAL VOICE AND RESPONSIBILITY: THE SUBJECT MATTER FOR RENEGOTIATION

The referendum is predicated on prior renegotiation of the terms of UK membership. It is the deal secured through such renegotiation that will serve as the backdrop to the political discourse leading to the referendum vote. A good deal and the government champions our continued membership of the EU, a bad deal and the government campaigns the other way, or finds it more difficult to convince the electorate of the reasons to stay in. Renegotiation is then a quintessential forum through which to express constitutional voice. It is the medium through which the body politic considers whether it is possible to reshape the terms of its membership in a broader community, the terms of which it is not comfortable with. If the renegotiation does not yield the desired outcome the state then has the exit option. Exercise of this constitutional voice is not however value free, it too entails constitutional responsibilities as will be seen from the ensuing discussion.

In the months after the Prime Minister's Bloomberg speech in which he promised the referendum there was much speculation as to the precise subject matter that would form the basis of this renegotiation.[21] David Cameron gave scant indication of what he would bring to the negotiating table in that speech, other than that there were serious things that needed to be improved in the modus operandi of the EU. The issues for renegotiation have now become clearer, and we shall return to this in due course. Before doing so, we need to take a step back and consider the government's balance of competence review.

The government established the balance of competence review in 2012.[22] It is the most comprehensive review of EU competence undertaken by any Member State. The object was to assess the impact of EU law broadly conceived on all areas of government action. To this end each government department considered the effect of EU law on its area. The reports analysed not only the extent of the impact, but whether the scope of EU power went beyond what was necessary in each area. The review was launched by the Foreign and Commonwealth Office in 2012 and was divided into four semesters.

There is little doubt that the review was launched with the hope in some quarters that it would provide the substance for subsequent renegotiation of the Treaties. The government would then have the ammunition to take to the bargaining table, whereby it could claim that the UK government had carried out an unimpeachable, detailed inquiry that revealed the excess of EU competence. Matters turned out rather differently. The inquiry conducted by government departments was indeed unimpeachable in terms of process, and well-judged in terms of substance, but it did not produce the ammunition that the Eurosceptics had hoped for. All of which goes to show that the best laid plans often go off the tracks.

21. The text of the Prime Minister's speech is available at: http://www.number10.gov.uk/news/eu-speech-at-bloomberg/.
22. Review of the Balance of Competences between the United Kingdom and the European Union, Cm 8415, July 2012, https://www.gov.uk/review-of-the-balance-of-competences.

In terms of process, it showed the UK civil service at its very best. It was told to conduct the review and did so. The civil service was however determined to ensure that the outcome would withstand serious scrutiny. It was not about to sully its reputation by authoring reports that might be regarded as politically biased. The process was therefore unimpeachable and uniform throughout. The lead department for the particular topic engaged in broad consultation. This took the form of publicising the review process; receiving written consultations; undertaking town-hall type meetings; and soliciting views of experts in day long discussions held in the department with those responsible for the study. The lead department produced a draft report based on the results of the consultation, including research that it had done. This draft report was then subject to rigorous scrutiny in a face to face meeting with a team from the Cabinet Office, which would test its compatibility against the evidence. This team was reinforced by two 'external challengers'. They were, as the title suggests, people from outside government with expertise in the area, who brought a critical eye to the draft report. The external challengers often had very different views concerning the EU, and there was therefore no necessary commonality between them. It was only after this process that the report was submitted to ministers for approval, which was generally given, the exception being the report on free movement that was subject to lengthy delays in the Home Office.

In terms of substance, the reports generally found that EU competence was pitched at about the right level. There were, as might be expected, questions about the wisdom of particular legislative initiatives, but that would inevitably be so in the context of a review into any area where a public authority wielded power, whether at national or EU level. The bottom line was that the Eurosceptics did not get the ammunition that they had hoped for from the review. While the civil service was instructed not to draw direct conclusions from the material, it is nonetheless clear from the reports that the general inference was that the distribution of competence was about right. This was not lost on commentators. Philip Stephens, reflecting on the first set of reports, noted that to the 'chagrin of some Eurosceptic colleagues the balance of competence review was coming up with the wrong answers' and that Brussels was 'neither sucking the lifeblood from British democracy nor stifling its economy with unnecessary regulation', but was rather 'serving the national interest'.[23] The same message was forthcoming in relation to the second set of reviews. Michael Emerson, Steven Blockmans, Steve Peers and Michael Wriglesworth concluded that the second 'set of reviews confirms the findings of the first set, and suggests a pattern; namely that there is no case for repatriation of EU competences at the level at which they are identified in the treaties'. This did not exclude the possibility that individual actions or laws might have been done better or not at all, 'but on the whole the EU institutions and its Member States are seen to have refined their respective competences, often 'shared

23. P. Stephens, 'The UK Audit of Relations with the EU is Coming up with Awkward Answers', Financial Times, 22 Jul. 2013, http://www.ft.com/cms/s/0/96074de6-f2d9-11e2-a203-00144feabdc0.html#ixzz2ZysCrmOo.

competences', in a reasonably sensible way.'[24] There were similar assessments about the later reviews.[25]

In a previous era it might have been possible to bury a report that did not cohere with what the government intended, although it would have been difficult to do that with a report of this size. The reality is that we live in an internet age, with the consequence that interring unwelcome reports produced after public input is simply not an option. There is no putting this particular genie back in the bottle. The reports have become known throughout the EU, not only in academic circles, but also among the political establishment in Member State capitals and in Brussels. The breadth of the balance of competence exercise ensured that Member States and the EU would be interested in the outcome. This will perforce impact on any future renegotiation, since it means that the other side have access to our data, which generally confirms that the balance of competence is about right. It is of course open to the government to contradict its own review on a particular topic, but this would be doubly difficult, in part because it signed off the review and in part because it would have to adduce convincing evidence as to why the detailed departmental assessment was to be doubted.

The difficulties for the government in deciding what to renegotiate are cast into sharp relief by the balance of competence review, which is in part why the Prime Minister was so unforthcoming about this until November 2015. These difficulties were further exacerbated by the fact that the Prime Minister sought a renegotiating strategy that would blunt the edge of a UKIP challenge, and satisfy its Eurosceptic members. We know what UKIP desires, which is exit from the EU. The best guide to the aspirations of the Eurosceptics is the manifesto of Fresh Start, a cross-party group with the objective of recasting the UK's relationship with the EU, although predominantly a vehicle for Conservative Party Eurosceptics. It produced a *Manifesto for Change, A New Vision for the UK* in Europe in January 2013, with a foreword written by William Hague.[26] The manifesto listed five principal changes to the existing Treaties: an emergency brake for any Member State regarding future EU legislation that affects financial services; repatriation of competence in the area of social and employment law to Member States; an opt-out for the UK from all existing EU policing and criminal justice measures not already covered by the Lisbon Treaty block opt-out; a new legal safeguard for the single market to ensure that there is no discrimination against non-Eurozone member interests; and the abolition of the Strasbourg seat of the EP. This was just the tip of the iceberg, since Fresh Start also sought a plethora of other changes, which were said to be attainable within the framework of the existing

24. M. Emerson et al., 'British Balance of Competence Reviews, Part II: Again, a Huge Contradiction between the Evidence and Eurosceptic Populism', EPIN Policy Network Paper, No. 40, 2014, p. 2. For the review of the initial set of reports, *See* M. Emerson & S. Blockmans, 'British Balance of Competence Reviews, Part I: 'Competences about right, so far"', CEPS/EPIN Working Paper No. 35, 2013, available at Http://www.epin.org.
25. M. Emerson et al., 'British Balance of Competence Reviews, Part III: More Reform than Renegotiation or Repatriation', EPIN Paper No. 42, December 2014.
26. http://www.eufreshstart.org/downloads/manifestoforchange.pdf.

Treaties.[27] Fresh Start published a shortened and revised version of its manifesto in November 2013, which included proposed Treaty amendment, and change within the existing Treaty fabric.[28] The list was much the same as in the earlier document, but there were additional demands which included: a UK opt-out from the EU Charter of Rights; a strengthened yellow card system so that it could be triggered by three national parliaments; the introduction of red cards for national parliaments, for existing and future legislation; introduction of a general emergency brake akin to the Luxembourg compromise that would enable a Member State to refer EU legislation enacted by qualified majority that would affect its fundamental interest to the European Council, which would decide by unanimity thus enabling the state to veto the measure; the ability to amend legislation speedily in the light of 'perverse' ECJ judgments; and extension of the double majority lock to protect non-Eurozone countries.

The Conservative leadership was thus caught between a rock and a hard place. The renegotiation has to bring about some meaningful change so as to placate Eurosceptics and stem UKIP, but the terms taken to the bargaining table must also be grounded in empirical reality as judged by what other states might be willing to accept. It is then no small wonder that the Conservative leadership remained reticent about what it would try to attain through renegotiation. It was left to commentators to trawl interviews given by the Prime Minister to discern what would be on the negotiating table.

Thus Michael Emerson deduced a number of objectives sought by the Prime Minister, as judged by an interview given to the Daily Telegraph in April 2014.[29] The objectives, which resonated with initiatives proposed by Fresh Start, included: no constant flow of power to Brussels; no to ever closer union; national parliaments being able to block unwanted EU legislation; business liberated from red tape; opening up of free trade with North America and Asia; no to unnecessary interference with our police and justice systems; free movement to take up work and not benefits; continued enlargement, with safeguards to prevent vast migrations; no to the euro; and no to a EU army. The extent to which these constituted a coherent platform from which to conduct renegotiation was doubtful to say the least. Consider in this respect Emerson's conclusion about the Daily Telegraph interview:[30]

> The Prime Minister's initial speech on Europe of January 2013 was full of radical rhetoric for renegotiating the EU's relationship with the EU, handing power back to the national level and reforming the EU itself. But it was very short on operational propositions. Nobody could know what he really wanted beyond general emotional aspirations, and indeed it seems that the Prime Minister himself did not know. His article in the Daily Telegraph of March 2014 shows where his thinking has since then got to, with the aid of his government's 'Balance of Competences Review' and numerous meetings with other European leaders.

27. The manifesto is analysed in detail in P. Craig, *The United Kingdom, the European Union and Sovereignty*, in *Sovereignty and the Law, Domestic, European and International Perspectives* Chapter 10 (R. Rawlings, P. Leyland & A. Young eds, Oxford U. Press 2013).
28. Fresh Start Project, *Mandate for Reform, Securing the Right Deal for the UK, Equipping the EU for a Globalized World*, November 2013.
29. M. Emerson, 'Cameron's Reality Check on Europe', EPIN Paper No. 38, April 2014.
30. *Ibid.* p. 6.

> Reading between the lines, it is evident that the case for repatriation of competences could not be supported either by the objective findings of his government's review, or from conversations with his colleagues in the European Council. This has left his agenda to be recomposed with a combination, on the one hand, of a number of rhetorical propositions that do not amount to operational issues at all, and on the other hand, a number of concerns that are shared quite widely by other Member States and are subjects of work in progress. All of this means that the Prime Minister seems to be on a course that will not risk hitting a brick wall of rejection by his colleagues, but neither will the likely outcome appear impressive in the rough marketplace of British public opinion.

We return then to the rock and the hard place adverted to earlier. If the Prime Minister sought seriously to address the agenda of his Eurosceptics he would enter negotiations playing a hand that was destined to fail. If he played a moderate hand he risked entering a bargaining forum in which he was destined to disappoint this powerful group. This tension was forcefully exemplified by the reception accorded to the Prime Minister's initiative in October 2014, when he finally placed something concrete on the bargaining table, viz the free movement of persons. The reaction was swift and predictable from the EU institutions, which emphasised the centrality of free movement to the EU, with the corollary that it was not up for grabs. It was, moreover, not readily apparent why the Prime Minister ever felt that he could secure the requisite unanimity for a Treaty amendment on this issue, when it would entail assent from a number of Member States that were the de facto target of the proposed limits on entry. The Prime Minister might have hoped that the larger states would line up behind his proposal, but this was always fanciful, and was quickly dispelled by the reaction of Chancellor Merkel, who made it clear that proposals of this kind would mean that the UK was marching towards the exit door. Curbs on benefit tourism might be considered, but direct attacks on the free movement principle would not.

The Prime Minister finally unveiled the UK's negotiating position on November 10 2015, which consists of four parts.[31]

First, there should be protection for countries outside the Eurozone. This was required in order to: protect the single market and ensure that all twenty-eight Member States decided its rules; to prevent discrimination against non-Eurozone countries; and to ensure that non-Eurozone countries did not have to shoulder additional costs from integration of the Eurozone. The Prime Minister asked European leaders to agree clear and binding principles that would protect non-Euro countries, and a safeguard mechanism to ensure that those principles were respected and enforced.

Second, there should be increased emphasis on competitiveness and the cutting of red tape, thereby removing unwarranted regulatory burdens on industry, the idea being that competitiveness should be written in the DNA of the EU.

Third, there should be change that impacted on sovereignty and subsidiarity. Thus the Treaty commitment to ever closer Union should no longer apply to Britain. For the Prime Minister this meant a clear, legally binding and irreversible agreement to end Britain's obligation to work towards an ever closer union. There should in addition

31. https://www.gov.uk/government/speeches/prime-ministers-speech-on-europe.

be some red card regime, such that if a certain number of national parliaments objected to a measure it could be prevented from becoming law, and there should also be greater emphasis on the application of the concept of subsidiarity. This third limb of the renegotiation package also contains proposals in relation to EU competence over human rights. The essence of the Prime Minister's reasoning was as follows. The government intends to scrap the Human Rights Act 1998, and to replace it with a British Bill of Rights, which would redefine the relationship between the UK and the European Convention on Human Rights. The Prime Minister therefore sought to minimize the extent to which this strategy could be undermined through the EU Charter of Rights, which contains many of the ECHR rights and which states that the meaning thereof is to be determined by the Strasbourg court. The UK would therefore include in its domestic law a provision whereby the EU Charter does not create any new rights, supplemented by an instruction to UK courts that they should not apply the EU Charter insofar as it contained 'spurious new human rights grounds'. The Prime Minister in addition expressed his attraction to the kind of ultra vires and identity locks used by the German Federal Constitutional Court.

The fourth and final part of the renegotiation package concerned free movement and immigration. The Prime Minister did not press for change to the basic right of free movement, acknowledging that it was a key part of the single market. He nonetheless sought change that would prevent what he termed abuse of the right to free movement, and facilitate greater control over migration in line with the Conservative manifesto. This meant ensuring that when new countries acceded to the EU free movement would not apply until their economies converged much more closely with existing member states and dealing with abuse of free movement. EU migrants should moreover have to live in the UK and contribute for four years before they qualified for in-work benefits or social housing,[32] and the practice of sending child benefit overseas should cease. The Prime Minister was cognizant that such changes could pose difficulties for other Member States, and said that he was open to different ways of dealing with them, while insisting that the basic demands should nonetheless be met.

Whether these demands can be realized in the renegotiation remains to be seen. Some will be easier to meet than others. Thus, seeking reduction in EU red tape is pushing at an open door. By way of contrast the changes to benefits for EU migrants raise complex legal issues and there is likely to be significant political opposition.[33] To take another example, the demand that non-Eurozone Member States should not have to bear the cost of aid to Eurozone states that are in financial difficulty would not be difficult to enshrine in legal terms, but the more general demand that there should not be discrimination against non-Eurozone states raises complex issues insofar as the

32. See however, https://www.ucl.ac.uk/news/news-articles/1114/051114-economic-impact-EU-immigration; C. Dustmann & T. Frattini, *The Fiscal Effects of Immigration to the UK* 124 Econ. J. F593 (2014) in which the authors calculate that migrants from new Member States contributed at a minimum GBP 5 billion more to the UK coffers than they took out, while the ne t contribution of migrants from the rest of the EU was in the order of GPB 15 billion.
33. S. Peers, *The Nine labours of Cameron: Analysis of the Plans to Change EU Free Movement Law*, 28 Oct. 2014, http://eulawanalysis.blogspot.co.uk/2014/11/the-nine-labours-of-cameron-analysis-of.html; Case C-333/13 *Dano*, 11 Nov. 2014.

Prime Minister might be seeking change over and beyond existing principles of non-discrimination. There are complex issues as to what changes require Treaty amendment, and what can be secured through other means.[34]

We should moreover be mindful about the renegotiation process. The general consensus is that most states would prefer the UK to stay in rather than leave, but this is seriously leavened by limits of patience with demands that are regarded as unsound in terms of the present and future ordering of the EU. This brings us back to the conception of constitutional responsibility adumbrated at the outset of this section. The argument in this context is simple and compelling. Renegotiation provides the window for constitutional voice. There is a nice question as to whether the conception of voice when exercised by an individual is predicated on its being used responsibly, although the better view is that it does. There is, however, no room for such meaningful disagreement when we shift to the collective dimension. The government exercises voice on behalf of its people, not just those who voted for it. It is there to represent the public interest, not just its own particular vision. To be sure the government of the day may well have a view as to what constitutes the public interest on a particular issue. This is entirely legitimate and part of the very raison d'etre of government. It does not however alter the point being made here. The government exercises voice on behalf of the people when engaged in renegotiation of the UK's treaty obligations, and must do so responsibly.

The specific content of this constitutional responsibility will perforce vary depending on the nature of the issue. It surely connotes at a minimum an obligation to present the case in relation to the EU in an even handed manner, notwithstanding the fact that this might not be agreeable to those with Eurosceptic leanings. This in turn should oblige the government to be open and honest about the results of the balance of competence review. The discourse concerning the terms on which to renegotiate has been conducted without reference to the fact that the most far-reaching review conducted by the UK government reached the conclusion that the balance of EU competence was generally correct and beneficial to the UK. The general public should surely be told this, and it is part of the government's constitutional responsibility to do so. The reality is to the contrary, the Conservative Party downplayed the results of the review and gave them the least possible publicity. The review was treated akin to Banquo's ghost, something that should be ignored in the hope that it would go away. This is attested to by the fact that the Prime Minister delayed release of the results of the first stage of the review until MPs had left for vacation in order to minimise their impact.[35] It is attested to once again by the temptation to 'spin' the results of the review, in a manner that distorts them whether intentionally or not. This is exemplified by ministerial blogs that focus predominantly on the fact that some balance of competence reviews were critical of specific EU regulatory initiatives, without making

34. S. Peers (*supra* n. 33); S. Peers, *Is it Possible to Reform the EU without Amending the Treaties?* 22 May 2015, http://eulawanalysis.blogspot.co.uk/2015/05/is-it-possible-to-reform-eu-without.html.
35. Stephens *supra* n. 23.

clear that this was in the context of a general conclusion that the balance of competence in the relevant area was nonetheless about right and beneficial to the UK.[36]

It might be contended by way of response that counter arguments can be made by those who favour the EU. This does not withstand examination. In empirical terms the government because of its very position has access to sources of publicity that others cannot match. In normative terms this argument denies the very nature of constitutional responsibility argued for here. It is predicated on the fact that it is constitutionally legitimate for a government to craft its renegotiation strategy and present it to the UK people without placing this in the context of the facts, which in this context assuredly includes the balance of competence review. If the government is minded to disagree with the conclusions that it has already signed off, it is then incumbent on it to present properly reasoned argument as to why this is so, and appeasement of Eurosceptic opinion, or attempts to head off the UKIP threat, do not come anywhere close to sufficing in this respect.

§5.04 CONSTITUTIONAL VOICE AND RESPONSIBILITY: THE CATCH 22 OF RENEGOTIATION

The discussion in the preceding section focused on the subject matter of renegotiation. There is, however, a further problem lurking in the wings. The difficulty resides in the dichotomy between negotiated agreement between the Member States at EU level and constitutional ratification of the terms thereof by the Member States. The nature of this conundrum can be simply explicated.[37]

Let us imagine that the UK, the other Member states and the EU institutions agree on the terms of a renegotiation package that entails some Treaty amendments. The compromise is praised in all quarters and the UK referendum is then conducted on the assumption that this package will take effect. The Prime Minister campaigns on the virtues of the deal that he has secured, and presents reasoned argument as to why it is in the UK interest to remain in the EU on these revised terms. The UK public agrees as reflected in an affirmative vote to remain in the EU; the Eurosceptics hope for more, but accept the outcome; and the UKIP threat is seen off. The Prime Minister basks in the glow of public esteem as a politician who stood up for UK interests and secured a deal that the others players were willing to accept. His strategy is viewed as the optimal blend of diplomacy and realpolitik, combined with the poker player's instinct as to when to bluff and when to fold. All is well in Westminster, Brussels and other centres of power.

36. *See*, e.g., David Lidington, http://blogs.fco.gov.uk/davidlidington/2014/04/04/boc-review-making-the-eu-work-for-you/.

37. I have serious doubts as to whether Treaty amendment can be avoided by recourse to agreements between heads of state of the kind discussed by Steve Peers *supra* n. 34 . It is doubtful whether the agreements in relation to Denmark and Ireland can be regarded as any kindof precedent in this respect, more especially since in this instance it would be used to achieve far-reaching change, while avoiding the normal safeguards built into the Lisbon Treaty when amendments are proposed., J-C. Piris, 'Brexit or Britin: is it really colder outside?', Fondation Robert Schuman, Policy Paper No. 369, 26 October 2015.

This beatific vision is however threatened by constitutional reality in terms of the Lisbon Treaty: insofar as the agreement secured between the UK and the other Member States requires Treaty amendment this can only take place when the revised Treaty has been ratified in accord with the constitutional requirements of each Member State.[38] The Lisbon Treaty does not specify a time-line by which this is to occur.[39] It is therefore perfectly possible for agreement to be secured on Treaty revision and for the UK referendum to have taken place before the outcome of the constitutional ratification process is known.

It might be argued that in these circumstances the requisite constitutional ratification would be forthcoming in the other Member States, and the respective national executives would ensure that this was so. This argument betrays a lack of understanding of EU history, which has been peppered with notable instances where a deal agreed by a national executive has foundered when it comes to national constitutional ratification, more especially where the constitution demands a referendum on approval, or where the deal must survive scrutiny by a constitutional court.[40] So, on this scenario the UK public would have voted on the basis of a deal that might not be delivered, and if it were not it would necessarily undermine a positive vote in the referendum.

It might be argued that there would be a collective imperative to ensure that national constitutional ratification in the other states preceded the UK referendum. Let us leave aside the very real difficulty of gaining agreement on this and making it a practical reality. There is a more compelling problem with this suggested scenario. Member States would on this hypothesis be asked to approve Treaty revision, which might also entail amendment to their national constitution, before the UK referendum had taken place. The obvious objection that would be voiced by other Member States is why they should bother to do this when it is unclear whether the UK public would vote to remain in the EU. The UK referendum might still result in a negative vote, in which case a proposed Treaty amendment designed to accommodate UK interests would in a literal sense be a waste of time, as would constitutional ratification thereof in twenty seven Member States.

§5.05 CONSTITUTIONAL CONSEQUENCES: FUTURE RELATIONS

If the referendum results in a no vote, this will signal the UK's exit from the EU, assuming that there is no post-referendum new deal offering something that might incline UK voters to change their mind. Some of what happens thereafter is predictable, some is not.

38. Article 48(4), Article 48(6) TEU.
39. Article 48(5) TEU only stipulates that if two years after agreement on Treaty amendment the revised Treaty has been ratified by four-fifths of the Member States, with difficulties encountered in one or more states, the matter shall be referred to the European Council.
40. *See*, e.g., the rejection of the Constitutional Treaty in the referenda in France and the Netherlands, and the rejection of the Reform Treaty in the referendum in Ireland.

[A] The 'Relatively' Predictable

The immediate aftermath is predictable insofar as the Lisbon Treaty contains provisions on exit that had not existed hitherto. Article 50 TEU provides that any Member State may decide to withdraw from the EU in accordance with its own constitutional requirements. It must inform the European Council of its intention to do so. The EU then negotiates and concludes an agreement with the state, in the light of guidelines provided by the European Council, which sets out the arrangements for its withdrawal, taking account of the framework for its future relationship with the Union.

The agreement is made in accordance with Article 218(3) TFEU, with the consequence that it is concluded on behalf of the EU by the Council, acting by a qualified majority, after obtaining the consent of the European Parliament. The Treaties cease to apply to the withdrawing state from the date of entry into force of the withdrawal agreement or, failing that, two years after the notification by the state of its intent to withdraw, unless the European Council, in agreement with the Member State concerned, unanimously decides to extend this period. The state seeking to withdraw does not participate in the discussions or decisions in the European Council or Council concerning it, and its vote is therefore not taken into account when calculating a qualified majority. If a State that has withdrawn from the EU seeks to rejoin, it must go through the procedure in Article 49 TEU concerning entry of new states.

All of the above will therefore take time. Those that imagined that exit will lead to a speedy repatriation of all competences to the UK should therefore adjust their time horizons. It is not going to happen fast. This is quite apart from the fact that many areas of UK law are wholly enmeshed with EU law. The unravelling exercise will take many years to complete. It will be for the UK government to decide whether it wishes to alter the relevant laws on a particular topic, given that it is no longer bound to their particular content by reason of EU membership. Put crudely the answer may be yes in some instances, no in others, or what is more likely in many instances is that there will be a via media whereby some of the content is retained because it is accepted, and some is altered. These choices will, moreover, often be markedly constrained by external forces in the manner set out below.

[B] The 'Relatively' Unpredictable

What is less readily predictable is the legal nature of relations between the UK and the EU thereafter. The principal options are joining the European Economic Area, as in the case of Norway; negotiating a series of free trade agreements, as in the case of Switzerland; or negotiating a new customs union relationship with the EU, as in the case of Turkey. The Prime Minister in his Bloomberg speech rejected all three options.[41] So too did the framers of the Fresh Start Manifesto, who concluded that such arrangements whereby the UK would be bound by trading rules in relation to which they had no input would be a 'disastrous position for the UK in terms of services

41. Bloomberg Speech *supra* n. 21.

trade'.[42] The Prime Minister reiterated his opposition to such options in his Chatham House speech, when he set out the terms of the UK renegotiation package.[43]

There are good reasons for rejecting these options, but it does rather beg the question as to the nature of the future relationship between the EU and the UK. The negative reaction to the principal options is not matched by indication of a positive alternative.[44] The implicit thinking seems to be either that some ad hoc deal will be put together between the EU and the UK, or that the UK will simply operate as a country outside the EU, trading with it in the same manner as most other countries in the world. The terms of any ad hoc deal between the UK and the EU cannot be predicted in advance, save for the fact that the other Member States will not come close to signing up to a deal whereby the UK secures the economic benefits of the single market without subscribing to the social obligations incumbent on other EU Member States.

This leaves the alternative option, viz the UK simply subsists as a country outside the EU, trading with it in the same manner as many other countries. This is certainly an option, but the assumption that we will thereby be free from EU rules relating to trade or indeed some other matters is a serious non-sequitur. The UK will continue to be bound by some of these provisions, either because the EU demands, for example, certain safety standards for all goods sold in the EU, or because the EU regulatory provisions have themselves been incorporated into global regulatory standards that thereby bind the UK wherever it trades. The UKIP vision of a UK freed from the EU, whereby all powers revert to the autonomous control of the nation state, is just that, a vision that bears scant relation to reality.

§5.06 CONCLUSION

The referendum will be highly significant for the future of the UK, irrespective of whether one supports the EU or not. The 'politics' preceding the referendum change almost daily, and that is so both internally within the Conservative party, and as between the UK government, other Member States and the EU institutions.This chapter has sought to canvass some of the principal issues surrounding the holding of such a referendum and to place those issues within a broader constitutional perspective. There are numerous dimensions to the debate about the EU, the terms that we should seek to renegotiate and the way in such any such referendum should be conducted. It has been argued that an important dimension that has been neglected hitherto concerns national constitutional responsibility, which has important implications for the way in which we think of the EU at present, and for the terms on which the renegotiation is conducted. It also has resonance for possible exit, in the sense that the government assuredly has a responsibility to explain to its citizens that many of the EU regulatory provisions will continue to apply to the UK irrespective of whether we are members thereof or not.

42. Fresh Start Manifesto *supra* n. 26, 6.
43. https://www.gov.uk/government/speeches/prime-ministers-speech-on-europe.
44. See Piris (*supra* n. 41) for discussion.

PART II Managing Alone?

CHAPTER 6

Which Options Would Be Available for the United Kingdom in the Case of a Withdrawal from the EU?

Jean-Claude Piris

§6.01 INTRODUCTION

The possibility that the United Kingdom (UK) might withdraw from the European Union (EU), after more than forty years of membership, looks unreal to many people,[1] but it has become less unrealistic.[2]

This is the case since the British Prime Minister, David Cameron, announced the holding of a referendum on the UK's membership of the EU before the end of 2017, should his political party remain in power after the May 2015 parliamentary elections. As the elections gave the Conservative Party a majority in the House of Commons, Mr Cameron confirmed that such a referendum will be organised. It seems that the referendum could take place earlier than planned, possibly before the summer of 2016. At the date of writing, the Government's bill is ready and the question proposed to the Parliament is: '*Should the United Kingdom remain a member of the European Union?*'. Therefore, the risk of a 'BREXIT' is not to be excluded. The Prime Minister has, in a letter addressed to Donald Tusk, President of the European Council, on 10 November 2015,[3] presented his suggestions of reforms of the EU in order to be able to have the best chances of success in the future referendum.

1. *See* the so-called Brexit Barometer launched at the beginning of 2015 by the think-tank 'Open Europe' (London), which has the ambition to assess the probability of Britain leaving the EU within the next British Parliament. On 27 Feb. 2015, their guess was: '*as things stand, we assess the prospects of Brexit at 17%, but we will be making regular adjustments*' (Open Europe website).
2. *See* Denis Macshane book: *Brexit, How Britain will Leave Europe*, (I.B. Tauris ed., 2015).
3. '*A new Settlement for the United Kingdom in a Reformed European Union*', published in the website GOV.UK, 10 Nov. 2015.

Paradoxically, the risk of a withdrawal is appearing at a time when the EU has been pushed by its Member States to evolve in directions which correspond to many, if not most, of the European policy objectives of the UK: the EU has been enlarged to many new Member States,[4] without much strengthening of its institutions; there is more flexibility for Member States to participate or not in some policies; in particular, the UK managed to keep access to the internal market, despite getting several permanent opt-outs on other major policies (the euro, Schengen, criminal justice and police cooperation); national control of the Member States on foreign and defence policies has been carefully preserved; the UK has been able to keep (with others) its budget rebate; the EU is liberalising external trade; the Commission and the Council control the respect of the principle of subsidiarity[5] better than they did in the past. Finally, the Lisbon Treaty, which does not contain any federalist symbol,[6] '*even marks a halt to the hopes of the "federalists"*',[7] and gave some powers to national Parliaments.[8]

These results have not been reached only because of the UK, but the UK has certainly been, in particular because of the high quality of the British diplomats and senior civil servants, a very influential Member State when it comes to shaping the EU as it is today.

In any case, most, if not all, other Member States of the EU would like the UK to remain an EU member. They will probably be ready, if needed, to help to try and find some ways and means to facilitate this. However, some of them will not do that at any price, as they have already made widely known.

§6.02 THE LEGAL FRAMEWORK

To begin with, if the UK decided to withdraw from the EU, on which legal basis and according to what legal procedure could this happen? The text of Article 50, a provision which was introduced in the Treaty on EU (TEU) by the Lisbon Treaty,[9] provides this legal basis and this procedure. It reads as follows:

> 1. *Any Member State may decide to withdraw from the Union in accordance with its own constitutional requirements.*
> 2. *A Member State which decides to withdraw shall notify the European Council of its intention. In the light of the guidelines provided by the European Council, the*

4. Nine Member States in 1973, after the accession of Denmark, the Republic of Ireland and the United Kingdom, and twenty-eight since the accession of Croatia in 2013.
5. According to which decisions must be taken as closely as possible to the citizen (*see* Article 1, second sub-paragraph, and Article 5(3) of the Treaty on European Union (TEU) as well as Protocol n°2 ''*On the Application of the Principles of Subsidiarity and Proportionality*'.
6. Contrary to the failed '*Treaty establishing a Constitution for Europe*': *see* Jean-Claude Piris, *The Constitution for Europe: A Legal Analysis* (Cambridge U. Press 2006).
7. *See* Jean-Claude Piris: *The Lisbon Treaty: A Legal and Political Analysis* 339 (Cambridge U. Press 2010).
8. *See* Article 12 TEU, Protocol n°1 '*On The Role of National Parliaments in the European Union*' and Protocol n°2 '*On The Application of the Principles of Subsidiarity and Proportionality*', especially Articles 6 and 7.
9. The Lisbon Treaty entered into force on 1 Dec. 2009.

Union shall negotiate and conclude an agreement with that State, setting out the arrangements for its withdrawal, taking account of the framework for its future relationship with the Union. That agreement shall be negotiated in accordance with Article 218(3) of the Treaty on the Functioning of the European Union. It shall be concluded on behalf of the Union by the Council, acting by a qualified majority, after obtaining the consent of the European Parliament.

3. *The Treaties shall cease to apply to the State in question from the date of entry into force of the withdrawal agreement or, failing that, two years after the notification referred to in paragraph 2, unless the European Council, in agreement with the Member State concerned, unanimously decides to extend this period.*
4. *For the purposes of paragraphs 2 and 3, the member of the European Council or of the Council representing the withdrawing Member State shall not participate in the discussions of the European Council or Council or in decisions concerning it.*
   A qualified majority shall be defined in accordance with Article 238(3)(b) of the Treaty on the Functioning of the European Union.
5. *If a State which has withdrawn from the Union asks to rejoin, its request shall be subject to the procedure referred to in Article 49.*

From paragraph 1 of that Article, it is clear that, in EU law, the decision of withdrawal is of a unilateral character. It belongs exclusively to the Member State concerned, without any need to be approved by the other Member States. It would not even need to be explained or justified. It must be taken by the Member State in question '*in accordance with its own constitutional requirements*'. The completion of this requirement can only be verified by the competent authorities of that State. This would probably be done before the notification of that State's intention to the European Council.[10]

The second paragraph of Article 50 provides for a procedure which allows the negotiation of a withdrawal treaty (WT) between the withdrawing State and the rest of the EU. If such a negotiation between the UK and the EU was successful, the date of the UK's withdrawal from the EU would then be the date of entry into force of the WT that they would have agreed on together. Otherwise, if such a WT was not concluded, the withdrawal would automatically happen two years after the notification of the UK's decision to the European Council.

Concluding a WT would be highly opportune, in order to settle, in particular, the new trade relationship the EU and the UK would have to establish among themselves. Ideally for the British economy (about half of the British trade is made with the rest of the EU), such an agreement should give the UK as much access as possible to the EU's internal market (actually, the EEA's market[11]).

10. A unilateral right for a Member State to withdraw from the EU, without any condition, results clearly from the will of the authors of the Treaty of Lisbon. This will is confirmed by the discussions in the European Convention on the corresponding article of the Constitution for Europe (draft Constitution, Volume I, CONV 724/03, Annex 2, p. 134). Article 50 is silent about the possibility or the interdiction for a Member State, after having notified a decision to withdraw, to change its mind and to cancel its notification within the two-year period referred to in that Article.
11. The European Economic Area (EEA) was established by several Agreements signed in 1992. It comprises now the twenty-eight EU Member States and three of the four Member States of the

In any case, at least some minimal transitional measures would be very opportune,[12] not to say necessary. This is because the economies of the UK and of the rest of the EU, after more than forty years of membership, have become closely intertwined and interdependent (share of trade in goods and services, share of investment, mobility of people, either studying, working or retired). As EU citizens, about two million British people live, study, work or are retired, in other EU countries, while about two million other EU citizens live in the UK. Many industries and enterprises are established both in the UK and on the continent. The exchanges of goods and services are intensive.

During the necessary period for negotiating, signing and ratifying a WT between the UK and the EU, the UK would remain a Member State of the EU and continue to participate in its activities under the same conditions as before. Its nationals would continue to exercise their full rights in all EU institutions. The only legal exception provided for in Article 50(4) is that the UK's representative in the European Council (the Prime Minister) and in the Council (Ministers) as well as in their preparatory bodies (Ambassador in the *COREPER*,[13] diplomats and civil servants in other bodies) would not be allowed to participate on the EU side in the negotiation of the future WT. In practice, however, it is highly probable, for political and psychological reasons, that the actual capacity of the UK to exercise an influence on the functioning of the EU and on decisions taken by the institutions would be seriously affected, including on matters unconnected with its withdrawal.

Contrary to a treaty of accession of a new Member State in the EU (which has to be based on Article 49 TEU), as well as to a treaty revising the EU Treaties (which has to be based on Article 48 TEU), neither a common accord in the Council, nor a ratification by the other Member States, are required by Article 50 TEU to conclude a WT. This is despite the fact that a WT would necessarily 'be accompanied by' some changes to the EU Treaties, *inter alia* to Article 52 TEU which is listing the names of the Member States. On top of the WT, a revision treaty would thus have to be adopted in parallel, on the basis of Article 48 TEU,[14] because Article 50 does not provide that the WT could contain amendments to the EU Treaties. Contrary to the revision treaty, the WT would not be primary law and, thus, would be subject to the jurisdiction of the EU Court of justice.

Given the complexity of the matter, it is highly probable that the delay of two years foreseen in Article 50 would not be sufficient. In that case, paragraph 3 of Article

---

European Free Trade Association (EFTA), i.e., Iceland, Liechtenstein and Norway. The EEA allows these three EEA EFTA States to largely participate to the EU's internal market. Switzerland, which is an EFTA Member, is not a member of the EEA. It has chosen, instead, to negotiate a number of bilateral specific agreements with the EU.

12. For an example, *see* the Research Paper 13/42 of the House of Commons Library, a document of 106 pages published in July 2013: '*It would not be possible to withdraw from, say, the Common Agriculture Policy overnight without causing enormous disruption for farmers*' (at page 11).
13. COREPER is the French acronym for 'Comité des Représentants Permanents des Etats Membres' (Committee of the Permanent Representatives of the Member States).
14. That 'revision treaty' should be ratified by all remaining Member States of the EU, in accordance with their respective constitutional requirements.

50 allows for that period to be extended.[15] A longer period might also be needed for the UK to prepare the national legislation which would be necessary to substitute EU acts.

Some parts of the WT could, if it was considered appropriate by both parties, be applied provisionally at the date of its signature,[16] while waiting for its conclusion by both Parties.

§6.03 AVOIDING BREXIT BY GETTING A SPECIAL EU MEMBER STATUS?

Before looking at what could happen in case of 'BREXIT', one should briefly examine another scenario, which was popular in some circles in London, until the 10 November letter of Mr Cameron. The idea was that the UK could legally remain a Member State of the EU, although it would obtain a special status. Such a special status could allow the UK to continue to participate both in the internal market and in the corresponding EU decision-making process, while obtaining the right not to participate in some, or in many, or even in any other EU policy. The current EU Treaties do not authorise such a possibility: they would therefore have to be modified. In accordance with Article 48 TEU, this would require a common agreement and a ratification of the modifications '*by all the Member States in accordance with their respective constitutional requirements*', which may require a referendum in some Member States, such as the Republic of Ireland.

The timing of the procedure to be followed would have been a serious difficulty: who should first ratify the amendments to the EU Treaties? The procedure would raise serious political difficulties, like any scenario requiring a modification of the EU Treaties.

In addition, that scenario would have raised serious questions of substance. Actually, the EU institutions and the other Member States would have imperative reasons for not accepting such a special status for the UK, because:

(i) this would affect the EU's decision-making autonomy on issues which are at the heart of its *raison d'être*, and thus might put into question its existence;
(ii) such a status would be extremely attractive for other States: it might open the door to similar requests from third countries, such as Switzerland, Norway, Iceland, Liechtenstein and the three 'States of a small dimension' (Andorra, Monaco and San Marino)[17] and probably also entail political difficulties in

15. According to Article 50(3) TEU, that decision would require the agreement of the UK as well as unanimity in the European Council (an abstention would not prevent unanimity: *see* Article 235(1) of the Treaty on the Functioning of the European Union (TFEU).
16. *See* Article 218 (5) TFEU.
17. The Council of the EU has decided, on 16 Dec. 2014, to authorise the Commission to open negotiations with Andorra, Monaco and San Marino on '*one or several Association Agreement(s)*' to provide for their increased participation in the EU's internal market and related horizontal and flanking policies. '*The Council will aim in these negotiations at the fullest possible implementation of the principles of the European single market, while taking into account the particular situation of these three countries in line with the Declaration on Article 8 TEU*'. The Declaration referred to was adopted by the Intergovernmental Conference which adopted

some EU Member States, such as Sweden, Denmark and others whose eurosceptic political parties could be tempted to play with this idea, risking thus to open another existential issue for the EU;

(iii) the hope that such a suggestion could be successful was partly based on an overly optimistic evaluation of the UK's actual leverage: while about 50% of its exports go to the rest of the EU, the rest of the EU sells only 10% of its exports to the UK.[18] Its power of negotiation would therefore not be as strong as some people think. Moreover, half of the EU's trade surplus with the UK is accounted for by just two Member States – Germany and the Netherlands – while a revision of the EU Treaties would require also the positive vote of the other twenty-five Member States, among them some which have a trade deficit with the UK.

Therefore, it is much more realistic to think that the EU would stick to its constant policy, if accepting to give access to the single market to the UK, in the hypothesis that it would no longer be an EU Member State. This constant policy requires that such an agreement must be accompanied by the obligation to follow the pertinent *acquis communautaire* and its dynamic evolution as decided by the EU, without the third State concerned having a right of decision on that evolution. It would be unreasonable to expect the EU to make an exception to these rules for the UK and to abandon the principle of autonomy of its decision-making. The principle according to which, in a single market, all economic operators must follow the same rules, that the interpretation of these rules must be the same for all, and that their implementation should be legally guaranteed, cannot have exceptions. By the way, this policy was always supported by the British authorities, both the Parliament and the Government, when applied to Norway, Switzerland, and others.

This also means that preserving the specific characteristics of EU/EEA law would be essential. One must recall that, as compared with classic international law, these specificities are primacy, direct effect, uniformity of interpretation, absence of reciprocity, control of implementation by an independent institution (the Commission) and adoption of sanctions (if needed) by an independent jurisdiction (the Court of Justice). These specificities make the internal market credible for the economic operators, whose trust is absolutely essential. This is why the preservation of the characteristics of the EU law would also be one of the key basic principles underlying the EU's negotiating position.

Thus, it is reasonable to expect that the conditions imposed by the EU will include the non-participation of British representatives in the legislative decision-making, both

---

the Treaty of Lisbon, and annexed to its Final Act. It reads as follows: '*The Union will take into account the particular situation of small-sized countries which maintain specific relations of proximity with it.*'

18. *See* the excellent Final Report of the Centre for European Reform (CER) on the UK and the EU's single market: '*The Economic Consequences of Leaving the EU*', published by the CER in London in June 2014 (92 pages).

in the European Parliament and in the Council. They might also include the acceptance of the role of the Commission and the Court of Justice, without a British national being a member of these institutions. They would certainly also include a financial contribution, inferior, but of a comparable magnitude to the current British contribution per head to the EU budget. These are the objectives aimed at by the EU in the 2014 negotiating mandate of a future institutional agreement with Switzerland. A different solution, in which a '*special status*' would '*exceptionally*' be conferred upon the UK, conceding advantages which have consistently been refused to Norway, Switzerland and others, would not be acceptable for the Member States and the institutions of the EU.

Thus, and even if this scenario left unaffected the Treaty's provisions on free movement of people,[19] its chances of success would have been very weak, not to say improbable. In any case, after the 10 November letter, it may be considered as dead and buried.

§6.04 THE SEVEN POSSIBLE OPTIONS AFTER 'BREXIT'

By contrast, the other scenario, in which the UK would choose to withdraw from the EU, would not depend on any decision taken by the EU's institutions or by its other Member States. It would be a unilateral decision which could be freely taken by the UK alone, without any possibility for others to oppose it, or even to delay it beyond the two year delay imposed by the EU Treaty. The challenge would be for the UK to build a new relationship with the rest of the EU. This seems unavoidable, as economy, geography and history are what they are. Moreover, the road to rejoin the EU, once having withdrawn, would not be easy and quick.[20]

Seven different options for a legal framework could be imagined to establish a new relationship between the UK and the EU after a BREXIT.

Unfortunately, none of these options would appear to be satisfactory for the UK.

19. As shown by the letter addressed by Prime Minister Cameron to the President of the European Council on 10 Nov. 2015, the British Government decided to choose this issue as one of its requests when negotiating, before the future referendum, with the EU. This political choice is linked with the progress in the polls of the United Kingdom Independence Party (UKIP), the British xenophobic and anti-EU political party. It is a risky choice, as it may, depending on the way it is formulated, lead the British Government to request a revision of the EU's Treaties. British requests on this issue would be extremely difficult to agree for some of the other twenty-seven Member States. It would raise psychological problems in all Member States having acceded the EU since 2004, which were supposed to be the best allies of the UK. It is however by no means certain that this position, which has been approved by a part of the Conservative Party, will be changed, despite the relative failure of the UKIP in the May 2015 elections.
20. According to Article 50(5) TEU, '*If a State which has withdrawn from the Union asks to rejoin, its request shall be subject to the procedure referred to in Article 49*'. This means that any 'ex Member-State' would have to follow the full procedure of accession, as a new applicant country, without any automatics or privileged right to 're-join'.

(1) According to a first option, the establishment of a new structured relationship between the EU and the UK would be provided for in a withdrawal treaty, adopted on the basis of Article 50 TEU, which could establish custom-made arrangements.

This is the treaty which is referred to in Article 50(2) TEU, which could be the legal support to establish in legal form some of the other options examined below on trade arrangements, but which could also contain provisional or permanent arrangements in all other policies and domains, aimed at making the UK's withdrawal less abrupt, by alleviating some of its most negative effects.

On the UK's side, the Government would obviously try to pick and choose among EU policies and, therefore, to follow a sectorial approach rather than a global one. In concrete terms, it would try to keep all benefits that EU policies bring to the UK. Thus, it would certainly try to keep the advantages given by the participation in the internal market. It would request to keep access to the internal market in all areas, or at least, on a case by case basis, in accordance with British economic interests in the different sectors, for example without agricultural and fisheries products.

At the same time, it would try to avoid, or, due to the impossibility to avoid them completely, rather to minimise, the budgetary, economic, legal and political costs of the withdrawal. Actually, the Government would have to try and show its population that the withdrawal, decided by the UK, would allow it to *'recover its full sovereignty'*. After all, this seems to be THE aim of a withdrawal! The Government would have to make this demonstration while avoiding losing too many benefits, and without endangering the country's economy, the way of life of its citizens and the role of the UK on the international scene.

As has already been mentioned, the UK's leverage in the negotiations to get as much access as possible to the EU's internal market would not be as strong as some people believe. On top of that, it should be stressed that the *'guidelines'*[21] of a possible agreement with the UK would require the *'consensus'*[22] of the European Council, i.e., of the Heads of State or Heads of Government of all the other twenty-seven EU Member States, some of which are running trade deficits with the UK.

On the EU's side, the institutions, and particularly the Commission, which would be the EU negotiator,[23] would demand to strictly preserve the decision-making autonomy of the EU. They will also demand to be given the legal capacity to control the respect by the UK of its future obligations. These two issues would be among the key basic principles on which the negotiating position of the EU would be based. Besides, the EU would resist a sectorial approach. On the contrary, the UK would strongly wish not to be bound by some EU policies anymore, such as perhaps the Common Agricultural Policy, the Common Fisheries Policy, the Economic, Social and Territorial Cohesion Policy, or the few EU texts which exist on Social Policy (as this policy remains largely decided at national level).

21. *See* Article 50(2) TEU.
22. *See* Article 15(4) TEU.
23. *See* Article 218(3) TFEU.

In the areas related to the EU's internal market which would be covered by the EU-UK agreement, the UK would be obliged by the EU, in order to preserve a single playing field for all economic operators in the internal market, to follow the pertinent EU legislation, without having a right to vote for their adoption and modifications. On top of that, the UK would also have to accept to pay a significant financial contribution, as shown by the examples of the current financial contributions of Norway and Switzerland.[24]

During the negotiation, each member of the EU Council would naturally act according to the interests of the State which he/she is representing, as well as to the interests of the EU. The decision to conclude a WT is to be taken by the EU Council by qualified majority voting, with the approval of the European Parliament,[25] which will have thus a right of veto. Except if the agreement extends to areas covered by Member States' powers, which should not normally be the case,[26] it would not need to be ratified by the EU Member States. However, an agreement would later have to be negotiated and signed with the EEA EFTA members (and ratified by the EU, by the UK, by the twenty-seven remaining EU Member States and by the three EEA EFTA States), in order to take into account the new relationship to be established between the EEA and the UK.

Finally, one may remember that, during or at the end of the negotiation, Article 218 (11) TFEU will allow '*a Member State, the European Parliament, the Council or the Commission (to) obtain the opinion of the Court of Justice as to whether an agreement envisaged is compatible with the Treaties*'. According to this provision, '*where the opinion of the Court is adverse, the agreement envisaged may not enter into force unless it is amended or the Treaties are revised*'. The use of that procedure would of course take time and be a cause of delay.

Thus, the negotiations of a withdrawal treaty would be extremely difficult.

(2) The second option would be for the UK to try and join Iceland, the Liechtenstein and Norway as a Member of the EEA.

The acceptance of the UK, which from the beginning looked very doubtful,[27] has now been clearly excluded by Mr David Cameron, in a speech given in Reykjavik (Iceland) on 28 October 2015. As shown below, the incentive for the EU to push the UK to join the EEA (which legally implies that the UK would also have had also to join the EFTA) would not have been obvious.

Such an option would have had the advantage of simplicity. The EEA Agreement allows the three EEA EFTA States (Iceland, Liechtenstein and Norway) to participate in a large part of the EU's internal market and to largely enjoy the four freedoms, without being committed to other EU policies, such as agriculture, fisheries, judicial affairs,

24. *See* below nn. 36 and 39.
25. *See* Article 50(2) TEU. The qualified majority in the Council would be calculated according to Article 238 (3, littera b) TFEU.
26. Unless it would demand UK's commitments on foreign policy or/and on defence policy or on other matters under the EU Member States' competences. In that case, the WT would be a '*mixed agreement*', which would have to be ratified not only by the EU and the UK, but also by each of the remaining twenty-seven other Member States.
27. *See* the Research Paper of the House of Commons 13/42, at p. 17.

foreign policy, etc. These countries have to follow the evolution of the EU legislation concerning the internal market as well as its evolution, without having the right to really influence its content much.

However, the EEA is currently not working in an optimal way. In a Commission Staff Working Document dated 7 December 2012,[28] the External European Action Service and the Commission complained about the increasing backlog of the three EEA EFTA States in putting into effect new EU legal acts. About 580 pertinent EU acts had not yet been integrated at the beginning of 2014,[29] some of them important, for example decisions of EU executive Agencies on financial services. In Conclusions adopted by the EU Council on 16 December 2014, the Council took a more conciliatory tone:

> *31. The Council expresses its satisfaction at the agreement between the EU and the EEA EFTA side, as noted by the EU and the EEA EFTA Ministers of Finance and Economy in their informal meeting of 14 October 2014, on the principles for the incorporation into the EEA Agreement of the EU Regulations establishing the European Supervisory Authorities in the area of financial services. The Council hopes that the technical work preparing the incorporation of these Regulations will be finalised as soon as possible.*

However, the Council added:

> *32. The Council nonetheless notes with concern the recurrent backlog and delays incurred during the entire process of incorporation of EU legislation into the EEA Agreement, as well as in the implementation and enforcement of relevant legislation in the EEA EFTA states. In this context, the Council strongly emphasizes the need for renewed efforts in order to ensure homogeneity and legal certainty in the European Economic Area.*

> *33. While welcoming efforts made by the EEA EFTA States over the last years to step up the pace of incorporation, the Council regrets that these efforts were still insufficient to effectively and comprehensively address the existing problems. It notes in particular that the questioning of the EEA relevance of EU legislation by the EEA EFTA states, the extensive use made of the possibility under the Agreement to request adaptations and exceptions, as well as delays in the clearance of constitutional requirements and in the implementation and enforcement of already adopted EEA legislation in the EEA EFTA states contribute to a fragmentation of the internal market and to asymmetric rights and obligations for economic operators. The Council encourages the EEA EFTA states to actively work towards a sustainable and streamlined incorporation and application of EEA relevant legislation as this is paramount to safeguard the overall competitiveness of the European Economic Area.*

---

28. Document SWD (2012) 425 Final '*A review of the functioning of the EEA*', available on the website of the European Parliament.
29. To be compared with 7000, which is the number of acts already integrated in EEA law since the entry into force of the EEA Agreement in 1994. It should be taken into account that this figure includes a number of texts which are less substantial than others, such as technical texts, modifications of previous ones, recommendations, etc.

It is true, nevertheless, that the advantages of avoiding an extremely complex negotiation would have been such that the EU might have envisaged that option.[30] However, looking at current discussions between the EU and Switzerland,[31] it is not impossible that, one day, the EU might request the EEA to negotiate a change of its institutional architecture, especially if the bad functioning noted by the EU Council would continue. And it is also a fact that the current EEA EFTA States themselves are complaining[32] that the EU does not take their interests and their constitutional problems sufficiently into account.

In any case, the main obstacle came, quite logically, from the UK itself. While the aim of its withdrawal from the EU would be to become ***less*** dependent on the EU power to legislate, it would have been politically difficult to accept:

(a) to integrate in the British legislation all new EU legal acts affecting the internal market[33], without having the right to substantially influence their content;
(b) the rule according to which the EEA EFTA States shall speak with one voice in the Joint Committee;[34]
(c) the powers conferred on the EFTA Surveillance Authority and on the EFTA Court;[35]
(d) and to pay to the EU a financial contribution of a comparable magnitude to as the contribution of a Member State[36] to the EU budget.

Finally, admitting a new State to the EEA would need an accession treaty to that organisation, which would have to be concluded, not only by the EU and the UK, as would be the case for a WT, but also by each of the thirty EEA Member States (twenty-seven from the EU and three from the EFTA).

It is therefore quite logical that Mr Cameron has decided that the loss of sovereignty which would accompany that option would not be acceptable for the UK.

---

30. Actually, the EEAS and the Commission suggested that option, initially and among others, to the European States of a small dimension with which they are now negotiating *'one or several association agreement(s)'* (Andorra, Monaco and San Marino), in application of the 16 Dec. 2014 Decision of the EU Council.
31. *See* the mandate of negotiation given to the European Commission by the Decision of the Council of the EU in its Decision taken on 6 May 2014 *'authorising the opening of negotiations between the European Union and the Swiss Confederation on an institutional framework governing bilateral relations'*, a new treaty which would impose on this country obligations of a comparable nature to, albeit going much further than, those accepted by the three EEA EFTA countries.
32. *See* the website of the Centre for European Policy Studies (CEPS, Brussels).
33. *See* Article 102 EEA Agreement.
34. *See* Article 93 EEA Agreement. This means that one of the EEA EFTA States might block the transposition into EEA law of a new EU law or of a modification of an existing one, even if the other EEA EFTA States would urgently need that transposition for economic reasons.
35. *See* Article 108 EEA Agreement.
36. According to the already quoted Final Report of the CER *The economic consequences of leaving the EU*, the financial contribution of the three EEA EFTA States to the EU was EUR 1.79 billion for the period 2009–2014. The Norwegian contribution per head to the EU during that period was, therefore, comparable to the British net contribution per head to the EU budget during the same period (9% less). Figures given in the Research Paper 13/42 of the House of Commons' Library are comparable: for the year 2011, 17% less per head for Norway as compared with the UK.

(3) The third option would be for the UK to rejoin the European Free Trade Agreement (EFTA), which it left in 1973.

This option would not be an adequate answer to the UK's needs: the UK would, like Switzerland, become a member of the EFTA, without becoming a member of the EEA. Given the development both of the EEA and of the bilateral relations of Switzerland with the EU, the Free Trade Agreement (FTA) between the EU and the EFTA States[37] has nearly become an empty shell: it now contains very little. Only trade for fish and some agricultural products are covered (no other goods, no services). This agreement has neither links with the EEA, nor with the 1972 Trade Agreement (modified several times) between Switzerland and the EU. Moreover, becoming a member of the EFTA would not give to the UK an automatic right to become a party to the FTAs concluded between the EFTA States (*and not by the EFTA itself*) and a number of third countries.[38]

(4) The fourth option for the UK would be to try and follow the current 'Switzerland model' of concluding sectorial treaties with the EU

Such an option would be unacceptable for the EU, given the fact that it is now insisting, in ongoing negotiations with Switzerland, that their current arrangements are not anymore acceptable.

This option would mean that the EU and the UK would aim at concluding as many sectorial bilateral agreements as needed: more than 120 agreements are currently in force between Switzerland and the EU, among them a few are very substantial.

Some in the UK think that such an option might be acceptable, despite the fact that Switzerland has no agreement with the EU on services, and in particular on financial services, while two-fifth of British trade is in services. However, such a shortcoming, if applied in the case of the UK, would definitely be serious.

The same observers stress that the framework of the arrangements between Switzerland and the EU has the big advantage to be based on classic international law. Switzerland is not bound by the judgments of a Court like the EU Court of Justice for the EU Member States, or the EFTA Court for the EEA EFTA countries. However, this does not fully reflect the reality: actually, in order to be able to export to the EU, Switzerland often finds itself in the same de facto situation as the EEA EFTA States, which means that it has to follow EU Regulations and Directives (including their interpretation by the EU Court of Justice) without participating in their making.[39]

More decisively, the relationship of Switzerland with the EU is most probably going to change. This is because the EU is unhappy with the present state of its relations with Switzerland. In its Conclusions adopted on 14 December 2010, the EU Council already described these relations as '*highly complex*', '*not ensuring the necessary*

37. There is no free trade agreement between the EU and *the EFTA as such*.
38. Contrary to what seems to be implied on page 17 of the Research Paper 13/42 of the House of Commons Library.
39. Switzerland also has to contribute financially to the EU. Its contribution per head is currently about 55% of the current net UK's contribution per head to the EU budget, taking into account that its access to the EU internal market is much narrower than that of the EEA EFTA States.

homogeneity', causing '*legal uncertainty*'. It added that this system '*has become complex and unwieldy to manage and has clearly reached its limits*'. In further Conclusions adopted two years later, on 20 December 2012, the EU Council reaffirmed:

> *that the approach taken by Switzerland to participate in EU policies and programmes through sectorial agreements in more and more areas in the absence of any horizontal institutional framework has reached its limits and needs to be consolidated. (...) further steps are necessary in order to ensure the homogeneous interpretation and application of the Internal Market rules. In particular, the Council deems it necessary to establish a suitable framework applicable to all existing and future agreements. This framework should, inter alia, provide for a legally binding mechanism as regards the adaptation of the agreements to the evolving EU acquis. Furthermore, it should include international mechanisms for surveillance and judicial control.*

Then, in February 2014, the Swiss people decided in a referendum to oppose unlimited immigration from the EU. The government decided that, consequently, it would have to impose restrictions on that immigration– although any restrictions would breach the treaties concluded with the EU. Thus, the Swiss government announced that it would not allow free movement of persons coming from Croatia, which accessed the EU in 2013. The EU rejected that move. It also rejected a subsequent proposal that Switzerland should be allowed to impose quantitative limits on a surge of immigrants from EU countries. The EU has already 'punished' Switzerland by excluding its people and universities from the Erasmus educational exchanges and from some of its research programmes. It is unclear how this stand-off will be resolved and when, but the EU said that, unless Switzerland rethinks the migration issue, it will start to lose access to the single market.

The dispute over free movement of persons confirmed the EU feeling that the current legal framework was failing. With the political wish to try and solve all problems in a single comprehensive 'package-deal', the EU Council decided, on 6 May 2014, to give the Commission a mandate to launch negotiations with Switzerland on '*an international agreement on an institutional framework governing bilateral relations with the Swiss confederation*'.[40]

This mandate is quite ambitious. If concluded, the new agreement would impose on Switzerland much stricter legal obligations than those of the EEA EFTA members:

(i) Crucially, this new agreement would not only apply to the future agreements to be concluded between the EU and Switzerland, but also to all important existing agreements concluded up to now between the EU and Switzerland[41], including all agreements '*related to the internal market*'.

(ii) The Council mandate aims at conferring on the European Commission the role to '*supervise the application of the agreements by Switzerland*'. '*The*

40. The text of the mandate has been leaked to the press.
41. Agreements on: free trade, free movement of persons, air transport, carriage of goods and passengers by rail and road, trade in agricultural products, mutual recognition in relation to conformity assessment, certain aspects of government procurement, simplification of inspections and formalities in respect of the carriage of goods and on customs security measures, cooperation in the field of statistics.

Commission should also be granted specific powers if required depending on each sector, such as investigatory and decision-making powers. These powers should reflect those already vested on the Commission in the field of the internal market' (for the EU Member States).

(iii) *'In relation with judicial control, each party should have the possibility to seize the Court of Justice, without the other party's prior consent, in case of dispute on the correct application of an agreement.'*. The *'decisions of the Court'* should be *'legally binding on both parties'*. *'The agreement should provide for the procedure to be followed if Switzerland departed from these decisions, leading, if no solution is found, to the termination of the agreement or the agreements concerned.'*

(iv) The mandate aims also at imposing on Switzerland *'a maximum time-limit for the implementation into the Swiss legal order'* of changes decided by the EU to the EU laws ('dynamic adaptation to the evolving acquis') within the scope of the agreements.

(v) The mandate makes moreover clear that *'negotiations on agreements giving Switzerland access to further sectors of the internal market should not be concluded before the conclusion of the agreement on an institutional framework'*.

In other words, the EU wants the Swiss-EU relationship to become much stricter than the EEA-EU model, even using directly the institutions of the EU itself. However, the negotiations are not finished. It is by no means a given fact that Switzerland, which might need to organise a referendum for the ratification of the 'horizontal agreement', will accept all requests of the European Union.

Nevertheless, and in any case, the current Swiss model is broken and will never be accepted again by the EU. On the other hand, it would be doubtful that the sovereignty-conscious UK would wish to follow any revamped version that the EU will negotiate with Switzerland.[42]

(5) The fifth option would be for the UK to negotiate a free trade agreement or an association agreement with the EU, like the EU has concluded with many countries.

That option is not likely to satisfy either British needs, or EU requirements.

On the one hand, there is no existing EU free trade or association agreement which has a scope as large in substance as would be desired and needed by the UK. On the other hand, no existing agreement of this kind provides for the surveillance and judicial instruments that the EU would insist on. Actually, there are no agreement (others than the EEA and the 'Swiss model') in which the EU conceded a substantive access to its internal market. In case it would concede such access to the UK, the EU would also in any case request that a part of the *acquis* would have to be adopted by the UK: labour market rules, health and safety, competition policy, product standards,

42. David Buchan, 'Outsiders on the inside: Swiss and Norwegian lessons for the UK', CER policy brief, September 2012.

consumer protection, technical specifications, etc. Without such conditions, the necessary acceptance by the EU Council would not appear to be possible.

Moreover, with such a scenario, the UK would also have to negotiate trade agreements with non-EU countries or organisations,[43] as it would not retain the rights and obligations provided for in the agreements concluded by the EU with third countries. However, it would be difficult for the UK to negotiate with third countries FTAs which would be as beneficial for its economy as the existing FTAs concluded by the EU. The UK would obviously have much less bargaining power than the EU, as it accounts for around respectively 2.47% and 6.64% of global exports of goods and services in the world in 2013 (these figures include the British imports from and exports to the other twenty-seven EU Member States), as compared to around respectively 16.44% and 24.75% for the EU[44] (these figures do not take into account the EU intra-trade between its twenty-eight Member States).

(6) The sixth option would be for the UK to negotiate a customs union with the EU, along the lines of the existing Association Agreement between Turkey and the EU.

This does not seem to be a good solution either, as it would not suit British needs.

The relations between Turkey and the EU provide the model of an Association Agreement comprising a customs union. If the UK accepted such an arrangement with the EU, it would not be free to adopt its own customs tariffs, because it would have to follow the decisions made by the EU. Besides, this option would not give access to the EU's internal market and would not cover services.

Moreover, as stressed in the CER Report[45] previously quoted:

> *Turkey must follow the EU's preferential agreements with non European countries. The UK would have no input into EU trade policy, but would have to comply with it. Not only would British-based manufacturers have to comply with EU products standards, but the UK would have to abide by large sections of the EU's acquis communautaire. Failure to do so could lead to the suspension of market access or the imposition of anti-dumping duties.(...) It is hard to see how this would be the best relationship for the UK upon quitting the EU.*

43. The EU has concluded many FTAs with third States or organisations, covering 35% of the world trade.
44. According to the WTO statistics available on its website at the time of writing, the figures for the share of the world trade during the year 2013 were the following (figures for the UK include the British exports to the other Members States of the EU, while figures for the EU include the UK's external trade outside the EU):

   - exports of goods: the UK exports 2 % of the world exports, the EU 15 %;
   - imports of goods: 3.5 % and 16.2 % respectively for the UK and for the EU;
   - exports of services: 6.4 % and 24.8 % respectively;
   - imports of services: 4.2 % and 20.1 % respectively.

45. London, July 2014.

(7) Finally, the seventh option would be that, in case no agreement were to be found on any of the six options above, the UK would become a third State vis-à-vis the EU, as the United States, China or other countries.

In such a case, what would happen in practice? BREXIT would have its full effects.

This deserves a more thorough analysis than the preceding options.

[A] BREXIT Would Negatively Affect British External Trade

If, after its withdrawal, the UK does not conclude any trade agreement with the EU, and simply relies on WTO rules to manage its trading relationship with the EU, it would have to build from scratch trading links both with the EU and with the rest of the world.

[1] Regarding British External Trade with the EU

The EU and its Member States would become third countries vis-à-vis the UK, and vice-versa. However, one should also take into account that, in order to be able to continue to be exported to the EU, some British products and services would still have to comply with EU standards. Thus, the UK would have to adopt a significant number of national laws and regulations in order for these goods and services to be in conformity with EU law, and in order to fill the legal void left by the inapplicability of the EU Regulations. The UK would have to re-establish customs controls at borders with EU. This would even include 'establishing' a border with the Republic of Ireland, unless the EU and the UK managed to conclude a special agreement on that issue before the date of the UK's withdrawal. The WTO rules would give the UK no more access to EU's market than what is currently enjoyed by countries that lack FTAs with the EU, such as Russia and China. The UK's goods and products would thus face the EU common external tariffs. In some highly price competitive markets, these tariffs would damage the UK's exporters. The EU's tariff on car engines, for example, is 10%. British firms shipping car engines to plants in the EU might reduce production in the UK and expand it in the EU.

[2] Regarding British External Trade with the Rest of the World

EU trade agreements, not only on goods and products, but also on air transport, financial services, etc. concluded both by the EU alone or with its Member States (mixed agreements) would no longer be legally binding for the relations between the UK and the third States having concluded them. A major problem, which would also exist with the other options, is that, being outside the EU, the UK would no longer be party to the FTAs negotiated by the EU with about sixty non-EU countries or organisations (together, these FTAs cover about 35% of world trade). The benefits from these FTAs would disappear on Day One of the withdrawal. The UK would need to negotiate new agreements with all these countries. However, the British government would face logistical problems to do that: it has not had any trade negotiators since 1973, having handed over trade deals to the EU, given the EU's exclusive competence in the area of common commercial policy.

Besides, and this is of more concern, it would be difficult for the UK to negotiate FTAs with third countries that would be as beneficial for its economy as the existing EU ones:

- First, the UK would have less bargaining power than the EU. The strongest powers get the best deals. Thus, in the China-Switzerland FTA, concluded in 2013, Switzerland has given China more access to its markets than vice versa. The EU is the biggest exporter and importer in the world, both for goods and for services, and thus gets better deals (see statistics above).
- Second, the British hand in negotiating FTAs would be weak, because it already has a relatively open economy. Therefore, in a negotiation with, say, China, China has less to gain from the removal of the UK's already-low trade barriers than has the UK from China's high ones.

The UK, as a member of that organisation, would benefit from the WTO rules on access to markets (most favoured nation clause), but they would give modest results. Since its creation in 1995, WTO has not concluded a significant multilateral trade agreement on lowering tariffs. It has done very little to liberalise either non-tariff barriers to trade in manufacturing, or the exchange of services – which is a big part of the UK's exports.

Thus, during a few years to say the least, British external trade would be negatively affected by a Brexit. A long period of uncertainty would be weighing on the British economy, until bilateral trade agreements between the UK and all its main partners, including of course the EU, come into force.

[B] BREXIT Would Have Also Negative Effects for the UK in Other Areas than External Trade

[1] First, on the UK's Legislation and Regulation

In the absence of the conclusion of any EU agreement with the UK, starting from the date of the entry into force of its withdrawal, the UK would be liberated from its legal obligation to implement EU law. This would concern EU regulations, directives, decisions, international treaties and other EU norms governing the internal market and the four freedoms. It would also concern existing EU law on all other EU policies. By the same token, the remaining twenty-seven Member States would no longer be bound to respect EU law in their dealings with the UK.

This would entail a lot of legislative activities in the UK. In order to plug the legal gaps which would open up when EU law ceased to apply, the British authorities would have to adopt new national laws. It would be urgent to do so, for example, on competition policy, the protection of consumers and of the environment, agriculture and fisheries, and so on. EU regulations are binding and directly applicable in the Member States, so when the UK left the EU they would normally no longer be in force on the date of withdrawal. The British Parliament would have to move swiftly to pass new laws in their place. EU directives, in contrast, set out the result to be achieved, but leave it to the Member States to adopt their own legislation. The UK would have to review national legislation that it had passed in order to implement EU directives and choose whether it wanted to abrogate, retain or modify them.

[2] Second, on Individuals

Brexit would affect the life of the about two million Britons living in other EU countries. It would not be possible for them to retain the advantages of the citizenship of the EU. The Treaty provides that one must hold the nationality of a Member State in order to be a citizen of the Union (Article 20(1) TFEU). There is nothing in the EU treaties or in the case-law of the Court of Justice which could be used to try to establish a theory of acquired rights of the citizens of a State that has left the EU. Thus, in the absence of any agreement between the UK and the EU, it would not be legally possible to build a theory according to which any '*acquired right*' would remain valid for dozens of millions of individuals (what about their children and their grandchildren?), who, despite having lost their EU citizenship, would nevertheless keep its advantages for ever.[46] This would also lead to absurd consequences.[47]

Thus, only EU laws granting nationals of any third country some rights would benefit UK citizens, for example, directives on family reunification, on long term residents, or on students.

Therefore, after a Brexit, public authorities, companies and individuals, from both the UK and the other EU Member States, would no longer benefit from the same rights. Companies and people from EU Member States that were established or permanent residents in the UK would no longer benefit from the protection of single market law. They would be in a new legal situation. Persons who had a right to permanent residence in other EU countries could probably keep it, as this right is derived from the European Convention on Human Rights. People would continue exercising their rights, based on their particular contracts and in conformity with local law. Those who did not have a right to permanent residence could be forced to leave.

The UK would therefore need to try and conclude urgently an agreement with the EU, in order to protect British citizens living in the EU. Any agreement would be based on classic international law and on reciprocity. The UK would not be able to negotiate separate deals with each of the twenty-seven – in a bid, for example, to exclude Central

46. *A contrario, see* Jochen Herbst, *Observations on the Right to Withdrawal from the EU: Who are the 'Masters of the Treaties?'* 6 German L. J. 1755 (2001). The reasoning of the author is (wrongly according to me) based on a single sentence in the judgment of the ECCJ Case C-26/62, the famous Van Gend and Loos judgment, which was not at all (obviously in a 1963 judgment!) concerning this question, but stating that Community law was a new legal order of international law which concerned not only the States but also their nationals, and that this law was becoming part of their '*legal heritage*' (I would add '*as long as they remain EU citizens, ie nationals of a Member State of the EU'!*).
47. As this would include the right of movement from and to all EU Member States as well as the right to vote and to be a candidate in the European Parliament (*see* Article 20 TFEU).

and Eastern Europeans. It would have to negotiate with the EU as a whole, which would not allow some of its Member States' citizens to be given a privileged treatment by the UK. All rights obtained in favour of British citizens residing in the twenty-seven Member States would have to be granted to their nationals residing in the UK.

Given that, post-Brexit, the probable British government's wish to impose restrictions on the right of EU citizens from some Central and Eastern EU Member States to come, live and work in the UK, Britons wanting to work, study or join their families on the continent would face equivalent difficulties in all the Member States of the EU. In the absence of an appropriate agreement, the ability of some Britons to remain on the continent could thus become difficult, especially if they were unemployed.

§6.05 WHAT WOULD BE THE BEST WAY TO AVOID BREXIT?

In order to avoid serious problems and uncertainties, a withdrawal of the UK from the EU should be accompanied by the establishment of a new comprehensive and structured relationship with the EU, through the conclusion of an international bilateral agreement.

The absence of such an agreement would have negative effects, especially for the UK's economy,[48] but also, even if to a lesser degree, for the rest of the EU. On top of that, a UK withdrawal would be politically catastrophic for the image of the EU, both in Europe and outside. Therefore, everyone has a strong interest in finding a solution which would allow the UK to remain a Member State of the EU. With smart diplomatic moves, reaching this objective is not excluded. This should include the adoption of some of the suggestions made in the 10 November 2015 letter of Mr Cameron. Actually, a number of European leaders probably consider that most of these suggestions could be answered positively, albeit not always in the legal shape desired by the British prime Minister.

Some options cannot be envisaged, at least for the time being: changing the EU Treaties is one of them. Then, Mr Cameron himself has already excluded not only the EEA membership, but also the scenario of the UK becoming 'half-a-Member' of the EU and the suggestion of 'a repatriation of Powers' from the EU to the Member States.

[A] The Importance of the Legal Shape of the Possible Answers

(1) For different reasons, changes to the EU Treaties look presently impracticable:

First, the political climate is not favourable:

> Many governments would refuse to open now the sensitive question of a Treaty change: the Greek crisis is not solved, the migrant crisis is divisive, and the EU's image is negative. Moreover, an attempt to change the EU Treaties would open a debate on the necessity to strengthen the constitutional basis of the eurozone,

48. This is even partly recognised by *The Europe Report: a win-win situation*, a report written by Gerard Lyons, the economic advisor of Boris Johnson, Greater London Authority, August 2014.

while the political situation does not allow this issue to be opened now. Any answer to the UK's list of suggestions should thus avoid to imply a Treaty change.

Second, the calendar also blocks a Treaty change:

The aim would be that the British accept, in a referendum, changes to the EU Treaties. But the other twenty-seven EU Member States would not ratify **before** the British referendum, without knowing if the British people would accept the changes, and Mr Cameron will not risk that British people vote in the referendum **before** knowing if the Treaty revision will be acceptable to the twenty-seven. There is no answer to this question: the British call that *'a catch 22 question'*.

Third, the idea to change the Treaties to 'rapatriate powers' to the Member States has been abandoned by Mr Cameron:

Actually, while the Reykjavik's speech of Mr Cameron on 28 October 2015 killed the idea to accede to the EEA (the so-called Norwegian model), his letter of 10 November 2015 also implicitly killed two other ideas: the idea of a special status of 'half a member' (see above § 6.03) and the idea of *'a repatriation of powers'*. That was an option suggested in 2013 by the British Government. The idea was to 'repatriate' competences from the EU back to the Member States. This necessarily implied a revision of the EU Treaties. In order to carefully prepare this scenario, the British Government had requested all pertinent services in Whitehall, as well as independent individuals and organisations, to analyse in detail, from an economic and legal point of view, the current share of powers between the EU and its Member States. The working hypothesis was that the Member States (including the UK of course) had been transferring too many legal powers to the EU, in too many sectors, in the successive EU Treaties.

As written by Michael Emerson in a book published in 2015:[49]

The British government has assembled the most comprehensive-ever assessment of the workings of the European Union, called the 'Balance of Competences Review'. This is based on 32 volumes and 3,000 pages of evidence submitted by 1,500 independent sources, now published in coherent analyses(...). The evidence shows that the sharing of competences between the EU and Member States has mostly been refined through years of negotiation and experience of reaching plausible balances.

This Report was written at a time when British authorities were (plausibly) convinced that the crisis in the eurozone would necessarily lead to a revision of the EU Treaties, in order to strengthen the eurozone's governance. They thought that this would then allow the UK to ask, at the same time, for amendments on 'repatriation of powers'. However, the eurozone decided not to go for a revision of the EU Treaties. It chose instead to limit itself to the conclusion of several 'intergovernmental agreements', treaties concluded only among the eurozone members and which are compatible with the EU Treaties. The situation was, and still is, that, whatever the legal and

49. *'Britain's Future in Europe: Reform, Renegotiation, Repatriation or Secession?'*, CEPS, Brussels, 192 pages).

political needs, the leaders of most countries of the eurozone are not ready to launch a politically dangerous new revision of the EU Treaties.

Fourth, the temptation of a 'disguised' Treaty change:

> Given the problem just described, some, including Mr Cameron, suggest to accept *'promises of future Treaty change'*. The Prime Minister asks in some cases to adopt solutions in *'a formal, legally-binding and irreversible way'*. The problem is that, **legally, making a promise legally binding transforms it into an actual Treaty change**: only the date of entry into force remains to be decided. Such a Treaty change could not be adopted without respecting, both the procedure set out in Article 48 TEU, and the procedures set out in the national Constitutions of all twenty-eight EU Member States. It would violate the rights of national Parliaments based on national constitutions: EU Treaty changes cannot be adopted by the sole Executive Powers.

(2) A legally binding instrument which respects the EU Treaties is legally possible:

> There is however a possibility to do something in a legally binding way, under the strict condition that it does not contradict, or modify, or add to the current EU Treaties as they are currently in force. This is what was done with the 11–12 December 1992 Decision of the Heads of State or Governments *'on Denmark and the EU'*[50], as well as with the 18–19 June 2009 Decision of the Heads of State or Governments *'on the concerns of the Irish People on the Treaty of Lisbon'*. These texts have a legal value, but they neither provide, nor 'promise' any **change** to the Treaties. As explicitly stressed in both texts, they are in conformity with the provisions of the EU Treaties and are just confirming and clarifying the meaning of existing Treaty provisions.[51] An intergovernmental agreement cannot change the meaning of a provision of the EU Treaties. This is the reason why the European Council could indicate, in its 2009 Conclusions, that the Decision on Ireland could later be transformed into a Protocol to the Treaties: it was fully respecting the EU Treaties.[52]

---

50. European Communities Official Journal, C348, 31 Dec. 1992, pp 1–4. *See also* Financial Times, 5 Jun. 2015: *'Creativity Will Not Allow Legal Procedures to be Bypassed'*, Jean-Claude Piris.
51. *See*, during the debates in the British House of Commons in January 1993, the Legal Assessment by Martin Howe, Michael Shrimpton and Leolin Price: *'it is clear beyond doubt that such an intergovernmental agreement cannot amend substantive Community law'(...) 'the Member States cannot alter Community law save in the modes authorised by the Treaties'*. *See*, however, Court of Justice of the EU, 2 March 2010, judgment C-135/08, *Rottmann*, paragraph 40. According to that judgment, where such a 'Decision of the Heads of State and Government, meeting within the European Council', is 'intended to clarify a question' it has 'to be taken into consideration' as an 'instrument(s) for the interpretation of the (EC) Treaty'.
52. *See* the Research Paper 09/75 of the House of Commons, 8 Oct. 2009: *'The Treaty of Lisbon after the Second Irish Referendum'* and, in particular, the quotation of the statements made in the House of Lords on the 1st July 2009 by the Minister for Europe, Ms Glenys Kinnock, confirming the Government's view that the second referendum on Ireland would be on the same Treaty of Lisbon, unchanged despite the adoption of the 'Decision of Heads of State or Governments': *'Those guarantees do not change the Lisbon Treaty; the European Council conclusions are very clear on them. The Lisbon Treaty, as debated and decided by our Parliament, will not be changed (...) Nothing in the Treaty will change and nothing in the guarantees will change the Treaty as Your Lordships agreed in'*. The Foreign Secretary, David Milliband, said to the House of Commons, on the 2 Jul. 2009, that *that legally binding text in the meaning of international law 'does not change the Lisbon Treaty and does not require ratification'*.

If there had been any discrepancy between one of these Decisions and the EU Treaties, the Decision in question would have been illegal and inapplicable.

Consequently, the adoption of measures which would not require a revision of the EU Treaties appears to be the only realistic and politically and legally acceptable solution.

Possible answers on the substance of the issues raised in Mr Cameron's letter:

> The EU should, as much as possible, give appropriate answers to the four 'baskets', already referred to by the Prime Minister in his *Bloomberg Speech* in January 2013 and in his *Telegraph* article in March 2014,[53] but now developed in his November 2015 letter:
>
> **-1)** **Economic Governance:** protecting non-Euro members from possible measures adopted by the Euro-members (*'we seek legally binding principles (...) and a safeguard mechanism to ensure these principles are respected and enforced'*).
>
> **-2)** **Competitiveness:** completing the internal market, establishing a digital market, a capital union, opening trade with third countries, cutting red tape, supporting growth and jobs... and adopt a comprehensive long term commitment bringing all this together.
>
> **-3)** **Sovereignty:** ending the UK's *'obligation'* for *'ever closer union'*, (*'in a legally binding and irreversible way'*), having an arrangement conferring new powers on national Parliaments to ensure better respect of subsidiarity by the EU (giving a group of them a veto on an EU legislation: 'red cards' instead of 'yellow cards') adopting concrete proposals to fully respect subsidiarity.
>
> **-4)** **Immigration:** inter alia, not giving too soon free movement of persons to the nationals of future EU Member States, and imposing on EU immigrants in the UK a period of four years of work before they qualify for in-work benefits or social housing.

[B] How Could the EU Meet Those Wishes?

[1] Economic Governance

This is the issue of the relations between the 'euro-ins' and the 'euro-outs' and on how to protect the rights of the non-euro EU Member States.

Most observers think that, in the medium term, the eurozone might be forced to integrate further, either through an EU Treaty revision or through a *Eurozone Treaty*, outside the EU Treaties but linked to them.[54] In such a case, non-eurozone EU members fear that the euro-ins might adopt decisions having a negative impact on them, especially concerning the single market. They fear that, even before, the nineteen euro-ins might take advantage of their number (which gives them a qualified majority of votes in the Council) to adopt EU measures that would not respect the integrity of the single market and the rights of the euro-outs. In order to reassure them, it is not

53. *See* Mr Cameron's 'Bloomberg speech', 23 Jan. 2013.
See his article in *The Telegraph*, 15 May 2014, as well as my comments on this article: *'Cameron Can Skip Treaty Change, Says Lawyer'*, *Financial Times*, London, 6 May 2014, p. 3.

54. *See* Jean-Claude Piris, *The Future of Europe: Towards a Two-Speed EU?* (Cambridge U. Press, 2012.

possible to change the voting rules in the Council, as this would necessitate amending the Treaties.[55] However, the euro-ins, or probably joined by some other EU members (the so-called pre-in eurozone members), could state that any future 'eurozone treaty' would confirm their legal obligations, under the control of the EU Court of Justice:

- to guarantee the rights of non-euro countries, including on the integrity of the single market;
- to respect the *acquis communautaire* and the exclusive and exercised powers of the EU under the Treaties;
- to respect the legal primacy of the EU Treaties and of the EU's law over the eurozone treaty;
- to accept to ensure openness of their activities; and
- to give the right to participate in meetings for those willing to join the euro within a given delay.

[2] Competitiveness

The mandate given by Jean-Claude Junker, the present President of the Commission, to his First Vice-President, Frans Timmermans, goes exactly in that direction, i.e., to cut 'red tape', to improve the respect of the principle of subsidiarity, and to try and help the Member States to boost growth and jobs. Frans Timmermans has certainly begun his task in a forceful manner. In any case, it must be recalled that, by definition, one piece of EU legislation replaces twenty-eight national laws (twenty-eight different red tapes…) and allows the single market to function better. Actually, preventing EU legislation from creating unnecessary and cumbersome obstacles to economic life is day-to-day work, which is taken more seriously today, both by the Member States and by the EU Institutions (see for example the Program 'REFIT'[56]), than was the case in the past. However, there is no simple legal option available to avoid red tape: this cannot be decided by a Treaty. A closer scrutiny of the Commission's legislative proposals by *national* authorities is the pre-requisite. Specific mechanisms might also be suggested, such as:

55. *See* the legally wrong suggestions made recently by the think-tank 'Open Europe' at http://openeurope.org.uk/intelligence/britain-and-the-eu/safeguarding-non-eurozone-states-rights-is-key-to-new-eu-settlement-heres-how-to-do-it/, which are clearly tending to modify the EU Treaties, while pretending they are not. They are based on a wrong interpretation of both the 'Ioannina Decision' (1994) and of the 'Ioannina-bis Decision' (2009): *see* Jean-Claude Piris, *The Lisbon Treaty* 222–225 (Cambridge U. Press 2010), (pm: a simple majority in the Council is at any time able to request to proceed to a vote in the Council, according to the QMV as defined in the Treaty. Both Decisions of 1994 (Article 6) and 2009 (article 11(1)) make it clear that the Rules of Procedure of the Council must always be respected. *See also*, the sole article of Protocol n°9, which means that a consensus in the European Council would be necessary in order to change this rule of the Rules of Procedure of the Council.
56. *REFIT* (Regulatory Fitness and Performance) is a programme of the European Commission. It aims at making EU law simpler and to reduce regulatory costs, thus contributing to a clear, stable and predictable regulatory framework supporting growth and jobs.

- improving the current Impact Assessment system, which could be conferred on an autonomous agency and could serve all three legislative institutions, the Commission, the Council and the Parliament;
- developing performance indicators;
- regularly assessing the actual effects of some EU Regulations or Directives after a few years of implementation;
- or even provide for a 'sunset clause' for some laws, which would no longer be in force after a few years, unless their duration was expressly renewed.

It should also be possible, without too many difficulties, to obtain a commitment from the Commission to submit proposals for legislation. One could, in particular, envisage the adoption of a calendar for the adoption of proposals in view of completing the internal market in services. This would be particularly important for the UK, given the share of services in its economy. This could be incorporated in a solemn Declaration of the European Council bringing together different proposals, agreements and measures on the Single Market and on the ways to help Member States *'to boost growth and Jobs'*.

[3] Sovereignty

- On the 'ever closer union':

The EU Treaties[57] mention a *'closer union among the peoples of Europe'*, not 'a closer Union of States'. In any case, the European Council has already shown its willingness on this issue, by stating in June 2014 that the political concept of an *'ever closer union'* should not be interpreted as a strict legal provision, and that it does allow for different '*paths*' (and not '*speeds*') of integration for the Member States. In the same vein, one could also recall that the EU Treaties give as an aim to the EU *'to deepen the solidarity between their peoples while* I add the EU *respecting their history, their culture and their traditions*' of the peoples of Europe (Preamble TEU). They also request the EU to '*respect its rich and linguistic diversity*' (Article 3(3) TEU) and *'to respect (...) the national identities of the Member States, inherent in their fundamental structures, political and constitutional, inclusive of regional and local self-government. It shall respect as well their essential State functions, including ensuring the territorial integrity of the State, maintaining law and order and safeguarding national security*' (Article 4(2)TEU).

It might be worth reminding the public of this, perhaps through some kind of a Solemn Declaration of the Heads of State or Government of the Twenty-Eight, recalling also that some Member States have a permanent derogation on the common currency and do not intend to join the euro.

- On national parliaments:

57. As well as the Treaty of Accession of the UK to the EU.

Article 12 TEU and Protocols n° 1 and 2, texts which were added to the Treaties by the Lisbon Treaty, confer interesting new powers on national parliaments (NP). According to the domain concerned, either one-third or one-quarter of NP may, based on control of subsidiarity, oblige the Commission to review a legislative proposal. It is true that this has rarely been used. Too short a period of delay is imposed on NPs, their cooperation is not organised in an optimal way and their opinions are not legally binding but only consultative ('yellow cards', not 'red cards': this means that national Parliaments do not have a collective right of veto, as their views do not have a legally binding effect). This could be improved in practice, without changing the Treaties:

- by offering practical facilities to NP (secretariat, services of interpretation);
- by interpreting and applying with flexibility the short delays that they have to react;
- by inviting the Commission to agree on a political commitment that, as a matter of principle, it will follow the NP conclusions agreed according to the figures provided for in Protocols 1 and 2, and that any exception would have to be justified in the European Council. In practice, that would transform the 'yellow card' almost certainly into 'a red card'. This is also a reason why this might be opposed by the European Parliament and some Member States.

[4] Immigration

The three precedent 'baskets' are objectively important issues to be looked at. They might be considered as more important for the UK in its future relations of the UK with the rest of the EU rather than the issue of immigration of EU workers in the UK. On this issue, it is sufficient to recall that the present EU legislation authorises Member States to adopt national measures against abuses in that domain. The EU Court of Justice reminded us of that in a recent judgment.[58] It is not established that the UK has taken all necessary domestic measures to that effect. If need be, the EU legislation could be made more precise on some points. However, suggestions made on freedom of movement of people would probably not be accepted by the other twenty seven EU Member States, as they would obviously violate the current EU Treaties. This includes suggestions aimed at allowing discrimination between EU citizens working in the UK, according to their nationality.[59] Thus, the suggestion to impose a delay of four years on EU immigrants working in the UK, before they could qualify for some social benefits or

58. Judgment of 11 Nov. 2014, Case C-333/13 Elisabeta Dano, *Florin Dano v. Jobcenter Leipzig*. However, the Court also recalled that: '*the status of citizen of the Union is destined to be the fundamental status of nationals of the Member States, enabling those among such nationals who find themselves in the same situation to enjoy within the scope ratione materiae of the FEU Treaty the same treatment in law irrespective of their nationality, subject to such exceptions as are expressly provided for in that regard*'.
59. *See* Article 18, first subparagraph, TFEU: '*Within the scope of application of the Treaties, and without prejudice to any special provisions contained therein, any discrimination on grounds of nationality shall be prohibited*', and Article 45(2) TFEU: '*Such freedom of movement shall entail the abolition of any discrimination based on nationality between workers of the Member States as regards employment, remuneration and other conditions of work and employment.*'

social housing, would be contrary to Articles 18 and 45 TFEU. It would affect the basic principles of free movement of persons, of equal pay, and of non-discrimination between EU citizens. A revision of the EU Treaties on this would not be accepted. Last but not least, such a move would directly psychologically affect the peoples of the Member States concerned, mainly the Central and Eastern European States that have joined the EU since 2004. One may think that this would not be conducive of a short and positive negotiation with the EU.

§6.06 CONCLUSION

None of the options available to the UK, in case of a Brexit, would look attractive.

Any option would take it in one of two directions:

- To get access to the EU's market, but at the same time becoming a kind of satellite of the EU, because then being obliged to transpose EU laws for the single market into its domestic law.
- To be cut off from the EU's market, by far its main market, and thus to be obliged to start trade negotiations with the EU as well as the rest of the world, without having much bargaining power.

Negotiating a new comprehensive agreement with the EU after a withdrawal, even if limited to trade and economic issues, would not be easy. None of the available options would satisfy, at the same time, both the British economic interests and its political wishes.

Nevertheless, the UK could not afford to leave unorganised its new relationship with the EU. In case of a Brexit, the absence of an agreement would affect many EU and British citizens. It would have substantive negative effect, especially for the UK's economy and also, to a lesser degree, for the economy of the rest of the EU.

Finally, it would certainly be extremely negative from a political point of view, either in Europe, or in the rest of the world, for the role of Europe and of its values and, thus, for the future prosperity and security of Europe as a whole... including, of course, the United Kingdom!

§6.07 POST-SCRIPTUM (19 DECEMBER 2015)

At its meeting of 17–18 December 2015, the European Council discussed the issues raised by Mr Cameron in his letter dated 10 November. The most difficult one is definitely the issue of workers coming from the EU to the UK. Mr Cameron continued to insist on being allowed to take measures aiming at reducing their number. He accepted not to question the EU principle of free movement of workers. However, he reiterated his proposal 'that people coming to Britain from the EU must live here and contribute for four years before they qualify for in-work benefits or social housing'.[60]

60. Letter addressed to Mr Tusk, President of the European Council, on 10 November 2015.

This would be a flagrant violation of the EU principles of non-discrimination (Article 18 TFEU) and of equal pay for equal work (Article 45(2) TFEU). Even if applied also to young Britons or to Britons coming back from foreign countries, this would remain a measure which would mainly have the aim and effect of discriminating against workers coming from other EU countries.

Resolving this delicate political and legal issue will not be easy. EU lawyers and diplomats would have to find an innovative and 'lateral' solution, which could be hailed by Mr Cameron as potentially giving the results he desires, albeit by other means. It could, for example, be based on the peculiarities of the architecture and financing of the British system of in-work benefits, as compared with the other member States' systems. It might instead allow temporary measures to deal with excessive flux of new-comers. The solution might also not be applicable immediately, but subject to the adoption of an amendment to the EU Treaties at a later time, when these Treaties will have to be modified for some other reason.

However, the December 2015 discussions have resulted in an optimistic consensus: 'Following today's substantive and constructive debate, the members of the European Council agreed to work closely together to find mutually satisfactory solutions in all the four areas at the European Council meeting on 18–19 February 2016.'[61]

Commitments are not taken lightly by the twenty-eight Heads of State or Government. Therefore, one could be optimistic that, regardless of the difficulties, the negotiations will be successful in February 2016. This would probably allow the British Government to organise the referendum in June.

61. Conclusions of the European Council, 17 and 18 December 2015, document EUCO 28/15, paragraph 20.

CHAPTER 7

The UK and the World: Environmental Law

Ioanna Hadjiyianni

§7.01 INTRODUCTION

'The important role that the EU plays in environmental law cannot be overstated'.[1] The EU has over the years engaged in extensive environmental policy action and developed considerable legislation addressing different kinds of environmental problems. The influence of EU environmental law is visible in the policies of both Member States and non-EU states and has often guided international developments in the field. Environmental law is thus a significant regulatory area in the debate on the exit of the UK from the EU because of the considerable influence of EU law on UK environmental policies and performance and because such influence will still largely occur even after a UK exit. This chapter examines the implications in the environmental legal field for the UK as a non-EU state – as a third country – both in relation to the EU and its Member States, and in relation to the rest of the world. It mainly focuses on environmental problems, which are either inherently transboundary, like climate change, or relate to cross-border activities, like trade.

Environmental problems are polycentric; involving different kinds of considerations and a multiplicity of actors. There are different characteristics of environmental problems that make them unique and complex to regulate. The analysis in this chapter is particularly guided by three characteristics. Firstly, many environmental problems are inherently transboundary, having effects beyond national borders and sometimes having global effects.[2] As such, they often require, or result in, international collective

1. Elizabeth Fisher, Bettina Lange and Eloise Scotford, *Environmental Law: Text, Cases and Materials* 115 (Oxford U. Press 2013).
2. Günther Handl, *Transboundary Impacts*, in *The Oxford Handbook of International Environmental Law* (D. Bodansky, J. Brunnee & E. Hey, eds, Oxford U. Press 2007). *Also see* Fisher, Lange and Scotford *supra* n. 1, Chapter 2.

action that signifies cooperation among states and actors to address these problems as effectively as possible, particularly when a single state cannot seek to achieve environmental protection on its own.[3] Secondly, regulating environmental problems involves different kinds of market considerations as environmental standards often influence the functioning of markets and affect flows of trade. Thirdly, building on the previous characteristic, regulating environmental problems involves addressing competitiveness considerations. This is because imposing national environmental standards can expose national actors to competitive disadvantages in relation to international competitors that do not have to abide by similar standards. The combination of these three inter-related characteristics affects what a state can do unilaterally in addressing such problems and is particularly relevant when thinking about the UK's position in regulating environmental problems.

In relation to global environmental problems, like climate change, or inherently transboundary problems like air pollution, the need for coordinated international action is essential and widely recognised. This is even in relation to the UK, which does not have direct physical boundaries with other States, besides Ireland. However, given the shortcomings of international environmental law and the slow development of multilateral regimes, alternative forms of coordinated action have emerged at regional and bilateral levels. The EU's environmental action forms part of these efforts and represents one of the most elaborate regional attempts to address environmental problems by pooling the efforts of twenty-eight different countries to pursue environmental protection goals within their borders, and influence the environmental policies of other actors in the international arena.

Furthermore, even for those problems that are not inherently transboundary in the conventional sense, in an increasingly globalised world, the approach taken in regulating environmental issues is not necessarily limited within national boundaries but is often greatly affected by third-country policies and international trends. National environmental regulation is influenced by what other countries are doing and this influence often leads to regulatory convergence[4] and policy transfer,[5] the migration of legal norms through transnational legal processes,[6] or even the creation of global environmental law.[7] The EU's role within such processes is particularly important, as it is both an important regulator and market, which greatly affects the policies of non-EU Member States – third countries – in the environmental field. In this regard, this chapter exposes and examines a legal phenomenon, particularly observed in EU environmental law, through which the EU's regulatory power extends beyond its borders, thus exhibiting an extraterritorial and potentially global reach.

---

3. Ellen Hey, *Common Interests and the (Re)constitution of Public Space*, 39 Env. Pol. & L. 152 (2009).
4. Daniel W. Drezner, *Globalization, Harmonization, and Competition: The Different Pathways to Policy Convergence* 12 J. Eur. Pub. Pol. 841 (2005).
5. Alasdair R. Young, *Political Transfer and "Trading Up"? Transatlantic Trade in Genetically Modified Food and US Politics* 55 World Pol. 457 (2003).
6. Gregory Shaffer & Daniel Bodansky, *Transnationalism, Unilateralism and International Law* 1 Transnatl. Env. L. 31 (2012).
7. Tseming Yang & Robert V. Percival, *The Emergence of Global Environmental Law* 36 Ecology L. Q. 615 (2009).

These considerations inform the discussion of the implications and consequences of UK exit from the EU and explain why the UK would still be largely influenced and in some ways bound by EU environmental law following an exit. It should be noted that this chapter is not meant to give a comprehensive account of how UK environmental law would substantively change and how it would be redrafted and restructured following an exit from the EU. Rather, while recognising that there are localised environmental problems in relation to which the UK could possibly gain more regulatory control, it focuses on environmental issues with important external dimensions.

In discussing the implications of a UK exit for environmental law, the chapter adopts the following structure. It first provides a brief overview of the impact of EU environmental law on the UK, while setting out the current EU legal and regulatory framework within which environmental competences are allocated, exercised and enforced. This discussion sets the foundations for understanding the role of the UK within this regime and the implications of exit as regards the relationship between the UK and the EU. The focus then turns to the position of the UK in relation to EU environmental standards in light of significant trade elements of EU environmental regulation. In this respect, the chapter unveils the expansive regulatory clout of EU environmental law and its continuing, albeit more indirect, influence on UK regulatory choices as a third country engaged in trade with the EU following the UK's exit. With a continued focus on the EU's expansive environmental regulatory power, the following section then explores the UK's position in relation to the rest of the world if it is no longer associated with the EU's 'green leadership'. The UK's loss of leverage within Multilateral Environmental Agreements (MEAs) and its loss of regulatory influence over third-country practices and policies reveal important constraints to UK unilateral action on environmental issues.

§7.02 THE UK AND THE EU

[A] EU Environmental Law and the UK

'Because the protection of the environment may require more, rather than less, action on the EU level, it seems that on that front the United Kingdom both faces and presents a serious problem'.[8] This passage amply summarises the complexities of this field of EU law in relation to the delineation of competences given the need for EU action in relation to transboundary and market-related environmental problems and the resistance of the UK to give up more powers to the EU in this field. EU action has seen an important increase in environmental regulation, which substantially limits the regulatory autonomy of the UK. This section maps the current legal and regulatory landscape within which the UK's position will be portrayed. In this respect it highlights the legal complexities surrounding the choice of the appropriate level of action in environmental

8. Francis Jacobs, *The Role of the European Court of Justice in the Protection of the Environment* 18 J. Env. L. 185, 205 (2006).

matters. While exit from the EU could provide flexibility and autonomy to UK environmental action, it is doubtful whether a unilateral path would always effectively address environmental protection goals.

EU environmental law is well embedded in UK environmental legislative frameworks, and even in UK environmental legal culture,[9] with much of UK environmental law now 'largely deriving' from EU law.[10] There is an overall recognition that the environment in the UK has mainly benefited from EU environmental action and the UK is no longer 'the dirty man of Europe'.[11] In certain areas in particular, the UK has made significant progress directly as a result of EU law, for example in relation to bathing and drinking water quality and cleaner power stations.[12] The overall beneficial relationship is dynamic and two-sided, with EU legislation often benefiting from UK input, especially in areas where UK action predated EU policies and in which the UK has set a good example to be followed, such as in the area of nature protection regulation[13] and climate change.[14]

Despite an overall recognition of the benefits of EU environmental law on UK environmental performance, there is however controversy in the UK about how much EU action is warranted in certain areas. For example, the UK government would like less EU regulation in areas where national sovereignty is cherished, for instance in relation to land use planning, noise, flooding and in the regulation of its energy mix and especially shale gas.[15]

Legally, the main controversies from a Member State perspective around EU environmental regulation are embedded in the allocation of competences. Competence constitutes the legal formulation that demonstrates the tensions in demarcating powers between the Member States and the EU. The complex compromise reached in the environmental sphere is expressed in terms of shared competence.[16] In addition, the landscape gets even muddier in seeking to determine the nature of competence in specific situations in areas of shared competence. There are situations where 'supervening exclusivity' arises, thus effectively turning areas of shared competence into

9. Fisher, Lange and Scotford *supra* n. 1, at 111.
10. Final Report Review of Balance of Competences: Environment and Climate Change, available at: https://www.gov.uk/government/consultations/eu-and-uk-action-on-environment-and-climate-change-review.
11. Chris Rose, *The Dirty Man of Europe: the Great British Pollution Scandal* (Simon & Schuster 1990). *See also* Catherine Burns, 'The Implications for UK Environmental Policy of a Vote to Exit the EU', available at: http://www.foe.co.uk/sites/default/files/downloads/eu_referendum_environment.pdf.
12. Burns *supra* n. 11.
13. The Habitats and Birds Directives were largely designed on the basis of the UK system. Stuart Bell, Donald McGillivray & Ole Pedersen, *Environmental Law*, Chapter 7 (8th edn OUP 2013).
14. The UK's ETS predated the EU ETS and provided important lessons for the creation of the EU ETS.
15. Review of Balance of Competences: Environment and Climate Change *supra* n. 10.
16. Consolidated Version of the Treaty on the Functioning of the European Union [2008] OJ 115/47 (TFEU) Article 4(2). Article 2(2) TFEU defines shared competence areas and specifies that 'The Member States shall exercise their competence to the extent that the Union has not exercised its competence. The Member States shall again exercise their competence to the extent that the Union has decided to cease exercising its competence.'

exclusive competence, both internally and externally.[17] Additionally, in the environmental context, there is provision for Member States to adopt stricter environmental standards as indicated in Article 193 of the Treaty on the Functioning of the European Union (TFEU).[18] However, this clause is not as straightforward and expansive as the wording might suggest and it is implicitly limited in various ways.[19] Furthermore, Member States are allowed to adopt or maintain national measures in relation to the protection of the environment alongside internal market harmonisation measures under certain conditions.[20] Although the framework for further action is unclear and relatively restrictive in areas of harmonisation, there are still possibilities for further action by Member States especially when the EU has not acted, or in maintaining pre-existing measures.[21] Overall, the legal landscape of the demarcation of competences raises complex questions when the UK prefers less EU action on certain issues[22] or when the UK seeks to pursue stricter action on others.[23]

Apart from controversies in the allocation of environmental competences, the internal functioning of the EU further complicates the legal and political framework in the environmental field. The multi-level nature of the structure and decision-making processes within the EU is especially perplexing in relation to the inter-sectoral and inter-institutional processes of environmental law.[24] The decision-making process relating to formulating environmental measures involves 'a range of venues'[25] including the different EU institutions and the multiple Directorates-General within those institutions. This process involves addressing diverse interests, particularly those of the different Member States as well as of other actors involved in the decision-making process at one stage or another, such as civil society, NGOs, lobby groups and industry. Within this process the UK's interests and preferences could be sidestepped or compromised, which explains why the UK would want to distance itself from this structure. Additionally, accommodating all the interests within the EU decision-making process is very difficult and often leads to political compromises that do not effectively

17. Alan Dashwood, *Mixity in the Era of the Treaty of Lisbon*, in *Mixed Agreements Revisited: The EU and its Member States in the World* (Christophe Hillion & Panos Koutrakos (eds) Hart Publishing 2010).
18. TFEU *supra* n. 16 Article 193, 'The protective measures adopted pursuant to Article 192 shall not prevent any Member State from maintaining or introducing more stringent protective measures. Such measures must be compatible with the Treaties. They shall be notified to the Commission.'
19. Such unilateral measures have to be based on Article 192 TFEU, respect free movement of goods principles and specifically Article 34 TFEU and are subject to the principle of loyal cooperation in Article 4(3) TEU. Fisher, Lange and Scotford *supra* n. 1, 130.
20. TFEU *supra* n. 16 Article 114. Fisher, Lange & Scotford *supra* n. 1.
21. Fisher, Lange & Scotford *supra* n. 1.
22. Such issues include regulation on flooding, noise pollution and land use planning, Review of Balance of Competences: Environment and Climate Change *supra* n. 10.
23. The UK had adopted stricter regime for the energy efficiency of buildings prior to EU action requiring new buildings to meet the zero carbon target from 2016 compared to the EU's target of 'nearly zero energy buildings' for new buildings by 2020. *See* Review of the Balance of Competences between the United Kingdom and the European Union Energy Report, 37 available at: https://www.gov.uk/government/consultations/energy-review-of-the-balance-of-competences.
24. Sebastiaan Princen, *Agenda Setting*, in *Environmental Policy in the EU. Actors, Institutions and Processes* 197 (Andrew Jordan & Camilla Adelle eds, 3rd edn, Routledge 2012).
25. *Ibid.*

address environmental problems.[26] This demonstrates how the EU may not always be well-placed to regulate such sensitive and complex issues, which are often linked to the UK's retained sovereignty, for example energy matters or other matters which the UK would have preferred to retain power in addressing local circumstances.

Nevertheless, despite the complexity of the EU's decision-making process and important legitimacy questions that may be raised about the EU's internal functioning in this area, the UK has multiple opportunities through which its government, industry and civil society can be heard in the formulation of EU environmental regulation and its subsequent updating. The UK has influenced the formulation of environmental policies at EU level on many occasions, both by providing a template for regulation,[27] and by introducing more flexibility in policies.[28] Overall, even if the UK's voice might not always be upheld,[29] following an exit the UK would lose its voice in the formulation of important environmental legislation, which may indirectly affect it in various ways, as discussed below.

Given the increasing European integration of environmental law, the complicated internal functioning of the EU and the fact that the UK's priorities are sometimes compromised within the EU structure, the UK could benefit from leaving the EU in some respects. This would be largely due to the UK gaining more flexibility and autonomy in regulating environmental problems. In particular, more flexibility would allow the UK to take more stringent measures in areas where it feels that it is being held back from more decisive action. The UK has already sought to address inadequacies of EU environmental law in certain areas through unilateral action in areas like climate change and the energy efficiency of buildings. However, not all the UK's unilateral actions have been successful. The adoption of the unilateral carbon floor price adopted by the UK has shown that unilateral measures to improve the EU Emissions Trading System (EU ETS) do not necessarily yield desirable results, especially in terms of reducing emissions and making the EU ETS more effective. Rather, such action could instead expose UK industry to competitive disadvantage towards EU competitors.[30] Therefore, even if the flexibility gained following an exit could be used by the UK to reinforce certain areas of environmental law, the effectiveness of unilateral action can be problematic.

At the same time, more flexibility does not necessarily mean good news for the protection of the environment as the UK could use such flexibility to lower its

26. Christoph Knill, *Taking Stock: The Environmental Problem-Solving Capacity of the EU' in Christoph Knill & Duncan Liefferink, Environmental Politics in the European Union: Policy-Making, Implementation and Patterns of Multi-Level Governance* (Manchester U. Press 2007).
27. The Integrated Pollution and Prevention Control Directive was largely influenced by integrated pollution control law of the UK. Bell, McGillivray & Pedersen *supra* n. 12.
28. As seen in the recently adopted 2030 climate change targets, which do not enclose a binding target on renewable energy on the EU as a whole without being binding at the national level after opposition from the UK. *See* Henriette Jacobsen and James Crisp, 'EU leaders adopt "flexible" energy and climate targets for 2030' available at: http://www.euractiv.com/sections/eu-priorities-2020/eu-leaders-adopt-flexible-energy-and-climate-targets-2030-309462.
29. The UK has sought to resist a ban on neonicotinoids pesticides to protect bees. *See* Burns *supra* n. 10.
30. Sandbag, 'The UK Carbon Floor Price', available at: http://www.sandbag.org.uk/site_media/pdfs/reports/Sandbag_Carbon_Floor_Price_190312.pdf.

environmental standards instead.[31] EU environmental action, whether in the form of binding legislation or general policy objectives, imposes external pressure on the UK in relation to environmental protection goals, whose priority can be variable on the national political agenda. Specifically in areas where the UK has consistently been in breach of EU environmental legislation such as air pollution standards, or where it has opposed stricter standards such as bans and strict labelling of GMOs, the EU has provided external pressure in engaging the UK to act on important environmental and health issues.

Additionally, apart from political and public external pressure, the EU legal system has also provided important avenues through which the UK can be held accountable for insufficient action. In particular, the EU provides important enforcement mechanisms, including Commission infringement actions against Member States,[32] and possibilities for private enforcement. In the environmental context in particular, the case law of the Court of Justice of the EU (CJEU) has been 'uniquely effective in terms of enforcement'[33] while the possibilities for private enforcement through directly effective legislation or the use of the duty of consistent interpretation of EU law have given both individuals and NGOs important enabling powers.[34] These possibilities have recently been employed in two cases – by an environmental NGO bringing a case against the UK before national courts,[35] and by the Commission initiating infringement proceedings in relation to the UK's persistent infringement of air pollution standards.[36] The national proceedings have now been concluded following a preliminary ruling by the CJEU, which left it to the national court to ensure compliance. To that effect, the Supreme Court has unanimously ordered the UK Government to draw up new air quality plans by 31 December 2015, in order to reduce NO_2 levels and comply with the Air Quality Directive limits.[37] As Lord Carnwath put it, 'the new Government, whatever its political complexion, should be left in no doubt as to the need for immediate action to address this issue. The only realistic way to achieve this is a mandatory order requiring new plans ... to be prepared within a defined timetable.'[38] The order made by the Supreme Court is of particular political significance especially given the time when it was granted – right before the general election – which ensures continuity of the obligation imposed on the government.

Although these EU judicial mechanisms may further limit the UK's autonomy, they reinforce effective implementation of UK commitments and require concrete action from the UK in relation to serious environmental and health problems. Furthermore, despite the fact that reception of EU environmental law within the UK judicial

31. Burns *supra* n. 11.
32. TFEU *supra* n. 16, Article 258.
33. Jacobs *supra* n. 8.
34. Daniel R. Kelemen, *Suing for Europe Adversarial Legalism and European Governance* (2006) 39(1) Comparative Political Studies 101.
35. *R (ClientEarth) v. Secretary of State for the Environment, Food and Rural Affairs* [2013] UKSC 25.
36. http://europa.eu/rapid/press-release_IP-14-154_en.htm.
37. European Parliament and Council Directive 2008/50/EC on Ambient Air Quality and Cleaner Air for Europe, [2008] OJ L152/1.
38. *R (ClientEarth) v. Secretary of State for the Environment, Food and Rural Affairs* [2015] UKSC 28, paragraph 31.

system was initially resisted, UK courts have gradually changed their approach and, as seen, are more willing to refer cases to the CJEU than in the early years of EU environmental law.[39] An important shift in approach can also be seen in terms of interpretation of EU environmental law by English courts, such as the Habitats Directive,[40] the Waste Framework Directive[41] and the Environmental Impact Assessment Directive,[42] which increasingly involves 'purposive interpretation' that enhances the rights derived from this legislation.[43] The combination of these enforcement mechanisms and the effects of EU legislation within the UK's legal and judicial system have yielded important steps forward in terms of public involvement and environmental integration.

Without the 'stick' elements provided by these enforcement mechanisms as well as external pressure from EU environmental laws, UK environmental policies could be more exposed to changing governmental positions and in relation to specific environmental problems would lack the necessary continuous commitment for long-term action. These governmental positions could be detrimental to the environment, the citizens and even in terms of providing certainty for investors in areas where it would be unclear what direction the UK might take.[44]

Overall, the influence of EU environmental law on UK laws has been extensive and largely positive. However, this is not to suggest that EU environmental legal solutions are perfect. Rather that despite shortcomings, the EU's environmental legal action is important and the UK's role within it crucial. Even though the competence issue often tilts in favour of the EU, the UK's position is strong in influencing the formulation of EU environmental policies and laws. This position could be more important than the UK's desire for more flexibility and autonomy in light of the extensive external influence of EU environmental law to be considered below. Indeed, leaving the EU does not necessarily mean that the UK would be entirely dissociating itself from EU environmental regulation. This partly depends on the type of cooperation agreement to be concluded between the UK and EU after the UK's exit and partly on the external influence of EU environmental law even in the absence of binding obligations to which the UK might commit as discussed in the next section.

---

39. Bell, McGillivray & Pedersen *supra* n. 13. However judicial reluctance is still noted which may warrant reform of the preliminary reference procedure in order to ensure better protection of the environment and greater effectiveness of EU law. See Veerle Heyvaert, Justine Thornton and Richard Drabble, *With Reference to the Environment: The Preliminary Reference Procedure, Environmental Decisions and the Domestic Judiciary,* (2014) 130(3) Law Quarterly Review 413.
40. *R v. Secretary of State for Trade & Industry & ORS, ex parte Greenpeace Ltd* (2000) Env L.R 221.
41. *R. v. Derbyshire County Council* [2001] Env. L.R. 26.
42. *Berkeley v. Secretary of State for the Environment* [2001] Env L.R 16.
43. Bell, McGillivray & Pedersen *supra* n. 13.
44. For example, it is uncertain whether the UK would maintain a sustainable use approach to waste management, which could create uncertainty for industry and investors. *See* House of Commons Library Research Paper 13/42, 1 Jul. 2013, 61 available at: http://www.parliament.uk/business/publications/research/briefing-papers/RP13-42/leaving-the-eu.

[B] Relationship with the EU after Exit: The UK as a Third Country

The discussion thus turns to the UK's position after exit vis-à-vis EU environmental legal obligations. Mainly due to trade considerations, the UK would directly or indirectly still be bound by some EU environmental standards. While much of EU environmental legislation would still substantially influence the UK industry and regulators, the UK would lose its direct voice in the EU's decision-making process within which such policies are formulated.

On the one hand, the extent and the ways in which EU environmental law would affect UK environmental regulation after exit depend on the kind of trade arrangement that would be concluded between the EU and the UK and any deriving obligations to be included in relation to other sectors such as the environment. The options of cooperation between the UK and the EU after exit are numerous,[45] with the UK most probably opting for preferential access to the EU market given that the EU is its largest trading partner.[46] The regulation of this access could take many forms, including some sort of bilateral free trade agreement similar to the one concluded by the EU with Switzerland, or an arrangement akin to the European Economic Area (EEA) Agreement.[47] Whatever the precise form and conditions of an EU-UK agreement, it would likely include obligations to abide by the '*acquis communautaire*' in the environmental field with possible exceptions as in the case of the EEA Agreement.[48] Especially bearing in mind that the UK would be the first former Member State, which would seek to be closely attached to the single market, the EU Member States would probably attach extensive conditions beyond trade in other fields of EU law. Such an arrangement would essentially mean that the UK would still be bound by the majority of EU environmental standards in place while at the same time losing its voice in the formulation of such policies in the internal decision-making process of the EU. Whatever the role of EEA countries for example in shaping EU environmental legislation and whatever role would be given to the UK in that respect, it would not have as many opportunities as it would by being a Member State to make its opinion heard by participating in the decision-making processes within EU institutions. This would be a very significant limitation to the UK's autonomy whereby the UK would have to comply with important environmental laws directly without however being involved in their formulation even within the EU's complicated structure. Thus what might essentially appear as an increase in flexibility would in essence be a further limitation to its autonomy.

On the other hand, even in the unlikely scenario where the UK would not be directly bound by EU environmental legislation as part of a trade agreement, either because such obligations would not be included in a trade arrangement or because the UK would not conclude a market access agreement, EU domestic environmental measures would still have important implications for it. The need for cooperative

45. *See* the discussion in Chapter 6 by Jean-Claude Piris.
46. 46% of UK's goods and services exports and 51% of the UK's imports in 2012 were to the EU, House of Commons Research Paper *supra* n. 44.
47. Burns *supra* n. 11.
48. *Ibid*.

action in addressing certain environmental problems, combined with the externalities of environmental regulations imply that even if the UK opts for a unilateral path in regulating environmental problems, this does not mean that it would be entirely detached from EU action in the field.

EU environmental law is increasingly characterised by a tendency of global reach.[49] In particular, this tendency is exhibited through the emerging legal phenomenon of internal environmental measures with extraterritorial implications (IEMEIs). IEMEIs consist of domestic measures unilaterally developed and adopted by the EU which are legally designed in such a way that their legal impact explicitly extends beyond EU borders. These measures are applied to non-EU operators through trade-related restrictions that regulate access to the EU market. Their common premise is the extraterritorial reach of the standards they impose that aim to address environmental problems that originate outside the EU's territory or stipulate restrictions on the basis of conduct or circumstances that take place beyond EU borders. This legal phenomenon is particularly relevant in the discussion of a potential exit of the UK from the EU as it comprises a broad spectrum of regulatory techniques through which the EU is extending its own environmental standards beyond its territory and which could structurally affect the UK as a third country in the future.

These measures can have important legal and regulatory implications for third countries and external actors and this largely relates to the importance of the EU as a market and regulator. EU law, including EU environmental law, increasingly gives rise to a 'Brussels effect' or 'unilateral regulatory globalisation' through which the EU is able 'to externalise its laws and regulations outside its borders through market mechanisms...'[50] This may occur both in terms of passively affecting business practice with foreign companies adjusting their practices and applying EU standards across their business - de facto Brussels effect - and/or third countries correspondingly changing their national laws - de jure Brussels effect.[51] In particular, the EU's laws on hazardous substances[52] and chemicals[53] have had significant influence for both business practice and third-country laws with some countries tailoring their regulatory approach to reflect EU terms[54] and others using EU policy as positive mode for

49. Joanne Scott, *Extraterritoriality and Territorial Extension in EU Law* 62 Am. J. Comp. L. 87 (2014).
50. Anu Bradford, *The Brussels Effect* 107 Nw U. L. Rev. 1.
51. *Ibid.*
52. European Parliament and Council Directive 2002/95/EC on the restriction of the use of certain hazardous substances in electrical and electronic equipment [2003] OJ L37/19. Also *see* European Parliament and Council Directive 2011/65/EC on restriction of certain hazardous substances in electrical and electronic equipment OJ [2011] 174/88.
53. European Parliament and Council Regulation 1907/2006/EC concerning the Registration, Evaluation, Authorisation and Restriction of Chemicals [2007] OJ L136/3 (REACH).
54. For example, the Directive on the restriction of the use of certain hazardous substances in electrical and electronic equipment *supra* n. 52 has led to policy changes that largely mirrored EU policy in China and Korea, Yoshiko Naiki, *Assessing Policy Reach: Japan's Chemical Policy Reform in Response to the EU's REACH Regulation* 22 J. Env. L. 171, 182 (2012).

reform.[55] In relation to chemicals regulation in particular, the EU has developed a unique regime, which has had far-reaching implications for third-country policies with some countries like Norway voluntarily adopting REACH[56] and other countries adjusting their own practices and policies accordingly.[57] This shows how the UK would probably be forced to maintain such well-established standards and possibly similar far-reaching standards in the future.

Adding to the passive externalisation of EU environmental law in this way, the EU is also increasingly structurally designing its internal measures by explicitly promoting action on environmental matters by third countries.[58] In particular, the EU is expanding the ways of regulating trade relations with third countries through the adoption of measures which impose restrictions on processes or conduct that occur outside EU borders. For example, the EU imposes restrictions on how harvesting of timber and production of biofuels occurs in third countries in measures regulating imports of such products in the EU.[59] Through such measures, EU environmental law exhibits 'territorial extension' through which the EU takes into account activities or processes occurring in third countries in determining compliance with EU law and thus extending its regulatory clout to activities occurring abroad.[60] The EU also imposes its own or equivalent standards in facilities located in third countries when they receive ships for ship recycling flying the flag of a Members State[61] or when they receive electrical and electronic waste from the EU.[62] Through these mechanisms, the EU ensures that EU operators do not evade EU obligations by exporting waste to third countries for example, but at the same time influences and sometimes directly dictates the kinds of process standards that third-country operators have to abide by when doing business with the EU.

Provoking action by third countries is also pursued through another legal mechanism increasingly employed in IEMEIs in the form of explicit links between the application of EU environmental law and legal developments that occur in third countries. These links are formulated in conditional terms making the unilateral

55. Japan adopted its own version of RoHS rather than mirroring it, *see* Naiki *supra* n. 54. *See* also Henrik Selin Stacy D. VanDeveer, *Raising Global Standards: Hazardous Substances and E-waste Management in the European Union* 48 Env.: Sci. & Pol. Sust. Dev. 6 (2006).
56. Regulation 1907/2006/EC *supra* n. 53.
57. Countries like Canada, Australia, China and Russia have adopted REACH-like legislation, Bradford *supra* n. 50, 28. Also *see* Joanne Scott, *From Brussels with Love: The Transatlantic Travels of European Law and the Chemistry of Regulatory Attraction* 57 Am. J. Comp. L. 897, 910 (2009).
58. Joanne Scott, *The Multi-Level Governance of Climate Change*' 1 Carbon and Climate L. Rev. 25 (2011).
59. European Parliament and Council Regulation 995/2010/EC laying down the obligations of operators who place timber and timber products on the market (EUTR) [2010] OJ L295/23. European Parliament and Council Directive 2009/28/EC on the promotion of the use of energy from renewable sources, [2009] OJ L140/16 (RED) Article 17.
60. Scott, *Extraterritoriality and Territorial Extension in EU Law, supra* n. 49.
61. European Parliament and Council Regulation 1257/2013/EU on ship recycling [2013] OJ L330/1.
62. European Parliament and Council Directive 2012/19/EC on waste electrical and electronic equipment [2012] OJ L197/38, Article 10. However, it should be noted that third-country facilities have to operate in accordance with equivalent conditions for waste treatment to count towards the recovery targets set by the Directive.

application of EU environmental law 'contingent' upon: the law of third countries; bilateral agreements agreed with the EU; or developments under international regimes.[63] These links can be explained in terms of 'escape routes'[64] either allowing third countries to 'escape' the obligations imposed by EU environmental law or to use alternative or supplementary routes to 'get to the destination' and comply with EU requirements. For example, the EU's inclusion of aviation emissions in the EU ETS was designed in conditional terms and provided for the non-application of the regime when third countries had a regime in place to address such emissions.[65] Additionally, the Renewable Energy Directive provides for the possibility of complying with the sustainability criteria on biofuels when a bilateral agreement is concluded with the EU containing provisions relating to issues covered by the sustainability criteria, or through the use of a private voluntary certification scheme, approved by the EU Commission.[66] At all stages, the EU retains a catalyst role in determining how compliance is to be achieved. Such action is often directed at specific issues and to specific countries, such as biofuels or timber producing countries, or aims to provoke action and enhance cooperation on specific controversial issues where multilateral action is weak. While the use of such measures is important in filling regulatory gaps in light of insufficient international environmental action, IEMEIs raise significant legitimacy concerns especially because they are imposed on third-country actors that do not usually have a voice in their formulation.

Overall, the discussion of this legal phenomenon is informative both by showing the constraints for the UK to effectively distance itself from existing EU policies and by exposing the position of the UK with relation to future environmental policies adopted by the EU. If the EU's activity, passively gives rise to far-reaching implications in terms of a 'Brussels effect' to countries such as the United States and Japan, similar implications and regulatory restrictions would probably occur in relation to an ex-Member State such as the UK. More importantly, the EU's extensive IEMEI activity is also characterised by an active pursuit of green leadership beyond EU borders as a means of 'incentivising regulatory engagement elsewhere'[67] and 'achieving extraterritorial effects and affecting multilateral negotiations'.[68] The EU could potentially use such mechanisms in the future to influence the UK's approach following an exit from

63. Joanne Scott & Lavanya Rajamani, *EU Climate Change Unilateralism* 23 Eur. J. Intl. L. 469 (2012).
64. Joanne Scott, *EU Global Action on Climate Change: Contingent Unilateralism and Regulatory Penalty Defaults* 2 SADC L. J. 1 (2012).
65. European Parliament and Council Directive 2003/87/EC establishing a scheme for greenhouse gas emission allowance trading within the Community [2003] OJ L275/32, Article 25a(1).
66. Directive 2009/28/EC *supra* n. 59, Article 18. In a similar vein the EU's Regulation on organic farming requires importers to comply with the requirements set out in the Regulation. It also provides that organic products that do not comply with EU standards could be allowed in the EU if they meet equivalent standards including the possibility for recognising countries with equivalent standards. *See* Council Regulation 834/2007 on organic production and labelling of organic products and repealing Regulation (EEC) No. 2092/91, [2007] OJ L189/1, Articles 32 and 33.
67. Scott, *The Multi-Level Governance of Climate Change*, *supra* n. 58, at 31.
68. Gracia Marin-Duran & Elisa Morgera, *Environmental Integration in the EU's External Relations: Beyond Multilateral Dimensions* 282 (Hart 2012).

the EU. This could occur in specific areas that might turn out to be problematic in the eyes of the EU when the UK is not a Member State thus influencing the content of UK environmental policies and promoting cooperation through the EU's own measures. As these measures tend to address issues with important trade components, it is becoming clear that the UK would not necessarily be able to simply distance itself from the extensive environmental action of the EU at least in relation to activities with transboundary market elements.

UK private and public actors currently have an important role within EU internal environmental legal processes and multiple opportunities for raising their concerns at the stage of conceptualisation and development of such regimes within the decision-making processes of the EU. In this way, these extensive regimes are not imposed on them indirectly by way of extension of EU environmental standards or by being used as bargaining chips in bilateral and international developments without their input at the initial stage of formulation.

On the basis of important market considerations and assuming a UK desire to be associated with the single European market, it seems that the UK, as a third country, would have to either directly or indirectly comply with at least some EU environmental standards by being engaged in trade relations with the EU. The implications of this could be far-reaching with the EU having additional ways of indirectly influencing UK environmental policy and provoking UK action while at the same time the UK's influence in formulating such extensive policies would be reduced.

§7.03 THE EU, THE UK AND THE WORLD

Having examined how the extension of EU regulatory power outside the EU could affect the relationship between the UK and the EU after exit, this section explores how this power could also affect the UK's relationship with the rest of the world. This section firstly sets out the benefits for the UK from EU membership in relation to external environmental action. It outlines the EU's important but often complex role in international environmental legal regimes while identifying benefits for the UK from being part of the EU bloc. It also highlights how the global reach of EU environmental law and its impact in third countries strengthens the UK's regulatory power and protects UK competitiveness. On the basis of these considerations, the section secondly identifies important limitations for UK unilateral action without the EU's external regulatory clout.

[A] Relationship with the World: The UK as a Member State

The EU's international environmental role is multifaceted. In the multilateral sphere, the EU is often portrayed as an important environmental actor whose action is at least 'influential' while also sometimes being presented as a 'green leader'.[69] The EU is an

69. R. Daniel Kelemen, *Globalizing European Union Environmental Policy*, 17 J. Eur. Pub. Pol. 335 (2010).

important environmental negotiator playing a crucial role in the negotiating process of important multilateral environmental agreements such as the Basel Convention, the Convention on Biological Diversity, the Kyoto Protocol and the Cartagena Protocol on Biosafety.[70] The EU's leadership role is usually associated with setting policy positions early in the negotiation process and inspiring policy change in third countries and under international regimes,[71] thus engaging in 'directional' leadership.[72]

Despite an overall good record as an international environmental negotiator however,[73] the EU has been criticised for lack of coherence and credibility in its leadership efforts.[74] As regards coherence in particular, vertical coherence between the EU and its Member States is often viewed 'at least as problematic'.[75] The internal functioning of the EU combined with the need to accommodate the interests of the different Member States as well as its complicated negotiating structure present real difficulties in maintaining and coordinating common positions in international negotiations. Especially in situations where both the EU and the Member States are parties to an agreement, a 'mixed agreement', the complicating shared nature of competences creates legal ambiguity both in relation to the limits of unilateral Member State action[76] and in terms of representation of the EU.[77] Even after the Lisbon Treaty, there is uncertainty about 'who has to do what'[78] and this might lead to situations where the EU is left without a clear negotiator.[79] If the UK were to leave the EU and act on its own in international negotiations, the UK would be able to dissociate itself from this uncertain

70. R Daniel Kelemen & David Vogel, *Trading Places: the Role of the United States and the European Union in International Environmental Politics* 43 Comp. Pol. Stud. 427 (2010).
71. Anthony R Zito, *The European Union as an Environmental Leader in a Global Environment* 2 Globalizations 363 (2005).
72. Bertil Killian & Ole Elgström, *Still a Green Leader? The European Union's Role in International Climate Negotiations* 45 Cooperation & Conflict 225 (2010).
73. Sebastian Oberthür, *The Role of the EU in Global Environmental and Climate Governance*, in *The European Union and Global Governance* 192 (Mario Telò, Routledge 2009).
74. John Vogler & Hannes R Stephan, *The European Union in Global Environmental Governance: Leadership in the Making?* 7 Intl Envtl Agreements: Pol. L. & Econ. 389 (2007).
75. Hans Vedder, *The Formalities and Substance of EU External Environmental Competence: Stuck between Climate Change and Competitiveness*, in *The External Environmental Policy of the European Union: EU and International Law Perspectives* (Elisa Morgera ed., Cambridge U. Press 2012).
76. Case C-246/07 *Commission v. Sweden* [2010] All E.R. (EC) 1198. EU Member States are precluded from adopting stricter standards within mixed agreements when an EU common strategy has been agreed on the basis of the operation of the duty of loyal cooperation in Article 4(3) TEU. *See* Geert De Baere, *'O, Where is Faith? O, Where is Loyalty?' Some Thoughts on the Duty of Loyal Co-operation and the Union's External Environmental Competences in the light of the PFOS Case*, 36 Eur. L. Rev. 405 (2011).
77. Tom Delreux, *The EU as an Actor in Global Environmental Politics*, in *Environmental Policy in the EU, Actors, Institutions and Processes* 299 (A. Jordan & C. Adelle eds, 3d ed., Routledge 2012).
78. Sijbren de Jong & Simon Schunz,, *Coherence in European Union External Policy before and after the Lisbon Treaty: The Cases of Energy Security and Climate Change* 17 Euro. For. Aff. Rev. 165, 175 (2012).
79. For example internal confusion on the representation of the EU resulted in the EU not having a voice at all at the first stage of negotiations on an international agreement on mercury, Geert De Baere, *International Negotiations Post Lisbon: A Case Study of the Union's External Environmental Policy*, in *The European Union's External Relations a Year After Lisbon* (Panos Koutrakos eds, Centre for the Law of EU External Relations 2011).

negotiating structure and burdensome internal negotiating processes as well as be able to present its own position without adjusting it to the EU's stand in mixed agreements.

Moreover, even in situations where the EU is not a party to an international agreement, EU law affects the action of the EU Member States both in the negotiating phase and after they have entered into such agreements. For example, in relation to the International Convention for the Regulation of Whaling, where the EU is merely an observer in the International Whaling Commission (IWC), EU law imposes strict requirements on what Member States can do,[80] not allowing them to commit to obligations that are less stringent than what EU law stipulates.[81] Even within the IWC, the EU Member States have opted to act together and vote en bloc and usually adopt common positions. This may sometimes mean that the UK is not able to promote its anti-whaling position, as it is required to compromise to adapt to the EU position.[82] Nonetheless, being able to act and vote as a bloc, increases the leverage of EU Member States in influencing the international position of an IWC of eighty-nine Member States, both when it comes to a vote within the IWC, and in negotiations by affecting other IWC Member States' positions.[83]

Therefore, the complexities related to the EU's international environmental role should not be over emphasised at the expense of its leverage and strength when acting as a bloc. The mere size and negotiating strength of the EU bloc combined with its long-standing commitment to multilateralism demonstrate the capacity of the EU to concretely influence the content and development of multilateral environmental agreements. For the UK, acting under the 'team EU' in climate change negotiations for example has provided it with more leverage to promote its position and expertise in regulating such controversial and complicated issues.[84] If the EU's complicated internal decision-making processes means that multiple interests have to be represented and compromised within the EU as discussed in section 2, when a decision-making platform on environmental issues is replicated at the international level, the venues, interests and voices at stake are of a much greater scale and the UK's voice could become isolated if not part of the EU's far-reaching voice.

Overall, despite the fact that the EU may not always be successful in promoting environmental action in all areas and is sometimes seen as struggling to maintain its role as a 'green leader', it remains an important international environmental actor. For example, it is the largest player consisting of developed countries globally that has consistently shown commitment to addressing climate change. In particular, the EU

80. Ludwig Krämer, Sandy Luk & Rowan Ryrie, 'The IWC Proposed Consensus Decision and EU law duties regarding whales' available at: http://www.clientearth.org/reports/marine-protection-clientearth-briefing-whaling-and-eu-law.pdf.
81. At the same time, this means that Member States could potentially commit to stricter requirements if no common EU position has been reached on the issue. Pieter Jan Kuijper et al., *The law of EU External Relations: Cases, Materials, and Commentary on the EU as an International Legal Actor* 812 (Oxford U. Press 2013).
82. For example, in relation to voting on a quota for Greenland.
83. The EU has recently led a demarche against Iceland's whaling practices, in collaboration with the USA, Brazil, Australia, Israel, New Zealand, Mexico and Monaco. *See* http://europa.eu/rapid/press-release_MEMO-14-529_en.htm.
84. Review on balance of Competences: Environment and Climate Change *supra* n. 10, at 45.

Member States have recently managed to agree on new emission reductions targets, which although less demanding than was hoped by civil society, present a strong position compared to positions of other big players and may affect negotiations in the next Conference of the Parties to the UNFCCC in Paris. The UK has overall benefited from being part of the EU in gaining international leverage in the environmental domain specifically by increasing its leverage in international negotiations having a greater voice at the international plane and particularly in influencing third-country positions.

The EU's external environmental action also extends beyond its official position in multilateral regimes. Indeed, the EU employs different kinds of external relations tools to support environmental multilateralism.[85] The EU has an extensive network of cooperation with third countries in environmental matters as a result of bilateral and inter-regional agreements which either focus on environmental issues or incorporate environmental clauses within other types of agreements, such as association agreements, external assistance policies and in the generalised system of preferences.[86] After exit, the UK would be distancing itself from this extensive external environmental action undertaken and coordinated by the EU. Additionally, the UK as a non-Member State would not be involved in important bilateral negotiations undertaken by the EU, which can affect environmental standards, such as the controversial Transatlantic Trade and Investment Partnership (TTIP). The UK has shown its commitment to be more actively engaged in the process specifically for ensuring that the EU's stringent environmental standards are upheld especially in areas where US standards are not equivalent.[87] This demonstrates the two-sided, reciprocal benefits that both the EU and the UK can derive from UK membership in terms of environmental protection. In this way the UK can play an important role in keeping the EU 'in check' when it is tempted to sacrifice its commitment to 'high level of environmental protection' for the sake of economic interests.

The extraterritorial and global reach of EU environmental law, through which the EU increasingly exercises structural leadership, also affects the position of the UK in the world. In particular, it should be recalled that the EU, through its economic power and the importance of its market, incentivises environmental action by third countries through its own internal environmental measures that have various extraterritorial implications. At the international level, in certain areas such as climate change for example, the EU is increasingly adopting a 'sticks and carrots' approach in international negotiations through the formulation of its internal policies in conditional terms and their employment as useful negotiating tools.[88] Several provisions within the EU ETS provide for revision of different aspects of the regime in case of an international

85. Marin-Duran & Morgera *supra* n. 68.
86. *Ibid.*
87. House of Commons Environmental Audit Committee: Environmental risks of the Trans-Atlantic Trade & Investment Partnership, available at: http://www.publications.parliament.uk/pa/cm201415/cmselect/cmenvaud/857/857.pdf.
88. Hans Vedder, *Diplomacy by Directive? An Analysis of the International Context of the Emissions Trading Scheme Directive*, in *Beyond the Established Legal Orders* 105 (Malcoln Evans & Panos Koutrakos eds, Hart 2011).

agreement being reached on the issues.[89] Additionally, the inclusion of aviation emissions in the EU ETS[90] is explicitly linked to developments at the international level, providing the possibility for revision of the scheme in case an international agreement is reached on the issue.[91] The explicit structural reference to international developments contributed to triggering negotiations to address aviation emissions within the International Civil Aviation Organisation (ICAO). In response, the EU suspended the application of the Aviation Directive for the time being in light of on-going negotiations. Such techniques further increase the leverage and influence exerted by the EU Member States within multilateral regimes thus advancing action on internationally stagnant issues while ensuring that EU unilateral action does not expose Member States to onerous competitive disadvantages.

Beyond driving multilateral developments, the implications of IEMEIs extend to considerable influence on the policies of third countries and induce engagement of third countries with the EU in regulating controversial environmental problems. Two main elements of IEMEI action, already discussed in section 7.02 are particularly relevant in this regard. First, the extension of EU environmental standards to processes occurring outside EU borders, and second the explicit links to legal developments under multilateral forums and to bilateral agreements to be concluded with the EU. Through these two particular features the EU is protecting the competitive position of EU companies and creates additional avenues of cooperation with third countries. The combination of these legal mechanisms creates reciprocal dynamic interactions between the application of EU environmental standards and developments taking place in third countries as a way of achieving environmental outcomes beyond the EU.

The UK benefits from this form of extraterritorial reach of EU environmental law in influencing third-country policies. For example in areas such as biofuels and timber the UK supports and benefits from such standards.[92] In relation to timber for example, the Timber Regulation is reinforcing the UK's efforts at tackling illegal and unsustainable timber by prohibiting the placing on the market of illegal timber, and imposing a due diligence obligation on traders who place timber on the market for the first time.[93] In this way, the Timber Regulation contributes at levelling the playing field with non-EU competitors. Additionally, it involves constructive ways of engaging producing countries, especially developing countries, in changing their regimes by founding the

89. *Ibid.* Also *see* Scott, *EU Global Action, supra* n. 64.
90. European Parliament and Council Directive 2008/101/EC amending Directive 2003/87/EC so as to include aviation activities in the scheme for greenhouse gas emission allowance trading within the Community, [2009] OJ L8/3.
91. European Parliament and Council Directive 2003/87/EC establishing a scheme for greenhouse gas emission allowance trading within the Community [2003] OJ L275/32, Article 25(a)(2).
92. On the basis of the similar reasoning other EU measures include requirements on organic farming, which allow for imports of organic products when they comply with the same or equivalent standards, thus protecting domestic producers that have to comply with strict standards. *See* Regulation 834/2007 *supra* n. 64 Articles 32 and 33.
93. Regulation 995/2010 *supra* n. 59.

assessment of the legality of timber on the law of the third country and providing the possibility for the conclusion of Voluntary Partnership Agreements with the EU.[94]

As regards biofuels, the sustainability criteria for biofuels, which also apply to biofuels imported from third countries, and specifically those that determine the origin of biofuels, require third-country producers to comply with requirements that have been developed by the EU.[95] Given the absence of an international regime on the issue, the EU platform is crucial in setting standards that may extend to third countries, initiating cooperative dialogue and affecting international efforts. Being a large user, producer and importer itself, with UK companies investing in third countries to produce biofuels to be exported to the EU, the UK has multiple interests at stake in having a say and influencing third countries' policies. Despite EU biofuels policy being flawed in some respects, there exists a comprehensive framework providing for multiple possibilities that the UK could use and benefit from in influencing third-country policies.

Through the practice of 'action-forcing contingent unilateralism'[96] and 'territorial extension'[97] of EU environmental law, the EU and its Member States maximise their efforts at the international level by employing the leverage of the EU as a market and regulator at multiple fronts. Having considered the EU's extensive external environmental action and the position of the UK as a Member State, the discussion shifts to the position of the UK vis-à-vis the rest of the world from outside the EU, starting from how the legal framework would look like after a UK exit.

[B] The Relationship with the World after exit: The UK as an Ex-Member State

Leaving the EU would not free the UK from its obligations towards third countries within international environmental law regimes, as the UK is a party to multilateral environmental agreements alongside the EU. However, EU policies often advance international regimes and impose stricter obligations as well as create further avenues of cooperation with third countries. After exit, the UK would not be involved with these but would rather merely be bound by international instruments without the enforceable and judicable methods of the EU. Additionally, in areas where there is no international agreement the UK would not be bound by EU environmental standards and obligations in its relations with third countries. Therefore, after exit from the EU the UK would be able to embark on its own in cooperating with third countries and would probably have to conclude many bilateral agreements on a variety of issues to

94. The UK has been actively involved in the procedure of VPAs. *See* WWF's EU Government Barometer on Illegal logging and Trade – 2014, available at: http://barometer.wwf.org.uk/what_we_do/government_barometer/scores_by_issues/question.cfm?issue=5.
95. Directive 2009/28/EC *supra* n. 57 Article 17(3), '...The Commission shall determine criteria and geographic ranges ...'. However, compliance with the sustainability criteria is not a compulsory condition for entry into the EU market. *See* Scott, 'The Multi-level Governance of Climate Change' *supra* n. 56.
96. Rajamani & Scott *supra* n. 63.
97. Scott, *Extraterritoriality and Territorial Extension in EU law*, *supra* n. 49.

that regard. The UK would no longer benefit from the extensive external action undertaken by the EU, its leverage on the international scene would probably be reduced and it would not have as much regulatory power to influence and cooperate with third countries in the environmental field. This is linked both to the reduction of the UK's international leverage within environmental forums and to the UK losing its role in influencing the formulation of EU environmental legal measures that extend beyond EU borders and indirectly affect third-country policies.

As has already been stressed, an important reason why the extensive external clout of EU environmental law is important for the UK relates to addressing competitiveness concerns in regulating environmental problems. By promoting the same or equivalent environmental standards to its trading partners through different legal mechanisms and through the 'Brussels effect', the EU ensures that its companies would not be exposed to a competitive disadvantage by having to compete with companies that apply lower standards.[98] In this way, the UK has gained considerable standard-setting power by being part of the EU and its operators are not exposed to competitive disadvantages to which they would have been, if the UK were unilaterally adopting such standards. After exit, the UK's position in the world would be exposed if the UK would unilaterally opt for strict environmental standards without the added 'protection' offered through the EU's external clout. On the other hand the UK could potentially take the opportunity to lower its environmental standards in order to attract more trade and investment. A closer examination of this reveals three important questions.

The first question relates to the *willingness* of the UK to lower its environmental standards. Even though the UK might be willing to lower its standards in relation to some controversial issues on which it has resisted strict EU regulation such as tar sands and shale gas, it would probably not be as eager to lower its standards in other areas. This is due to the long-standing commitment of the UK in certain areas like climate change, the likely public opposition that the UK would be exposed to and the existing industry investment in the UK in complying with EU environmental standards[99] and in promoting low-carbon technologies.

The second question raised concerns the *capacity* of the UK to attract trade and investment by lowering its environmental standards and in particular to deviate trade and investment from the EU in this way. Although the UK is very attractive for foreign investment, its attractiveness might be lowered if the UK would not grant access to the single market of the EU and lowering environmental standards would not necessarily outweigh the benefits of having access to the single market.[100] Furthermore, given the extensive implications of IEMEIs for business practices and policies in third countries,

98. Bradford *supra* n. 50, 39.
99. This argument is particularly made in relation to recent investments made in complying with REACH within the harmonised system, *See* House of Commons Research Paper *supra* n. 44, 62.
100. John Springford & Simon Tilford, *The Great British Trade off, The Impact of Leaving the EU on the UK's Trade and Investment*, Centre for European Reform, January 2014, available at: http://www.cer.org.uk/sites/default/files/publications/attachments/pdf/2014/pb_britishtrade_16jan14-8285.pdf.

it would be relatively difficult for third countries to deviate from the standards to which they have adapted in terms of ensuring compliance with EU standards. Bradford stresses that one of the reasons of occurrence of the 'Brussels effect' is that it makes sense, economically and practically, for non-EU operators to extend EU standards across the board even when not doing business with the EU.[101] If the UK adopts a different regime, would it be able to project such a regime outwards in such a way as to reduce the effect of EU environmental global reach? In this respect, an interesting area is the regulation of trade in GMOs. The UK would have the option to relax its regime and enhance its relationship with GMO producing countries outside the EU context. Even though this might potentially open more avenues of cooperation with GMO producing countries, it should be noted that even if the EU is not the largest GMO export market, its approach has led to a limited Brussels effect being felt by non-EU GMO producers and has restricted transatlantic trade in GMOs.[102] It is doubtful whether by relaxing its own regime the UK would be able to move away from this influence, as multinational companies might still be reluctant to purchase crops that would lead to liabilities under the EU regime.

The third question touches upon the discussion in section 2 and the *ability* of the UK to distance itself from EU policies in the first place. If the EU's environmental action through IEMEIs continues to extensively influence third countries, not only would the UK lose its leverage in influencing its non-EU competitors, but there would also be added pressure for the UK to adapt to new EU standards. In any event, if by maintaining its trading relations with the EU, UK companies would have to comply with EU environmental obligations to a certain extent, this might then induce such companies to expand such standards across their business along similar lines of a 'Brussels effect'.

§7.04 CONCLUSION

Overall, even though the environment might not be the first area that comes to mind when thinking about an exit of the UK from the EU, environmental law is an important regulatory field where non-membership of the EU would have real and visible impacts on the UK's legal and policy framework and in relation to which the UK has largely benefited from being a Member State. The global reach of much of EU environmental law and the far-reaching implications it has on third countries significantly affects the UK. Following exit, the UK would be directly or indirectly bound by extensive EU environmental legislative measures that would be adopted without its contribution. Additionally, the UK would significantly lose leverage in the environmental field internationally, both in influencing international negotiations and in terms of the standard-setting power the UK currently enjoys by being part of the EU's global environmental regulatory power from which both the EU and the UK benefit.

101. Bradford Identifies Legal, Technical and Economic Non-divisibility of such Standards, *supra* n. 50.
102. Bradford, *supra* n. 50.

CHAPTER 8

The EU's External Relations: A Question of Competence

Daniel Denman[*]

For lawyers who take an interest in the EU's external relations, one concept is fundamental: competence. We are forever considering what is within the EU's competence, what is within its exclusive competence, what Member States may do on their own, what they are prevented from doing on their own, and so forth. For us, questions about the EU's external relations are inextricably connected to questions about the breadth of and limits on its external competence.

But it is striking that outside legal circles, whenever there are discussions about the EU's role in the wider world, the word 'competence' rarely appears. Indeed, there is a commonly held view that these technical arguments may impede the ability of the EU and its Member States to act effectively in the wider world. So when the government's 'Review of the Balance of Competences between the United Kingdom and the European Union' published a report on Foreign Policy in July 2013,[1] the executive summary said:

> ... the evidence raised few issues in the balance of competence in non-CFSP areas of the EU's foreign policy, such as international trade and energy... But the evidence argued that the complicated web of different sources of EU foreign policy competence, creates scope for disagreements over interpretation. In particular, contributors noted tensions among the Member States and the EU institutions over how international agreements should be negotiated for the EU and how EU foreign policy should be represented at meetings of other international organisations.
>
> ... Most of the evidence argued that it was strongly in the UK's interests to work through the EU in a number of policy areas. The key benefits included: increased impact from acting in concert with 27 other countries; greater influence with

* The views expressed are personal, and do not necessarily reflect the views of the UK government.
1. https://www.gov.uk/government/uploads/system/uploads/attachment_data/file/227437/2901086_Foreign_Policy_acc.pdf.

> non-EU powers, derived from our position as a leading EU country; the international weight of the EU's single market, including its power to deliver commercially beneficial trade agreements; the reach and magnitude of EU financial instruments, such as for development and economic partnerships; the range and versatility of the EU's tools, as compared with other international organisations; and the EU's perceived political neutrality, which enables it to act in some cases where other countries or international organisations might not.
>
> ...
>
> Again according to the evidence, the comparative disadvantages of operating through the EU are: challenges in formulating strong, clear strategy; uneven leadership; institutional divisions, and a complexity of funding instruments, which can impede implementation of policy; and sometimes slow or ineffective decision-making, due to complicated internal relationships and differing interests. One commentator summarised it thus: 'The issue is not legal competence, but competence in general.' Some argued that the EU is at its most effective when the Member States, in particular the UK, France and Germany, are aligned and driving policy.

It has also been suggested that a more pragmatic attitude to questions of competence would better serve the interests of both the EU and the Member States. Some point to the success of the so-called Team EU in environmental negotiations, where questions about competence take second place to getting the right people in the room to conduct the negotiations. The report by the Balance of Competences Review on Environment and Climate Change, published in February 2014,[2] said:

> The position with regard to negotiating under the UNFCCC and the Kyoto Protocol is slightly different; the Member States negotiate together, as part of 'Team EU.' This team draws on expertise from both the European Commission and Member States and negotiating positions are agreed by consensus in Council Conclusions prior to the main negotiating sessions.
>
> In order to maximise the influence of the EU and its Member States in negotiations under the UNFCCC, a political decision was taken to negotiate as a bloc, with agreement on EU positions reached by consensus among Member States and the European Commission... Members of the Commission and representatives from some Member States work together in a 'Team EU' arrangement.
>
> ... Nearly all respondents who addressed the question considered that it was important for the UK to remain part of 'Team EU' in the negotiations in the UNFCCC...

So why, if at all, do questions about competence matter? There is of course a point of principle: the EU and its institutions should act within the constraints set out in the Treaties, irrespective of the practical implications. That is an entirely legitimate political position for the Member States or the institutions to take. And take it they do. Listed in the annex are a good dozen live or recently concluded cases in the CJEU about external relations that the UK government is either involved in or watching closely. A couple take the form *Member State v. Council;* there are also a *Parliament v. Council*, half a dozen *Commission v. Council*s, and latterly some *Council v. Commission*s. In all of them, the applicant is arguing that its prerogatives have not been respected.

2. https://www.gov.uk/government/uploads/system/uploads/attachment_data/file/284500/environment-climate-change-documents-final-report.pdf.

But it is also incumbent on those of us who advise about these matters to make sure we consider and explain what difference the demarcation of competence makes. This is not a straightforward exercise, which is all the more reason for us to make sure we do it properly. In particular, it can be perilous to rely on short cuts and generalisations.

For instance, a Member State might overestimate the risks to its future autonomy if it should ever allow the EU to act externally on its own behalf. But it is open to question to what extent allowing the EU to exercise its shared competence in respect of one international agreement necessarily limits Member States' freedom of action in relation to other possible agreements. Article 3(2) of the Treaty on the Functioning of the European Union (TFEU) provides that an exercise of shared competence will sometimes prevent the Member States from exercising that competence themselves, but it is not an automatic consequence. The Court has said that working out whether the EU has acquired exclusive competence to enter into an international agreement requires 'a comprehensive and detailed analysis of the relationship between the envisaged international agreement and the EU law in force'.[3] Only once that analysis has been conducted is it possible to assess to what extent the EU's exercise of competence in one instance might limit the Member States' freedom of action in other circumstances.

Conversely, overgeneralisations can lead to overconfidence about the extent to which Member States have protected their position. For example, it is sometimes assumed that the Member States' autonomy in international affairs is sufficiently protected if they become parties to 'mixed' international agreements in their own right, alongside the EU, rather than allowing the EU to participate on its own. There are good practical reasons for having mixed agreements: it is only possible to build a team of experts if the experts are able to attend the negotiations, which is why it is important to Member States that they have a seat at the international table. That is only possible, or at least it is more straightforward, if the Member States are represented in their own right alongside the EU.

However, if the Member States are concerned about protecting their position, it can be rash for them to assume they have done enough just by making sure they are party to a mixed agreement alongside the EU. It is necessary to think more broadly about the legal implications of the agreement, and in particular to think about what might happen after the agreement is concluded and comes into force. In the '*Brown Bears*' case,[4] the CJEU held that it may have jurisdiction to consider the whole of a provision in a mixed agreement if the provision is mostly concerned with matters that are for the EU, even if the provision also covers areas where the Member States rather than the EU are exercising competence. The CJEU's decision seems to have been born of pragmatism rather than strict principle: as Advocate General Sharpston said in her Opinion in the case, the Court appears to have become increasingly frustrated with the EU and the Member States for not being clear which parts of a mixed agreement bind

3. *See* most recently Opinion 1/13, EU:C:2014:2303, paragraph 74.
4. *Lesoochranárske zoskupenie*, C-240/09, EU:C:2011:125.

the EU and which bind the Member States.[5] That lack of clarity is itself perhaps a sign that questions about the demarcation of competence are too often regarded as having been resolved at the end of negotiations, when in fact international agreements continue to have saliency long afterwards.

Then there is the more general concern, referred to in the Balance of Competences report on Foreign Policy, that insisting on theoretical purity may carry a practical cost.

For instance, if I may use a partisan example, it might be thought that the Commission's insistence on preserving the widest possible influence and discretion can be to the detriment of the EU's ability to act effectively on the international stage. Case C-425/13 *Commission v. Council*[6] is a challenge to the procedure by which the Council authorised the Commission to negotiate an emissions trading agreement with Australia. (Ironically, the change in government in Australia makes it very unlikely that this agreement will happen for the foreseeable future.) Under Article 218 TFEU, the Council decides the EU's negotiating position and the Commission represents it. The Commission argues, however, that the Council's role is limited to giving the Commission an initial negotiating mandate and then approving or disapproving the text that the Commission comes back with; in its view, the Council has no role in between. Quite apart from the arguments of legal principle, this seems odd. It must be in the interests of efficient negotiation that the body with the final say about whether the agreement should be concluded is able to tell the negotiator whether it is minded to agree the text that is likely to emerge. It hardly helps the EU's international reputation if the Commission spends years negotiating a detailed text that the Council then rejects, so that the Commission has to return to its international interlocutors with its tail between its legs and start again.

As these examples show, there is not always a clear distinction between questions of principle and questions of pragmatism. But for all the difficulties in disentangling them, it is important that as far as possible we try to do so. It is not for me as an unelected official to say how the balance should be struck between principled concerns about policing the boundaries of competence and a practical desire to achieve the best substantive outcome in the EU's external activities. But it seems to me that however that balance is to be struck, those of us who advise the decision-makers must do what we can to ensure their decisions are based on the clearest possible information.

ANNEX: RECENT AND FORTHCOMING CJEU CASES ON EXTERNAL MATTERS

Parliament v. Council, C-658/11, EU:C:2014:2025. The Court annulled a Council decision on the signature and conclusion of an agreement with Mauritius about the

5. C-240/09, EU:C:2010:436, paragraphs 55–56.
6. *See* now the judgment, given since the text of this chapter was written: *Commission v. Council*, C-425/13, EU:C:2015:483. The CJEU upheld the Commission's action in part, and annulled some elements of the Council's decision.

transfer of suspected pirates, because the Council had not kept the Parliament fully informed during negotiations.

Commission v. Council, C-103/12 and C-165/12, EU:C:2014:2400. The Court annulled a Council decision approving a declaration on granting fishing opportunities in EU waters to Venezuelan vessels. It said the decision should have had a legal basis requiring the Council to obtain the Parliament's consent rather than just consulting it.

Commission v. Council, C-114/12, EU:C:2014:2151. The Court annulled a decision of the Council and the Member States about the negotiation of a Council of Europe Convention on the protection of the rights of broadcasting organisations. It decided the EU had exclusive competence in this area, so the Member States should not participate in the negotiations in their own right.

Commission v. Council, C-137/12, EU:C:2013:675. The Court annulled a Council decision concerning signature of the European Convention on the legal protection of conditional access services. It considered the legal basis for the decision should have been Article 207 TFEU (the common commercial policy), not Article 114 TFEU (the internal market).

Commission v. Council, C-377/12, EU:C:2014:1903. The Court annulled a Council decision concerning signature of the Framework Agreement on Partnership and Cooperation with the Philippines. According to the Court, the whole agreement concerned development cooperation, so the decision should not have included separate legal bases for readmission, transport and the environment.

Germany v. Council, C-399/12, EU:C:2014:2258. The Court dismissed a challenge to the Council decision establishing the EU's position in the International Organisation of Vine and Wine (OIV). The decision had been adopted on the correct legal basis.

Opinion 1/13, EU:C:2014:2303. The Court held that the EU had exclusive competence to accept the accession of a third State to the Hague Convention on the civil aspects of international child abduction.

Opinion 2/13, EU:C:2014:2454. The Court said that the proposed agreement on the accession of the EU to the ECHR was not compatible with the EU Treaties.

UK v. Council, C-81/13, EU:C:2014:2449. The Court dismissed the UK's challenge to the Council decision on the EU's position in the EEC-Turkey Association Council with regard to the adoption of provisions on the coordination of social security systems. It considered the legal basis for the decision was incorrect, but the mistake did not affect the content of the decision or the procedure for its adoption. See also the UK's unsuccessful challenges in *United Kingdom v. Council*, C431/11, EU:C:2013:589, and *United Kingdom v. Council*, C-656/11, EU:C:2014:97.

Commission v. Council, C-28/12, EU:C:2015:282. The Court upheld the Commission's challenge to the Decision of the Council and the Member States on the signature and provisional application of the Air Transport Agreement with the USA, on the grounds that the decisions should have been taken by the Council and the Member States separately.

Commission v. Council, C-425/13, EU:C:2015:483. The Court partially upheld the Commission's challenge to certain provisions of the Council decision authorising the opening of negotiations on linking the EU emissions trading scheme with an emissions trading system in Australia, on the grounds that the decision gave the Council too much control over the conduct of the negotiations.

Council v. Commission, C-660/13, forthcoming. A challenge to the Commission's decision on the signature of the addendum to the memorandum of understanding on a Swiss financial contribution. The Council maintains that the Commission needed the Council's authorisation before signing the addendum.

Council v. Commission, C-73/14, EU:C:2015:663. The Court dismissed the Council's challenge to the Commission's decision to submit a 'Written statement by the European Commission on behalf of the European Union' to the International Tribunal for the Law of the Sea. The Court accepted that the Commission could submit the statement without the Council's approval.

Opinion 1/15, forthcoming. A request by the European Parliament for the Court's opinion about whether the EU-Canada agreement on the transfer of Passenger Name Records is compatible with the EU treaties and the Charter of Fundamental Rights – so a case about substance rather than procedure.

Opinion 2/15, forthcoming. A request by the Commission for the Court's opinion about whether the EU has competence to sign and conclude the Free Trade Agreement with Singapore alone, without the involvement of the Member States.

Opinion 3/15, forthcoming. A request by the Commission for the Court's opinion about whether the EU has exclusive competence to conclude the Marrakesh Treaty to facilitate access to published works for persons who are blind, visually impaired, or otherwise print disabled.

Commission v. Council, C-389/15, forthcoming. A challenge to the Council's decision authorising the opening of negotiations on a revised Lisbon Agreement on Appellations of Origin and Geographical Indications as regards matters falling within the competence of the EU. The Commission maintains that the entire agreement falls within the EU's exclusive competence.

CHAPTER 9

Judicial Protection and the UK's Opt-Outs: Is Britain Alone in the CJEU?

Maria Kendrick

§9.01 INTRODUCTION

Divergence of views on the policy areas and laws of the EU, between its constituent Member States, is not a new phenomenon. Differentiated application of EU laws, put in place by Treaty Protocols, has been a feature of the Union since the Treaty of Rome. There are now various mechanisms of flexible integration in the Union. One of the most significant is that found in Articles 20 TEU and 326 to 334 TFEU, on enhanced cooperation. The constitutional impact of the mechanisms of differentiated integration and their theoretical underpinnings have and continue to be discussed at length in political and legal academic literature. However, what is discussed with comparative infrequency is the fact that these mechanisms are being tested in the judicial forum.

In considering some of the key cases involving the United Kingdom and flexibility mechanisms, this chapter will critique the Court's often haughtily detached decisions, which leave Member States opting out without judicial protection. However, in fairness to the Court, it will also be argued that the Member States do not crown themselves in glory in their use of the system. This chapter will therefore submit that the judicial forum should be used as a system in which the non-participating Member States are protected, as are the mechanisms of flexible integration, and that responsibility lies equally with all of the parties involved; the Member States, the EU institutions and the Court. This would not only be beneficial for the Union in the long run but essential for the preservation of the rule of law through a complete and coherent system of legal remedies and procedures.

§9.02 FLEXIBILITY AND ITS MECHANISMS

Dougan has 'roughly' defined flexibility as 'the possibility that one or more Member States may chose or even be obliged to remain permanently outside the scope of certain activities pursued within the Union's legal framework.'[1] Until the Treaty of Amsterdam, differentiation generally served more as a method to assist in the implementation of European Union law, for instance through minimum harmonisation or transitional measures, rather than as a method by which Member States, in disagreement with the general direction of the European exercise or with whole sections of policy ideology, could choose to 'opt-out' of what was not suited to taste. The drafters of the Amsterdam Treaty included a general mechanism of flexibility between some, but crucially not all, Member States. Gaja identifies two basic reasons for this; first, 'certain Member States are reluctant to take part in some form of integration in a given field while other States wish to pursue it' and the 'second reason stems from the fact that certain States are viewed as incapable of taking part in further integration because of their political, economic or social conditions'.[2] However, due to the offensive nature of, at least, the latter reason, the general mechanism made no distinction between these two reasons.[3] It was thought that reluctant Member States may not want to advertise their reluctance and that incapable Member States would want to disguise their incapacity.[4]

Generally, flexibility is now achieved through a number of mechanisms including: opt-outs or opt-ins, within or outside of various Protocols, enhanced cooperation, derogations, transitional provisions upon accession, abstentions, constructive abstentions and passerelle clauses. It should also be noted that on five occasions prior to the first authorisation of a new enhanced cooperation, the Treaty provisions which apply

1. Michael Dougan, *The Unfinished Business of Enhanced Cooperation: Some Institutional Questions and Their Constitutional Implications* in Andrea Ott and Ellen Vos (eds), *Fifty Years of European Integration: Foundations and Perspectives* (TMC Asser Press 2009) 157.
2. G. Gaja, *How Flexible is Flexibility under the Amsterdam Treaty?,* 35 CMLRev 855, 858 (1998).
3. *Ibid.*, 860.
4. J. Weiler, *Prologue: Amsterdam and the Quest for Constitutional Democracy* in David O'Keefe and Patrick Twomey (eds), *Legal Issues of the Amsterdam Treaty,* (Hart Publishing, Oxford, Portland Oregon 1999) 3. For a navigation around the terminology in this area see A. Stubb, *A Categorization of Differentiated Integration,* 34 JCMS 283 (1996). The Treaty of Nice followed by the Treaty of Lisbon made some changes to the mechanisms of flexibility. The motivations behind the genesis of enhanced cooperation as well as the other mechanisms of flexibility inevitably vary between individual Member States and indeed different political parties within those States. However, one motivation in particular that stands out in the literature is to avoid a deadlock in decision-making within the Council. Some examples of the literature are: Foreword by AG Maduro in Andrea Ott and Ellen Vos (eds), *Fifty Years of European Integration: Foundations and Perspectives* (TMC Asser Press 2009); David O'Keefe and Patrick Twomey, *Legal Issues of the Amsterdam Treaty* (Hart Publishing, Oxford, Portland Oregon 1999) *Introduction by the Editors* XXXV; Michael Dougan, *The Unfinished Business of Enhanced Cooperation: Some Institutional Questions and Their Constitutional Implications* in Andrea Ott and Ellen Vos (eds), *Fifty Years of European Integration: Foundations and Perspectives* (TMC Asser Press 2009); C. D. Ehlermann, *Increased Differentiation or Stronger Uniformity* in T.M.C Asser Instituut *Reforming the Treaty on European Union – The Legal Debate* J. A. Winter, D. M. Curtin, A. E. Kellermann and B. De Witte (eds) (Kluwer Law International, The Hague, Boston, London 1995); H. Wallace, *Flexibility: A tool of integration or a restraint on disintegration?* In Neunreither and Weiner (eds) *Amsterdam and Beyond: Institutional Dynamics and Prospects for Democracy* (Oxford University Press, Oxford 1999).

to allow a Member State to join an established enhanced cooperation which is already in progress were used to permit the United Kingdom to opt-in to an area covered by one of its Protocol opt-outs.[5]

Whatever mechanism used or measure deployed, the Member States adopt an incongruous stance. On the one hand, there is the obtainment of an opt-out and a reliance on those negotiated provisions in order to keep them out of a measure they do not want to be part of or bound by. Whereas, on the other hand, there is the reluctance to be the subject of a forced exclusion and even isolation from an area that they may want to join in, or at least not be shut out of completely, especially in terms of future negotiations and deliberations. It is understandable that Member States, which find themselves in either of these positions, or in both as is regularly the case with the United Kingdom, have been looking to the CJEU for judicial protection.

§9.03 JUDICIAL PROTECTION

There are a number of cases involving the United Kingdom, either as an applicant or intervenor, in actions for annulment of legislative or administrative acts, relating to a flexibility mechanism. As the CJEU is the most significant forum post the enactment of a measure, it is important to ascertain the Courts' approach to such challenges. Moreover, Member States' consequently need to carefully consider their position when litigating in the CJEU in order to ensure that they, and indeed their opt-outs, receive judicial protection. As David Cameron is embarking on a renegotiation mission, the aim of which is to secure further opt-outs for the UK, it is increasingly important that the UK learns to get this right. However, the following cases demonstrate that this is far from easy and the success rate of the UK is mixed.

Most litigious challenges involving flexibility mechanisms relate either to the choice of the legal basis of a measure, the decision authorising an enhanced cooperation, or the exclusion of a non-participating Member State. The latter situation is typically where a Member State does not participate in certain EU competences by virtue of an opt-out, commonly contained in a Protocol, but is prevented or excluded from participation in either current or future measures where the provisions of the Protocol allow for inclusion. Applications for inclusion are subject to procedural and substantive conditions, which become the subject of litigation. Space precludes a detailed analysis of every case and even every recent case. Suffice it for present

5. S. Peers, *Divorce, European Style: the First Authorization of Enhanced Cooperation*, 6(3) E.C.L. Review 339, 343 (2010). Philippart, Edwards and Stubb categorise flexibility in three basic forms: first, 'a general system of rules for any closer cooperation that meets certain preconditions' or as Stubb terms it 'enabling clauses', second, pre-determined flexibility which is 'closer cooperation in particular fields with special arrangements'. Stubb calls this pre-defined flexibility and considers that it covers Protocols and Declarations including Schengen, and third, case-by-case flexibility, which includes constructive abstention and for Philippart and Edwards also opt-outs: E. Philippart and G. Edwards, *The Provisions on Closer Cooperation in the Treaty of Amsterdam: The Politics of Flexibility in the European Union*, 37 JCMS 87, 89 (1999). A. Stubb, *Dealing with Flexibility in the IGC* in Best et al (eds) *Rethinking the European Union: IGC 2000 and Beyond* (EIPA, the Netherlands 2000) 145, 148-150.

purposes to take a pertinent example of each of the three categories identified as illustrative of the Court's position.[6]

[A] Choice of Legal Basis

As it is the choice of the legal basis of a measure which dictates whether a Protocol opt-out applies, if a Member State does not succeed in utilising the EU institutions in their legislative capacity, to have a measure adopted on the basis of a Treaty Article, which allows it to avail itself of its opt-out, that Member State can find itself implementing provisions it thought it had not signed up for. The option for a Member State in this situation is to seek to have the measure annulled. In this respect, it is notable that applicant Member States do not always seek to challenge the detailed contents of the measure itself. It may not mind if the provisions apply to other Member States. Rather, the intention is to insist on the opportunity to opt-out.

A recent report by the House of Lords European Union Committee[7] reviewed the United Kingdom Government's strategic approach to litigating in the CJEU. The review was conducted in relation to the specific opt-out provisions of Protocol 21 of the Treaty of Lisbon.[8] This Protocol applies to the Area of Freedom, Security and Justice. The report details the approach of the Government to challenging the choice of legal basis as: requiring the Protocol opt-out to be considered first and then the aim of the specific contested measure afterwards. In the Government's view the opt-out should be prioritised. The report suggested that the Court's approach is to look at the Protocol and measure in reverse order to that of the UK's view. The Court therefore does not prioritise the Protocol opt-out. In fact, according to the report, the CJEU focuses on the ultimate aim of the measure, without necessarily referring to the Protocol.

The EU institutions themselves have engaged in litigation on this issue. In the relatively recent case of *Commission v. Parliament and Council*[9] the United Kingdom intervened in support of the Defendants[10] in an action to annul Directive 2011/82/EU facilitating the cross-border exchange of information on road safety related traffic offences.[11] The choice of Treaty Article as the legal base was between Article 91(1)(c) TFEU, which specifically provides the basis on which 'measures to improve transport

6. See generally on the role of the European Court of Justice in relation to flexibility: C. Lyons, *Closer Co-operation and the Court of Justice,* in G. de Búrca and J. Scott (eds) *Constitutional Change in the EU: From Uniformity to Flexibility* (Hart Publishing, Oxford, Portland Oregon 2000) 95 to 113.
7. House of Lords European Union Committee, *The UK's opt-in Protocol: implications of the Government's approach,* HL Paper 136, http://www.parliament.uk/business/committees/committees-a-z/lords-select/eu-law-and-institutions-sub-committee-e/news/opt-in-protocol-report-publication/ last (accessed 24 March 2015).
8. Article 1, Protocol (No21) ON THE POSITION OF THE UNITED KINGDOM AND IRELAND IN RESPECT OF THE AREA OF FREEDOM, SECURITY AND JUSTICE, C 326/295.
9. 2014 EUECJ C-43/12, not yet published.
10. The UK was accompanied by a further six intervening Member States, namely Belgium, Ireland, Hungary, Poland, Sweden and the Slovak Republic.
11. Directive 2011/82/EU of the European Parliament and of the Council of 25 October 2011 facilitating the cross-border exchange of information on road safety related traffic offences, OJ 2011 L 288, p. 1.

safety' can be laid down. Alternatively, Article 87(2) TFEU was available as a legal base, covering a range of possible measures for 'the collection, storage, processing, analysis and exchange of relevant information; ... support for the training of staff, and cooperation on the exchange of staff, on equipment and on research into crime-detection; ... common investigation techniques in relation to the detection of serious forms of organised crime.' The Commission had initially proposed Article 91(1)(c) TFEU[12] as the correct legal basis. As the legislative process progressed the Council and European Parliament reached an agreement to replace Article 91(1)(c) TFEU as the legal basis of the Directive with Article 87(2) TFEU. Consequent on this substitution, Protocol Number 21, which provides the UK with an opt-out in respect of the Area of Freedom, Security and Justice then applied. As a result, the UK was deemed not to be taking part in the Directive's adoption nor would it be bound by or subject to its application.

It was argued on behalf of the Commission *inter alia* that because the Directive put in place a mechanism for the exchange of information between the Member States on road safety related traffic offences, whether of an administrative or criminal nature, both the goal and the content of Directive 2011/82 fell within the field of transport policy and consequently Article 91 TFEU. This Article should therefore have been used as the legal basis of the Directive.[13] On the contrary, the Defendants, supported by the intervening Member States, submitted *inter alia* that the precise aims of the Directive are to collect information concerning offences, in order to help deter them, which are measures for which the European Union has competence under Article 87 of the TFEU.[14]

The Court held that the measure could not validly be adopted on the basis of Article 87(2) TFEU.[15] In coming to this conclusion, it applied its familiar test that 'the choice of legal basis for a European Union measure must rest on objective factors that are amenable to judicial review; these include the aim and content of that measure'[16] and then went on to reaffirm that when examining a measure to establish its aim, content and purpose, if a twofold purpose is revealed and 'if one of those is identifiable as the main or predominant purpose or component, whereas the other is merely incidental, that measure must be based on a single legal basis, namely that required by the main or predominant purpose or component'[17]. The Court concluded that the main aim of the Directive was the improvement of road safety,[18] which the Court considered a 'prime objective'[19] of the transport policy of the European Union. The Court admitted

12. The proposal was actually made under Article 71(1)(c) EC however the Treaty of Lisbon numbered the Article 91(1)(c) and as the Court refers to the latter numbering throughout its judgment for ease of reference this chapter will use the Lisbon numbering.
13. C-43/12 paras 19 to 20.
14. C-43/12 para. 27.
15. C-43/12 para. 50.
16. C-43/12 para. 29 citing case C411/06 *Commission v. Parliament and Council* EU:C:2009:518, para. 45 and case C130/10 *Parliament v. Council* EU:C:2012:472, para. 42 and the case-law cited.
17. C-43/12 para. 30 citing case C137/12 *Commission v. Council* EU:C:2013:675, para. 53 and the case-law cited.
18. C-43/12 para.36.
19. *Ibid.*

that the Directive does establish a system for the cross-border exchange of information, but as that system related to information on the subject of road safety related traffic offences, the prime objective of this system was to enable the European Union to pursue the goal of improving road safety.[20]

The Court also looked at its previous interpretations of Article 91(1)(c) TFEU and what provisions had been adopted on the basis of that Article. It considered that measures aimed at improving road safety and transport safety which, in its opinion included the Directive, is apt to be adopted under Article 91(1)(c) TFEU.[21] In light of the similarly interpretive exercise it had conducted in relation to Article 87(2), the Court had satisfied itself that this was a stable interpretation.[22]

The Court consequently deprived the United Kingdom of the opportunity to avail itself of its Protocol 21 opt-out. It therefore appears, from the perspective of the United Kingdom, that in this instance protection of its opt-out was actually provided by the Council and European Parliament. At least this can be said to have been the position initially, by virtue of their action in changing the legal basis from Article 91(1)(c) TFEU to Article 87(2) TFEU. When it came to litigation, judicial protection was not, from the point of view of the Defendants and the intervening Member States, available.

This judgment came much, as the recent House of Lords report documents, to the dissatisfaction of the then UK Coalition Government, which suggested that despite its loss it would not change its approach in the CJEU.[23] According to Theresa May MP, the Court was, and continues to be, silent as to the scope of Protocol 21 and therefore the decision does not directly impact on or change the then Government's policy on its future strategy for litigating in regards to its opt-out. However, the report and the expert evidence provided to the Committee disagreed and confirmed essentially that whether or not the opt-out can be used is a matter of judicial interpretation as to the aim and predominant purpose of the relevant measure.

Given the opaque nature of the Treaty, and the fact that the parties to this case were the institutions themselves, if not even they can agree on the predominant purpose of a measure, what hope is there for the Member States? It may actually be

---

20. C-43/12 para. 37.
21. C-43/12 paras 43 and 44 referring to joined cases C184/02 and C223/02 *Spain and Finland v. Parliament and Council* EU:C:2004:497, para. 30.
22. C-43/12 para. 48.
23. Theresa May MP's answer, when giving evidence, in response to question 49 as to the impact of the case law on Title V on the Government's opt-in policy 'in none of the decisions on *Turkey*, the *Philippines*, *road safety*, *Swiss social security* and *conditional access* did the court rule on whether JHA content alone could trigger the opt-in or whether incidental JHA content requires a JHA legal base. It has singularly so far avoided addressing what we feel is the fundamental issue of the correct interpretation of Protocol 21. ... it may very well be that there is some difference of opinion and that some members of the court actually believe that Protocol 21 is not an exception but is actually part of the founding principles. I am not party to their decisions or why they have come to this decision, but the fact that they have not addressed this Protocol 21 issue suggests to me that there may be some discussion, or they feel there is an arguable point, about the correct interpretation of Protocol 21.' House of Lords European Union Committee Report, para. 162 and fn 157, oral evidence available at http://data.parliament.uk/writtenevidence/committeeevidence.svc/evidencedocument/eu-justice-institutions-and-consumer-protection-subcommittee/the-uks-optin-and-international-agreements/oral/17552.html (last accessed 31 March 2015).

hoped that the change of Government in the UK may see a wiser, less naïve approach to operating in the judicial forum. UK Recognition that the judges have their own view on things and that a dogmatic adherence to what has proven to be an unsuccessful policy could leave you alone in the CJEU, without being able to use your opt-out, would be a good start.

[B] Decisions Authorising Enhanced Cooperation

It must be noted that the enhanced cooperation provisions contained in the Lisbon Treaty provide for two stages in the operation of the mechanism. First, it is necessary for the Member States that wish to embark on cooperation in a given area to obtain a decision authorising usage of the mechanism. The substantive and procedural hurdles for obtaining authorisation include: that there are at least nine Member States wishing to participate; the non-participating Member States should be able to join later i.e. that a spirit of openness applies to operation of the mechanism; that the authorising decision be adopted by the Council as a last resort (when it has established that the objectives of such a cooperation cannot be attained within a reasonable period by the Union as a whole); that the enhanced cooperation shall reinforce the process of integration; and the request for authorisation does not relate to one of the Union's exclusive competences.[24] Once authorisation has been granted, on which the vote in Council referred to by Article 20(2) TEU and Article 329(1) TFEU is by qualified majority of all Member States, whether participants or non-participants, the second stage in the process is to adopt measures that implement the subject matter of the specific cooperation. The decision authorising the enhanced cooperation is therefore crucial, because it dictates which Member States are excluded and which are included in the cooperation. This is not only of paramount importance to those Member States that wish to embark on further integration in a specific policy area, but as the next case under analysis demonstrates, it has significant consequences for those Member States which do not, or cannot, participate.

Despite its reputation for being a reluctant participant, the United Kingdom has shown willing to engage in enhanced cooperation. In *Spain and Italy v. Council* and *Italy v. Council*[25] the United Kingdom was among the initial twelve Member States that wished to engage in enhanced cooperation on the subject of unitary patent protection. Although the UK was included in the enhanced cooperation, the case is still important for the UK because it shows the attitude of the Court to protection of non-participants to enhanced cooperation, which could equally apply to the UK in another instance. The specific background to the case is thus: twelve Member States, namely, Denmark, Germany, Estonia, France, Lithuania, Luxembourg, the Netherlands, Poland, Slovenia, Finland, Sweden and the United Kingdom, initially addressed requests to the Commission, by letters dated 7, 8 and 13 December 2010, indicating that they wished to establish enhanced cooperation between themselves in the area of the creation of

24. Article 20 (1) and (2) TEU, supplemented and supported by Articles 326 to 334 TFEU.
25. 2013 EUECJ Joined cases C-274/11 and C-295/11. This chapter will refer to the lead case, *Spain and Italy v. Council* C-274/11 published in the electronic Reports of Cases.

unitary patent protection. The request was submitted on the basis of the existing proposals, which had been supported by the same Member States during negotiations, but which were not proving successful during the legislative procedure involving the whole of the Union. They asked the Commission to submit a proposal to the Council to that end. In the meantime, thirteen more Member States, namely, Belgium, Bulgaria, the Czech Republic, Ireland, Greece, Cyprus, Latvia, Hungary, Malta, Austria, Portugal, Romania and Slovakia, wrote to the Commission indicating that they also wished to participate in the envisaged enhanced cooperation. Spain and Italy, were the two Member States which argued, in two joined cases challenging the Council's Decision to authorise enhanced cooperation, that they were being excluded because they were not able to adopt the language provisions proposed.[26] The United Kingdom, along with nine other Member States, the European Parliament and the Commission, intervened in support of the Council.

There were four main pleadings[27] submitted on behalf of the applicant Member States: first, lack of competence, second, misuse of power, third, what the applicants termed 'infringement of an essential procedural requirement' whereas the Court termed it 'breach of a condition that a decision authorising enhanced cooperation must be adopted as a last resort',[28] and fourth, infringement of the Treaty and any rule of law relating to its application. Taking the first argument, the applicants submitted that to provide uniform protection of intellectual property rights, as referred to in Article 118 TFEU, fell within the exclusive competence of the Union, as provided for in Article 3(1)(b) TFEU, concerning 'the establishing of the competition rules necessary for the functioning of the internal market'. Therefore, the Council lacked competence to authorise the enhanced cooperation in question, because authorisation cannot be granted in relation to an exclusive competence.[29] Italy added that Articles 3 to 6 TFEU do no more than set out a non-binding classification of the spheres of the Union's competences. Therefore, it would be permissible for the Court to treat as exclusive the competences conferred by Article 118 TFEU without relying on the list in Article 3(1) TFEU.[30]

Contrarily, the Council, with the intervenors in support, argued that the rules governing intellectual property fall within the ambit of the internal market, in the sphere of which the Union enjoys a shared competence under Article 4(2)(a) TFEU.[31] The Council therefore maintained that it had competence to authorise the enhanced cooperation proposed.

The Court rejected the argument of the non-participating Member States and approached its determination as to whether those competences were non-exclusive,

26. Council Decision 2011/167/EU of 10 March 2011, authorising enhanced cooperation in the area of the creation of unitary patent protection including language provisions, OJ 2011 L76, p. 53.
27. An additional plea was numbered the fifth plea after the cases were joined and was considered by the Court. Space precludes consideration of this plea. This article will focus on the four most pertinent.
28. C-274/11 para. 9.
29. C-274/11 and C-295/11 paras 10 to 11.
30. *Ibid.* para. 14.
31. *Ibid.* para. 15.

and therefore may be exercised by way of enhanced cooperation, by considering the first paragraph of Article 118 TFEU. The Court decided that competence to create European intellectual property rights and to set up centralised authorisation, coordination and supervision arrangements were conferred by the first paragraph of Article 118 TFEU. As a result, where the second paragraph of that Article provides for the establishment of language arrangements for those rights, the competence conferred is as provided by the first paragraph of that Article. The two are 'closely bound up' together.[32] As those competences fall within the ambit of the functioning of the internal market, the Court held that in accordance with Article 4(2) TFEU, competence shared between the Union and the Member States applies to, *inter alia*, the area of the internal market. Under Article 2(6) TFEU, the scope of, and arrangements for, exercising the Union's competences are to be determined by the provisions of the Treaties relating to each area and that for 'competition rules necessary for the functioning of the internal market' determination is by Part Three, Title VII, Chapter 1 of the TFEU, in particular in Articles 101 TFEU to 109 TFEU. The court was keen to avoid unduly extending the scope of Article 3(1)(b) TFEU and so concluded that the competences conferred by Article 118 TFEU fall within an area of shared competences for the purpose of Article 4(2) TFEU and are non-exclusive for the purpose of the enhanced cooperation mechanism.[33]

As to the second argument of misuse of power on the part of the Council, it was submitted on behalf of Spain and Italy that all enhanced cooperations must contribute to the process of integration. In this case, however, they maintained that the true object of the contested decision was not to achieve integration but to exclude Spain and Italy from the negotiations on the issue of the language arrangements for the unitary patent. Thus, depriving them of their right conferred by the second paragraph of Article 118 TFEU. The applicants alleged that the enhanced cooperation procedure had been used to keep Member States out of difficult negotiations and to circumvent the requirement of unanimity. They considered that this was an incorrect use of the enhanced cooperation procedure, which was actually designed to be used when one or more Member States is or are not yet ready to take part in the entirety of a legislative action of the Union.[34] In response, the Council submitted that if Spain and Italy do not play a part in this enhanced cooperation, it is because they have refused to do so and not because they have been kept out of negotiations. The Council pointed out that Recital 16 in the preamble to the contested decision stresses that creating protection by a unitary patent would promote the objectives of the Union and strengthen the process of integration. The parties intervening in support of the Council concurred with this view. They emphasised that those areas that require unanimity are by no means excluded from the spheres in which it is permissible for enhanced cooperation to be established. It is also a 'procedure that makes it possible to overcome the problems

32. *Ibid.* paras 16 to 26.
33. *Ibid.* paras 16 to 26.
34. *Ibid.* paras 27 to 29.

relating to blocking minorities'.[35] It was perhaps not that wise for the UK to point out this advantage.

The Court held[36] that the Articles which provide for the enhanced cooperation mechanism do not proscribe use of enhanced cooperation in areas where a competence must be exercised unanimously. Nor does the requirement that the enhanced cooperation mechanism be used as a last resort relate solely to instances where one or more Member States is simply not ready to participate. There are many valid and applicable reasons why the provision 'the objectives of such cooperation cannot be attained within a reasonable period by the Union as a whole' can occur.[37]

The Court therefore held in relation to this plea that the Council's decision was certainly not an attempt to circumvent the unanimity requirement provided for in Article 118 TFEU nor an attempt to exclude Spain and Italy as the Member States which did not join in making the request for authorisation of enhanced cooperation. The argument that there had been misuse of power by the Council was deemed to be unfounded, the Court actually found that the Council had contributed to the process of integration. Spain and Italy had yet another argument rejected.[38]

With regard to the third pleading, it was submitted that the Council had failed to give reasons, providing instead an 'excessively laconic explanation ... why the Council considers the conditions laid down by the ... Treaties in the sphere of enhanced cooperation have been satisfied'.[39] The Court re-phrased this pleading to essentially be an argument that the Council had not properly satisfied itself that the condition that enhanced cooperation can only be authorised as a last resort had been fulfilled, this had been demonstrated by the Council's poor explanation in this regard, and there had therefore been a breach of the condition laid down in Article 20(2) TEU. However, the Court decided that the Council is the best placed of all the institutions to assess the state of negotiations as to whether the condition relating to adoption of a decision as a last resort had been satisfied. Such decisions would consequently only be subject to a limited examination by the Court.[40] In this instance, the Court was satisfied that, having regard to the applicants' participation in the negotiations and to the detailed description of the fruitless stages before the contested decision became the subject of the enhanced cooperation, it cannot be concluded that the decision was vitiated by any failure to state reasons capable of resulting in its annulment.[41] The Council and the intervening Member States had successfully maintained an insistence that deadlock had been reached in the negotiations.

Finally, Spain and Italy argued that there had been an infringement of four separate Articles of the Treaties: Article 20(1) TEU, Article 118 TFEU, Article 326, second paragraph, TFEU and Article 327 TFEU. For present purposes and for reasons of space, this chapter will concentrate on those arguments which on the one hand,

35. *Ibid.* para 32 see generally paras 27 to 32.
36. *Ibid.* para. 33 citing C442/04 *Spain v. Council* [1998] ECR I3517, para. 49.
37. *Ibid.* para. 36.
38. *Ibid.* paras 33 to 41.
39. *Ibid.* para. 45.
40. *Ibid.* paras 47 to 58.
41. *Ibid.* paras 52, 53 and 58.

approach the issues of integration and uniformity, and on the other hand, consider most specifically the position of a non-participating Member State to an enhanced cooperation. In relation to the former, according to Spain and Italy, the Council was wrong to consider that the proposed enhanced cooperation would create a higher level of integration.[42] They disagreed with the Council's and the intervening Member States' observation that whereas both national patents and European patents validated in one Member State or more confer only national protection, the unitary patent contemplated by the enhanced cooperation would at least give undertakings uniform protection in twenty five Member States. The Court however was not convinced by Spain and Italy. It accepted that an enhanced cooperation would at least make it possible to draw closer to the objective of securing uniformity in the internal market therefore resulting in furtherance of integration.[43] It is unsurprising that the Court sided with the Council and the participating Member States on this point as it is hardly likely to adjudicate essentially against the express provisions of the Treaty. But where does this leave the non-participant Member States if they do not feel able to join in at a later date?

In citing Article 327 TFEU, the non-participating Member States complained that their rights had been infringed. They argued that, contrary to that Article, the enhanced cooperation did not respect their rights as non-participating Member States because their right to take part in the enhanced cooperation in future was compromised as they were unable to accept the terms of the proposed measure.[44] The response from the Council and the intervening Member States was to reiterate that the Treaty makes it quite possible for the non-participating States to join the enhanced cooperation later, consequently rendering this argument otiose.[45] The Court again decided not to uphold the application. According to Article 327 TFEU, the Court held, even if those taking part in the cooperation prescribe rules with which those non-participating States would not agree if they did take part in it, this 'does not render ineffective the opportunity for non-participating Member States of joining in the enhanced cooperation'.[46]

The Court appears to err on the side of protecting those involved in the enhanced cooperation rather than the non-participants, concluding that the non-participants are protected by virtue of the fact that they can apply to join the enhanced cooperation in future, regardless of how difficult or even impossible this may be. This has obvious consequences for uniformity and integration in the Union. However, this chapter's stance is that the numerous opt-outs and exceptions to participation in the Union's competences, granted not just to the UK, demonstrate that absolute uniformity is not required for the Union to function. Furthermore, the Treaty provisions and the Court's judgment ring true if the integration objective can actually be progressed by allowing a way around deadlock in negotiations in contentious policy sectors as a 'last resort'.

However much this particular judgment may have been good news for the United Kingdom, it does indicate that should they have been on the other side of the litigation

42. *Ibid.* para. 60.
43. *Ibid.* paras 61 and 63.
44. *Ibid.* para. 79.
45. *Ibid.* para. 80.
46. *Ibid.* paras 81 to 83.

they may have felt like a 'second class' Member State. Criticism of the judgment in a manner none too favourable from the perspective of judicial protection has been made on the basis that the 'last resort' requirement 'which should be considered satisfied only when it is impossible to adopt common legislation within the foreseeable future'[47] was actually signalled by the Court to be in essence a political assessment due to the Court's acceptance that it is the Council which is the best placed to decide if the requirement has been met with 'only to a limited degree of external judicial scrutiny'.[48] This may leave non-participating Member States unprotected by the Court and therefore exposed.

[C] Exclusion of a Non-participating Member State

The exclusion of a non-participating Member State can occur mainly in two instances, either the State is not participating in an enhanced cooperation, as discussed in the section above, or the operation of a long standing opt-out contained in a Protocol means that the Member State does not participate in an area of EU policy. The United Kingdom has several such Protocols, including one in relation to the Schengen acquis. The Schengen provisions, initially an example of intergovernmental cooperation, were incorporated into the Union legal order by the Treaty of Amsterdam. Intergovernmental agreements were not in the past untypical as a way of achieving flexibility, and / or, as Tuytschaever states, as a way of preventing a deadlock in decision making on politically sensitive policy areas within the Union:

> On the most general level, there is of course the fact that the ... issues ... go to the heart of national sovereignty. Practice shows beyond any reasonable doubt that this increases the sensitivity of the delegations and results in a stronger adherence to their individual negotiating positions. This may be an obstacle to establishing an overall vision of how to deal with issues and reduce negotiations in a quagmire of detail. Or, as it has done in the past, it may ultimately force a limited number of Member States to abandon any hope of attaining a workable compromise in the field and to start working together on an intergovernmental basis (which some of them did by means of the Schengen Agreement).[49]

The UK's Schengen Protocol does make it possible for the UK to participate in the policy area covered by its opt-out, but only in compliance with the procedure laid down in the Protocol, specifically Articles 4 and 5. *United Kingdom v. Council*[50] concerned an action for annulment by the UK of Council Regulation 2252/2004 on standards for security features and biometrics in passports and travel documents issued by Member States.[51] The UK argued that it had been refused permission by the Council to

---

47. Editorial Comments, *What do we want? 'Flexibility! Sort-of ...' When do we want it? 'Now! Maybe...'*, 50 CMLRev 673, 676-7 (2013).
48. *Ibid.*
49. F. Tuytschaever, *Differentiation in European Union Law* (Hart Publishing Oxford, Portland Oregon 1999) 74.
50. 2007 EUECJ C-137/05 [2007] ECR I-11593.
51. Council Regulation (EC) No 2252/2004 of 13 December 2004 on standards for security features and biometrics in passports and travel documents issued by Member States OJ 2004 L 385, p. 1.

participate in the adoption of the measure and that the Council's refusal equated to a breach of Article 5 of the Schengen Protocol.[52] The Council's submissions in response were very illuminating in terms of outlining its perspective, in this instance on Schengen, but which could equally in theory be applied to almost any opt-out regime within the Union. It submitted that the objective of Article 5, is not to confer a right to participate on the UK, but to reassure the Member States participating in the Schengen acquis that their measures will not be jeopardised by the reluctance of other Member States to join in. The Council submitted further that the interpretation of Article 5(1) proposed by the United Kingdom would deprive the vetting procedure in Article 4 of the protocol of its effectiveness, because a Member State which had not been successful in participating by utilising Article 4 of the Schengen Protocol could then try again by using the procedure contained in Article 5. Consequently 'the integrity of the Schengen acquis would … no longer be guaranteed'.[53]

The Court held in favour of the Council to the exclusion of the UK. The question the Court had to answer was whether the content and aim of Regulation 2252/2004, was to build upon the Schengen acquis, or not, as this would dictate whether the UK could avail itself of a right to participate. The Court concluded that because the Regulation has the objective of combating fraud with travel documents and has sought to achieve this by harmonising and improving minimum security standards, it categorised the measure as one from which the United Kingdom was to be excluded from participating.[54] In a rather damning commentary on the Court's judgment in this case,[55] Chalmers has criticised the Court's decision to uphold the Council's exclusion of the United Kingdom as being 'difficult to give due credit to the legal incoherence, intellectual poverty and political myopia'[56] of the judgment. Whilst the present writer considers this rather strong, it does highlight the difficulty inherent in trying to assimilate the Court's approach. This is particularly so with regard to the position of the non-participating Member States, which rely on the Court for their inclusion in the deliberations on the adoption of acts. Therefore, planning their own policies, including litigation policies, in the light of the Court's approach. The present writer does consider the judgment a disappointing one because the Court at one point in the judgment acknowledges that the classification of Regulation No 2252/2004 as a measure developing provisions of the Schengen acquis will have a direct effect on the right of the

52. C-137/05 see especially paras 32 to 36.
53. *Ibid.* paras 37 and 38.
54. C-137/05 and J. J. Rijpma, Case note, *Case C-77/05, United Kingdom v. Council, Judgment of the Grand Chamber of 18 December 2007, not yet reported, and Case C-137/05, United Kingdom v. Council, Judgment of the Grand Chamber of 18 December 2007, not yet reported,* 45 CMLRev 835, 844 (2008).
55. And case C-77/05 [2007] ECR I-11459 decided by the Court on the same day. Space precludes separate analysis of this case in this chapter however as the reasoning of the judgments are similar pertinent points from both judgments have effectively been considered.
56. D. Chalmers, *Editorial. Cut off from Europe – the fog surrounding Luxembourg,* 33(2) ELJ 135, 136 (2008). For an alternative prediction as to the Court's reasoning particularly in enhanced cooperation cases see F. Amtenbrink and D. Kochenov, *Towards a More Flexible Approach to Enhanced Cooperation,* in Andrea Ott and Ellen Vos (eds), *Fifty Years of European Integration: Foundations and Perspectives* (TMC Asser Press 2009) especially 198.

UK to participate[57] then continues to exclude the UK in a judgment that is sparse in detail and reasoning. Chalmers summarises the effect this could have on integration: '[In the Lisbon Treaty] all 27 member States agreed to a series of unilateral Protocols and Declarations so that there is barely a Member State who adheres just to the Treaty. ... The Court's rulings attach unanticipated penalties to asymmetric integration that are quite at odds with the tenor of these reforms.'[58] This judgment is disappointing from the UK's point of view because it has been historically difficult to get the UK to participate in some areas of EU policy. Therefore, on the occasions where the UK not only agrees to participate but does so in an area where it has already opted out, it would have been invaluable to have the court's assistance, if not protection, to ensure the UK is included in these circumstances.

Moreover, flexible arrangements were required in order to achieve the incorporation of Schengen into the union legal order due to political sensitivities, in fact it was 'only possible due to the fact that a number of Member States were granted important opt-ins and opt-outs.'[59] The Court's position in this evolution was touched upon by Advocate General Trstenjak in *United Kingdom v. Council,*[60] the judgment which was decided on the same day as the present case under discussion. The Advocate General stated that 'the Court is called on to interpret protocols which relate in particular to closer cooperation. The traditional concept of European integration flows from the notion of unity of integration, that is to say the creation of uniform rules that are valid in all the Member States.'[61] However, the Advocate General outlines that what she perceives are the causes of a change from uniformity to flexibility in integration are essentially extensions of competences and enlargements of the Union, 'which involve greater heterogeneity of structures and interests. Enhanced cooperation is a legal expression of the balancing exercise between making the Union wider and making it deeper.'[62] Therefore, judicial protection in cases where the protocols regulate the position of non-participating Member States is crucial in encouraging integration within the Union legal order, not just from the perspective of the United Kingdom but for all Member States.

Contrary to the progressive movement of the Union towards flexible integration and therefore flexible accommodation of the differing views of the Member States, the Court's judgment indicates an approach which is not sufficiently protective of the non-participatory Member States. Rather, Rijpma considers that the Court concluded that the exclusion of the UK was justified possibly because it 'wanted to bring back into focus the underlying rationale of the Schengen *acquis*, namely the free movement of EU citizens as part of the wider single market project. ... The Court in so doing sent out a

57. C-137/05 para. 55.
58. D. Chalmers, *Editorial. Cut off from Europe – the fog surrounding Luxembourg,* 33(2) ELJ 135, 136 (2008).
59. J. J. Rijpma, Case note, *Case C-77/05, United Kingdom v. Council, Judgment of the Grand Chamber of 18 December 2007, not yet reported, and Case C-137/05, United Kingdom v. Council, Judgment of the Grand Chamber of 18 December 2007, not yet reported,* 45 CMLRev 835, 835 (2008).
60. C-77/05.
61. C-77/05 Opinion of AG Trstenjak para. 83.
62. *Ibid.*

clear signal disapproving of a "pick and choose" approach regarding the Schengen *acquis*.'[63]

The consequential impact of these judgments on the Union as a whole and as a group of Member States combining efforts in a joint enterprise is unfortunate in its negativity. It could be argued in favour of the United Kingdom's inclusion that it would reinforce solidarity between Member States, solidarity being a broader value underpinning Member States' cooperation in general. On the basis that the Protocols and enhanced cooperation authorisations referred to in the above analysed cases are actually integrative mechanisms, not least because the Lisbon Treaty states as such, but also by acting as a safety valve for those Member States that want to join in with most, but not all, of the European project, the fact that these judgments evidence insufficient judicial protection for the non-participant Member States when availing themselves of the provisions negotiated importantly as part of or annexed to the Treaty itself, is unfortunate to say the least. It is this that could have a detrimental effect on solidarity in the Union, not the existence of opt-outs. Furthermore, as it seems to be difficult to confidently ascertain in such a complex situation when a State can avail itself of an opt-out, and even an opt-in, because it is not sufficiently certain or predictable as to when judicial protection will be engaged, the consequence this may have on the continued membership of the States involved is a regrettably if not irresponsibly negative one.

There are also constitutional ramifications for the Union legal order arising from the Court's approach. In the momentous *Les Verts* judgment it was expressed that the Treaty is the basic constitutional charter,[64] according to which the Court must function. Concomitant with this statement is the principle that the Union is based on the rule of law, therefore each actor – the Union institutions, the Member States and the CJEU – is responsible for the inviolability of the system, that is the complete and comprehensive system of legal remedies and procedures. How does this apply to mechanisms of flexibility? There should not be inequality in the protection afforded by the Court to the Member States, whether fully participating, opting out or opting back in again, or to the institutions in those circumstances. Lenaerts identifies that one of the fundamental elements of *Les Verts* is the fact that 'it fell to the Court of Justice to uphold the observance of equal judicial protection in the Community legal order notwithstanding the Member States' lack of consensus on the matter'.[65] In that specific case the protection was of the European Parliament, which was not provided with standing in the Single European Act. This chapter submits that the principle similarly applies to other EU institutions and the Member States. The operation of an opt-out should not

63. J. J. Rijpma, Case note, *Case C-77/05, United Kingdom v. Council, Judgment of the Grand Chamber of 18 December 2007, not yet reported, and Case C-137/05, United Kingdom v. Council, Judgment of the Grand Chamber of 18 December 2007, not yet reported,* 45 CMLRev 835, 836 (2008).
64. Case 294/83 *Parti écologiste 'Les Verts' v. European Parliament* [1986] ECR 1339, para. 23.
65. Koen Lenaerts, *The Basic Constitutional Charter of a Community Based on the Rule of Law,* in Maduro and Azoulai (eds) *The Past and Future of EU Law: The Classics of EU Law Revisited on the 50th Anniversary of the Rome Treaty,* Hart Publishing, Oxford and Portland, Oregon 2010, p. 297.

divest a non-participating Member State of its protection. Of course this does not dilute the Member States' responsibility. It is essential for the preservation of the rule of law within the Union for which judicial protection is a requisite that each actor plays their part. However, in order to ensure a coherent and complete system so that 'in effect, the court verifies that the institutions are acting in conformity with the rules of the Treaty ... and that the proper legal basis setting forth the decision-making procedure to be followed in the adoption of such measures has been used'[66] and to avoid a lacuna, which compromises the completeness of the system, judicial protection and equality before the court must apply not just to individuals but also to non-participating Member States. The constitutional significance of this system cannot be overstated. For the CJEU to not play its part, protecting the Member States when they utilise the flexibility mechanisms, would compromise the coherence of the system and consequently preservation of the rule of law in the Union.[67]

§9.04 STAYING IN, EVEN WHEN NOT OPTING IN

Despite the criticism of the Court's judgments discussed in this chapter, it ought to be acknowledged that the UK has benefitted from the outcome of some of the judgments, even if they would not necessarily have been pleased had they been supporting the opposing side. This highlights the fact that in the Union system judicial protection in the CJEU is not a one way street. The onus is not solely on the Court. Member States are also responsible for ensuring that they use the system well in order to obtain judicial protection. The practical reality is that after the recent UK general election, which saw a majority Conservative government elected, David Cameron is embarking on a mission to negotiate more British opt-outs. Consequently, the more opt-outs the UK has, the more proficient it needs to become at utilising the system of judicial protection, because whether the UK government likes it or not, they will inevitably become more reliant on it.

Becoming proficient at utilising the judicial protection available in the CJEU is still preferable to opting to leave the Union altogether. For example, there has been a long standing provision in the Treaty that all Members of the Council may participate in the deliberations over a legislative measure which is part of an enhanced cooperation.[68] It is doubtful that a Member State that wished to withdraw its membership would be assured of such involvement in any policy area negotiations, especially those part of a flexibility arrangement. European Union law is pervasive and therefore it would be counter-productive for the United Kingdom to leave a position from which there is an opportunity to influence its direction. An Article 50 TEU negotiated withdrawal package could see the UK lose control and influence over the laws it would still inevitably be bound by through trading and generally operating in the EU sphere.

66. *Ibid.* p. 298 and further see T. Tridimas *The General Principles of EU Law* Second Edition, Oxford EU Law Library, Oxford University Press 2006.
67. Further on coherence see Case C-461/03 *Gaston Schul Douane-expediteur BV* [2005] ECR I-10513.
68. Presently in Article 330 TFEU and Article 20(3) TEU.

There would be a real risk of reform packages and EU laws being presented as a *fait accompli*. At least flexibility within the Union framework, through the enhanced cooperation provisions, means that all Member States can be closely involved in the policy processes,[69] extra-Union flexibility is not necessarily a desirable model.

In any event, an Article 50 TEU withdrawal would inevitably see the United Kingdom negotiate a package deal with the rest of the Union over the mass of laws and administrative provisions that already regulate its relations. To make this withdrawal package workable for all parties there would need to be access to the CJEU. For the UK to be able to litigate over the arrangements and agreements reached through both the withdrawal negotiations and the operation of future dealings with the EU, it would need to be provided with legal standing before the Court. The UK would consequently be equally reliant on CJEU judicial protection of its rights and interests whether or not it chooses to withdraw from the Union. Whatever the arrangement, the CJEU would not lose its significance.

Perhaps, in the humble suggestion of the present writer, the UK government may benefit from a greater concentration on putting itself in the Court's shoes. The Secretary of State for Foreign and Commonwealth Affairs has recently stated that any renegotiation package David Cameron achieves will probably require Treaty change in order to protect it from an adverse judgment in the CJEU.[70] Working with rather than battling against the system would surely be preferable to the political difficulties associated with obtaining agreement to change the Treaty or receiving adverse judgments.

The consequence of not using the system of judicial protection well enough can be illustrated by *Spain v. Council*,[71] the Grand Chamber judgment delivered on 5 May 2015, which is the action to annul the implementing enhanced cooperation Regulation[72] following on from the *Spain and Italy v. Council*[73] challenge to the authorisation decision for enhanced cooperation on unitary patent protection, discussed above. It will be recalled that Spain was unsuccessful on numerous grounds in challenging the authorisation decision and similarly submitted a comparably long list of pleadings, including: infringement of the principle of non-discrimination on the ground of language; infringement of the principles set out in the *Meroni* judgment; lack of legal basis for Article 4 of the contested regulation; infringement of the principle of legal certainty; and infringement of the principle of the autonomy of EU law. Again each pleading was rejected by the Court, which is not at all surprising. Concerns about infringements of the principle of non-discrimination, on the ground of language or otherwise, in relation to the operation of the enhanced cooperation mechanism have been alleviated by the Court and recognised by academia some years ago. Arguments

69. Editorial Comments, *What do we want? 'Flexibility! Sort-of ...' When do we want it? 'Now! Maybe...'*, 50 CMLRev 673, 679 (2013). Also see S. Peers, *Divorce, European Style: the First Authorization of Enhanced Cooperation*, 6(3) E.C.L. Review 339, 357 (2010).
70. BBC Andrew Marr Show, Sunday 7 June 2015.
71. C-147/13 *Spain v. Council* not yet reported.
72. Council Regulation (EU) No 1260/2012 of 17 December 2012 implementing enhanced cooperation in the area of the creation of unitary patent protection with regard to the applicable translation arrangements OJ 2012 L 361, p. 89.
73. C-274/11 and C-295/11.

that a mechanism enshrined in the Treaty and therefore agreed by all Member States can operate in a discriminatory manner against those States which have agreed to it has proven historically to be a non-starter.

Space precludes detailed analysis of the Court's reasoning on every pleading. Suffice it for present purposes to suppose that what is noteworthy about this case is that it demonstrates that if a Member State is not skilful at litigating in the CJEU at the first opportunity, particularly as far as enhanced cooperation is concerned, it is demonstrably more difficult to challenge the disliked legislation at a later date. The UK therefore needs to get better at utilising the system of judicial protection.

§9.05 CONCLUSION

The above discussion on the system of judicial protection demonstrates that Britain is not necessarily alone in the CJEU, however, it should certainly become more adept at using the judicial forum. It should not be forgotten that it is the most important post legislative forum and that Britain's reliance on it is unlikely to dissipate as David Cameron embarks on negotiating further opt-outs. This is still the case even though the House of Lords European Union Committee has concluded that it is 'highly unlikely'[74] that the CJEU will change its approach to interpretation in this area, especially where it relates to determining the legal basis of a measure.

This chapter submits that the Court should also look to review its position in order to maintain a comprehensive and coherent system of judicial protection, which crucially provides for adherence to the rule of law in the Union. This does not absolve the Member States, including the UK, from their obligation to maximise the utility in the system. Rather, for the system to work both practically and constitutionally each actor has to play their part. For the flexibility mechanisms, which at the end of the day assist in fulfilling the integrative objective of the Union, to work, the importance of the proper functioning of the system cannot be underestimated. This will continue to be the case for the UK in, or out, of the Union.

74. House of Lords European Union Committee, *The UK's opt-in Protocol: implications of the Government's approach*, HL Paper 136, p. 6.

CHAPTER 10

Criminal Law

John R. Spencer

§10.01 INTRODUCTION

This short chapter, like Caesar's Gaul, *divisa est in partes tres*. The first part reminds readers of what EU criminal law is. The second part describes the UK's current attitude towards it, which could fairly be described as 'semi-detached'. And the third part attempts to sketch out what the UK's practical position in relation to EU criminal law might be if, downstream of the referendum now promised by our politicians, the UK should withdraw from the EU. The first two parts of the chapter deal with matters on which I have already written extensively elsewhere, and here I necessarily repeat, though more concisely, things that I have previously said. Readers keen to learn more about these topics are referred to the materials listed in the footnote below.[1]

§10.02 WHAT EU CRIMINAL LAW CONSISTS OF?

The phrase 'EU criminal law' suggests a separate body of criminal law, with its own courts, prosecutors and criminal procedure, as exists (for example) in the United States

1. *EU Criminal Law – the Present and the Future?*, in *A Constitutional Order of States? Essays in Honour of Alan Dashwood* Chapter 18 (Anthony Arnull ed., et al. Hart Publishing 2011); *EU Criminal Law*, in *European Union Law* Chapter 25 (Catherine Barnard & Steve Peers, eds, OUP 2014),; 'The UK and EU Criminal Law: should We be Leading, Following or Abstaining?', in *Globalisation, Criminal Law and Criminal Justice* Chapter 7 (Valsamis Mitsilegas, Peter Alldridge & Leonidas Cheliotis eds, Hart Publishing 2014); *Who's Afraid of the Big, Bad European Public Prosecutor?* Chapter 14, 14 Cambridge Y.B. Eur. Leg. Stud. (2011–2012); *Opting out of EU Criminal Law: What is Actually Involved?*, A. Hinarejos, J.R. Spencer & S. Peers, *Opting out of EU Criminal Law – What is Actually Involved?* CELS Working Paper, New Series, No. 1 (September 2012), online at http://www.cels.law.cam.ac.uk/Media/working_papers/Optout%20text%20final.pdf; *Opting out of EU Criminal Justice?* [2012] 7 Archbold Rev. 6–9 ; *Opting Out of EU Criminal Justice: Withdrawal, or an Exercise in Smoke and Mirrors?* [2013] 8 Archbold Rev. 6–9.

of America. In fact it is something less focussed and much more amorphous. At present, it consists of a collection of rules created to regulate a collection of different but connected issues, most of which stem from what might be called the 'fifth freedom' – the unwanted consequence of one of the EU's key policies. Central to the EU's economic policies are freedom of movement for workers, services, goods and capital, usually called 'the four freedoms'. An inevitable side-effect of implementing these has been the emergence of a fifth freedom – free movement of criminals and crime. The consequence of this is the growth of crimes that have trans-border aspects to them, and to deal with these, a greater degree of cooperation between the criminal justice systems of the Member States is obviously required. A large part of EU criminal law is directed towards achieving this improved cooperation. A further factor in the growth of EU criminal law has been the need to protect certain key interests of the EU itself. So, for example, the EU has adopted legislation requiring all Member States to make it a criminal offence to counterfeit the common currency,[2] and similarly, to ensure that the criminal justice systems of all Member States are able to punish those who commit frauds on Community finances.[3]

This body of legislation is marked by a tension between what are usually called the 'vertical' and 'horizontal' methods. The 'vertical method' means imposing a single, uniform solution on all the Member States from the top down. The obvious example in this area is OLAF, the EU's central anti-fraud agency, which has powers to investigate budgetary frauds through the European Union. The 'horizontal method', by contrast, means seeking a solution under which the EU encourages and facilitates the legal systems of the different Member States, and their respective criminal justice agencies, to deal with the problem on their own. Here the obvious example is the European Arrest Warrant: a speedy and simplified system of extradition, designed to make it easier for the different national criminal justice systems to prosecute offenders who live, or lurk, in other Member States, and thereby deal more easily with trans-border crime. Criminal justice, as everybody knows, is something which nation states traditionally see as a matter for themselves, and in respect of which they particularly resent foreign interference. This being so, it is hardly surprising that, as far as criminal justice is concerned, the 'horizontal method' is usually the one preferred.

Before Lisbon, the legal basis for EU criminal law was two-fold: first, the 'Third Pillar' provisions of the old-style Treaty of European Union, originating from the Treaty of Maastricht in 1992, and significantly added to by the Treaty of Amsterdam; and secondly, the Schengen Treaty – originally adopted outside the framework of the EU, but brought within the EU framework by the Amsterdam Treaty in 1997. By the relevant Articles in Title VI of the old-style TEU, and the legislation made under them, the UK, like other Member States, was bound. And though most of the inhabitants of the UK are probably unaware of this, the UK was also bound by a substantial part of the Schengen provisions. The Schengen Treaty, as is widely known, was in essence an

2. Council Framework Decision of 29 May 2000 on increasing protection by criminal penalties and other sanctions against counterfeiting in connection with the introduction of the euro, OJ L 140/1.
3. Council Act of 26 Jul. 1995 drawing up the Convention on the protection of the European Communities' financial interests.

arrangement under which the contracting States agreed to open their borders to one another – an arrangement which the UK declined to join. However, with a view to coping with the enhanced mobility of crime and criminals that was expected to result from open borders, the Schengen Treaty also contained a list of 'tough on crime' measures designed to enhance the control of cross-border crime; and in these measures the UK decided to participate. Post-Lisbon, the legal basis for future EU criminal law is now primarily a suite of Articles in Title V of Part 3 of Chapter Four of the Treaty on the Functioning of the European Union. The extent to which the UK is bound by this, and by criminal justice legislation made under it, will be explained in the second part of this chapter.

In concrete terms, EU criminal law consists of legislation and (in some cases) associated case law relating to five different things.[4]

First, there is the body of law creating and regulating a series of EU bodies designed to deal in various ways with crime. Of these there are at present three, and there may shortly be a fourth. There is OLAF, the EU anti-fraud agency, already mentioned. Though this has wide powers to investigate frauds, its ability to bring to justice the authors of any criminal frauds that it detects is limited, because although it can investigate 'fraud, corruption and any other illegal activity affecting the financial interests of the [EU]'[5] it cannot prosecute the authors if it catches them. For this, it must rely on the prosecuting authorities of the Member States, to which, if it thinks action should be taken, it must then transfer the file. There is Europol, the European Police Office.[6] The role of Europol is to support the law enforcement agencies of the Member States, and to facilitate cooperation between them. To this end, it acts mainly as a clearing-house for information. Unlike OLAF, it has no power to carry out its own investigations. Then there is Eurojust,[7] which (in essence) does for public prosecutors what Europol does for the police. Lastly, for the future there is a possible European Public Prosecutor – currently referred to as the EPPO, or European Public Prosecutor's Office.[8] If the negotiations currently underway reach fruition, the EPPO will be an official EU agency responsible, within those Member States that have joined the project, for bringing prosecutions for frauds against the EU budget. What largely drives

4. A much fuller description of the various legal instruments is given in my chapter in Barnard and Peers, *European Union Law* (2014), *supra* n. 1. For more detailed information on EU criminal law generally *see* André Klip, *European Criminal Law – an Integrative Approach* (2nd edn, Intersentia 2011), Valsamis Mitsilegas, *EU Criminal Law* (Hart Publishing 2009) and Steve Peers, *EU Justice and Home Affairs Law* Chapters 9–12 (3rd edn OUP 2011).
5. Article 1(1) of the OLAF Regulation (Regulation (EU, EURATOM) No. 883/2013 of the European Parliament and of the Council of 11 Sep. 2013 concerning investigations conducted by the European Anti-Fraud Office (OLAF) and repealing Regulation (EC) No. 1073/1999 of the European Parliament and of the Council and Council Regulation (Euratom) No. 1074/1999, OJ OJ L 248/1).
6. Council Decision of 6 Apr. 2009 establishing the European Police Office (Europol) (2009/371/JHA), OJ L121/37, 15 May 2009.
7. Council Decision of 28 Feb. 2002, [2002] OJ L 63/1; Council Decision 2009/492/JHA of 16 Dec. 2008 on strengthening Eurojust and amending Decision 2002/187/JHA, [2009] OJ L 138/14.
8. Proposal for a Council Regulation on the establishment of the European Public Prosecutor's Office, COM(2013) 534 final Brussels, 17 Jul. 2013. For the earlier history, see J.R. Spencer, 'Who's Afraid of the Big, Bad European Public Prosecutor?', (2011–2012) 14 CYELS Chapter 14.

the EPPO proposal is the worry that, when files from OLAF are transferred to them, the public prosecutors of the Member States (or some of them) show little enthusiasm for acting on them – understandably preferring to devote their limited resources to dealing with national crime.

Secondly, there is a body of law designed to facilitate cooperation between the police forces of the different Member States. Of this, the best-known example is the 2002 instrument that created a legal basis for joint investigation teams, or 'JITs';[9] but there are others which are equally important. These include the 'Swedish Framework Decision', which requires Member States to provide information and intelligence to law enforcement agencies from other Member States in the same way as, within that Member State, one agency would make it available to another,[10] and the instrument creating a scheme called 'ECRIS' (European Criminal Records Information System), under which Member States are obliged on request to supply, in a standard shape and form, details of a given person's criminal convictions.[11]

Thirdly, there is an important body of legal instruments designed to facilitate cooperation between the prosecutors and the criminal courts of the different Member States. These are said to operate by creating a system of 'mutual recognition', whereby the criminal courts of the different Member States formally recognise and give effect to one another's judgments and orders more or less automatically – as has long been the case in the field of civil justice. Recognition may be passive, as with the instrument that requires the criminal courts of the Member States to give the same weight to previous convictions imposed by criminal courts in other Member States as it does to those imposed by its own.[12] Or it may be active, as where recognition of the foreign order or judgment requires positive steps to be taken. Of the instruments requiring mutual recognition in the active sense, by far the best known – and the most controversial – is the instrument that created the European Arrest Warrant.[13] There are a number of others. The most recent is the Directive, adopted in April 2014, creating what is called the European Investigation Order.[14] When this comes into force, it will require the courts of the Member States to give quasi-automatic recognition to one another's orders seeking evidence – for example, search warrants.

Fourthly, there is a group of instruments which attempt to secure some degree of harmonisation in areas of substantive criminal law in areas where it is felt that a common approach is required in the face of a common problem. These instruments usually require all Member States to ensure that their codes of criminal law penalise

9. Council Framework Decision 2002/465/JHA of 13 Jun. 2002, [2002] OJ L 162.
10. Council Framework Decision 2006/960/JHA of 18 Dec. 2006 on simplifying the exchange of information and intelligence between law enforcement authorities of the Member States of the European Union, [2006] OJ L 386/89.
11. Council Framework Decision 2009/315/JHA of 26 Feb. 2009, [2009] OJ L 93.
12. Council Framework Decision 2008/675/JHA of 24 Jul. 2008 on taking account of convictions in the Member States of the European Union in the course of new criminal proceedings.
13. Council Framework Decision 2002/584/JHA of 13 Jun. 2002 on the European arrest warrant and the surrender procedures between Member States, [2002] OJ L 190/1.ates of the European Union in the course of new criminal proceedings.
14. Directive 2014/41/EU of the European Parliament and of the Council of 3 Apr. 2014 regarding the European Investigation Order, OJ L 130/1.

certain specified activities, and also provide maximum penalties severe enough to act as a deterrent. In this spirit the EU has adopted instruments on terrorism,[15] drug-dealing,[16] child sexual abuse and pornography,[17] cybercrime,[18] bribery,[19] money-laundering,[20] people-smuggling,[21] people-trafficking,[22] and frauds in relation to electronic payments; and with the interests of the EU itself in mind, the EU has also adopted measures requiring Member States to make counterfeiting the Euro a criminal offence, as well as frauds against the budget. Among these criminal law measures is the Framework Decision requiring Member States to penalise certain forms of racism and xenophobia: an instrument much criticised by UK eurosceptics, who claimed that it would force the UK to create new offences restricting our ancient traditions of free speech.

Fifthly and finally, there is a smaller group of instruments the aim of which is to secure some degree of harmonisation in criminal procedure. These include instruments designed to ensure that the victims of criminal offences are treated with a certain minimum degree of respect and consideration, and a group of instruments requiring Member States to provide certain minimum levels of protection and practical help to suspects and defendants. These pro-defendant measures have been adopted in execution of a rolling programme, published in 2009, and known as the 'Roadmap'. The underlying idea (or part of it) is to foster the programme of 'mutual recognition': national criminal courts will, it is hoped, be readier to give automatic recognition to judgments and orders from criminal courts in other Member States if they feel confident that defendants in those systems are treated fairly and that safeguards exist to minimise the risk of their being wrongly convicted.

§10.03 THE UK'S ATTITUDE TOWARDS EU CRIMINAL LAW: PAST AND PRESENT

Having started rather slowly after Maastricht, EU criminal law developed rapidly from 1997, once the Treaty of Amsterdam had amended the criminal law provisions of the old-style TEU by adding to the feeble range of possible instruments a new and stronger instrument, the Framework Decision: a measure which, like Directives under the First Pillar, had to be implemented by all Member States without the preliminary step of ratification by the Member State concerned. During the twelve years from Amsterdam to Lisbon in December 2009 a Labour government was in power at Westminster and this was broadly favourable to the growth of EU criminal law. During this period, it

15. Council Framework Decision 2002/475/JHA of 13 Jun. 2002 on combating terrorism, [2002] OJ L 164/3.
16. Council Framework Decision 2004/757/JHA, [2004] OJ L 335.
17. Directive 2011/92/EU of the European Parliament and of the Council of 13 Dec. 2011 on combating the sexual abuse and sexual exploitation of children and child pornography, and replacing Council Framework Decision 2004/68/JHA, [2011] OJ L 335/1.
18. Directive 2013/40/EU, OJL 218/8.
19. Council Framework Decision 2003/568/JHA, [2003] OJ L 192/54.
20. Council Framework Decision 2001/500/JHA, [2001] OJ L 182.
21. Council Framework Decision 2002/946/JHA, [2002] OJ L 328.
22. Directive 2011/36/EU, [2011] OJ L 101/1.

should be recalled, 'Third Pillar' criminal justice measures could only be adopted by unanimity, which meant that every Member State had (in effect) the power to veto a measure by refusing to vote for it; and far from blocking measures, the UK government was content to join in the creation and adoption of a long list of measures, in the manufacture of some of which – notably the European Arrest Warrant – it took a leading part. Most of these measures were, broadly speaking, aimed at strengthening the powers of the police and prosecutors rather than providing guarantees for defendants. When in the mid-2000s there were moves towards the adoption of an EU measure aimed to provide minimum rights for suspects and defendants, the UK initially used its political muscle to block them – although in 2009 it eventually withdrew its opposition and supported the 'Roadmap' mentioned in the paragraph above. In similar spirit, in 2005 the UK, whilst retaining border controls, opted into the more repressive parts of the Schengen convention, designed to cope with the unwanted side-effects of open borders.

One significant feature of the Third Pillar arrangements, as we have just seen, was that every Member State had in effect a veto over the adoption of new measures; and a second significant feature was that, though Member States were theoretically bound to implement Third Pillar criminal justice measures, they were in practice free to disregard them with impunity, because the European Court of Justice had no power to entertain infringement proceedings against Member States which failed to implement them. Under the Lisbon Treaty, all this was due to change. In future, criminal justice measures could be adopted by qualified majority voting, and Member States that failed to implement them would in future be liable to be hauled before the Court of Justice (now renamed the CJEU) in infringement proceedings. For good measure, the Lisbon Treaty also provided that, as from December 2014, any remaining Third Pillar criminal justice measures would also become enforceable through infringement proceedings.

Neither of these changes was welcome to the UK, and by exercising diplomatic pressure during the negotiations it managed to insulate itself from both of them. Under Protocol 21, which it negotiated in league with the Republic of Ireland, neither the UK nor the Republic of Ireland are bound by any new criminal justice measures (or indeed any new civil justice measures) adopted under Title V of Part Three of Chapter Four of the TFEU unless they have expressly opted in. And, this time acting alone, by Article 10 of Protocol 36 the UK enabled itself to avoid, albeit in a roundabout way, the future jurisdiction of the CJEU in respect of any remaining Third Pillar criminal justice measures. This labyrinthine provision gave the UK the right, at any time before June 2014, to denounce en bloc, and with effect from December 2014, all the remaining Third Pillar criminal justice measures; though subject to the right then to seek readmission one by one to any of those measures which, on reflection, it decided it wished to belong to after all. If readmitted to one of these measures, the UK would have to accept the jurisdiction of the CJEU as part of the package; and a fortiori, the UK accepts the jurisdiction of the Court in respect of any post-Lisbon criminal justice measure that it elects to opt into under Protocol 21.

The Lisbon Treaty came into force in December 2009 and six months later, following a general election, the Labour government was replaced by a Coalition of

Conservatives and Liberal Democrats, the Conservatives being in the driving seat. To stitch this Coalition together was not easy, given how widely these parties differed on a number of important issues – not least, on Europe and the EU, towards which the Liberal Democrats are basically favourable, whereas the Conservatives are much less so, with a large bloc of eurosceptic MPs loudly hostile to the EU and all its works. Unsurprisingly, the change of government caused the UK's attitude towards EU criminal law to become significantly more incoherent. The consistent policy of the previous government, to put it provocatively, could be summed up as 'at one with Europe in repression'. But the main feature of Coalition's policy, by contrast, has been its inconsistency.

When it came to office, the Coalition published an official policy on EU criminal law which at least gave an appearance of coherence. In its 'Programme for Government' it said:

> We will approach forthcoming legislation in the area of criminal justice on a case-by-case basis, with a view to maximising our country's security, protecting Britain's civil liberties and preserving the integrity of our criminal justice system. Britain will not participate in the establishment of any European Public Prosecutor.

Acting on the last sentence of the statement, one of the first moves of the new Government was to cause Parliament to erect a statutory obstacle to the UK's ever participating in the creation of a European Public Prosecutor. The European Union Act of 2011, while it remains in force, disables the UK from acceding to any future treaty change that would increase the powers of the EU unless this has been approved by an Act of the Westminster Parliament, preceded by a national referendum. Going further, the Act also imposes a 'referendum lock' on the UK's participation in a list of other possible measures for which the existing Treaties already provide a legal basis – among them the European Public Prosecutor.

The reason for this, as I have explained elsewhere, is the hostile reaction of the eurosceptic press towards the *Corpus Juris* project – the document in which the idea of a European Public Prosecutor was first floated back in 1997; which the *Daily Telegraph* and other eurosceptic newspapers painted as a 'Brussels Plot' to force the UK to abandon its traditional common law adversarial system of criminal justice in favour of a horror its own imagining called the 'Napoleonic system', allegedly in force in Continental Europe. This misrepresentation of the *Corpus Juris* project is bizarre, as will be clear from even the most cursory examination of the original document. Unsurprisingly, this view of the matter was immediately endorsed by the more extreme among the UK's eurosceptics – the UK Independence Party making use of the supposed threat to the common law as an argument in favour of the UK's withdrawal from the EU. More surprisingly, this view was also accepted and rapidly internalised by those who are influential in the Conservative Party. And in consequence, the European Public Prosecutor found itself, together with the Euro, on the list of developments to be subjected to the 'referendum lock'.

Despite taking this extreme position on the European Public Prosecutor, in other respects the Coalition government seemed at first prepared to continue the cooperative policy of its predecessor in matters of EU criminal law. Thus in the summer of 2010 the government exercised the UK's right under Protocol 21 to opt the UK into the proposal to create, on the same principles as the European Arrest Warrant, a European Investigation Order – the effect of which, as we have seen, will be to require the courts of Member States to enforce one another's orders for the gathering of evidence; a decision which provoked the outrage of the *Daily Telegraph*, which reported it under the headline 'Britons to be Spied on by Foreign Police'. At first the Coalition government also continued the policy the previous government had belatedly adopted of supporting the EU 'Roadmap' of new measures intended to provide further guarantees for suspects and defendants. This initially cooperative mood changed, however, once the eurosceptic wing of the Conservative Party, backed by the *Daily Telegraph*, discovered the Protocol 36 opt-out, and began to press the government to exercise it.

The campaign to persuade the Government to invoke the Protocol 36 opt-out began in earnest on 6 February 2012 when the *Daily Telegraph* published a letter signed by over 100 back-bench Conservative MPs. Calling for the UK to exercise the opt-out in order to liberate itself from the impending control of the CJEU over matters of criminal justice, this letter raised the spectre of the European Public Prosecutor and the EU Commission's supposed 'ambitions for a pan-European code of Euro-crimes'. The MPs' call was taken up by the journalist Philip Johnson with a supportive article entitled 'We have European opt-outs, so why not use them?' In the course of 2012 these clinching arguments convinced the Prime Minister, David Cameron, who, in answer to a random question fired at him by a Sky news journalist while on a trade mission to Brazil, announced, out of the blue, that the UK would exercise the opt-out: 'That has to be done before the end of the year, and the opt-out is there. We'll be exercising that opt-out'. Some weeks later this casual announcement was followed by a more considered statement from the Home Secretary, Teresa May, who said that the Government was 'minded' to do this; in other words, that it was considering it, but had not finally made up its mind. This second announcement was greeted by the *Daily Express* with the ecstatic headline: 'BRITAIN'S FIRST STEP TO EU EXIT – government to claw back 130 powers from Brussels'.

If pleasing to the eurosceptics on the Conservative back-benches, all this was anything but pleasing to the Liberal Democrats and to their leader, the Deputy Prime Minister, who (it was widely rumoured) had not been consulted in advance. Behind the scenes – and to some extent in public – they made it plain that they would not support the exercise of the opt-out unless it were accompanied by a sizeable 'wish-list' of measures the UK would then seek to opt back into. In exercising this pressure they were joined by the police, who were particularly worried about the prospect of losing the European Arrest Warrant. And so it was that, instead of the opt-out process being completed the end of the 2012, as David Cameron had blithely suggested when he made his unguarded comments in Brazil, there was a long delay; during the course of which the House of Lords EU Committee conducted an enquiry, which concluded that:

> the government have not made a convincing case for exercising the opt-out and that opting out would have significant adverse negative repercussions for the internal security of the UK and the administration of criminal justice in the UK, as well as reducing its influence over this area of EU policy.

Undeterred, at the end of July 2013 that the Government eventually served formal notice upon Brussels that the Protocol 36 opt-out was invoked. And when doing so, it indicated that, whilst withdrawing permanently from rather less than 100 measures, the UK would seek readmission to some 35. Prominently excluded from the list were nearly all the measures related to substantive criminal law – including of course the Framework Decision on racism and xenophobia, but also including the ones requiring Member States to punish bribery, money-laundering, drug-smuggling and terrorism: so ensuring the UK would be free to decriminalise these activities as well, should at some future date it feels the urge to do so. But on the other hand, the opt-back-in list did include most of the measures the importance of which is practical rather than symbolic. Prominent among the 'opt- back-ins' were nearly all of the mutual recognition instruments, including the Framework Decision creating European Arrest Warrant: the measure which the Tory eurosceptics were as keen to get rid of as the police were anxious to retain.

This outcome raised the obvious question: 'If we are going to opt back in again to all the important measures, what is the point of having opting out?' In consequence the government's position attracted at one and the same time the derision of the Labour Party and the exasperation of the Tory eurosecptics. With some justice, it might be thought, Yvette Cooper, the Shadow Home Secretary, castigated the government's policy thus:

> That is the historic transfer of powers that the Home Secretary boasted about – the great liberation from Europe and the great cause for celebration that she promised . . . We have the power not to do a whole series of things we plan to carry on doing anyway, the power not to follow guidance we already follow, the power not to take action we already take, the power not to meet standards we already meet, the power not to do things that everyone else has already stopped doing and the power not to do a whole series of things we want to do anyway.'

And in an angry speech in a later Parliamentary debate, the prominent Tory eurosceptic Jacob Rees-Mogg quoted the florid rhetoric the Prime Minister had used against the European Arrest Warrant when, as an opposition MP twelve years before, he had opposed the Extradition Bill designed to implement it. How can the public be expected to have confidence in our politicians, Rees-Mogg said, if 'in opposition they have backbone and in government they are jellyfish.'

The end of the story was even more undignified. Having initially promised that both Houses of Parliament would have a proper chance to debate its 'wish-list' of proposed opt-back-ins, in November 2014 the Government contrived to provoke the Tory eurosceptics even further by back-tracking and offering the House of Commons a debate the scope of which was restricted to those measures on the wish-list for the implementation of which a piece of secondary legislation was required. The resulting debate was angry and confused, though in the end the Government secured the vote it needed. The Opposition then exploited the Government's embarrassment by devoting its 'opposition day' – a periodic half-day in the Parliamentary calendar in which the Opposition can choose the topic for a House of Commons debate and vote – to holding the full debate and vote the Government had tried so clumsily to avoid; at the end of which a majority of the House of Commons solemnly voted its support for the Government's proposal to seek readmission to what was by then being called 'the magic 35'. And finally, just before the date in December 2014 when the Protocol 36 opt-out was due to take effect, the readmission package was finally agreed by the Council and the Commission.[23]

In response to the political pressures that caused it to invoke the Protocol 36 opt-out, by the end of its time the Coalition government had distanced itself from the EU's efforts towards the development of EU criminal law. In March 2014 the Minister of Justice told Parliament that the UK would not take part in the next stages of the implementation of the 'Roadmap' on defence rights: proposed EU Directives on the presumption of innocence, safeguards for child defendants, safeguards for vulnerable defendants, and legal aid.[24]

In May 2015 the General Election gave the Conservative Party a majority. As this chapter is revised to go to press the Prime Minister is trying to 'renegotiate' the UK's relationship with the EU, with a view to putting the 'new deal' – if there is one – before the electorate in a national referendum on to whether the UK should stay in the EU or leave. And of all this the outcome is, of course, uncertain.

§10.04 THE EFFECT OF WITHDRAWAL

So what would happen to this body of law (or what remains of it after the Protocol 36 opt-out) if, following the promised referendum, the UK then withdrew completely from the EU?

The procedure for Member States to withdraw from the Union is set out in Article 50 of the (post-Lisbon) TEU. This provides for the terms of withdrawal to be negotiated according to the procedure set out in Article 218(3) –the procedure designated for making treaties with third party states and international organisations – and then 'concluded on behalf of the Union by the Council, acting by a qualified majority, after obtaining the consent of the European Parliament'. Assuming the UK used this procedure to withdraw, and did not simply make a unilateral declaration of independence, then it is almost certain that the eventual 'exit package' would contain provisions dealing with the future position of the UK in relation to the body of legal instruments of which EU criminal law is composed; and the matter would then be regulated by these provisions. As to what these provisions might contain it is only possible to speculate. At one extreme, it is possible – though unlikely – that they would say that the UK continued to participate in these instruments, and to that extent continued to accept the jurisdiction of the CJEU; and if that were the case it would be 'business as before'. It seems much more likely, however, that the terms negotiated for a 'Brexit' would be the opposite: that after a given date, all these instruments would cease to apply to the UK, and that as part of the deal, the jurisdiction of the CJEU over the UK would also cease. The rest of this chapter will be based on that assumption.

23. For the details, see the two Council Decision of 1 Dec. 2014, 2014: 2014/857/EU and 2014/858/EU, OJ L345, vol 57, 1 Dec. 2014.
24. Hansard, House of Commons, 18 Mar. 2014, col 702.

In the first part of this chapter, EU criminal law was said to consist of five different but related matters: rules setting up and regulating new European bodies designed to co-ordinate the fight against crime, rules designed to facilitate cooperation between the police forces of the Member States, 'mutual recognition' rules designed to facilitate cooperation between prosecutors and the criminal courts, rules designed to harmonise certain aspects of substantive criminal law, and rules designed to harmonise certain aspects of criminal procedure. In what follows, the implications of a 'Brexit' on those terms will be analysed, taking each of the areas in turn.

All three of the European crime-fighting bodies that currently exist – OLAF, Europol and Eurojust – have concluded formal arrangements for cooperation with a range of non-EU states, and it is likely that similar arrangements would be quickly set in place for the UK if it withdrew from the EU. The UK would then continue to work with these bodies, and to make use of them, according to the terms of those agreements. However, it would henceforth do so, obviously, on the basis of something akin to 'second class citizenship'. Thus Europol and Eurojust are collegiate bodies, run by a college of representatives from each Member State, and if the UK were no longer a Member State it would no longer participate in the college. Difficult questions arise as to the future relationship between the UK and the EPPO, should there ever be one – even if the UK remains an EU Member State. On the one hand, as was explained in the first section of this chapter, the UK's official revulsion towards the idea of a European Public Prosecutor has been given statutory expression by the provisions of the European Union Act which impose a 'referendum lock' on any future participation of the UK in the project. But on the other hand, a supposedly sacred principle of criminal procedure in England and Wales (and in Northern Ireland, though not in Scotland[25]) is the right of private prosecution; and in principle, private prosecutions can be instituted by legal persons as well as natural persons. So even if the EPPO continues to be an agency that the UK formally shuns and avoids, it seems – astonishingly – that a future European Public Prosecutor would be at liberty to institute criminal proceedings in any part of the country south of the river Tweed.

For the EU instruments designed to facilitate cross-border police cooperation and the EU instruments designed to facilitate cross-border cooperation between prosecutors and criminal courts the legal issues arising from a 'Brexit' are similar, and for present purposes they can be treated together. And in this connection, it is necessary to distinguish between two situations: where, after withdrawal, a Member State tried to make use of the instrument to secure cooperation from the UK, and where, after withdrawal, the UK tried to use the instrument to secure cooperation from another Member State.

Taking first the case where another Member State sought to make use of the instrument, the UK's obligation under EU law to take the requested step would obviously exist no longer. However, depending on the way in which the duty to take the step in question had been incorporated into UK national law, there might still exist an obligation under UK law. The obvious example here is the European Arrest Warrant.

25. Where the public prosecutor in Scotland (the Crown Office and Prosecutor Fiscal Service) has, in effect, a monopoly and private prosecutions are severely restricted.

The Framework Decision creating this instrument was implemented in the UK by Part I of the Extradition Act 2003. As if drafted by a eurosceptic, this piece of legislation studiously avoids all mention of the European Union (and indeed of the European Arrest Warrant) and creates, by statute, the sort of speedy regime of extradition which the Framework Decision requires, which it makes available not to 'EU Member States', but to what the Act calls 'Part I territories' – defined as other countries to be designated as such by the Secretary of State.[26] If the UK withdrew from the EU, Parliament would then be free to amend the implementing legislation in any way it liked, and the Minister would then be free to delete any or all of the Member States from the list of Part I territories. But as long Part I of the Extradition Act 2003 retained its present shape, and the Secretary of State continued to designate the other Member States as 'Part I territories', the UK courts would presumably continue to execute their European Arrest Warrants.

How far the UK could continue to make use of EU legal instruments designed to enable the authorities of one Member State to require some step to be taken by the authorities of another would depend in turn on the way in which the other Member State had chosen to implement the EU instrument. If the other Member State had implemented (for example) the European Arrest Warrant using the same legislative techniques as the UK in Part I of the Extradition Act 2003, then presumably its courts would in turn continue to execute European Arrest Warrants issued by the UK. But that many Member States have done so seems unlikely and that all have done so is inconceivable. The articles of the French *Code de procédure pénale* which implement the Framework Decision on the European Arrest Warrant, for example, begin as follows : *Les disposition du présent chapitre sont applicables aux demandes d'entraide entre la France et les autres Etats membres de l'Union européenne*. So the consequences of the UK's withdrawal from the EU would almost certainly be that, as far as the UK is concerned, all the EU instruments designed to facilitate cooperate between the police, prosecution agencies and criminal courts would cease to operate.

Unless withdrawal were immediately followed by the closing of borders and the suspension of free movement, the disappearance of this group of legal instruments without replacement would lead to serious law-enforcement problems. This point was made, forcefully and publicly, by the UK police when it began to look as if the government was about to exercise the Protocol 36 opt-out; and it was because the government accepted the arguments of the police that it was prepared to brave the fury of the Tory eurosceptics and include almost all the Third Pillar instruments on police cooperation and mutual recognition in its wish-list of opt-back-ins – including the particular bête noir of the Tory eurosceptics, the European Arrest Warrant. So if free movement were to continue in its present form – or even in some more restricted form – this group of instruments would need to be replaced.

Those who wanted to see the UK ditch this group of instruments as part of the Protocol 36 opt-out argued that, insofar as they served a useful purpose, they could be replaced by 'inter-governmental' instruments negotiated individually between the UK

26. For a comment on the drafting of these provisions, see J.R. Spencer, *Implementing the European Arrest Warrant: a Tale of How Not to Do It* 30 Statute L. Rev. 184–202 (2009).

and each other Member State. A simple exercise with a pocket calculator (or even a pencil and paper) suggests that this would be easier said than done. If the UK withdrew from the EU, the number of Member States with which it would then need to negotiate separate agreements would be 27. To ensure the UK was still able to deal with trans-border crime the government negotiated the UK's readmission to some 35 Third Pillar instruments. Taking this as the number of topics on which it would necessary to secure cooperation, the number of inter-governmental instruments to be negotiated would be 945!

In response to this, the point is often made that the task of setting up a network of inter-governmental arrangements would actually be much easier because there is already in existence a collection of inter-governmental Conventions drawn up within the framework of the Council of Europe. These pre-date the EU instruments on police cooperation and mutual recognition from which the UK would now withdraw. They were the legal basis on which the Member States formerly conducted this sort of business with each other before EU criminal law came into being, and continue to be the legal basis on which the Member States (including the UK) conduct this sort of business with those countries in Europe which do not belong to the EU. So if the UK withdrew from the EU, it could resume police and judicial cooperation with the other Member States on the basis of this group of inter-governmental instruments.

This would alleviate the problem to some extent – but would not solve it. As I and my colleagues pointed out when discussing the effect of the UK's possible withdrawal from this group of measures in the context of the Protocol 36 opt-out:

> As a fall-back, the UK's relations with other Member States would be governed by Council of Europe instruments on criminal law, but in some areas (such as pre-trial release) there are no instruments; in other areas (such as the validity of criminal judgments and the recognition of probation and parole orders), the UK (and some other Member States) have not ratified the instrument concerned, and in still other areas (such as the Second Protocol to the mutual assistance convention) the UK has ratified the treaty concerned but some other Member States have not. In any event, none of the Council of Europe measures establish a system which is as effective as the EU's rules, as the EU measures were specifically designed to improve the Council of Europe rules by setting out deadlines, providing for standard forms, limiting the exceptions to the rules and so on.[27]

Opponents of the European Arrest Warrant have made much of the possibility of replacing it by expedited arrangements for extradition made under the 1957 Council of Europe Convention on Extradition. But among other practical drawbacks, the 1957 Convention permits the contracting states, if they so wish, to stipulate that they will not extradite their nationals – as did a number of important countries, now Member Members of the EU, in the days before the European Arrest Warrant – including France, Germany and Poland. So in those days, if a national of one of those countries committed a crime in the UK and then fled back to his country of origin, the only way

27. *Opting out of EU Criminal Law: What is Actually Involved?*, *supra* n. 1, at §152. For a more detailed examination, see the House of Lords EU Committee, 13th Report of Session 2012–2013, April 2013), *EU Police and Criminal Justice Measures: the UK's 2014 opt-out*, HL Paper 159.

of bringing him to justice was to persuade that country to prosecute him for it there: the practical difficulties of which meant that such crimes often went unpunished. In the light of this, it is unsurprising that, in its evidence to the House of Lords inquiry into the Protocol 36 opt-out, the Association of Chief Police Officers said that the abandonment of this set of measures would be 'a massive step back for UK policing which would benefit no one'.[28]

The fourth group of instruments which go to make up EU criminal law are those designed to harmonise certain aspects of substantive criminal law. For these, the UK's withdrawal from the EU would make little or no practical difference to the legal position as it exists within the UK. First, most of them are Third Pillar measures covered by the Protocol 36 opt-out, in respect of all but one of which the UK did not seek readmission – in consequence of which they have vanished from the UK legal scene already. Secondly, the one remaining Third Pillar measure which the UK re-joined, and the handful of post-Lisbon instruments affecting substantive criminal law which the UK has already exercised its right under Protocol 21 to join, relate to forms of behaviour which it is inconceivable that the UK would ever wish to decriminalise, or even render less severely punishable: child pornography,[29] child abuse,[30] cybercrime,[31] and people-trafficking.[32] Thirdly, in the unlikely event that the UK did wish to decriminalise some form of behaviour to which one of these EU instruments applies, it would usually find its liberty constrained by other international obligations. To quote again from what I and my colleagues said in the context of these instruments and the Protocol 36 opt-out:

> But even this hypothetical 'liberation' to decriminalise such acts would be very limited in practice, because as regards almost all of the offences in question the UK would remain bound by a number of treaties of the Council of Europe, the United Nations and the OECD which it has ratified, which require the UK to criminalise essentially the same activity which the EU measures require it to criminalise (terrorist-related acts, drug trafficking, counterfeiting currency, corruption/bribery, people-smuggling, cyber-crime and money laundering). For instance, even if the UK used the block opt-out to denounce its EU obligations as regards corruption (i.e., bribery), it would still be bound by other treaties in this field which it has ratified, drawn up within the framework of each of these other international organisations...[33]

The UK's withdrawal from the EU would mean that the UK also ceased to be bound by the handful of EU measures intended to harmonise rules of criminal procedure across all Member States. But once again, the practical effects on the legal

28. House of Lords, *supra* n. 41, at §125.
29. Council Decision 2000/375/JHA to combat child pornography on the internet.
30. Directive 2011/92/EU of the European Parliament and of the Council of 13 Dec. 2011 on combating the sexual abuse and sexual exploitation of children and child pornography, and replacing Council Framework Decision 2004/68/JHA. OJ L 335/1.
31. Directive 2013/40/EU of the European Parliament and of the Council on attacks against information systems and replacing Council Framework Decision 2005/222/JHA, OJ L 218/8.
32. Directive 2011/36/EU of the European Parliament and of the Council on preventing and combating trafficking in human beings and protecting its victims, and replacing Council Framework Decision 2002/629/JHA, OJ L 301/1.
33. *Supra* n. 27, at §31.

situation within the UK would be minimal or non-existent. The EU measures in this area which currently apply to the UK are these: (i) The 2008 Framework Decision which regulates the status, in national proceedings, of previous convictions imposed in other Member States in respect of earlier offences;[34] (ii) Article 54 of the Schengen Convention, which deals with the related issue of prosecutions for offences which have previously been the subject of criminal proceedings in another Member State; (iii) the 2012 Directive providing certain guarantees for victims of crime;[35] (iv) two Directives, stemming from the 'Roadmap' programme, providing certain guarantees for suspects and defendants: the 2010 Directive on the right to interpretation and translation,[36] and the 2012 Directive on the right to information.[37] Short of a fascist takeover, no part of the UK is likely to wish to deprive suspects and defendants of the right to interpretation, translation or information, or even to change the law to make it generally possible for criminal offences to be prosecuted twice. And short of a complete takeover of the government by criminals, no part of the UK is ever likely to wish to change the law so that previous convictions imposed in foreign jurisdictions are in future disregarded, or to undermine the position of victims of crime. Furthermore, attempts to do some of these things would put the UK in contravention of its obligations under the European Convention on Human Rights; though any government that was minded to make major inroads on the existing rights of suspects and defendants would presumably have denounced the European Convention long before.

In practical terms, the most worrying consequences for criminal justice of the UK's withdrawal from the EU would be those stemming from the fact that instruments facilitating cooperation between the criminal justice agencies of the UK and the other Member States would no longer operate. These were created as a necessary response to the problem of trans-border crime, a problem which has inevitably become more acute in consequence of the EU's policy of free movement. If, as part of a future 'Brexit', the 'four freedoms' ceased to operate and the UK were to isolate itself from its neighbours, like a sort of European North Korea, the problems they were designed to cope with would be less acute. But in economic terms, the cost of isolation would be a high one.

34. 2008 Council Framework Decision 2008/675/JHA of 24 Jul. 2008 on taking account of convictions in the Member States of the European Union in the course of new criminal proceedings.
35. Directive 2012/29/EU of the European Parliament and of the Council of 25 Oct. 2012 establishing minimum standards on the rights, support and protection of victims of crime, and replacing Council Framework Decision 2001/220/JHA, OJ L 315/57.
36. Directive 2012/64/EU of the European Parliament and of the Council of 20 Oct. 2010 on the right to interpretation and translation in criminal proceedings, OJ L 280/1.
37. Directive 2012/13/EU of the European Parliament and of the Council of 22 May 2012 on the right to information in criminal proceedings.

CHAPTER 11

From EU Citizens to Third-Country Nationals: The Legacy of *Polydor*

Marja-Liisa Öberg[*]

§11.01 INTRODUCTION

Since its foundation, the EU has been the main driving force behind economic integration in Europe. The economic impact of the EU's Internal Market – the core of the European cooperation project – is significant.[1] It affects not only the Member States but all countries in the EU's neighbourhood. The large majority of the neighbouring countries pursue economic cooperation with the Union, often entailing regulatory cooperation. The instruments of the EU's cooperation with third countries vary in depth and breadth, yet have a general tendency of deepening the participation of third countries in the internal market. The prospect of the UK, an EU Member State possibly wishing to withdraw from the Union raises a myriad of legal questions.[2] One of the most important among them concerns the future relationship between the EU and the UK. Throughout its membership in the EU, the UK has been reluctant to join a number of EU policies which has resulted in a significant number of opt-outs. Many of the current opt-outs, such as the economic and monetary union and certain parts of the Area of Freedom, Security and Justice, do not concern the Internal Market specifically. Others, such as the opt-out from the Charter on Fundamental Rights affect equally the application of Internal Market *acquis* within the UK.[3] Yet even if Britain decides to go

* The author would like to thank Professors Marise Cremona and Loïc Azoulai for their useful comments on an earlier draft of the chapter. All errors remain the author's.

1. An earlier version of this chapter appears in (2016) *European Public Law* Issue 1.
Gráinne De Búrca, 'Differentiation within the Core: The Case of the Common Market', in Gráinne De Búrca & Joanne Scott (eds), *Constitutional Change in the EU: From Uniformity to Flexibility?* 133–171 at 133 (Hart Publishing 2000).
2. Until now, the closest example is the withdrawal of Greenland in 1985.
3. The actual effect of Protocol 7 of the Lisbon Treaty on the application of the Charter of Fundamental Rights of the EU to Poland and to the United Kingdom falls short of that of a true

as far as bid farewell to its membership in the Union, the country is unlikely to wish to cut all ties to the Internal Market.

Ideally, leaving the EU and renegotiating a new instrument of cooperation with the Union would allow the UK to restrict future integration to an *à la carte* selection of preferred fields only. By discarding less favoured domains while adopting – or continuing to adopt – chosen parts of the EU *acquis* Britain could, in theory, maintain access to chosen areas of the internal market.

There are a number of examples of third countries participating in the EU's Internal Market by means of international agreements. The prime example of such deep cooperation is the 1994 Agreement establishing the European Economic Area (EEA) concluded between the European Community and its Member States and three states of the European Free Trade Area (EFTA) – Iceland, Liechtenstein and Norway.[4] Other such agreements exporting EU Internal Market *acquis* to third countries include the series of bilateral agreements concluded between the EU and Switzerland and the 1963 association agreement concluded between the European Economic Community (EEC) and Turkey (hereinafter 'EEC-Turkey Agreement'). Despite the different scope of the EU's cooperation with the EFTA States and Turkey, all of the agreements provide a stake for non-Member States in the Internal Market (see Piris, chapter 6).

Joining the EEA or concluding an agreement or set of agreements similar to those concluded by the EU with Switzerland and Turkey, respectively, is one alternative for a Member State leaving the Union. Questions of political feasibility aside, on the one hand, the state may wish to continue to participate in the Internal Market but only adopt *acquis* which it deems desirable. On the other hand, however, cherry-picking may lead to unfavourable outcomes with respect to the areas which the withdrawing state does not wish to deviate from. The weaker the link between the objectives and content of the *acquis* in the Internal Market and in the international agreement exporting *acquis* to a third country, the weaker the guarantee that similarly or identically worded *acquis* will be given uniform interpretation in- and outside the EU.

The general idea of unity in the Internal Market goes hand in hand with the uniform interpretation, implementation, application and enforcement of common rules. In order for individuals and economic operators across the expanded EU Internal Market to enjoy the same rights the international agreement must extend to third countries all relevant *acquis* as well as ensure uniform interpretation and effective implementation and enforcement of the *acquis*. It is thus not a given that the adoption of Internal Market *acquis* by a third country equals full membership in the Internal Market. Some of these reasons for this are substantive, others procedural and institutional in nature. The current analysis is specifically restricted to the former category and the question of guarantees to identical interpretation of provisions identical in substance in an expanded Internal Market.

---

opt-out: Catherine Barnard, *The 'Opt-Out' for the UK and Poland from the Charter of Fundamental Rights: Triumph of Rhetoric over Reality?*, in *The Lisbon Treaty* 257–283 at 281 (Stefan Griller & Jacques Ziller eds, Springer 2008).

4. Discussed in detail in an article by Ciarán Burke and Ólafur Ísberg Hannesson, forthcoming in 22 *European Public Law* (2016).

This chapter considers the possible effects of 'Brexit' on British nationals who would no longer be EU citizens. Any Member State withdrawing from the Union is unlikely to cut all ties to the Internal Market. It is almost inevitable that a departing State would need to set up a bilateral or multilateral arrangement for the purpose of continuing to participate in the Internal Market. The analysis compares the legal status of the citizens of a withdrawing state vis-à-vis EU citizens and examines whether and under what conditions third-country nationals are conferred rights and obligations in the EU Internal Market which are equal to those enjoyed by EU citizens. In this context, the possibility of using the Polydor doctrine to empower third-country nationals to an extent comparable to EU nationals is explored.

§11.02 DEFINING 'EUROPEAN INDIVIDUALS'

The proclaimed aim of the EU internal market is to 'unite national markets into a single market having the characteristics of a domestic market'.[5] This objective is achieved by granting free movement of persons, goods, services and capital, the freedom of establishment and equal conditions for competition. The scope of the free movement rights is specified by the Treaties and secondary EU law, and interpreted by the EU and Member State judiciaries in the light of the objectives of the Treaties and general principles of EU law. As a result, individuals within the EU enjoy, regardless of their country of origin, the same set of free movement rights across the Union.

The European Communities specifically intended to join together not only the contracting states but also their nationals. The 'ever closer union between the peoples of Europe' as articulated in the Preamble to the EEC Treaty has proven crucial to the development of EU law.[6] The 'peoples of Europe' have progressively become the European individuals who are specifically empowered by the Treaties, often so directly without Member State legislation.[7] The distinction between the actors – the states and the peoples – which has assumed great importance in the narrative of the EU plays an equally important role in determining whether identical *acquis* functions in the same manner within the EU and beyond. Arguably, the expansion of the internal market entails the creation of 'European individuals' outside the EU.[8]

International cooperation and the increasing practice of norms export by the EU challenges the common assumption that the 'European individual' is, if not an EU citizen, then at least someone physically present in the EU. EU citizenship itself does not define 'European individuals' in the Internal Market context. Introduced by the Maastricht Treaty in 1992, the concept of EU citizenship has granted the right to move

5. Case 270/80 *Polydor v. Harlequin* [1982] ECR 329, paragraph 16. Also Case 15/81 *Schul* [1982] ECR 1409, paragraph 33.
6. Recital 1, Preamble of the Treaty Establishing the European Economic Community (Rome Treaty).
7. Case 26/62 *Van Gend en Loos* [1963] ECR 1.
8. On 'European individuals' in the context of EU citizenship, see Loïc Azoulai, *Transfiguring European Citizenship: From Member State Territory to Union Territory*, forthcoming in Dimitry Kochenov (ed.), *EU Citizenship and Federalism: The Role of Rights* (Cambridge U. Press 2015).

and reside freely within the EU to all EU citizens[9] but has not altered the substantive content of the free movement rights within the Internal Market. In addition to European citizens who derive rights and obligations directly from the EU Treaties there is an increasing number of persons who have been granted a comparable set of free movement rights in the Internal Market by virtue of international agreements. In situations where an international agreement confers on third-country nationals a similar set of rights as to EU nationals those third-country individuals, too, can be considered European individuals – not by virtue of their country's membership in the EU but due to Internal Market *acquis* applying to them. Inversely, insofar as the internal market is extended to third-country nationals EU citizens, too, enjoy corresponding rights *vis-à-vis* third countries. The situation is comparable to that of expanding the Union through accession yet in this case integration is merely limited to the Internal Market or to parts thereof.

§11.03 EXPORTING INTERNAL MARKET *ACQUIS: 'SO CLOSE, YET SO FAR AWAY'*

Uniform rights, however, do not only depend on the similarity of the provisions but also on their uniform interpretation. Uniform interpretation of rules underpins the concepts of unity of the EU legal order and effectiveness of EU law. Institutional considerations aside, the issue comes down to whether different courts – the judiciary of the EU, of the Member States and the third countries – give the same effect to *acquis* which is identical in substance on the EU and Member State levels. In an internal market expanded to third countries the interpretation of identical *acquis* is, on the one hand, provided by the EU judiciary and Member States' courts. On the other hand, the provisions are applied and interpreted by the non-EU judiciaries – third-country national courts or judicial bodies set up by the international agreements. In the EEA these two dimensions are referred to as the 'EU pillar' and the 'EFTA pillar'. For example, the outcome of the application of a provision of free movement depends largely on whether the national court follows the interpretation of the Court of Justice or whether the Court itself interprets the *acquis* contained in international agreements in the same vein as the underlying EU *acquis*. The present analysis is restrained to the EU-side of the coin and the conditions under which the Court of Justice is willing to regard third-country citizens as 'EU individuals' on the basis of *acquis* that is identical in substance.

Interpretation methods are adopted by the interpreting bodies themselves. With the ultimate aim of securing the effectiveness of EU law, the Court of Justice often uses teleological interpretation to construe the meaning of the provisions of EU law.[10] Does

9. Article 21 TFEU, subject to limits and conditions elaborated by the Treaties and implementing measures.
10. Nial Fennelly, *Legal Interpretation at the European Court of Justice*, 20 Fordham Intl L. J. 656, 664 (1996). Teleological interpretation is, of course, not the only method which the Court uses. See Koen Lenaerts & José A. Gutiérrez-Fons *To Say What the Law of the EU Is: Methods of Interpretation and the European Court of Justice*. 9 EUI Working Paper (2013), http://cadmus.eui.eu/bitstream/handle/1814/28339/AEL_2013_09_DL.pdf?sequence=1 (accessed 9 Feb. 2015).

this mean that the Court is inclined to extend the effectiveness-driven method of EU interpretation also to the *acquis* exported to third countries by international agreements? The answer to the question lies primarily in the landmark decision of the Court of Justice in *Polydor*[11] and a determination of whether the *Polydor* doctrine applies to the international agreements exporting Internal Market *acquis* to third countries.

[A] The *Polydor* Doctrine

The *Polydor* case demonstrated that identical wording of provisions contained in the EU Treaties and in international agreements does not entail automatic uniformity of interpretation. The case concerned the interpretation of a provision of a free trade agreement concluded between the EEC and Portugal in 1972, before the latter joined the EEC. Two British companies were selling in the UK records which they had imported from a Portuguese producer. The records did not comply with UK copyright laws and, subsequently, a copyright infringement action was brought against the companies. The defendants relied on the provision in the EEC-Portugal FTA, equivalent to similar provisions in the EEC Treaty, on the abolition of restrictions to trade in goods which have been lawfully placed on the market in Portugal. The Court refused to interpret the provision of the EEC-Portugal FTA in a manner identical to the corresponding provisions of the EEC Treaty.

The Court maintained that the interpretation of the EEC Treaty follows from the objectives and purpose of the EEC Treaty.[12] The provisions of the EEC-Portugal FTA must be given their own interpretation in the light of the specific objectives of that Agreement. A comparison between the objectives of the EEC Treaty and the EEC-Portugal FTA revealed the narrower scope of the latter.[13] Subsequently, a mere similarity between the provisions of the EEC-Portugal FTA and the EEC Treaty does not justify an extension of the interpretation given in the context of the EEC Treaty to the provisions of the FTA.[14] UK undertakings could not, therefore, exercise their right of free movement of goods between Portugal and the UK quite to the same extent as they would have been able to within the EEC. The *Polydor* doctrine is moreover fully in line with Article 31 of the Vienna Convention on the Law of Treaties according to which the provisions of an international agreement must be interpreted in the light of objectives of that agreement.

The *Polydor* doctrine has had a crucial impact on all attempts to construct 'European individuals' beyond the EU by means of exporting internal market *acquis*. In order for third-country nationals to enjoy the same rights as conferred on EU citizens by the Treaties, the international agreements exporting the *acquis* must contain similarly worded provisions as well as demonstrate an equivalence of objectives pertaining to the Internal Market. A mere free trade agreement does not entail such similarity of objectives nor does it provide a guarantee for identical interpretation.

11. *Supra* n. 5.
12. *Ibid.* paragraph 16.
13. *Ibid.* paragraphs 16–18.
14. *Ibid.* paragraphs 15, 18.

[B] The Application of the *Polydor* Doctrine

The Court has elaborated on the principle that evolved in *Polydor* in a number of subsequent cases, seeking to establish whether similar provisions should be given the same interpretation by assessing the aims pursued by each provision in their particular context and a comparison between the objectives and context of an international agreement and the EU Treaties. In some instances the Court considered that provisions of free trade agreements and association agreements satisfied the above criteria and were thus interpreted in a manner identical to the provisions of the EU Treaties,[15] in others it did not.[16] The determination is always made with reference to each provision separately and does not extend to any international agreement in its entirety.

In *Pabst & Richarz*, for example, the Court contended that a provision of the EEC-Greece Association Agreement, which was similar in wording to Article 95 of the EEC Treaty on the prohibition of fiscal barriers to trade, 'fulfils, within the framework of the Association between the Community and Greece the same function as that of Article 95' due to its purpose of preparing the entry of Greece into the EEC.[17] Consequently, the Court ruled that the 'objective and nature' of the EEC-Greece Association Agreement and the wording of the specific provision required that within the Community spirits originating from Greece must be treated equally *vis-à-vis* spirits originating from the Member States.[18]

In some instances the institutional context of the international agreement, too, plays a role in establishing the comparability of the legal contexts of the EU Treaties and an international agreement. In *A*, the Court claimed that the same interpretation of the provisions on the free movement of capital within the Community cannot be extended to capital movements between the Community and third countries insofar as the mutual assistance between competent authorities does not extend to the third countries in question.[19] The Court maintained this requirement even with respect to the EEA Agreement.[20]

---

15. For example, Case C-207/91 *Eurim-Pharm* [1993] ECR I-3723 concerning the EEC-Austria Free Trade Agreement; Case C-162/00 *Pokrzeptowicz-Meyer* [2002] ECR I-1049 concerning the EC-Poland Association Agreement; Case C-438/00 *Deutscher Handballbund* [2003] ECR I-4135 concerning the EC-Slovakia Association Agreement; Case C-171/01 *Wählergruppe Gemeinsam* [2003] ECR I-4301 concerning the EEC-Turkey Association Agreement; and Case C-265/03 *Simutenkov* [2005] ECR I-2579 concerning the EC-Russia Partnership Agreement.
16. E.g., Case C-312/91 *Metalsa* [1993] ECR I-3751 concerning the EEC-Austria Free Trade Agreement; Case C-63/99 *Gloszczuk* [2001] ECR I-6369 concerning the EC-Poland Association Agreement; Cases C-235/99 *Kondova* [2001] ECR I-6427 and C-101/10 *Pavlov and Famira* [2011] ECR I-5951 concerning the EC-Bulgaria Association Agreement; and Case C-257/99 *Barkoci and Malik* [2001] ECR I-6557 concerning the EC-Czech Association Agreement.
17. Case 17/81 *Pabst & Richarz KG v. Hauptzollamt Oldenburg* [1982] ECR 1331, paragraph 26.
18. *Ibid.*, paragraph 27.
19. Case C-101/05 *A* [2007] ECR I-11531, paragraphs 60–63.
20. Case C-72/09 *Établissements Rimbaud* [2010] ECR I-10659, paragraph 40; Judgment of the Court of Justice in Case C-48/11 *Veronsaajien oikeudenvalvontayksikkö v. A Oy* of 19 Jul. 2012, nyr, paragraph 34. In the former, the conditions for administrative assistance were not satisfied, in the latter they were.

§11.04 TURKISH, SWISS AND EEA NATIONALS: 'EUROPEAN INDIVIDUALS'?

There is abundant case law of the Court of Justice on the interpretation of provisions of international agreements including those which replicate EU *acquis*. The Court's interpretation of three (sets of) agreements – the EEC-Turkey Association Agreement, the bilateral agreements concluded between the EU and Switzerland and the EEA Agreement – illustrate this point. Each of these agreements has a different scope and aim at a different level of integration. The following analysis focuses specifically on the possibility to considering Turkish, Swiss and EEA-EFTA nationals 'European individuals' in the light of the *Polydor* doctrine.

[A] The EEC-Turkey Agreement

The EEC-Turkey Agreement was concluded with the aim of promoting trade and economic relations between Turkey and the EU and, ultimately, creating a customs union.[21] The specific *acquis* which Turkey is obliged to adopt under the Agreement is specified in the decisions of the Association Council. Together with the Agreement the latter form the 'law of association'.[22] The specific means of approximation include the adoption of legislation 'equivalent' to the EU *acquis* as well as accession to multilateral conventions on intellectual, industrial and commercial property rights.[23] Although the 'law of association' contains extensive parts of the legislation in force within the Union it falls short of all four free movement rights. A case in point is the free movement of workers between the EU and Turkey which has not been realised to this date[24] in spite of the programmatic declaration on the progressive achievement of this right in Article 12 of the Association Agreement.[25]

The *Polydor* doctrine established that in order for the Court of Justice to interpret similarly worded provisions in international agreements in line with the interpretation of EU law, the substantive content of the respective provisions, the objective of the agreement and the institutional and procedural context must be comparable. On several occasions, the Court had ruled that the free movement of Turkish workers in the EU is limited and does not comprise a general freedom of movement which is granted to EU citizens.[26] The Court's judgment in *Demirkan* is a good example in delimiting the scope of the free movement provisions in the EEC-Turkey Agreement.[27]

21. Articles 2 and 5 EEC-Turkey Agreement.
22. Edgar Lenski, *Turkey (including Northern Cyprus)*, in *The European Union and Its Neighbours: A Legal Appraisal of the EU's Policies of Stabilisation, Partnership and Integration* 283–313 at 289 (Steven Blockmans & Adam Łazowski eds, T.M.C. Asser Press 2006).
23. Articles 2-3 of Annex 8 to the Decision 1/95 of the EC-Turkey Association Council.
24. *Supra* n. 21, at 294–296.
25. Case 12/86 *Demirel v. Stadt Schwäbisch Gmünd* [1987] ECR 3719, paragraph 23.
26. For example, Case C-171/95 *Tetik* [1997] ECR 1-329, paragraph 29; Case C-37/98 *Savas* [2000] ECR 1-2927, paragraph 59; Case C-171/01 *Wählergruppe Gemeinsam*, *supra* n. 15, paragraph 89; Case C-325/05 *Derin* [2007] ECR I-6495, paragraph 66.
27. Judgment of the Court of Justice in Case C-221/11 *Demirkan* of 24 Sep. 2013, nyr.

Demirkan concerned a standstill clause in the Additional Protocol to the EEC-Turkey Agreement which restricted the contracting parties to adopt new barriers to the freedom to provide services after the conclusion of the agreement. The standstill clause became binding on Germany in 1973 but, nevertheless, in 1980 Germany introduced a visa requirement for Turkish nationals travelling to Germany. In *Soysal*, the Court found that the visa requirement infringed the standstill clause by erecting new barriers to the freedom of Turkish nationals to provide services in the EU.[28] Demirkan, a Turkish national, applied for a German visa to visit a relative in Germany but her application was rejected by the German authorities. The applicant challenged the rejection in a German court arguing that because the visa requirement restricted her freedom to receive services in Germany it also violated the standstill clause. The Court rejected the argument.

Previously, in *Luisi and Carbone* the Court had interpreted the 'freedom to provide services' as entailing a passive dimension – the freedom of movement for the purpose of receiving rather than providing services.[29] In *Demirkan*, the Court decided not to extend the interpretation given in *Luigi and Carbone* to the EEC-Turkey Agreement. Resorting to the *Polydor*-doctrine, the Court found that the 'purely economic purpose' of the EEC-Turkey Agreement fell short of the purpose of the EU Treaties to 'bring ... about freedom of movement for persons of a general nature'.[30] Pursuant to the Court, the protection of passive freedom to provide services is part of the specific internal market objective – one which distinguishes the EU Treaties from the EEC-Turkey Agreement.[31] *Demirkan* clearly demonstrates that it is not a given that a fundamental freedom retains the same scope as within the EU when extended to non-EU nationals.

[B] EU-Switzerland Bilateral Agreements

Following a negative referendum in 1992 Switzerland was the only EFTA state to remain outside the EEA. Instead, Switzerland has concluded with the EU over 100 bilateral agreements which cover almost the entire field of the EU internal market. The objective of the EU-Swiss relationship based on bilateral agreements is not straightforward. From the perspective of exporting the *acquis*, the most significant of the bilateral agreements are the packages 'Bilateral I' signed in 1999 and 'Bilateral II' signed in 2004. On the one hand, Switzerland has agreed to adopt all EU *acquis* in the fields covered by the bilateral agreements thus resulting in very deep cooperation. On the other hand, although more far-reaching than the EEC-Turkey Agreement, the depth of integration of the bilateral agreements is smaller than that of the comprehensive EEA Agreement. The bilateral agreements notably exclude, in addition to some policy fields, to a smaller or greater extent the free movement of capital and services, and the freedom of establishment.

28. Case C-228/06 *Soysal and Savatli* [2009] ECR I-1031, paragraphs 57–58.
29. Joined Cases 286/82 and 26/83 *Luisi and Carbone* [1984] ECR 377, paragraph 16.
30. Case C-221/11 *Demirkan, supra* n. 27, paragraphs 44, 51, 53.
31. *Ibid.*, paragraph 56.

There are two possibilities for analysing the application of the *Polydor* doctrine to the EU-Switzerland bilateral agreements. On the one hand, each of the bilateral agreements is separate and has its own objectives. On the other hand, however, each bilateral agreement contributes to the comprehensive management of EU-Switzerland relations and must, thus, be seen in the overall context of the set of agreements.[32] In *Grimme*, the Court adopted the latter, comprehensive way of analysis.[33] The Court found that the objectives of the EU-Swiss bilateral agreements as regards the internal market were not comparable to those of the EEA Agreement. The Court noted that Switzerland, by rejecting the EEA Agreement and refraining from implementing the free movement of services and establishment, did not 'join the internal market of the Community' which is an 'area of total freedom of movement analogous to that provided by a national market'.[34] Therefore, the provisions of the EU-Switzerland bilateral agreements cannot automatically be interpreted in line with the corresponding provisions of EU Treaties unless the agreement in question provides so explicitly.[35] AG Mazák in *Bergström* referred to *Grimme* to conclude that there is no automatic equivalence of interpretation between the EU internal market provisions and the provisions of the EC-Switzerland bilateral agreements but that the latter instead need to be interpreted in the light of the objectives of the bilateral agreements.[36] Surely, this does not preclude the possibility of identical interpretation provided that in the relevant fields the objectives of the Treaties and of the bilateral agreements are comparable.

In his Opinion in *Ettwein*,[37] AG Jääskinen reiterated the Court's reasoning in *Grimme*. The AG found that as regards the internal market and the four freedoms the aims of the EEA Agreement are identical to those of the EU Treaties; identically worded provisions of the EEA Agreement should, therefore, be given the same interpretation as the underlying EU rules.[38] By rejecting the EEA Agreement in 1992, Switzerland also discarded the 'project of creating an integrated economic whole with a single market based on common rules between its members'.[39] Instead, the EC-Switzerland agreement on the free movement of persons, which was the subject of the Opinion, merely aims at the strengthening of relations 'without any prospect of extending the application of the fundamental freedoms *in toto* to the Swiss Confederation', thus excluding identical interpretation from taking place automatically.[40] The Court of Justice in *Ettwein* interpreted the relevant provisions of the EC-Switzerland agreement in the light of the agreement itself without comparing the objectives of the agreement with

32. This applies in particular to the 'Bilateral I' set of seven agreements which are bound together by a so-called guillotine clause. All of the agreements entered into force together and none of them can be terminated individually.
33. Case C-351/08 *Grimme* [2009] ECR I-10777.
34. *Ibid.*, paragraph 27.
35. *Ibid.*, paragraph 29; Case C-541/08 *Fokus Invest* [2010] ECR I-1025, paragraph 28; Case C-70/09 *Hengartner and Gasser* [2010] ECR I-7233, paragraph 42.
36. Opinion of AG Mazák in Case C-257/10 *Bergström* [2011] ECR I-13227, paragraph 45.
37. Opinion of AG Jääskinen in Case C-425/11 *Katja Ettwein v. Finanzamt Konstanz* of 18 Oct. 2012, nyr.
38. *Ibid.*, paragraph 39.
39. *Ibid.*, paragraph 36.
40. *Ibid.*, paragraphs 36–37, 65.

those of the EU Treaties or the EEA Agreement.[41] In spite of the lack of automaticity, the Court deemed the objectives in the particular case comparable and interpreted the relevant provisions of the EC-Switzerland agreement in light of its previous judgments given in the EU context.

[C] The EEA Agreement

The EEA Agreement comes closest to the level of integration in the EU internal market. The objective of the EEA Agreement is to promote trade and economic relations between the contracting parties by setting up a 'dynamic and homogeneous' EEA based on the free movement of goods, persons, services and capital and equal conditions for competition.[42] To realise the EEA, the EEA Agreement is continuously updated to reflect the developments in the internal market *acquis*. The EEA Agreement covers almost the entire internal market with the exception of the common customs tariff, common commercial policy and common agricultural and fisheries policies. Homogeneous interpretation of EEA *acquis* with EU *acquis* is moreover pursued by Article 6 EEA Agreement which provides that provisions of the EEA Agreement which are identical in substance to EU *acquis* must be interpreted in conformity with the pre-1994 case law of the Court.

Already before the conclusion of the EEA Agreement, its objectives were subject to scrutiny by the Court of Justice. In Opinion 1/91 the Court, implicitly referring to the *Polydor* doctrine, found that the identical wording of the provisions of the EC Treaty and the EEA Agreement does not necessarily lead to their identical interpretation unless the objectives of both treaties justify such analogous interpretation.[43] Even though the internal market objectives of the EU and the EEA are roughly identical the Court found that the free trade and competition rules in the EEC Treaty 'far from being an end in themselves' serve the purpose within the Community of 'making concrete progress towards European unity'.[44] Provisions 'identical in their content or wording' in themselves do not guarantee homogeneity between the EEC Treaty and the EEA Agreement.[45]

The Court's conclusions in Opinion 1/91 regarding homogeneity were, however, not fully endorsed. In *Opel Austria*, the Court of First Instance (CFI, now General Court) rejected the Council's argument on the existence of major differences between the EU Treaties and the EEA Agreement that would preclude an identical interpretation of Article 10 EEA Agreement and the corresponding provision in the EC Treaty.[46] The CFI recognised the difference between the aims and context of the EEA Agreement and Community law yet did no perceive them as standing in the way of achieving homogeneity in the EEA. Instead, the CFI deemed the integration objectives of the EEA

41. Judgment of the Court of Justice in Case C-425/11 *Katja Ettwein v. Finanzamt Konstanz* of 28 Feb. 2013, nyr.
42. Article 1 and Recital 4 of the Preamble of the EEA Agreement.
43. Opinion 1/91 *EEA I* [1991] ECR I-6079, paragraph 14.
44. *Ibid.*, paragraphs 15–18.
45. *Ibid.*, paragraph 22.
46. Case T-115/94 *Opel Austria v. Council* [1997] ECR II-39, paragraphs 105–106.

Agreement to 'exceed those of a mere free-trade agreement', thus justifying the inapplicability of the *Polydor* doctrine.[47] The CFI argued that the conclusions of Opinion 1/91 referred to the envisaged judicial system of the EEA and its effect on the autonomy of the EU legal order rather than the identical interpretation of similar provisions.[48] The EEA Agreement contains certain safeguard clauses that allow the Joint Committee to refuse the entry of post-1994 *acquis* into the EEA legal order, thus leading to derogations from substantive uniformity between the EU and the EEA legal order. The CFI, however, regarded the possibility of derogations not to be of importance for the purpose of interpreting Article 10 EEA Agreement.[49] Certain substantive derogations in the composition of the *acquis* should not render the objectives of the EEA Agreement incomparable to EU law.

The arguments of the CFI in *Opel Austria* were refuted by AG Cosmas in *Andersson*.[50] The case concerned the interpretation of Article 6 EEA Agreement with a view to determining whether secondary EU law and principles established in the case law of the Court of Justice – in this case the *Francovich* doctrine – can be applied in the EEA legal order. Noting the 'fundamental differences' between the EU and the EEA legal systems the AG contended that the contexts are too different to transfer to the EEA the fundamental principles of primacy, direct effect and state liability.[51] The analysis of AG Cosmas can be considered correct but must be regarded in the specific context of the applicability of fundamental principles in the EEA Agreement. Undoubtedly an important aspect in the process of constructing 'European individuals' outside the EU, it pertains the effect of the *acquis* outside the Union rather than the identical set of rights and obligations which is the focus of the present chapter. As concerns the comparability of the objectives of the EEA Agreement and the EU Treaties for the purpose of interpreting Article 10 EEA Agreement, AG Cosmas fully endorsed the CFI's conclusions in *Opel Austria*.[52]

The 'notorious' differences in character between the EU and the EEA Treaties once noted by AG Fennelly[53] have not been upheld in subsequent case law. In *Ospelt*, both AG Geelhoed and the Court of Justice agreed that the objective of 'the fullest possible realisation of the free movement of goods, persons, services and capital within the whole European Economic Area' adds up to an extension of the EU internal market to the EEA EFTA States.[54] To the extent that the EU Treaties and the EEA Agreement feature similar provisions on the free movement of capital as well as similar objectives and context, the provision itself and permissible restrictions must 'as far as possible' be given identical interpretation.[55]

47. *Ibid.*, paragraphs 106–107.
48. *Ibid.*, paragraph 109.
49. *Ibid.*, paragraph 110.
50. Opinion of AG Cosmas in Case C-321/97 *Andersson and Wåkerås-Andersson* [1999] ECR I-3551.
51. *Ibid.*, paragraph 49.
52. *Ibid.*, at note 44.
53. Opinion of AG Fennelly in Case C-110/95 *Yamanouchi* [1997] ECR I-3251, paragraph 30.
54. Opinion of AG Geelhoed in Case C-452/01 *Ospelt* [2003] ECR I-9743, paragraph 69; Case C-452/01 *Ospelt* [2003] ECR I-9743, paragraph 29.
55. Opinion of AG Geelhoed in Case C-452/01 *Ospelt*, *supra* n. 54, paragraphs 69–71.

Commentators, too, agree that the *Polydor* doctrine does not apply to the EEA Agreement to the effect of precluding identical interpretation of provisions which are identical in substance.[56] On the one hand, compared to the EEC-Portugal FTA, the EEA Agreement envisages much deeper cooperation. On the other hand, Article 6 EEA Agreement precludes conflicting interpretations, at least with regard to pre-signature case law. Moreover, although the EEA Agreement does not include a reference to the peoples of the EU and the EEA EFTA States as did the original EEC Treaty, the preamble of the EEA Agreement does speak of 'the important role that individuals will play in the EEA through the exercise of the rights conferred on them by this Agreement and through the judicial defence of these rights'.[57] Importantly, Recital 8 was only added to the preamble of the draft EEA Agreement after the Court had given its Opinion 1/91.[58] Compared to both the EEC-Turkey Agreement and the EU-Switzerland bilateral agreements, therefore, objectives of the EEA Agreement do, indeed, to the extent of the internal market constitute a pre-determined guarantee for identical interpretation of *acquis* which is identical in wording. The type of the agreement plays hereby no particular role as all of the agreements discussed above have been concluded as association agreements.[59]

[D] *Three Rounds of United Kingdom v. Council:* The EEA, Switzerland and Turkey Agreements Compared

The three recent judgments in cases *United Kingdom v. Council* provided a unique occasion to compare the objectives of the EEA Agreement,[60] the EC-Switzerland Agreement on the Free Movement of Persons,[61] and the EEC-Turkey Association Agreement.[62] Although the judgments do not concern the interpretation of identical provisions they illustrate the considerations of the objective and context of the international agreements which can and certainly will be taken into account should a question of identical interpretation arise at a different point in time.

Each of the cases concerns an annulment action brought by the UK government against a Council decision on the position to be taken on behalf of the EU in accordance with Article 218(9) TFEU by the bodies who amend the three international agreements. The amendments in question concerned the adoption into the EEA Agreement, the

56. Sven Norberg, *The European Economic Area* in *Oliver on Free Movement of Goods in the European Union* 487–506 at 493 (Peter Oliver ed., Hart Publishing 2010); Carl Baudenbacher, *The EFTA Court and Court of Justice of the European Union: Coming in Parts But Winning Together*, in *The Court of Justice and the Construction of Europe: Analyses and Perspectives on Sixty Years of Case-law* 183–203 at 191 (T.M.C. Asser Press 2013).
57. Recital 8, Preamble of the EEA Agreement.
58. Halvard Haukeland Fredriksen, *The EFTA Court 15 Years on*, 59 Intl & Comp. L. Q. 731, 750 (2010).
59. Among the bilateral agreements concluded with Switzerland, agreements belonging to 'Bilateral I' are association agreements but not those of the 'Bilateral II' package. The Agreement on the Free Movement of Persons is part of 'Bilateral I'.
60. Judgment of the Court of Justice in Case C-431/11 *UK v. Council* of 26 Sep. 2013, nyr.
61. Judgment of the Court of Justice in Case C-656/11 *UK v. Council* of 27 Feb. 2014, nyr.
62. Judgment of the Court of Justice in Case C-81/13 *UK v. Council* of 18 Dec. 2014, nyr.

EC-Switzerland Agreement and the EEC-Turkey Agreement Regulation No. 883/2004 on the coordination of social security systems which replaced Regulation No. 1408/71. The UK government claimed that the decisions were adopted on a wrong legal basis. Instead of the Internal Market legal basis of Article 48 TFEU, the UK argued that the contested Council decisions should have been adopted on the basis of Article 79(2) TFEU regulating EU immigration policy. From the latter the UK may opt out.

In all cases, the Court firmly overruled the UK's arguments regarding the amendments as immigration policy measures. The first judgment delivered in Case C-431/11 concerned the EEA Agreement. The Court, firstly, cited its earlier judgment in *Ospelt* on the objectives of the EEA agreement to extend the internal market to EEA EFTA States and found that the contested Regulation served precisely the purpose of providing to EEA citizens the same social conditions for the exercise of their free movement rights as those enjoyed by EU citizens.[63] In the case of the EC-Switzerland agreement, the Court did not use the language of extending the internal market to Switzerland, probably due to the Swiss refusal to become party to the EEA Agreement. Instead, the Court referred to the objective of the agreement to 'bring about between [the EC and Switzerland] the free movement of persons on the basis of the rules applying in the Community'.[64]

Both the EEA and the EC-Switzerland agreements already contained EU *acquis* on the approximation of social security systems with a view to ensure the effectiveness of the free movement provisions. An update in EU *acquis* was necessary to incorporate changes introduced by the Lisbon Treaty. In order to ensure the balance of rights between EU citizens and the citizens of Iceland, Liechtenstein, Norway and Switzerland and 'with the result that nationals of the EEA States concerned benefit from the free movement of persons under the same social conditions as EU citizens' required a due update in the EEA and EU-Swiss *acquis* on the free movement of persons but the scope of the amendment in itself was not significant.[65]

The same does not hold true for the EEC-Turkey Agreement. The objective of the EEC-Turkey Agreement is narrower than the fullest possible realisation of the free movement of persons, stating merely the wish of the contracting parties to secure between them the freedom of movement for workers in progressive stages, one of the stages being the incorporation of the contested Regulation into the Agreement.[66] As set out in *Demirkan* and other case law, there is no general freedom of movement between the EU and Turkey, nor have the parties completed the progressive introduction of the free movement of workers provided in Article 12 of the Agreement. In the judgment, the Court referred extensively to the previous judgments in the cases concerning the EEA Agreement and the EC-Switzerland Agreement. The comparison of the three agreements led to a conclusion that regarding the free movement of persons the

63. Case C-431/11 *UK v. Council, supra* n. 60, paragraphs 50 and 58.
64. Case C-656/11 *UK v. Council, supra* n. 61, paragraph 55.
65. *Ibid.*, paragraph 58.
66. Case C-81/13 *UK v. Council, supra* n. 62, paragraphs 43, 45.

objective of the EEC-Turkey Agreement was neither comparable to that of the EEA Agreement nor the EC-Switzerland Agreement.[67]

The Court contended that the EEA EFTA States and Switzerland can be 'equated with a Member State for the purposes of the application of those regulations' whereas Turkey cannot.[68] Even the fact that Regulation No. 1408/71 had been incorporated into the EEC-Turkey Agreement and the Additional Protocol similarly as to the EEA and the EC-Swiss agreements, it did not have the same effect of extending to Turkey the rules on the coordination of social security systems.[69] As a result, Turkey was not covered by the extension of the internal market in the way of the EEA EFTA States and Switzerland. In the case at hand this meant that the Council decision in question could not be adopted solely on the internal market legal basis of Article 48 TFEU but in conjunction with Article 217 TFEU which is the legal basis for association agreements.[70] The additional legal basis was meant to emphasise the distinction between the EEC-Turkey Agreement and the EEA and EC-Switzerland agreements yet is somewhat puzzling as all of the agreements are association agreements. The Court highlighted that the legal basis of Article 48 TFEU may only be used on its own for adopting Internal Market measures within the EU or in external action *vis-à-vis* non-EU Member States that 'can be placed on the same footing' as EU Member States.[71] The difference between the decisions does not lie within actual divergences in the application of Regulation 883/2004 in the third countries concerned but rather in the perceived differences in the level of integration of the third countries into the Internal Market. In this case, individuals of Iceland, Liechtenstein, Norway and Switzerland were, indeed, placed on an equal footing with EU citizens thus justifying their position as 'European individuals' outside the EU. In the case of Switzerland, this generalisation cannot automatically be carried on to all of the bilateral agreements because the EU-Swiss cooperation lacks uniformity in the crucial elements of the Internal Market – the four freedoms.

In Opinion 1/91, the Court contended that the fundamental freedoms were only one of several possible means to achieve the Internal Market and economic and monetary union and, eventually, greater European unity.[72] A reading of Opinion 1/91 in combination with the judgments in the above cases *United Kingdom v. Council*, however, reveals that the Court is not likely to restrict the application of EU *acquis* in countries covered by agreements which envisage deep regulatory integration. By 2014, the Court's careful approach towards the EEA Agreement has been replaced by recognition of the possibility of truly extending the Internal Market beyond the EU also in the light of the *Polydor* principle. The facts of the cases above did not require the Court to comment on the interpretation of EU *acquis* in the respective agreements yet the Court's affirmation of an extended Internal Market encourages one to assume that it is unlikely for the Court to impede the functioning of the expanded Internal Market

67. *Ibid.*, paragraph 57.
68. *Ibid.*
69. *Ibid.*, paragraph 58.
70. *Ibid.*, paragraphs 59–66.
71. *Ibid.*, paragraph 59.
72. Opinion 1/91 *EEA I*, *supra* n. 43, paragraph 19.

by refusing to interpret EEA or even EU-Swiss *acquis* which is identical in substance to the underlying EU *acquis* differently from the latter.

§11.05 CONCLUSION

The EU is becoming an ever closer union among the peoples of Europe and is likewise expanding the Internal Market integration to non-Member States. In the meantime, the fundamental freedoms – the cornerstone of the Internal Market – do not exist independently of the nuances provided by the Court of Justice. In order for an exported set of Internal Market *acquis* to function as a true extension of the Internal Market it must be ensured that national courts and especially the Court of Justice are willing to extend to the exported *acquis* the same interpretation that it gives to provisions of EU law. The Court's ruling in *Polydor* has long raised doubts as to the viability of the practice of exporting EU *acquis* from the perspective of thereby achieving a homogeneous legal space which includes both identical rules as well as identical interpretation of those rules.

Recent case law, however, has shown that early concerns have largely been unfounded. A comparison between three rather different agreements which export EU *acquis* to third countries reveals that it is possible to pass the 'objectives and context' test of *Polydor*. The question which remains is whether the equivalence of the objectives and context of an international agreement to the EU Treaties can be pre-determined such as appears to be the case with the EEA Agreement or whether the objectives and context have to be compared separately in each new case. Due to the incomplete application of the fundamental freedoms in the EU-Swiss relationship, for example, the provisions of each of the bilateral agreements must be analysed in the light of their own objectives. In those areas where integration is more advanced, such as the free movement of persons and goods, the Court is more likely to interpret provisions of the bilateral agreements in line with EU *acquis* than in areas such as the free movement of services. The EEC-Turkey Agreement generally lags behind the EEA and EU-Swiss agreements in terms of the depth of integration envisaged. Each provision of the EEC-Turkey Agreement must be fully proven in accordance with the *Polydor* doctrine without, of course, precluding an outcome of identical interpretation. It applies equally to all international agreements exporting the *acquis* that the interpretation of different provisions within the same agreement may vary. In some fields, non-EU individuals may be in a comparable situation to EU individuals whereas in other cases an identical interpretation is precluded by the purpose served by the particular provision in the EU and in the international agreement, respectively.

The possible application of the *Polydor* doctrine must also be considered by Member States wishing to leave the EU yet retain a stake in the Internal Market, perhaps even full membership. The option of switching from an 'opt-out' scenario to a full 'opt-in' scenario may seem tempting at first but may have serious consequences for the areas from which one does not wish to deviate. Identical interpretation of EU *acquis* which means identical scope of rights and obligations for the market participants is only automatically guaranteed in an EEA-type agreement pursuing deepest possible integration. Each divergence from the *acquis* that is reflected in the objectives and context of the instrument chosen will reduce the possibility to foresee the actual scope of the exported *acquis* following an interpretation by the Court.

From the perspective of the EU and the Court of Justice it is possible to construct 'European individuals' outside the EU legal order yet the required level of integration of the overall framework with the EU is deep. An opt-out from one policy area of the EU Treaties does not affect the scope of the rest of the *acquis* and the Member State who thus opts out does not lose the 'same footing' with other Member States. Where a Member State, however, decides to leave the Union and reject cooperation in certain fields, especially one of the four fundamental freedoms such as in the case of Switzerland, its 'equal footing' will be challenged to the extent of the individuals concerned losing their equal position *vis-à-vis* EU nationals. Cherry-picking outside the Union is, therefore, much trickier than inside.

CHAPTER 12

Britain Alone! The Implications and Consequences of United Kingdom Exit from the European Union: Social Policies

Aileen McColgan

§12.01 INTRODUCTION

The implications of EU membership for individual rights, particularly those concerned with employment and the broader regulation of discrimination, have been extremely significant. Here I will consider the relationship between such membership and the development of individual social rights, in particular pertaining to employment and equality, and the possible legal repercussions in this area of exit. For the reasons set out below I will suggest that, though much of the UK's discrimination legislation has developed organically rather than being transplanted from the EEC/EU, any departure from the EU would pose significant threat to its existence and, in particular, its efficacy. As for other, employment-focused, social rights such as those concerned with the regulation of working time and the protection of agency workers, the likelihood is that exit from the EU would result in more or less comprehensive repeal.

A significant number of employment-related rights derive directly from EU law. Among these are prohibitions on discrimination against part-time and fixed-term workers; protection (albeit limited) accorded to agency workers; entitlements to paid holiday and to maximum weekly hours; protection of employment rights for employees affected by transfers of undertakings and parental leave rights. There is significant cause to question whether any or all of these provisions would survive UK exit from the EU in the event (as is likely) that such would occur within the context of a Conservative or Conservative-dominated coalition Government. Certainly Prime Minister David Cameron singled out the Working Time Directive (2003/88/EC,) for criticism in his

January 2013 speech on the future of Europe.[1] And although the 2015 Conservative manifesto is silent on the question of which social policy rights the party regards as inappropriate it does state that an incoming Conservative government would 'cut a further GBP 10 billion of red tape over the next Parliament through our Red Tape Challenge and our One-In-Two-Out rule',[2] while UKIP's manifesto singles out the Working Time Directive as 'actively restrict[ing] the British work ethos and therefore our economy' and blames the growth of zero-hours contracts on the Temporary Agency Work Directive (2008/104/EC).[3]

§12.02 AN HISTORICAL ACCOUNT OF DOMESTIC DISCRIMINATION/EQUALITY LAW

The likely fate of EU-derived employment rights such as those mentioned above, in the event of a UK exit from the EU, is fairly clear. More difficult to assess, I would suggest, is the position as regards discrimination law properly so called (i.e., the wide-ranging prohibitions on discrimination on grounds, *inter alia*, of sex, race, disability, sexual orientation, religion or belief and age now consolidated (with amendments) into the Equality Act 2010 in Great Britain, and their equivalent provisions which continue to apply in Northern Ireland.

The relationship between EU membership and the legal regulation of discrimination in the UK is not a straightforward one. It is the case that the Equal Pay Act 1970, one of the earliest modern anti-discrimination statutes,[4] was provoked by the UK's impending membership of what was then the EEC. But the Race Relations Act 1965, which prohibited direct race discrimination by service providers in 'places of public resort' (not including shops) and the Race Relations Act 1968, which extended this prohibition to cover employment, housing, and the provision of goods, facilities and services, were unconnected with prospective membership. The former was a reaction to overt race discrimination in the form of colour bars applied, in particular, to Caribbean immigrants. The years that followed immediately upon its implementation saw the ending of an unofficial colour bar on black workers by British Rail at Euston Station following publicity regarding its operation, together with reports that similar bars continued to apply at other stations including Camden and Broad Street. In 1968 the exodus of East African Asians from Kenya into the UK resulted in the 1968 Commonwealth Immigration Act which required British subjects (at the time a very large category indeed) to demonstrate a 'close connection' with the UK as a condition of entry. That Act was, to the condemnation of Enoch Powell (then shadow defence spokesman) accompanied by the Race Relations Act of the same year which aimed to facilitate the integration of those immigrants who had already arrived, or would be permitted to enter the UK under the new regime.

---

1. http://www.bbc.co.uk/news/uk-politics-21013771 (accessed 4 May 2015).
2. https://www.conservatives.com/manifesto (accessed 4 May 2015).
3. http://www.ukip.org/manifesto2015 (accessed 4 May 2015).
4. I am not here concerned with early Acts such as the Papists Act 1778 and Roman Catholics Relief Act 1829, or the 1918 or 1928 Representation of the People Acts.

The Sex Discrimination Act 1975 post-dated the UK's accession to the European Communities but preceded the adoption of the Equal Treatment Directive (Directive 76/207/EEC), whose provisions would later require amendments to the 1975 Act. The European Council had in 1974 resolved on a social action programme which prioritised the taking of action to achieve equality between men and women in the sphere of employment, but the 1975 Act was not driven by any EU imperative. It had been preceded by proposals circulated by a Conservative government in 1973[5] which suggested that legislation should have the objectives of widening the range of opportunities open to women, that unfair sex discrimination in areas such as employment and training should be challenged, and that there should be an investigation into whether further measures were required to help women contribute to society on equal terms with men.

The Labour Party tethered its proposed legislation on sex discrimination to the race discrimination provisions in the 1974 White Paper *Equality for Women*, which was published between the two general elections of 1974, and in which it indicated the intention 'to harmonise the powers and procedures for dealing with sex and race discrimination so as to secure genuine equality of opportunity in both fields'. Home Secretary Roy Jenkins made clear his view that the Sex Discrimination Bill, and the Bill that would become the 1976 Race Relations Act, were aspects of a coherent policy of reform,[6] a 'comprehensive code of law against racial and sex discrimination'.[7] The 1975/6 package of legislation was drawn up more with an eye on the US than on the European Communities. The 1968 RRA had been influenced by the report of the Street Committee which had examined the approach taken in the US, and elsewhere, to anti-discrimination legislation.[8] But the US approach proved particularly influential in the 1970s in the legislative prohibition of indirect discrimination, which followed a visit by Roy Jenkins to the US in 1974 where he was made aware of the significance of the decision in *Griggs v. Duke Power Co*[9] which allowed challenge to be made to broad institutional practices as well as individual acts of deliberate and/or overt discrimination.[10] Both the Sex Discrimination Act 1975 and the Race Relations Act 1976 prohibited this form of discrimination.

The Sex Discrimination Act, as it was passed, owed little or nothing to the UK's membership of the EEC. Notwithstanding the fact that the Act became the vehicle in Britain for the transposition of the Equal Treatment Directive 1976 (Directive 76/207),

5. *Equal Opportunities for Men and Women – Government Proposals for Legislation*, Department of Employment, 1973.
6. *See* for example his statement to the House of Commons in July 1974 Hansard, vol 877, col 1298.
7. Speech to the annual conference of the Community Relations Commission in September 1975, published in the CRC *Journal*, October 1975.
8. H. Street, G. Howe & G. Bindman, *Report on Anti-discrimination Legislation. London: Political and Economic Planning* (1967) and *see* G. Bindman, *The Law and Racial Discrimination: Third Thoughts*, III Brit. J. L. & Soc. 110–114 (1976).
9. 401 U.S. 424 (1971).
10. G. Bindman & S. Grosz, *Indirect Discrimination and the Race Relations Act*, in Runnymede Trust, *A Review of the Race Relations Act 1976: Proceedings of a one-day seminar in London, 30 March 1979* (London: Runnymede Trust), 21. The visit also resulted in the amendment of the Bill to permit a small measure of positive discrimination – see J. Gregory, *Sex, Race and the Law – Legislating for Equality* 48 (Sage 1987) and Hansard, vol 889, col 514 & vol 906, col 1558.

and was subject to many express amendments to this end, neither the Directive nor any subsequent gender equality directives have matched the material reach of the 1975 Act which extended its prohibitions on sex discrimination beyond employment (broadly defined to include vocational training and access to self-employment, trade union membership, etc) to cover, *inter alia*, education and access to goods, facilities and services.[11]

A year after the Sex Discrimination Act was adopted the Race Relations Act 1976 became law. The White Paper which had preceded it, *Racial Discrimination*,[12] recognised (p. 2) the commonplace nature of employment-related discrimination notwithstanding the 1968 Act, its impact on unemployment rates for some BME groups, and (p. 3) the concentration of the BME population in poor, over-crowded private sector rental accommodation. In words which, for the most part, continue to resonate in 2015, the White Paper expressed concern over the fact that the passage of time had not eradicated the disadvantages experienced by immigrant communities:

> 11. The possibility has to be faced that there is at work in this country, as elsewhere in the world, the familiar cycle of cumulative disadvantage by which relatively low-paid or low-status jobs for the first generation of immigrants go hand in hand with poor and overcrowded living conditions and a depressed environment [which has the effect that] ... the second generation finds themselves trapped in poor jobs and poor housing. If, at each stage of the process, an element of racial discrimination enters in, then an entire group of people are launched into a vicious downward spiral of deprivation. They may share each of the disadvantages with some other deprived group in society; but few other groups in society display all their accumulated disadvantages...
>
> It is the Government's duty to prevent these morally unacceptable and socially divisive inequalities from hardening into entrenched patterns. It is inconceivable that Britain, in the last quarter of the 20th century, should confess herself unable to secure for a small minority of around a million and a half coloured [sic] citizens their full and equal rights as individual men and women (pp.3-4).

By the time the RRA 1976 was passed domestic legislation on discrimination was significantly more advanced than EEC provisions. And more recently, while EU Directives[13] resulted in the implementation in the UK of legislative prohibitions on (broadly) employment-related discrimination on grounds of sexual orientation, religion or belief (in 2003) and age (in 2006), and extensive amendments to domestic provisions regulating discrimination on grounds of race (broadly defined), sex and disability, the UK's legislation on sex, race and disability legislation was significantly in advance of that in most EU states at the dates of adoption of Directives 2000/43/EC and

11. The Gender (Goods and Services) Directive (2004/113/EC) excludes education, though it applies to the provision of some goods and services.
12. http://filestore.nationalarchives.gov.uk/pdfs/small/cab-129-184-c-93.pdf (accessed 3 May 20 15).
13. Council Directives 2000/34/EC (the Race Directive) and 2000/78/EC (the Employment Equality Directive).

2000/78/EC and the Disability Discrimination Act 1995 had itself helped to give shape to the prohibition of disability discrimination in the latter Directive.[14]

Directive 2000/78/EC required Member States to adopt prohibitions on employment-related discrimination on grounds of disability, age, sexual orientation and religion/belief. Its sister directive, 2000/43/EC, required the broader prohibition of race discrimination in the context (as well as employment, broadly defined) of social protection, including social security and healthcare; social advantages; education; access to and supply of goods and services which are available to the public, including housing. And while this Directive, like Directive 2000/78/EC, required amendments to be made to the UK's existing prohibitions[15] as well as (in the case of Directive 2000/78/EC) the adoption of new legislative prohibitions on discrimination on grounds of sexual orientation and religion/belief,[16] the UK went significantly further than the Directives required in extending the prohibitions on discrimination on grounds of sexual orientation, religion or belief and (in GB, though not Northern Ireland) age beyond the context of employment. Further, and importantly, the development of the 'public sector equality duty' (PSED) now found in section 149 of the Equality Act 2010 has taken place entirely independently of EEC/EU imperatives.

The PSED has its roots in section 71 RRA 1975 which imposed duties on local authorities (alone) 'to make appropriate arrangements with a view to securing that their various functions are carried out with due regard to the need – (a) to eliminate unlawful racial discrimination; and (b) to promote equality of opportunity, and good relations, between persons of different racial groups'. The provision was something of a dead letter, attempts by local authorities to rely upon it as a basis for anti-apartheid actions having been rejected by the courts on a number of occasions and no successful judicial review having been brought against a local authority on the basis of it.[17] Section 71 was amended by the Race Relations (Amendment) Act 2000 which was passed in the aftermath of the racist murder of Stephen Lawrence and the publication of the MacPherson inquiry's Report, which made far-reaching findings of institutionalised discrimination in relation to the police, and which resulted in a spotlight being turned on the practices of other public bodies to sometimes unflattering effect.[18] MacPherson's findings proved the death knell to the immunity previously enjoyed by public authorities in respect of discrimination in the exercise of public powers,[19] new section 19B RRA prohibiting race discrimination in the carrying out of public functions.

14. Albeit that the latter applied to a narrower material scope (employment, broadly defined) while the DDA also applied to education, the provision of goods, facilities and services, housing and transport.
15. In the case of Directive 2000/43/EC, to the RRA 1976, in the case of Directive 2000/78/EC to the DDA 1995.
16. Except in NI where the Fair Employment and Treatment Order 1998 (and before it the Fair Employment Acts 1976 and 1989) already prohibited discrimination on grounds of religious or political opinion, albeit it required some amendment.
17. *Wheeler v. Leicester CC* [1985] AC 1054, *R v. Lewisham LBC Ex p. Shell UK* [1988] 1 All ER 938.
18. *See* A. McColgan, *Discrimination Law: Text, Cases and Materials*, Chapter 7 (Hart 2000).
19. The House of Lords had decided in *R v. Entry Clearance Officer, Bombay, ex p Amin* [1983] 2 AC 818, a case concerning the materially identical provisions of the SDA, that public authorities were only bound by the RRA when they exercised functions equivalent to those of private bodies, and not when they were engaged in the activities of the 'state' as such.

A Liberal Democrat amendment to the Bill in the House of Lords in January 2000[20] provoked a Government announcement in the same month that a statutory duty on public authorities to promote equality would be included in the Bill.[21]

Post amendment by the 2000 Act, section 71 RRA required that every body listed in Schedule 1A of the Act 'shall, in carrying out its functions, have due regard to the need – (a) to eliminate unlawful racial discrimination [[22]]; and (b) to promote equality of opportunity and good relations between persons of different racial groups'. The DDA and then the SDA were amended to similar (though not identical) effect in 2005 and 2007 respectively, and these PSEDs were brought together in section 149 of the Equality Act 2010 which applies similarly in respect of sexual orientation, religion/belief and age.

§12.03 THE IMPACT OF EU LAW ON DOMESTIC DISCRIMINATION LAW

It is clear from the foregoing that, other than in respect of legislative prohibitions on employment-related discrimination on grounds of age, sexual orientation and religion or belief, the UK has not required to be prodded into taking legislative steps to regulate discrimination by the EU or its predecessor. The same has proven true as regards the protection of trans-men and women (though the impetus for this came from the 'other Europe'[23]), and the recognition, successively, of same-sex civil partnerships and same-sex marriage. This is not to say, however, that EU membership has not proved extremely important in the development of legal protections against discrimination in the UK. It is by no means clear that the legislative prohibitions on discrimination relating to sexual orientation, religion or belief and age would have been put in place when they were had EU law not driven this, although they would likely have eventually found their way into the statute books. But of equal if not greater importance has been the role of the CJEU in clarifying the scope and effect of the EU provisions and, through that, of domestic law (whether by judicial interpretation or necessary legislative amendment).

In *Marshall v. Southampton & South West Health Authority*[24] the ECJ (as it then was) ruled that the UK's differential retirement ages for men and women were incompatible with the Equal Treatment Directive. In *Marshall v. Southampton & South West Health Authority (No. 2)*[25] it ruled that the cap on compensation then applied in discrimination claims breached the requirement that sanctions be effective. In *Bilka-Kaufhaus v. Weber von Hartz*[26] the Court ruled that the prohibition on gender-based pay discrimination applied to indirect, as well as to direct, discrimination, and in

20. *Ibid*, vol 608, col 773-788.
21. *See* Race Relations Amendment Bill (HL) Bill, Commons Library Research Paper http://www.parliament.uk/briefing-papers/RP00-27/race-relations-amendment-bill-hl-bill-bill-60-of-1999 2000 p. 24 (accessed 3 May 2015).
22. After 1 Oct. 2010 'discrimination and victimisation'.
23. *Goodwin v. United Kingdom* (1996) 22 EHRR 123.
24. C-152/84 [1986] 2 ECR 723.
25. C-271/91 [1993] ECR I-04367.
26. C-170/84 [1986] ECR 1607.

Barber v. Guardian Royal Exchange Assurance Group[27] that occupational pensions were 'pay' to which the requirement for equal pay without discrimination based on sex applied. In *Webb v. EMO Air Cargo (UK) Ltd*[28] it ruled that pregnancy discrimination must be prohibited as sex discrimination, which the SDA did not at the time do, and in *P v. S & Cornwall*[29] that the prohibition on sex discrimination extended to protect a trans-woman from discrimination connected with her gender reassignment. In *Levez v. Harlow Pools Ltd*[30] the ECJ ruled that the then-rigid time limits for equal pay claims were not compatible with EU law and in *Coote v. Granada*[31] that workers must be protected against victimisation by former employers arising out of complaints of sex discrimination. These decisions all proved to be of substantial, and some of them of profound, importance to domestic law, and this is not even to take into account the Court's rulings on infringement actions brought in respect of UK domestic law by the Commission[32] which resulted in amendments to the SDA and Equal Pay Act.

Domestic discrimination law is now consolidated in Great Britain (though not Northern Ireland) into the Equality Act 2010 which imposes the PSED discussed above and regulates discrimination, victimisation and harassment because of race (broadly defined), sex, sexual orientation, gender reassignment, pregnancy and maternity, marriage and civil partnership, religion or belief, age and disability across a range of activities including employment, education, public functions, membership organisations and the provision of goods, facilities and services.[33] In the event of the UK's exit from the EU it is not inevitable that the edifice of domestic equality law would crumble.

§12.04 DOMESTIC LAW AND THE COALITION GOVERNMENT

[A] Introduction

It is of course true, however, that such departure would have the effect of removing from domestic equality legislation the underpinning provided by EU law both in its current form and with the benefit of likely, if not imminent, extensions in scope (in the case of age, disability, sexual orientation and religion or belief) beyond the scope of employment to cover social advantages and social protection, education and access to

27. C-262/88 [1990] ECR I-1889.
28. C-32/93 [1994] ECR I-3567.
29. C-13/94 [1996] ECR I-02143.
30. C-326/96 [1998] ECR I-7835.
31. C-185/97 [1998] ECR I-5199.
32. *Commission of the European Communities v. UK* C-61/81[1982] ECR 2601, which required the extension of the EqPA to provide for equal pay for work of equal value; and C-165/82 [1983] ECR I-3431, which required the removal of miscellaneous exceptions to the SDA's prohibition of sex discrimination.
33. There are some variations between the grounds as regards protection, harassment related to neither sexual orientation nor religion/belief being prohibited as such in access to goods, facilities or services and discrimination in relation to marriage/civil partnership being regulated only in relation to employment (broadly defined).

goods and services.[34] This may well prove of increasing significance given the general hostility of many of those on the right to 'red tape' and the 'compensation culture'. Certainly the prohibitions on discrimination in relation to pregnancy and maternity, and disability in particular impose 'burdens on business', as do restrictions on indirect discrimination related to sex and religion.[35] And the regulation of discrimination on grounds of nationality and national origin can interfere with the freedom of employers and (for example) education providers and private landlords to perform any policing functions regarding immigration which the state might wish to delegate.

It is important to acknowledge that five years of coalition government have not resulted in radical amendment to substantive domestic equality law. This may well, however, have been in large part the result of the Liberal Democrats' relative enthusiasm for the legislation. And it is worthy of note that a number of the innovations contained in the Equality Act 2010, which was passed in the dying days of New Labour's regime, were scrapped by the incoming Government. Among these were the regulation of 'dual discrimination' and the protection of workers from third party harassment. The first of these was never brought into force and the second, implemented in October 2010 by the incoming Government, was repealed in October 2013 with the implementation of the Enterprise and Regulatory Reform Act 2013.[36] The Coalition Government had also announced as early as November 2010 that it would not implement section 1 of the 2010 Act, which would impose a duty on public authorities to take into account, in strategic decision-making, to 'have due regard to the desirability of exercising [their functions] in a way that is designed to reduce the inequalities of outcome which result from socio-economic disadvantage'. Home Secretary Theresa May, in stating that she was 'scrapping Harman's law for good', denounced the provision as 'ridiculous'.[37] (It remains on the face of the Act.[38]) A similar approach was taken to section 78 of the Act, which provides the basis for mandatory gender pay audits.[39] Any assumption that gender pay inequality has been 'solved' should be disproved by the fact that the UK, for the first time, lost its position within the world's

34. Note the Proposal for a Council Directive of 2 Jul. 2008 on implementing the principle of equal treatment between persons irrespective of religion or belief, disability, age or sexual orientation. For discussion of this and the position across Europe see A. McColgan, *National protection beyond the two EU Anti-discrimination Directives* (European Commission 2013), http://ec.europa.eu/justice/discrimination /files/final_beyond_employment_en.pdf (accessed 3 May 2015).
35. This because of the obligations it imposes as regards the accommodation of family life, religious observations etc.
36. Section 65 of which amended section 40 Equality Act 2010.
37. 'Theresa May scraps legal requirement to reduce inequality', *Guardian* 17 Nov. 2010, http://www.theguardian.com/society/2010/nov/17/theresa-may-scraps-legal-requirement-inequality (accessed 3 May 2015).
38. This being the case, the decision in *R v. Secretary of State for the Home Department, ex p Fire Brigades Union* [1995] 2 AC 513, [1995] 2 All ER 244 makes it clear that the Home Secretary remains under a continuing obligation to consider whether to implement the provision.
39. Though tribunals were given the power from 1 Oct. 2014 to order such audits where an employer loses an equal pay claim.

twenty most gender-equal countries in October 2014 after women's average wages fell by GBP 2,700 in a year (men's wages remaining constant).[40]

[B] Discrimination Questionnaires

The matters mentioned immediately above were beyond the scope of EU law and within domestic government's freedom of manoeuvre. It is by no means fanciful to suggest that exit from Europe would result in other amendments to the scope of domestic law. Particularly significant as regards possible future directions of travel for a government untrammelled by the demands of EU law have been the recent changes to the enforcement of equality/discrimination law. Discrimination/equal pay questionnaires, which had been in operation since the 1970s, were abolished as of April 2014 notwithstanding an 83% majority against this proposal in responses to the government's consultation document.[41] The questionnaires facilitated early engagement with potential or actual claims because tribunals could draw adverse inferences from the employer's failure to answer questions posed, and/or from evasive or equivocal answers. Acas has issued non-binding, good practice guidance which points out that employees remain entitled to ask questions of employers, albeit without the benefit of the previous statutory standard forms and time limits which applied under the questionnaire procedure.[42] And tribunals remain free to draw inferences from failures to answer on employers' part, and/or from evasive or otherwise unsatisfactory answers. But the abolition of the questionnaires indicates a degree of hostility to discrimination claims. Thus, according to the foreword in the Government's response to the consultation:

> ... Overall, we do not think that responses to the consultation have provided arguments to persuade us that our proposals were wrong... The procedures for obtaining information – including the Government's role in them – are prescriptive and potentially threatening to employers. The consultation provided evidence of the procedures operating as intended, but also of abuse... we think that ultimately an employer should be free to decide on whether to act or to take the risk of not acting. We have therefore decided to proceed with the repeal of these provisions where a suitable opportunity arises ...

The executive summary queries 'whether the existing legislation is a proportionate way of dealing with the enforcement of discrimination law', referring both to the questionnaire procedure and to Tribunals' power to make wider recommendations

---

40. 'UK drops out of gender equality top 20 after women's wages fall' *The Independent* 28 Oct. 2014, http://www.independent.co.uk/news/uk/home-news/uk-drops-out-of-gender-equality-top-20-after-womens-wages-fall-9821990.html (accessed 4 May 2015). The UK fell from 18 to 26 place in a year, behind Nicaragua, Rwanda, the Philippines, Bulgaria and Burundi as well as 'obvious suspects' such as (in order) Iceland, Finland, Norway, Sweden and Denmark, according to the World Economic Forum's Global Gender Gap Report.
41. https://www.gov.uk/government/uploads/system/uploads/attachment_data/file/136235/consultation -response.pdf (accessed 2 May 2015).
42. *Asking and responding to questions of discrimination in the workplace*, http://www.acas.org.uk/media/pdf/m/p/ Asking-and-responding-to-questions-of-discrimination-in-the-workplace.pdf (accessed 4 May 2015).

(see further below). Noting the level of opposition to the proposed repeal of the questionnaire procedure, the Executive Summary went on to state that '[r]esponses which agreed to the proposed repeals came mostly from private and not-for profit sector employers and business representative organisations' with responses disagreeing with the proposals coming mainly from 'unions, equality lobby groups, staff associations, the judiciary and members of the public ... In the light of this response, the Government will seek an opportunity to repeal both the wider recommendations provisions and the obtaining information provisions'. It is difficult to escape the conclusion that the change was ideologically driven.

§12.05 TRIBUNAL POWERS OF RECOMMENDATION

Another assault on the enforcement of equality claims has been the removal of the power granted to tribunals in Great Britain for the first time by the Equality Act 2010 to make recommendations, by way of response to successful discrimination claims, which extend beyond the relationship between claimant and employer. The Act provides (section 124) that a tribunal which has found a breach of the employment-related prohibitions on discrimination may, together with or instead of making a declaration and/or awarding compensation,[43] make an 'appropriate recommendation' which is in turn defined as 'a recommendation that within a specified period the respondent takes specified steps for the purpose of obviating or reducing the adverse effect of any matter to which the proceedings relate *(a) on the complainant; (b) on any other person*'. As of 1 October 2015 the italicised words are to be removed, courtesy of the Deregulation Act 2015,[44] and the words 'on the complainant' inserted between 'adverse effect' and 'of any matter'. This change was proposed, together with the removal of the prohibition on third party harassment and the abolition of statutory questionnaires, in May 2012 following the Government's 'red tape challenge'.

The consultation document did not put forward any rationale for the abolition of the power to make wider recommendations save to assert that 'Employers remain concerned that the remedy [which was thought to have been used in only one case to that date] might be unnecessary'.[45] The British Chambers of Commerce were reported to have suggested that 'the power is not required because employers often make changes to their policies and practices, anyway, as a result of a tribunal finding, without the need for a recommendation'. And it was said that the power 'requires employment tribunals to be able to formulate proposals which go beyond the case in question, and which affect an employer's business more generally – in effect, taking on the role of an equality consultant' and that 'The view of this consultation is therefore that the wider recommendations provision is not likely to serve a practical purpose or

43. Such being almost inevitable in a successful discrimination claim – see *Ministry of Defence v. Sullivan* [1994] ICR 193.
44. Section 2(1)(a).
45. https://www.gov.uk/government/uploads/system/uploads/attachment_data/file/136232/consultation-document.pdf, p. 9.

to be an appropriate or effective legal remedy for employment tribunals ... [and accordingly that] this provision is an unnecessary burden on business'.

The sole example of the use of the wider power of recommendation from which then which the consultation document drew involved a recommendation made by a tribunal which had found that a claimant had been subject to pregnancy and maternity discrimination that: 'within 6 months, the respondent appoint external consultants to implement a programme of training for all managers and all members of HR team relating not only to the respondent's existing maternity policies but also in relation to its particular statutory legal obligations to employees in their protected period and that the programme of training be completed within a 12 month period' and that 'the respondent redraft its equal opportunities policy to include maternity and pregnancy as a protected characteristic'.[46]

It is difficult to take issue with the substance of these recommendations. But the Impact Assessment which accompanied the consultation document, and which was dated December 2011, stated that:

> [w]e understand that employers continue to have fears of inappropriate or excessive recommendations although we are unaware of any wider recommendations having been made since the commencement of these provisions in October 2010[[47]]... The policy objective is to reduce any regulatory burden on employers that the power of employment tribunals to make wider recommendations may impose. The intended effects are to ensure that, if the results of the forthcoming consultation on the need for employment tribunals to have the power to make wider recommendations identify these provisions as unnecessary, disproportionate or ineffective, steps will be taken to remove these provisions from the legislation without affecting strong and effective enforcement.

That assessment concluded from the fact (as was understood in December 2011) that no wider recommendations had been made, that '[t]here is ... no evidence, so far, to show that the extended power is necessary or that it is an appropriate or effective remedy'.[48] This conclusion was drawn notwithstanding the fact that the transitional arrangements applicable to the Equality Act 2010 were to the effect that tribunals could only make wider recommendations in respect of discrimination claims which pertained at least in part to acts of discrimination occurring after 1 October 2010.[49] (It is, further, worthy of note that only 60% of cases received in the period October 2010 to December 2010 proceeded to a hearing within twenty-six weeks.[50])

46. *Stone v. Ramsay Health Care UK Operations Ltd* ET/1400762/11.
47. It is clear from p. 53 of the consultation document that this statement was based on employer responses to the *Discrimination Law Review* (2007) from which the conclusion was drawn that '... to do nothing, employer fears of excessive or inappropriate recommendations will continue'.
48. *Supra* n. 45, at 50.
49. Equality Act 2010 (Commencement No. 4, Savings, Consequential, Transitional, Transitory and Incidental Provisions and Revocation) Order 2010 Articles 2(1), 7, 9(f) & 15.
50. https://www.gov.uk/government/uploads/system/uploads/attachment_data/file/218516/quarerly-tribs-stats-q3-2010-11.pdf, table 1.4.

Only 12% of those who responded to the Consultation Paper were in favour of repealing the wider powers of recommendation with 79% against.[51] As in the case of the statutory questionnaires, however, the government moved from the statement that '[v]ery few of the responses, both those opposed to and those in favour of repeal have offered significant quantifiable evidence or specific evidence based on actual situations and outcomes, to support their views' to the conclusion that 'In the light of this response, the Government will seek an opportunity to repeal' the relevant provisions.

The Consultation Response indicated that three additional cases in which wider recommendations had been made had been brought to the attention of its drafters by respondents. In all three, as in the case identified in the Consultation document itself, the recommendations had involved equalities training for specific categories of staff. The Consultation Response acknowledged '[t]he types of wider recommendations made in the four cases identified since the launch of this consultation are in our view, common-sense straightforward recommendations... [which] all relate to improving an employer's human resource practices or providing equality training to staff and [which] in the Government's view ... are basic remedial actions which we would expect most employers at the sharp end of a tribunal finding to undertake in any case',[52] further that 'there is no evidence to suggest that the wider recommendations made so far are disproportionate or ineffective', though it went on to state that 'in the absence of evidence of follow up action on whether a wider recommendation has been implemented, we cannot reach any conclusions on this'.[53]

It is difficult to rationalise the abolition of a power used so modestly and so apparently appropriately by tribunals in the twenty-two months between implementation and close of the consultation period, not least in view of the fact that its removal would have the effect that no recommendations could be made where claimants are no longer in employment (a situation which, according to the Government's own impact assessment, applies to as many as 72% of claimants).[54] Indeed the Consultation Response made no real effort to provide any such rationalisation, asserting only that 'We believe that any employer who is not observant enough to make a connection between the two [i.e., unfavourable finding and necessary remedial action] may well not take notice of the tribunal's recommendation and will therefore run the risks associated with that in any event'.[55]

Having remarked on the lack of evidential basis for or against repeal, opponents of repeal arguing 'the need not to act prematurely before the provision had a chance to demonstrate effectiveness' and proponents arguing that 'the power is rarely used and is therefore unnecessary and that employers often put right flawed employment practices of their own accord following a tribunal finding against them and therefore the power is unnecessary', the Consultation Response acknowledged that 'there was no quantifiable evidence to support the latter view'[56] but stated (notwithstanding the

51. *Supra* n. 41.
52. *Supra* n. 41, §24.
53. *Ibid.* §23.
54. *Supra* n. 45, p. 49.
55. *Supra* n. 41, §24.
56. *Ibid.* §28.

overwhelming view of the consultation responses against repeal, and its own conclusions on the actual recommendations made to date) that 'employers still show considerable concern about the potential for inappropriate recommendations'. By way of conclusion, while:

> [t]he Government considers that ... the types of recommendations made highlight wider issues around lack of awareness and knowledge by employers of equality and employment law, the wider recommendations provision is not the right way to address this issue. We think a better approach is through the practical non-legislative measures proposed by the Government in May 2012 as part of the Red Tape Challenge equalities package announcement. We intend .... to work with businesses, particularly small businesses and their representative organisations to increase understanding of compliance and best-practice in avoiding risk of adverse tribunal decisions; and through very short, straightforward web-based guidance for small businesses on equality law areas known to be particularly difficult for them.

The 'Red Tape Challenge equalities package' announced by Home Secretary Theresa May in May 2012 consisted in consulting on the repeal of the various measures here discussed, and others; a review of the PSED; and the curtailment of the powers and budget of the Equality and Human Rights Commission (EHRC) (whose budget has been cut from GBP 70 million in 2007 to under GBP 18 million in 2015/16[57]).[58] It is worth remarking, in passing, that the PM made clear a few months later in his speech to the CBI conference his view of the PSED: 'We have smart people in Whitehall who consider equalities issues while they're making the policy. We don't need all this extra tick-box stuff. So I can tell you today we are calling time on Equality Impact Assessments. You no longer have to do them if these issues have been properly considered.'[59] Even leaving aside Cameron's willingness to jump the gun on the outcome of a review which in fact concluded that it was too early to draw any conclusions on the operation of the PSED,[60] it is not obvious which aspects of May's package are being relied upon in the Consultation Response as the 'practical non-legislative measures' suggested as an alternative to the power of tribunals to make wider recommendations.

57. The budget cuts announced as a result of the 2010 Spending Review, which reduced the budget to GBP 26.8M in 2014–2015, provoked a letter from the UN Commissioner on Human Rights warning the Home secretary that the Commission would lose its financial autonomy, and its UN 'A' grade rating, if cuts to its budget continued: http://www.theguardian.com /society/2012/oct/26/budget-cuts-rights-watchdog-un-status.
58. https://www.gov.uk/government/speeches/equalities-red-tape-challenge-and-reform-of-the-equality-and-human-rights-commission-outcome (accessed 4 May 2015).
59. The full text of the PM's speech is at http://blogs.spectator.co.uk/david-blackburn/2012/11/david-camerons-speech-to-the-cbi (accessed 4 May 2015). This statement either ignored, or displayed the PM's failure to grasp, the fact that the PSED does not require equality impact assessments, as distinct from proper consideration of equality issues.
60. https://www.gov.uk/government/publications/the-independent-steering-groups-report-of-the-public-sector-equality-duty-psed-review-and-government-response (accessed 4 May 2015).

§12.06 TRIBUNAL FEES

The extensive discussion of the decision to curtail tribunal powers to make recommendations is intended to call into question the rationale for this decision, and to found a suggestion that it best understood as part of a deliberate retrenchment on the part of the Government from effective equality measures. Of more practical significance to most discrimination claimants, however, was the introduction in July 2013 of tribunal fees. The Employment Tribunals and the Employment Appeal Tribunal Fees Order 2013 requires the payment of GBP 250 on submission of a discrimination claim and a further GBP 950 in advance of any hearing, with additional fees of GBP 400 and GBP 1200 payable in respect of any appeal to the EAT. Fees may be remitted for claimants on very low incomes, but most claimants will be required to meet them as a condition of the claim.[61] The number of employment cases filed fell by 64% in October 2012–September 2014 compared with the figures for the previous year.[62] Sex discrimination claims fell by 83%, equal pay claims by 77%, sexual orientation and religion or belief claims by 64% and 60% respectively and race, disability and age claims by 58%, 54% and 43%.[63] Notably, in view of the assertion by Matthew Hancock, Minister for Education and Business, in April 2014 that the 79% drop in tribunal applications to that date demonstrated that blameless employers had been subject to many false allegations prior to the introduction of tribunal fees,[64] the success rate of those claims brought has not changed in the period since fees were introduced.[65]

[A] The Threat to Equality Law

The introduction of tribunal fees has clearly had a devastating impact on discrimination claims. The response of the domestic courts to attempted legal challenges to the introduction of these fees is considered below. It is not here being suggested that any significant proportion of Conservative MPs share the view of Nigel Farage, leader of UKIP, that race discrimination laws should be repealed.[66] But it is strongly arguable, notwithstanding the occasional expression of support by the PM, May and assorted others for gay marriage, equality and apple pie,[67] that elements within the Conservative party are constitutionally ill-disposed towards discrimination legislation. One example is Cameron's speech to the 2012 CBI conference (see above). Another is the 2012

---

61. Of the 43,961 claims accepted in the period (down from 187,441 in the previous year), fees were remitted on 3,913 occasions (note that remissions made in respect of issue and hearing fee count as two remissions, so the number of claimants whose fees were partly or wholly remitted was lower than the number of remissions) http://www.parliament.uk/business/publications/research/briefing-papers/SN07081/employment-tribunal (accessed 4 May 2015, p. 12).
62. *Ibid*, at 1.
63. *Ibid*, at 12.
64. 'Minister hails 80pc fall in employment tribunals' *Telegraph* 26 Apr. 2014.
65. *Tribunal Statistics: April to June 2014 (Tables)*, Ministry of Justice, September 2014, Table 2.3.
66. http://www.channel4.com/news/nigel-farage-race-discrimination-laws-scrapped.
67. *See* 'Marriage Equality Tops David Cameron's Proudest Achievements', http://www.advocate.com/politics/marriage-equality/2015/01/10/marriage-equality-among-david-camerons-proudest-achievements (accessed 4 May 2015).

'Red-Tape Challenge' which was, as Angela O'Hagan remarked in the UK's Comment paper to the European Commission's 'Exchange of good practices on gender equality', 'premised on the assertion that equalities legislation and accompanying practices such as equality impact assessment represented a burden on business and employers'.[68]

Exit from the EU, resulting as it would (if at all) from the actions of a Conservative or Conservative Coalition Government, threatens any elements of discrimination law which are seen as business-unfriendly. It would also allow such a Government to continue the assault on the enforcement of whatever equality/discrimination laws remained, unconstrained by any external requirement for effectiveness. I would suggest that enforcement is the area in which the Coalition Government (possibly more precisely the Conservative Party constrained only minimally by the junior Liberal Democratic element of the Coalition) has most clearly signalled its destructive intention. It is platitudinous to state that legal rights (whether related to discrimination, housing, child custody or anything else) are meaningful only to the extent that they are capable of enforcement. This is a truth, however, which the current Government seems at best wilfully blind to, at worst eager to exploit.

One example is the institution of tribunal fees: it stretches credibility to suggest, for example, that a worker owed GBP 400 in holiday pay will spend GBP 160 on an application to the tribunal and a further GBP 230 by way of a hearing fee even if s/he can be relatively confident (though not certain) that recovery in the event of a successful claim (should the employer choose to pay[69]) will include reimbursement by the employer of those fees. This being the case, the introduction of tribunal fees at the current level has served to render that worker's entitlement to that holiday pay entirely empty. Another example concerns the PSED: apparently thwarted by the failure of the 'independent steering group' on the PSED to recommend changes to the Act, the Government lit on its suggestion for consideration of 'whether there are quicker and more cost-effective ways of reconciling disputes relating to the PSED' to consult on the possibility of removing judicial review as the enforcement mechanism for the PSED.[70] (It is worth pointing out that at the time of this consultation (September 2013) the Government had already decided to remove legal aid from the permission stage of judicial review applications unless permission was granted,[71] and to slash the rates paid to lawyers for legally aided judicial review claims.)

At least 79% of respondents to the September 2013 consultation on judicial review opposed any move to remove the PSED from the scope of judicial review. The Government's Consultation Response did not, however, discount this possibility, recording instead that matter was being considered by the Government's Equalities

68. http://ec.europa.eu/justice/gender-equality/files/exchange_of_good_practices_at/uk_comments_paper_at_2014_en.pdf, p. 3.
69. A November 2013 study conducted for Department of Business, Innovation and skills found that only 49% of claimants recovered their compensation in full, with another 16% making partial recovery: https://www.gov.uk/government/uploads/system/uploads/attachment_data/file/253558/bis-13-1270-enforcement-of-tribunal-awards.pdf (accessed 4 May 2015).
70. https://www.gov.uk/government/uploads/system/uploads/attachment_data/file/264091/8703.pdf §§106-109 (accessed 4 May 2015).
71. This was subsequently ruled unlawful in *R (Ben Hoare Bell Solicitors and others) v. Lord Chancellor* [2015] EWHC 523 (Admin).

Office.[72] (The Chair of the Steering Group subsequently made it clear to the Joint Committee on Human Rights that 'in his view the PSED should continue to be legally enforceable', and recommended that any '"quicker" and more "cost-effective" mechanism ... must retain the ultimate legal enforceability of the duty by judicial review, rather than be an alternative to it'.[73]) Absent any confirmation to the contrary from the Equalities Office the PSED must still be considered under threat.

[B] Conclusion: Europe as the Guarantor of Rights?

None of this is to suggest that EU membership acts as a guarantee even of those individual rights required to be afforded as a result of EU membership. The introduction of tribunal fees in July 2013 has been mentioned above. Attempts to rely on EU law to challenge them have thus far not succeeded. In *R (Unison) v. Lord Chancellor* (2014), Unison argued that the imposition of the fees breached the principles of effectiveness and equivalence (also that their introduction breached the PSED and amounted to indirect discrimination against minority groups such as women, ethnic minorities and disabled people).[74] The 2014 case predated the publication of the first official tribunal statistics covering the period from July 2013 but the evidence that there was pointed to a steep decline in applications. The High Court rejected the argument that the fees made it 'virtually impossible, or excessively difficult' to exercise rights conferred by EU law. It made reference to the remission system and the fact that the fees were paid in two stages, with a period of time in between, from which it concluded that prospective claimants even of modest means could pay them,[75] and ruled that it was more appropriate to 'wait and see' what the impact would be. The Court suggested that the Lord Chancellor would change the system if an apparent fall in applications relied upon by Unison proved to be the case, particularly as regards discrimination claims. It also ruled that the appropriate comparator cases for an argument about equivalence were ordinary breach of contract claims rather than (as Unison argued) small claims. This being the case, fees were comparable save that tribunal claimants were (largely) protected from the threat of having to bear the costs of the other side if the claim failed, and would if successful normally be able to recover the costs of the fees paid from the employer.

Shortly after the decision in the Unison case the official statistics disclosed a drop of around 80% in tribunal claims generally, and sex discrimination claims in particular, in the first six months after fees were imposed. In May 2014 the Court of Appeal granted

72. https://www.gov.uk/government/uploads/system/uploads/attachment_data/file/281330/8811.pdf, §40, and annex A §112 (accessed 4 May 2015).
73. Thirteenth Report of 2013–14, 'The implications for access to justice of the Government's proposals to reform judicial review' §129, http://www.publications.parliament.uk/pa/jt201314/jtselect/ jtrights/174/17410.htm (accessed 4 May 2015).
74. [2014] EWHC 218 (Admin), [2014] IRLR 266.
75. This in the basis of evidence which suggested that, even after remission, a variety of sample discrimination claimants would have to pay as much as 163% of monthly disposable income to have a claim heard in the ET, with an additional 197% of disposable monthly income in the event of an EAT hearing, *ibid.* §37.

Unison leave to appeal the decision of the High Court. The appeal was stayed and pending the outcome of a fresh application for judicial review which relied on the evidence regarding the severe (and subsequently sustained) drop in Tribunal claims. This too, however, was destined to fail; in December 2014 the High Court decided, in *R (Unison) v. Lord Chancellor* (*No.2*) that the introduction of Tribunal fees did not breach the principle of effectiveness and was not otherwise unlawful.[76] The Court accepted that the statistics showed that the fees had made claimants less willing to bring claims, but ruled that, in the absence of evidence that they had made any **particular** individual unable to bring a claim, it was not open to the Court to conclude that the fees rendered any EU employment rights ineffective.

It might be suggested, in light of the decisions in the Unison challenges, that the UK's membership has had little protective impact to date in securing access to justice for discrimination claimants. That would overlook, however, the impact of factors such as the removal of the compensation cap in discrimination claims, the shift in the burden of proof and the evolution of indirect discrimination which has resulted from EU legislative and case law developments. Nor is it by any means certain that the decisions of the High Court in the Unison challenges are reflective of the true position under EU law. The Court of Appeal upheld the High Court decisions in the Unison cases[77] but permission has been sought to appeal to the Supreme Court which may take a different view.

76. [2014] EWHC 4198 (Admin), [2015] ICR 390.
77. [2015] IRLR 911.

CHAPTER 13
The Death of Social Europe

Keith D. Ewing

§13.01 INTRODUCTION

We live in counter-revolutionary times. The great social democratic experiment that created Social Europe as a progressive force in global politics appears to be over. The economic crisis has provided an opportunity for a major shift in the balance of economic power between capital and labour, and has created in turn a political crisis for the labour movement throughout Europe and beyond. It has also created a crisis of legality, as the opportunity to drive home neo-liberal counter-revolutionary measures is being exploited in apparent violation of the legal obligations of EU Member States, and perhaps also EU institutions. This is despite the bold claims by Hayek – and other authors of neo – liberalism – about the singular importance of the 'great principles known as the Rule of Law'.[1] Legality it seems is a casualty of even the most civilised revolutionaries.

The counter-revolution – the displacement of social democracy by neo-liberalism – has led to major changes in several legal disciplines, and it is in the process of turning labour law upside down. Perhaps the greatest impact for European labour law, however, is the coordinated attack on collective bargaining structures, an attack which is all the greater for the fact that collective bargaining is thought to be fundamental to social democracy – partly because it is a route to engagement and participation in economic decision-making, and partly because it is a principal lever for income

1. F.A. Hayek, *The Road to Serfdom* 54 (Routledge 1944). On Hayek's influence on the development of British labour law, *see* K. Ewing, *Trade Unions and the Constitution: The Impact of the New Conservatives*, in *Waiving the Rules – The Constitution under Thatcherism* (C. Graham & T. Prosser, eds, Open U. Press 1988) and Lord Wedderburn, *Freedom of Association and Philosophies of Labour Law* 18 Indus. L. J. 1 (1989). On Hayek and the rule of law, *see also* F.A. Hayek, *The Constitution of Liberty* Chapter 16 (U. Chicago Press 1960).

redistribution and equality.[2] This chapter addresses first the steps that were taken carefully to build and support the integration of collective bargaining procedures at multiple levels in the European project, and secondly the more recent steps taken to destroy the structures that facilitated that integration in the first place.

§13.02 THE BIRTH OF SOCIAL EUROPE

The starting point for an understanding of Social Europe is a speech by Jaques Delors, then President of the European Commission, to the British Trades Union Congress in September 1988. Delors said:

> It would be unacceptable for Europe to become a source of social regression, while we are trying rediscover together the road to prosperity and employment. The European Commission has suggested the following principles on which to base the definition and implementation of these rules:
>
> First, measures adopted to complete the large market should not diminish the level of social protection already achieved in the Member States.
>
> Second, the internal market should be designed to benefit each and every citizen of the Community. It is therefore necessary to improve worker's living and working conditions, and to provide better protection for health and safety at work.
>
> Third, the measures to be taken will concern the area of collective bargaining and legislation.[3]

From its origins in 1957, the European Economic Community was understood to be a business-oriented venture, in which the social rights of the citizens of the Member States appeared very much a secondary concern.[4] It is true that a social dimension emerged in the 1970s;[5] but progress froze soon thereafter, and it was not until Delors' leadership that Social Europe began seriously to grow. Delors had the wisdom to realise that support for the European project was conditional, and that it could be neither commanded nor demanded. So after setting out his vision for a social dimension in what was undoubtedly a multi-layered political speech, Delors made what appeared to be a promise, which won over the hitherto sceptical British trade unionists in his audience. Delors promised:

> The establishment of a platform of guaranteed social rights, containing general principles, such as every worker's right to be covered by a collective agreement …[6]

---

2. On which *see* S. Hayter, *Want to Tackle Inequality? Shore Up Collective Bargaining*, 3 Mar. 2015: http://iloblog.org/2015/03/03/want-to-tackle-inequality-shore-up-collective-bargaining/. *See also* S. Tailby & S. Moore, 'Collective Bargaining: Building Solidarity Through the Fight against Inequalities and Discrimination' (2014) 32 *Cuadernos de Relaciones Laborales* 361.
3. TUC, Annual Report 1988. Coincidentally, we were reminded of the importance of this speech by a *BBC News* item on Sunday 24 Aug. 2014, when parts of the speech were broadcast in a feature edited by Professor Vernon Bogdanor, including in particular the passage dealing with collective bargaining.
4. C. Barnard, *EU Employment Law* Chapter 1 (Oxford U. Press 2012).
5. *See* B.A. Hepple, *The Crisis in EEC Labour Law* 16 Indus. L. J. 77 (1987).
6. TUC Annual Report, *supra*.

– Embedding 'Collective Bargaining' as a Source of Law

Delors' promise was kept for about twenty years thereafter, beginning with the Maastricht Treaty in 1992, with its anticipation of an ambitious framework for the integration of trade unions into the law-making processes of the EU on the one hand, and decision-making within corporations operating in the EU on the other.[7] Social dialogue between the representatives of capital and labour was to become a way of making law at the Union level, and also a way of transposing it at national level.[8] So in TFEU, Articles 154 and 155 we have what Julia Lopez Lopez describes as a 'neo-corporatist and coordinated model of capitalism', which 'survives' at EU level, with 'norms and instruments that have an enormous impact back at the national level, setting a minimal floor of rights and principles for both national-level legislation and judges'.[9] These begin with an obligation on the Commission to promote dialogue between management and labour, to consult generally about social policy and to consult also about specific proposals.[10]

But more importantly, this 'neo-corporatist' model not only anticipates agreements between management and labour on a potentially wide range of matters. It also creates procedures for the conversion of these agreements into law, imposing duties on Member States affecting all employers and all workers. By virtue of what is now TFEU, Article 155, some of these agreements concluded at EU level could be implemented at the joint request of both sides 'by a Council decision on a proposal from the Commission', with the European Parliament to be 'informed'. For those of us schooled in the traditions of liberal democracy, the by-passing of Parliament in this way was remarkable, and it was perhaps inevitable that the procedure would be challenged on grounds of democratic legitimacy.[11] But the European Court of First Instance dismissed the challenge, taking the view that:

> the principle of democracy on which the Union is founded requires - in the absence of the participation of the European Parliament in the legislative process - that the participation of the people be otherwise assured, in this instance through the parties representative of management and labour who concluded the agreement which is endowed by the Council, acting on a qualified majority, on a proposal from the Commission, with a legislative foundation at Community level. In order to make sure that that requirement is complied with, the Commission and the Council are under a duty to verify that the signatories to the agreement are truly representative.[12]

7. *See* B. Bercusson, *Maastricht: A Fundamental Change in European Labour Law* 23 Indus. Rel. J. 177 (1992).
8. For the origins of this 'Social Dialogue' process, *see* B. Hepple, *European Social Dialogue – Alibi or Opportunity* (Institute of Employment Rights 1993).
9. J. Lopez Lopez, *Solidarity and the Resocialisation of Risk*, in *Resocialising Europe in a Time of Crisis* 357 (N. Countouris & M. Freedland eds, Cambridge U. Press 2013).
10. TFEU, Article 154.
11. Case T-135/96, *UEAPME v. Council of the European Union* [1998] ECR – II 02335. *See* B. Bercusson, *Democratic Legitimacy and European Labour Law* 28 Indus. L. J. 153 (1999).
12. *UEAPME, ibid.* at paragraph 89.

Questions of democratic legitimacy thus resolved, the social dialogue procedure led to a number of legislative instruments, dealing with parental leave, part-time work and fixed-term work.[13] Although we may quibble about the content of these instruments, the main point for present purposes relates to the process, and to what Lopez Lopez refers to as the 'crucial role' of the European Trade Union Confederation (ETUC) in constructing this group of agreements, providing 'evidence of the governance role played by unions' at the highest level.[14] As a party to these agreements the ETUC effectively performed a primary legislative function, producing instruments that have general application. In doing so the ETUC took part in a procedure that allowed their affiliates to be parties to the implementation of the agreements at national level by a similar process. The preamble to *Parental Leave Directive (96/34/EC)* provides for example that 'Member States may entrust the social partners, at their joint request, with the implementation of this Directive, as long as such Member States take all the steps necessary to ensure that they can at all times guarantee the results imposed by this Directive'.

Yet although there was thus provision for making law by social dialogue, and at the same time provision for the implementation of law at national level by collective agreement (subject to requirements imposed by the ECJ),[15] no provision was made to ensure that the infrastructure existed at national level to enable collective bargaining to perform this implementation function.[16] This is despite the fact that 'European social dialogue will not succeed if it is not constructed atop strong collective bargaining structures supported by strong trade unions in Member States.'[17] Nevertheless, European labour law presumed the existence of a regulatory framework in national law but did not demand it – for example through a Directive that would require Member States to put such a framework in place. With the benefit of hindsight this was a mistake. But at the time, it must have seemed generally unnecessary to address at Community level that for which provision was already made in many Member States. Indeed in many of the EU-15, the right to bargain collectively was included in the national constitution, perhaps reflecting the economic orthodoxy at the time these constitutions were drafted – usually between the mid-1940s and mid-1970s.[18]

---

13. But not temporary and agency work on which agreement between the social partners proved impossible, as the preamble to Directive 2008/14/EC makes very clear.
14. *Solidarity and the Resocialisation of Risk*, *supra*, at 360.
15. *See* B. Bercusson, *Collective Bargaining and the Protection of Social Rights in Europe*, in *Human Rights and Labour Law – Essays for Paul O'Higgins* Chapter 5 (K.D. Ewing, C.A. Gearty & B.A. Hepple eds, Mansell 1994).
16. The closest we got to a right to bargain collectively – whether in the implementation of EU law or otherwise – was the provision in the non-binding Charter of the Fundamental Social Rights of Workers of 1989 that 'Employers or employers' organisations, on the one hand, and workers' organisations, on the other, shall have the right to negotiate and conclude collective agreements under the conditions laid down by national legislation and practice'.
17. Alan Bogg & R. Dukes, *The European Social Dialogue – From Autonomy to Here*, in Countouris & Freedland (eds), *supra* n. 9, at 492.
18. *See further*, K.D. Ewing, *Economic Rights*, in *The Oxford Handbook of Comparative Constitutional Law* Chapter 50 (M. Rosenfeld & A. Sajo eds, Oxford U. Press 2013).

So, if we take the constitutions of Greece, Spain and Portugal we find that:

- 'general conditions of work shall be determined by law and supplemented by collective agreements arrived at by free collective bargaining' (Greece, Article 22);
- 'law shall guarantee the right to collective labour negotiations between the representatives of workers and employers, as well as the binding force of agreements' (Spain, Article 37); and
- 'trade union associations have the powers to exercise the right of concluding collective agreements', though 'the rules governing the powers to conclude collective labour agreements and the scope of their provisions are laid down by law' (Portugal, Article 56).[19]

Otherwise, with the exception of the United Kingdom, most Member States already had robust collective bargaining procedures, most Member States had multi-employer regulatory systems of collective bargaining in place, and according to the OECD in 1994 most Member States had high levels of collective bargaining density.[20] In this way, European labour law was built upon national labour law, reflecting Bercusson's important insight that European labour law was a synthesis of laws and practices developed at different levels, being altogether greater than the sum of its parts.

– Integrating Collective Bargaining as a Regulatory Process

What we have so far then is collective bargaining embedded at the highest level as an instrument for making EU law, and collective bargaining with an important role in the implementation of EU law, whether made under the social dialogue procedure or otherwise. There are other pieces of engagement in what was to become a complex jigsaw, in which EU law operated in conjunction with collective bargaining structures at national level, recognising their importance and encouraging their development. This would take place additionally in two ways, the first acknowledging the regulatory nature of collective bargaining as a source of established norms at national level, taken as *standards to be complied with as a matter of EU law*. The second was to acknowledge that collective bargaining not only provided an opportunity for the transposition of directives, but as a regulatory method also provided *an opportunity for flexible transposition* of at least some directives.

Beginning with the acknowledgement of collective bargaining as a legitimate regulatory source, this is best illustrated by the *Posted Workers Directive (96/71/EC)*. The directive addresses the problem of workers being posted by their employer from a low wage country to work for a limited period in a high wage country, with the directive being designed to ensure that the workers in question are not paid low wage

19. The Portuguese constitution also guarantees trade unions the right to participate in the preparation of labour legislation, the management of social security institutions, the monitoring of the implementation of economic and social plans, and to be represented on bodies engaged in the harmonisation of social questions (Article 56).
20. OECD, *Economic Outlook 1994*, Chapter 5 – dealing with *Collective Bargaining Levels and Coverage*.

rates in the high wage environment. Employers posting workers are thus required to observe wage rates and certain other mandatory terms and conditions of employment at least as good as those operating in the host country. Under Article 3(1) of the Directive, the terms and conditions in question are those laid down by:

- law, regulation or administrative provision; and/or
- collective agreements or arbitration awards which have been declared universally applicable within the meaning of paragraph 8.[21]

Although the second indent is restricted in scope to a limited group of workers listed in an Annex to the Directive (mainly construction and building services),[22] it is nevertheless the case that in this way – albeit to a limited extent – collective bargaining is treated not only as a source of rights, but also as a source *equal in status* to legislation.

It is, of course, true that not all collective agreements enjoy this status, as the ECJ controversially made clear in the *Laval* case.[23] This aspect of the directive effectively applies only to those countries where collective agreements have a genuinely regulatory impact in the sense that they are 'declared universally applicable', as provided by Article 3(8), which means 'collective agreements or arbitration awards which must be observed by all undertakings in the geographical area and in the profession or industry concerned'.[24] It is also provided that:

> In the absence of a system for declaring collective agreements or arbitration awards to be of universal application within the meaning of the first subparagraph, Member States may, if they so decide, base themselves on:
>
> - collective agreements or arbitration awards which are generally applicable to all similar undertakings in the geographical area and in the profession or industry concerned, and/or
> - collective agreements which have been concluded by the most representative employers' and labour organizations at national level and which are applied throughout national territory.[25]

But despite their restricted application, it is nevertheless impossible to exaggerate the significance of these provisions, again from the perspective of liberal democracy. This was made very clear by the Irish Supreme Court in 2013, openly challenging the legitimacy of collective bargaining procedures of the kind acknowledged in

21. There is a qualification in the sense that this indent applies only 'insofar as they concern the activities referred to in the Annex'. The Annex deals mainly with construction and building services.
22. The categories can be extended (Article 3(10). But *see Case C-319/06, Commission v. Luxembourg* [2008] ECR I-4323.
23. On which *see Case 341/05, Laval un Partneri Ltd v. Svenska Byggnadsarbetareförbundet, Svenska Byggnadsarbetareförbundets avdelning 1, Byggettan and Svenska Elektrikerförbundet* [2007] ECR I-11767.
24. On the problems caused in systems with weak regulatory bargaining systems, *see* C. Barnard, *British Jobs for British Workers: the Lindsey Oil Refinery Dispute and the Future of Local Labour Clauses in an Integrated EU Market* 38 Indus. L. J. 245 (2009).
25. Posted Workers Directive (96/71/EC), Article 3(8).

Article 3(8), as conflicting with the ultra-liberal values that underpin the Irish Constitution, and in particular the requirement that legislative effect can be given only to rules made by the Oireachtas (Parliament).[26]

Yet there is more to engagement than the recognition of the legitimacy of a process and the obligations it creates. There is also the desire to work with the process, not only to apply standards developed in national law, but also to implement standards in national law developed by EU law itself. This is a phenomenon best illustrated by the *Working Time Directive (2003/88/EC)*, which introduced a maximum working week of forty-eight hours (subject to an opt-out now enjoyed by a number of Member States), the right to paid annual leave, and the regulation of daily and weekly rest breaks. In introducing these measures the directive anticipates a central role for collective bargaining, not just for the purposes of direct transposition, but also for the purpose of determining the substantive terms to be attributed to the directive. In this way the law of working time is a complex web in which EU legislative standards interact with national collective bargaining arrangements, and in which collective agreements at national level become instruments for the flexible implementation of standards. But more than that, in this way EU law both relies upon and encourages the development of national collective bargaining arrangements, which are now essential to the operation of EU law, the latter dependent on these structures being in place.

A good example of how national bargaining arrangements are thus hard - wired into European law relates to rest breaks, with the Working Time Directive providing that the Community norm is to be established at national level using collective bargaining as the preferred regulatory tool, with legislation the less preferred fall-back. Thus Article 4 of the directive provides that:

> Member States shall take the measures necessary to ensure that, where the working day is longer than six hours, every worker is entitled to a rest break, the details of which, including duration and the terms on which it is granted, shall be laid down in collective agreements or agreements between the two sides of industry or, failing that, by national legislation.

This inter-weaving of EU law with national collective bargaining arrangements is also seen in the way in which collective bargaining procedures under the national law of Member States may be used as instruments for derogating from certain standards established by the directive.[27] In this way a different kind of preferred status is given to collective bargaining over legislation, a preferred status enhanced by the possibility that derogating collective agreements may be extended to other workers and employers

26. *See McGowan v. Labour Court* [2013] IESC 21, turning largely on law making by collective bargaining in a system where the constitution provides that 'The sole and exclusive power for making laws for the State is hereby vested in the Oireachtas: no other legislative authority has power to make laws for the State' (Article 15.2.1).
27. Directive 2003/88, Article 18: 'Derogations may be made from Articles 3, 4, 5, 8 and 16 by means of collective agreements or agreements concluded between the two sides of industry at national or regional level or, in conformity with the rules laid down by them, by means of collective agreements or agreements concluded between the two sides of industry at a lower level'. There is however a requirement of equivalent protections being introduced in some cases, or appropriate protection where this is not possible.

in accordance with national legislation and/or practice;[28] that is to say workers and employers who are not parties to the collective agreement in question.[29] European law is not now simply recognising the legitimacy of extending collective agreements *erga omnes* (as in the Posted Workers Directive), but despite constitutional objections in Ireland, is openly embracing the process at national level for the development of its own standards.

– Entrenching Collective Bargaining as a Fundamental Right

As we focus on (i) law-making by collective bargaining, and (ii) the integration into EU law of national collective bargaining procedures, there is one major piece of the jigsaw puzzle missing. This is (iii) the existence of a right to bargain collectively as a fundamental social right at EU level. For all the importance given to collective bargaining practices in European labour law, the burden of making those practices real lay with national law.[30] That, however, changed to some extent when the right to bargain collectively was swept into the EU Charter of Fundamental Rights in 2000, along with other labour rights. The EU Charter is hugely symbolic, not least because it includes social and economic rights in the same document as civil and political rights, and purports to give them the same formal legal status.[31] Although the inclusion of both categories of rights is not unusual in the national constitutions of Member States beyond its eccentric common law fringe, this is the first time such an inclusion is to be found in a treaty of this nature. It is true of course that Council of Europe instruments – the ECHR and the Social Charter – cover much the same ground. But despite claims in the preamble to the latter about the indivisibility of human rights, it is clear if only from the manner of their enforcement that the latter Charter is subordinate to the Convention.

So far as the right to bargain collectively is concerned, there are two important provisions of the EU Charter. The first and most obvious is Article 28, which provides as follows:

> Workers and employers, or their respective organisations, have, in accordance with Community law and national laws and practices, the right to negotiate and

28. On the principle of extension, *see* ILO Recommendation 91 (Collective Agreements Recommendation, 1951), Article 5(1) providing that '(1) Where appropriate, having regard to established collective bargaining practice, measures, to be determined by national laws or regulations and suited to the conditions of each country, should be taken to extend the application of all or certain stipulations of a collective agreement to all the employers and workers included within the industrial and territorial scope of the agreement'.
29. It is notable that in providing for collective bargaining in these ways, the Working Time Directive reflected a view of collective bargaining being a uniquely regulatory process, the ECJ eschewing a representative role for trade unions in some decisions under the Directive: *Joined Cases 397-01 to 403-01, Pfeiffer v. Deutsches Rotes Kreuz, Kreisverband Waldshut eV* [2004] ECR I-08835.
30. As pointed out above (n. 17), the right to bargain collectively was recognised by the Charter of the Fundamental Social Rights of Workers in 1989. But this was a programmatic statement of intent rather than a legally binding instrument. *See* B. Bercusson, *The European Community's Charter of Fundamental Social Rights of Workers* 53 Modern L. Rev. 624 (1990).
31. *See* C.C. Murphy, *Using the EU Charter of Fundamental Rights Against Private Parties after Association de Médiation Sociale* Eur. Hum. Rights L. Rev. 170 [2014].

> conclude collective agreements at the appropriate levels and, in cases of conflicts of interest, to take collective action to defend their interests, including strike action.

Note the substance of the right. It is the right of workers individually and their organisations. It is a right defined by Community law and by national laws and practices. And it is a right which is open as to the levels at which it may be exercised – enterprise, sector, or national. But note too that Article 28 does not on its own fill the gap in European labour law described above, to the extent that it does not create a free-standing right. Instead, it is heavily contingent on Community law and national laws being in place to give effect to the right. At the time of the Lisbon treaty giving the Charter legal effect in 2009, there was no Community law guaranteeing the right to bargain collectively, apart from the quite specific forms of engagement explained above. To that extent Article 28 appeared to be rather empty of substance.

Article 28 does not, however, stand alone. Also important for the right to bargain collectively is Article 12 of the Charter, which provides that everyone has a right to freedom of association, said to imply 'the right of everyone to form and to join trade unions for the protection of his or her interests'. The latter has become unexpectedly significant in view of the provisions of Article 52(3), which provides that:

> In so far as this Charter contains rights which correspond to rights guaranteed by the Convention for the Protection of Human Rights and Fundamental Freedoms, the meaning and scope of those rights shall be the same as those laid down by the said Convention. This provision shall not prevent Union law providing more extensive protection.

The reason why the latter is important is the decision of the European Court of Human Rights (ECtHR) in *Demir and Baycara v. Turkey*,[32] which brought to life the European Convention on Human Rights (ECHR), Article 11. This is significant because the ECHR, Article 11 corresponds to the EU Charter, Article 12, thereby bringing the 'meaning and scope' provisions of Article 52(3) into play. In the *Demir* case, the ECtHR appeared to impose a duty on Member States to have in place collective bargaining regimes consistent with ILO Convention 98 (which all Member States have ratified).[33] According to the Court:

> having regard to the developments in labour law, both international and national, and to the practice of Contracting States in such matters, the right to bargain collectively with the employer has, in principle, become one of the essential elements of the 'right to form and to join trade unions for the protection of [one's] interests' set forth in Article 11 of the Convention, it being understood that States remain free to organise their system so as, if appropriate, to grant special status to representative trade unions.[34]

32. [2008] ECHR 1345, (2009) 48 EHRR 54.
33. On ILO Convention 98, *see* B. Gernigon, A. Odero & H. Guido, *ILO Principles Concerning Collective Bargaining* 139 Intl. Lab. Rev. 33 (2000).
34. *Demir and Baycara*, *supra*, at paragraph 154.

One effect of *Demir and Baycara v. Turkey* relates to its impact on the relationship between the EU Charter, Articles 12 and 28. The effect of that influence could work in one of two ways. One possibility is that Article 28 of the EU Charter has become redundant because of the higher standard of protection that Article 12 of the Charter must now provide, as a result of Article 12 having the same meaning and scope as the ECHR, Article 11. An alternative possibility is that Article 12 informs the meaning of Article 28, so that when Article 28 refers to a right in accordance with Community law, that Community law must include Article 12 of the Charter, which must have the same meaning and scope as ECHR, Article 11. Whichever possibility prevails, the overall effect of *Demir and Baycara v. Turkey* is that the EU Charter may now go some way closer to providing the missing piece in the jigsaw puzzle referred to above. Although there may be no direct obligation under EU law to have 'legislation necessary to give effect to the provisions of the international labour conventions already ratified' by the Member State in question,[35] such an obligation arises from the EU Charter, Article 12, as informed by the jurisprudence of the ECtHR (albeit through a perhaps unanticipated consequence of the Charter).

By this circuitous and indirect route, ILO Convention 98 is thus indirectly incorporated into EU law, and with it the rich jurisprudence on collective bargaining produced by the ILO supervisory bodies.[36] This determines not only the scope of the right, but also when it may lawfully be qualified.[37] As such, these unanticipated developments address the need to ensure that the regulatory role of collective bargaining in European law has a guaranteed legal base in the domestic law of Member States, without which that regulatory role would be impossible to perform. But although perhaps unanticipated, this ought not to be controversial. Almost exactly two years before the Lisbon treaty came into force, the ECJ had already recognised the importance of core international labour conventions as part of the general principles of law of the EU.[38] But following *Demir and Baycara* this can no longer be a token gesture, even if it is the case that ILO minimum standards fall some way below the standards currently operating in most EU Member States.[39]

Rowing Back on *Demir and Baycara*?

It is well known that *Demir and Baycara v. Turkey* [2008] ECHR 1345 was an important breakthrough for labour rights under the ECHR. It is well known, however, that the ECtHR has been the subject of intense political criticism from those (notably in the British government) unhappy about some of its more liberal decisions. The decision in

35. *Ibid.* at paragraph 157.
36. On which *see* Gernigon, Odero & Guido, *supra*.
37. *See Demir and Baycara*, *supra*, at paragraph 166.
38. *Laval un Partneri Ltd*, *supra*, at paragraph 90 – referring there not to ILO Convention 98, but to its sibling Convention 87.
39. But *see* now *National Union of Rail, Maritime and Transport Workers v. United Kingdom* [2014] ECHR 366, (2015) 60 EHRR 10, where there are suggestions that the *Demir and Baycara* decision may be 'reinterpreted': *see* esp paragraph 86. For discussion, *see* Alan Bogg & K.D. Ewing, *The Implications of the RMT Case* 43 Indus. L. J. 221 (2014).

> *National Union of Rail, Maritime and Transport Workers* [2014] ECHR 346 may be a signal that the Court is listening to that criticism, and that it is unwilling to open up new areas of conflict with national governments.
>
> The case concerned a challenge to two aspects of the United Kingdom's strict anti-strike laws. The first related to the detailed notice requirements that trade unions must give to employers before industrial action may lawfully be taken. The second related to the ban on all forms of solidarity action. The Court held – controversially – that the first aspect of the claim was inadmissible, and that there had been no breach of ECHR, Article 11 in relation to the second aspect, even though the effect of the ban was to prevent the union from taking collective action in support of a small group of workers whose pay and conditions were being cut.
>
> The Court held that the right to strike fell within Article 11, but declined to say whether it was an 'essential' element of trade union activity. It also held that solidarity action fell within Article 11 but also held that a total ban could be justified under Article 11(2), thereby acknowledging the existence of a right that could never lawfully be exercised. In reaching this conclusion, the Court drew a distinction between core and accessory action, suggesting that solidarity action fell within the latter rather than the former category. A wider margin of appreciation would be allowed in respect of conduct deemed accessory.
>
> In an important passage, the Court said: 'The applicant relied heavily on the *Demir and Baykara* judgment, in which the Court considered that the respondent State should be allowed only a limited margin (see paragraph 119 of the judgment). The Court would point out, however, that the passage in question appears in the part of the judgment examining a very far-reaching interference with freedom of association, one that intruded into its inner core, namely the dissolution of a trade union. It is not to be understood as narrowing decisively and definitively the domestic authorities' margin of appreciation in relation to regulating, through normal democratic processes, the exercise of trade union freedom within the social and economic framework of the country concerned' (para 86).

§13.03 THE DEATH OF SOCIAL EUROPE

Jacques Delors kept his promise. We have evidence of a clear trajectory and evidence too of real outcomes. We have: (i) an institutionalised process of making law by a form of 'collective bargaining', (ii) a well developed process of engaging with collective bargaining at national level to implement and adapt legal obligations, and (iii) the entrenchment of the right to bargain collectively as a fundamental right. Collective bargaining is deeply embedded within the institutional structures of the European Union, supporting and exploiting the social democratic inheritance of most Member States.

So where did it all go wrong? How has it unravelled so quickly? The starting point for an understanding of the decline is Mario Draghi's by now infamous announcement of the death of Social Europe in an interview in the *Wall Street Journal* in 2012. According to Draghi, head of the European Central Bank, 'the European Social Model has already gone'.[40] These remarks expressed in the 'bible of global finance',[41] have been hotly disputed and perhaps even deeply resented.[42] But if the trajectory of collective bargaining and the reasons for that trajectory are any guide, he may be right. As a distinguished banker, he is to be taken at his word.

– Economic 'Coordination' and Collective Bargaining 'Deregulation'

We do not speak any more about he EU making law by social dialogue or collective bargaining, save only to mourn the passing of an era, it being some time since the social dialogue procedure was successfully engaged. The contemporary focus is on new economic governance arrangements, and the subordination of labour rights generally - and for our purposes collective bargaining specifically – to more closely coordinated national economic policies. These have been presented as part of the Europe 2020 growth strategy, with the scrutiny and surveillance of national economies. This scrutiny and surveillance is conducted under procedures established by TFEU, Articles 119–121,[43] taking the labour lawyer deep into very unfamiliar and at times terrifying territory. Referring to TEU, Article 3, the latter treaty provisions provide for not only the 'close coordination of national economic policies' (TFEU, Article 119), but also an obligation to comply with 'broad guidelines', setting out the economic policies for the Member States' (TFEU, Article 121). The guidelines are to be found in a Council Recommendation, of which the Parliament is to be 'informed', Member States then subject to 'surveillance' to ensure compliance.

So what do the guidelines say and how do they address collective bargaining arrangements in Member States? In line with the foregoing, the Council adopted Commission-proposed guidelines for 2010–2014 on 13 July 2010.[44] So far as relevant, Guideline 2 provided:

> Member States should encourage *the right framework conditions for wage bargaining systems* and labour cost developments consistent with price stability, productivity trends over the medium-term and the need to reduce macroeconomic imbalances. Where appropriate, adequate wage setting in the public sector should be regarded as an important signal to ensure wage moderation in the private sector in line with the need to improve competitiveness. *Wage setting frameworks, including minimum wages, should allow for wage formation processes that take into account differences in skills and local labour market conditions and respond to large divergences in economic performance across regions, sectors and companies within a country.*

40. *Wall Street Journal*, 24 Feb. 2012.
41. P. Mabille, *Draghi Buries European Social Model, La Tribune*, 27 Feb. 2012.
42. *See Lord Monks, Social Europe is Far From Dead Europe's World (Spring 2014)*.
43. Note also the provisions of the Euro-plus Pact: 'Each country will be responsible for the specific policy actions it chooses to foster competitiveness, but the following reforms will be given particular attention: (i) respecting national traditions of social dialogue and industrial relations, measures to ensure costs developments in line with productivity, such as: review the wage setting arrangements, and, where necessary, the degree of centralisation in the bargaining process, and the indexation mechanisms, while maintaining the autonomy of the social partners in the collective bargaining process': European Council, Conclusions, 24–25 Mar. 2011.
44. Council Recommendation of 13 Jul. 2010 (Broad guidelines for the economic policies of the Member States and of the Union) (2010/410/EU), Guideline 2.

Guideline 2 needs to be read carefully. 'Wage bargaining systems' of course is a reference to collective bargaining. What appears to be suggested here is not that such systems need to be developed and expanded where they do not already exist (in line with the 'social market' and 'social justice' ambitions of TEU, Article 3), but that existing procedures should be made to operate with greater flexibility, notwithstanding the (unacknowledged) potential consequences for the regulatory impact of these systems.

Despite the acknowledgement in TFEU, Article 120 of the objectives of the EU as set out in TEU, Article 3, there is little evidence in the guidelines of a desire to be moved by the commitments found in the TEU, Article 3 such as the commitment to a *social* market rather than a *free* market, or to social *justice* rather than social *injustice*. On the contrary, a major driving force behind the coordination and surveillance of national economies is 'international competitiveness', a point reinforced by Guideline 7. Introduced on 21 October 2010 to complement Guideline 2 above, Guideline 7 refers specifically to 'competiveness' as part of the context for encouraging '*the right framework conditions for wage bargaining*', a term used in Guideline 2 which is repeated in Guideline 7.[45] Whether we like it or not this has become a prescription for collective bargaining deregulation by a technocratic process about which most citizens in most Member States are largely unaware. Indeed, the prescription is now being swallowed, the guidelines being used to 'reform' collective bargaining procedures, 'reform' for this purpose meaning deregulation, deregulation for this purpose meaning the decentralisation of bargaining activity.[46]

What does this mean for collective bargaining procedures in practice? The main consequence so far has been a pre-meditated assault on multi-employer, sector-wide collective agreements, which in many Member States are then extended to non-participating firms, in the manner discussed above.[47] The assault on these arrangements is all the more remarkable for the fact that it seems to be ideologically inspired rather than evidence led, a Commission document noting that '*it is difficult to find a robust relationship between the centralisation of wage bargaining and economic outcomes*'.[48] But not only is this deregulation by stealth apparently unsupported by evidence, it is being pursued in the knowledge that it will lead to greater inequality between European citizens, in a manner which can hardly be consistent with TEU, Article 3. It is thus openly accepted that '*there is robust evidence that higher levels of bargaining coverage and more centralised or coordinated bargaining, as well as high*

45. Emphasis added. So far as relevant, Guideline 7 reinforces the message in Guideline 2: 'In order to increase competitiveness and raise participation levels, particularly for the low-skilled, and in line with economic policy guideline 2, Member States should encourage the right framework conditions for wage bargaining and labour cost development consistent with price stability and productivity trends': Council Decision of 21 Oct. 2010 (Guidelines for the employment policies of Member States) (2010/707/EU).
46. European Commission, *Wage Setting Systems and Wage Developments* [nd], http://ec.europa.eu/europe2020/pdf/themes/26_wage_setting_02.pdf.
47. *Ibid.* 'The existence of a procedure for legal extension of collective agreements, making them binding to non-unionised employees or non-signatory firms, can significantly broaden the coverage of collective agreements'.
48. *Ibid.*

union density, are associated with a compression of the wage distribution and a reduction of earnings inequality'.[49] This seems only to add to the enthusiasm of the authors of deregulation.

Since 2010, four countries in particular have been the targets of this deregulatory impulse, in response to Commission concerns that their collective bargaining systems – of a type 'widespread in the EU'[50] - were creating wages that were 'too high'.[51] The first of these countries was **Italy**, told in 2011 that 'bargaining at firm level can play a significant role, which may also help to address regional labour market disparities', and encouraged to make greater use of opening clauses in collective agreements to derogate from the sectoral wage agreed at national level.[52] In the same year, concern was expressed that 'the ongoing labour market reform in **Spain** needs to be complemented by an overhaul of the current unwieldy collective bargaining system', and that the 'predominance of provincial and industry agreements leaves little room for negotiations at firm level'.[53] In the following year, **Belgium** was told that it too had to 'reform' the system of wage bargaining, in order to facilitate 'the use of opt-out clauses from sectoral collective agreements to better align wage growth and labour productivity developments at local level'.[54] This is only the beginning, **Portugal** told much the same in 2014,[55] even if there is welcome evidence of resistance.[56]

49. *Ibid*. Emphasis added.
50. *Ibid*.
51. *Ibid*: 'As a result of extension of collective agreements, wages may not be able to fully adjust to differences in productivity across firms or geographical areas within the same sector. The more important these differences are, the stronger the risk that the extension results in a misallocation of labour, with too high wages (and low employment, output) in low-productivity firms. Extension mechanisms are also likely to reduce the responsiveness of nominal wages to shocks, as wages are less responsive to local conditions'.
52. Council Recommendation of 12 Jul. 2011 (National Reform Programme 2011 of Italy) (2011/C-215/02).
53. Council Recommendation of 12 Jul. 2011 (National Reform Programme 2011 of Spain) (2011/C-212/01). Indeed the 'automatic extension of collective agreements, the validity of non-renewed contracts and the use of ex-post inflation indexation clauses contribute to wage-inertia, preventing the wage flexibility needed to speed up economic adjustment and restore competitiveness' (*ibid*.). For the implications of Spain's rapid de-regulation of its collective bargaining system, *see* ILO, Committee on Freedom of Association, *Report No. 371, Case No 2947* (Spain) (2014), paragraphs 317–465.
54. Council Recommendation of 10 Jul. 2012 (National Reform Programme 2012 of Belgium) (2012/C-219/02).
55. European Commission, *Recommendation for a Council Recommendation on Portugal's 2014 National Reform Programme*, COM (2014) 423 Final. Portugal was told to 'Explore, in consultation with the social partners and in accordance with national practice, the possibility of firm-level temporary opt-out arrangements from sectoral contracts agreed between employers and workers' representatives'.
56. Thus, concerns continue to be expressed that 'a number of obstacles continue to prevent firms and workers from engaging in firm-level negotiation. If properly implemented, the agreement could also make effective the possibility of derogating from national collective contracts, which was formally introduced by the 2011 inter-sectoral agreement but rarely implemented': European Commission, Commission Staff Working Document, Country Report Italy 2015, (COM (2015) 85 final.

– Austerity and Collective Bargaining 'Destruction'

Coordination of economic policy is, however, not the only way by which the Commission is now intervening in national collective bargaining systems. The financial assistance packages introduced after the Euro-crisis in 2010 are a second and more dramatic source of collective bargaining de-regulation. Whether directly or indirectly this has led to major initiatives in Ireland, Romania and Greece, where entire collective bargaining structures have been abolished, in the latter two cases in circumstances that violate the international obligations of the countries concerned. In the case of **Ireland**, in return for financial assistance the government undertook in a Memorandum of Understanding (2010) to 'introduce legislation to reform the minimum wage', and take steps to 'prevent distortions of wage conditions across sectors associated with the presence of sectoral minimum wages in addition to the national minimum wage'.[57] Specific measures included an independent review of the two regimes that provided for wage determination on a sectoral basis, namely Joint Labour Committees on the one hand and Registered Employment Agreements on the other.[58] The latter were recently declared unconstitutional.[59]

An altogether more dramatic assault on collective bargaining structures has taken place in **Romania**. Again in a Memorandum of Understanding (2011), Romania undertook 'reforms to the wage-setting system allowing wages to better reflect productivity developments in the medium term'.[60] The principal means by which this was done appears to have been Law 62/2011, which was as controversial for the manner of its introduction as for its content. So far as the latter is concerned, however, the new law abolished national collective bargaining arrangements, and imposed tight restrictions on sectoral and enterprise based bargaining. So far as sectoral bargaining is concerned, this could be established in sectors only where the employers taking part

57. European Commission, *Memorandum of Understanding on Specific Economic Policy Conditionality (Ireland)* (3 Dec. 2010): http://ec.europa.eu/economy_finance/articles/eu_economic_situation/pdf/2010-12-07-mou_en.pdf.
58. Department of Jobs, Enterprise and Innovation, *Report of the Independent Review of Employment Regulation Orders and Registered Employment Agreement Wage Setting Mechanisms* (2011). The terms of reference of the independent review – which were to be agreed with the Commission – were to consider 'whether minimum wages and working conditions more stringent [than] those guaranteed by the national minimum wage for the worker categories covered by [Employment Regulation Orders] are justified on the grounds of fairness'. The review concluded that 'the current JLC/REA regulatory system should be retained', though radically overhauled to make it 'more responsive to changing economic circumstances and labour market conditions' (p. 2).
59. *McGowan v. Labour Court*, above. Although having operated successfully for 67 years, the extension procedures were nevertheless found to violate a provision of Ireland's apparently ultra-liberal constitution, which confines law-making powers to the legislature. The High Court had previously ruled that the JLC system of wage determination was unconstitutional: *John Grace Fried Chicken Ltd v. Catering Joint Labour Committee* [2011] IEHC 277. *See* the brilliant blog-post by P. McMahon, Joint Labour Committee System Declared Unconstitutional', 8 Jul. 2011 (drawing parallels with New York's 'sick chicken' case, *ALA Schechter Poultry Corp v. United States*, 295 US 495 (1935)): http://www.extempore.ie/2011/07/08/joint-labour-committee-system-declared-unconstitutional/. Ireland has been left without any legal support for collective bargaining.
60. European Commission, *Memorandum of Understanding between the European Commission and Romania* (June 2012), paragraph 37. These steps were to be taken 'while respecting the autonomy of social partners, national traditions and practices' (*ibid.*).

employed a majority of the workers in the sector in question. The effect of this requirement was to make collective bargaining at this level 'so difficult that no sector-level agreement has been concluded'.[61] So far as enterprise based bargaining is concerned, the threshold here was that the union in the enterprise must have in membership more than 50% of the workers in the enterprise in question. According to the ILO Committee of Experts, there has been a 'drastic decrease' in the number of enterprise agreements as a result.[62]

Unlike in the case of Ireland, the changes introduced in Romania have been the subject of scrutiny by the ILO Committee of Experts (though Ireland has recently fallen foul of ILO standards for other reasons).[63] The latter body has expressed concern about the compatibility of the changes with ILO Convention 98, and requested the government to amend the legislation to guarantee the application of freedom of association principles.[64] However, proposals to do just that met some resistance from the IMF and the European Commission in a confidential document leaked to the International Trade Union Confederation.[65] Thus, strongly urging the Romanian authorities 'to limit any amendments to Law 62/2011 to revisions necessary to bring the law into compliance with core ILO conventions', the IMF and European Commission representatives warned that:

> The re-introduction of national collective labour agreements with automatic erga-omnes extension risks resulting in a misalignment of wages and productivity developments across firms, sectors and occupations. We strongly urge the authorities to ensure that national collective agreements do not contain elements related to wages and/or reverse the progress achieved with the Labor Code adopted in May 2011 (e.g., on working time regulation).[66]

A yet more dramatic assault on collective structures has taken place in **Greece**,[67] these being more far-reaching and more explicit than the demands imposed elsewhere. So under the direction of the Troika:

> it was decided to follow a two-step approach after consultation with the authorities (in particular with the Ministry of Labour) and social partners. Firstly, the government will launch a social pact with social partners to forge consensus on decentralization of wage bargaining (to allow the local level to opt-out from the

61. ITUC, 'IMF and EC Apply Behind-the –Scenes Pressure on Romania to Halt the Restoration of Core Labour Rights', 21 Nov. 2012: http://www.ituc-csi.org/imf-and-ec-apply-behind-the-scenes.
62. ILO, 102nd Session, *Report of the Committee of Experts on the Application of Conventions and Recommendations* (2013).
63. On the current situation regarding Ireland, *see* ILO, 102nd Session, *Report of the Committee of Experts on the Application of Conventions and Recommendations* (2013).
64. ILO, 102nd Session, *Report of the Committee of Experts on the Application of Conventions and Recommendations* (2013).
65. ITUC, 'IMF and EC Apply Behind-the–Scenes Pressure on Romania to Halt the Restoration of Core Labour Rights', *supra*.
66. http://www.ituc-csi.org/IMG/pdf/romania.pdf. Steps by the authorities to ensure that national collective bargaining does not include pay would not be consistent with ILO Convention 98, as the ITUC pointed out.
67. *See* A. Koukiadaki & L. Kretsos, *Opening Pandora's Box: The Sovereign Debt Crisis and Labour Market Regulation in Greece* 41 Indus. L. J. 276 (2012).

> wage increases agreed at the sectoral level), the introduction of sub-minima wages for the young and long-term unemployed, the revision of important aspects of firing rules and costs, and the revision of part-time and temporary work regulations. Secondly, the government will enforce the required changes in the wage-setting mechanisms and labour market institutions.[68]

These demands led to a number of important changes to Greek law, so that both sector and enterprise-based agreements could make provision less favourable than that contained in the national agreement. Moreover, ad hoc associations of employees could negotiate these latter arrangements where there were no trade unions, this latter provision a response by the Greek government to the concerns of the Troika that enterprise-level agreements were not sufficiently widespread. One reasons for the absence of such agreements is that there were very few trade unions at enterprise level, with enterprise agreements applying only to enterprises with more than fifty workers.

It is not possible here to do justice to the full range and scope of the changes that were introduced in Greece as a result of 'austerity'.[69] Suffice it to say that in 2012 the ILO Committee of Experts examined the changes introduced in Greece, following a visit to Athens in 2011 by an ILO High Level Mission, which had produced a very detailed and troubling report. On the basis of evidence produced by the High Level Mission and other information provided by the Greek trade unions, the Committee of Experts concluded that the decentralising measures were 'likely to have a significant – and potentially devastating – impact on the industrial relations system in the country'.[70] The Committee also expressed the fear 'that the entire foundation of collective bargaining in the country may be vulnerable to collapse under this new framework'. This was partly because 90% of the (private sector) workforce was employed in small enterprises, in a system where trade unions cannot legally be formed in enterprises with less than 20 employees. In these circumstances:

> granting collective bargaining rights to other types of workers' representation which are not afforded the guarantees of independence that apply to the structure and formation of trade unions and the protection of its officers and members is likely to seriously undermine the position of trade unions as the representative voice of the workers in the collective bargaining process.[71]

68. European Commission, *The Economic Adjustment Programme for Greece* (2010), paragraph 31. These changes were accepted 'Despite the fact that we support Collective Bargaining and Agreements between social partners (a longstanding European value and position recently included in the proposed new Treaty changes): George Papandreou to Christine Lagarde, Jean-Claude Juncker, Olli Rehn and Mario Draghi, 15 Feb. 2012.
69. For full details *see* International Labour Office, *Report on the High Level Mission to Greece (Athens, 19-23 September 2011)* (Geneva, 2011).
70. ILO, 101st Session, *Report of the Committee of Experts on the Application of Conventions and Recommendations* (2012).
71. *Ibid*. For continuing concerns, *see* ILO, 103rd Session, *Report of the Committee of Experts on the Application of Conventions and Recommendations* (2014): 'national occupational collective agreements have gone down from 43 in 2008 to seven in 2012 whereas firm-level collective agreements have increased from 215 in 2008 to 975 in 2012 (706 signed by associations of persons and 269 signed by trade unions)'. These procedures appear to be a clear breach of ILO Convention 98, Articles 2 and 3.

– *TTIP and Collective Bargaining 'Decentralisation'*

We are witnessing collective bargaining 'deregulation' and 'destruction' in the interest of 'competitiveness' and 'austerity'. But there is a third consideration likely to pull in the same direction, adding to the pressures for greater decentralisation from sector to firm. This is 'free trade', the growth of the oxymoronic 'free' trade agreements, most notably the proposed EU-US Free Trade Agreement (or the Transatlantic Trade and Investment Partnership as it is officially known).[72] TTIP is a highly controversial initiative, not least because of its secrecy, its likely content, and the manner of its enforcement (in some though not all areas). In the United Kingdom, much of the debate has been concentrated on the National Health Service, and the possible implications TTIP will have for a socialised health service. But that is not the only concern, as reflected in motions submitted to the TUC Annual Congress in 2014, with one from the GMB union expressing anxiety that TTIP will 'potentially undermine labour standards, pay, conditions and trade union rights as the US refuses to ratify core ILO conventions and operates anti-union 'right to work' policies in half of its states'.[73]

The context here is that TTIP is one of a number of free trade agreements negotiated by the United States with a large number of countries since the collapse of proposals for a global free trade deal. There is of course the North American Free Trade Agreement between the US, Canada and Mexico, as well as bilateral agreements with Singapore, Australia and a host of other countries.[74] US ambitions are now much greater, and it seems that the idea of a de facto global free trade area for US business will be realised by the bolder free trade agreements now being negotiated, one being TTIP and the other being a parallel and equally controversial agreement for the Pacific Rim, also currently the subject of negotiations. It is not the purpose here to consider the wisdom or otherwise of US trade policy. But it is to be noted that the US is not alone in expanding the global reach of free trade, with similar initiatives also being taken by the EU and others.[75] The EU has already concluded a free trade agreement with Korea in which provides by Article 13.4 that:

> The Parties, in accordance with the obligations deriving from membership of the ILO and the ILO Declaration on Fundamental Principles and Rights at Work and its Follow-up, 1998, commit to respecting, promoting and realising, in their laws and

72. *See further*, K.D. Ewing & J. Hendy QC, Written Evidence to Business, Innovation and Skills Committee, Transatlantic Trade and Investment Partnership Inquiry, 28 Jan. 2015.
73. A 'right to work' state is a State that permits workers not to join a trade union where the union has been certified as a bargaining agent following a vote in which a majority of workers vote in favour of union representation. It means that those who opt – out enjoy the significant benefits of unionisation (in terms of higher pay and better conditions) without making a contribution. Council of Europe states are effectively right to work states to the extent that compulsory membership of a trade union as a condition of employment is prohibited by both the European Convention on Human Rights (as construed by the European Court of Human Rights) and the European Social Charter (as construed by the European Committee of Social Rights). *See* H. Colllns, K.D. Ewing & A. McColgan, *Labour Law* Chapter 12 (Cambridge U. Press 2012).
74. Many of these agreements may be found on the ILO website: http://ilo.org/global/standards/information-resources-and-publications/free-trade-agreements-and-labour-rights/lang--en/index.htm.
75. *Ibid.*

> practices, the principles concerning the fundamental rights, namely freedom of association and the effective recognition of the right to collective bargaining.

Given that there is likely to be a similar labour chapter in TTIP, why is there any concern that these agreements will affect collective bargaining arrangements? We could begin by asking how meaningful are the commitments to labour standards by our trade partners. Take the United States, an ILO member since 1980.[76] The United States has ratified only 14 ILO Conventions, and only two of the eight fundamental conventions.[77] And while the United States claims that federal law is broadly consistent with ILO standards, there is a long line of decisions of the Freedom of Association Committee that would suggest otherwise. The latter Committee has criticised the extent to which US labour law (i) denies the right to freedom of association to public sector workers, and (ii) denies trade union officials access to workplaces while trying to organise workers with a view to securing certification as a bargaining agent.[78] In addition, the Freedom of Association Committee has criticised the US for denying workers the right to strike by allowing lawful strikers to be replaced. In an important complaint citing a number of companies that had replaced lawful strikers, the Committee said that:

> The right to strike is one of the essential means through which workers and their organisations may promote and defend their economic and social interests. The Committee considers that this basic right is not really guaranteed when a worker who exercises it legally runs the risk of seeing his or her job taken up permanently by another worker, just as legally. The Committee considers that, if a strike is otherwise legal, the use of labour drawn from outside the undertaking to replace strikers for an indeterminate period entails a risk of derogation from the right to strike which may affect the free exercise of trade union rights.[79]

The commitment to respect labour standards by countries such as the USA that have not ratified the relevant ILO Conventions is not a compelling commitment, particularly when the countries in question are clearly in breach of ILO obligations. The fact is that existing free trade agreements contain hollow commitments on labour rights – commitments to undertakings that are not observed, that no one has any greater intention of observing, with no procedures to ensure compliance.[80] But perhaps more importantly, even if these obligations were complied with it is a commitment to comply with the minimum standards of the ILO, not the prevailing standards of most EU Member States. The danger is obvious. In this free trade area there will be an inevitable

---

76. The USA had previously been a member of the ILO from 1934 to 1977. Curiously it was not a founding member.
77. This does not include either of the freedom of association conventions, 87 or 98.
78. For a brief consideration of these cases, *see* KD Ewing, *International Regulation*, in *Comparative Employment Relations in the Global Economy* Chapter 23 (C. Frege & J. Kelly eds, Routledge 2013).
79. ILO, Committee on Freedom of Association, *Report No 284, Case No 1523* (United States) (1991).
80. The point is reinforced by experience of the EU-Korea Free Trade Agreement – Korea has ratified only 24 ILO Conventions and only four of the eight fundamental conventions. It has a poor record before the ILO Freedom of Association Committee: *see* ILO, Committee on Freedom of Association, *Report No. 359, Case No 2602* (Korea) (2008). Korea's commitment to freedom of association is hard to take seriously in light of the foregoing case.

demand from US corporations to do in Dortmund what they do in Delaware, just like they demanded to do in Dagenham what they did in Detroit. In the same way, European corporations will demand the same power to do in Tuscany what they can already do in Texas. This will lead inevitably to more permissive and flexible procedures as a result, with even more pressure to de-centralise pay bargaining arrangements, putting even more pressure on sector-wide agreements in EU Member States, as ever more urgent demands grow to move the locus of collective bargaining to the enterprise.

Why? Because the US operates a highly decentralised system of collective bargaining, with the sector-wide initiatives pioneered by Roosevelt's National Industrial Recovery Act having been declared unconstitutional shortly after enactment.[81] US labour law (which has been imported by a number of countries, notably Canada, another free trade partner) effectively mandates enterprise or company level collective bargaining, which in turn is associated with low levels of coverage, though makes collective bargaining arrangements difficult to establish for reasons that need not be explored here, with only about 10% of US workers thought to be protected by a collective agreement.[82] This contrasts with what was the EU norm under active sector-wide bargaining arrangements, when at one time collective bargaining density in the EU-15 (excluding the United Kingdom) was well above 70% in the case of most Member States. If it is the case – as in my view it is likely - free trade leads to regulatory convergence in the form of enterprise level collective bargaining, the British experience should stand as a salutary warning to the rest of Europe. The gradual decentralisation of collective bargaining in the United Kingdom under Thatcher inspired initiatives since 1980, and the subsequent adoption of US style collective bargaining laws under the Blair government, has seen collective bargaining density collapse from 82% in 1980 to just over 20% today.[83]

§13.04 CONCLUSION

In relation to collective bargaining it is quite obvious what is going on. To this end a very important insight is provided by an ECOFIN Report, in which a number of employment related recommendations were made. These included:

> *decrease* the bargaining coverage or (automatic) extension of collective agreements.

81. *ALA Schechter Poultry Corp v. United States*, 295 US 495 (1935). For context, *see* A.J. Badger, *FDR-The First Hundred Days* (Hill & Wang, 2008).
82. The Supreme Court of Canada has recently confirmed that the right to bargain collectively is constitutionally protected by the Canadian Charter of Rights and Freedoms: *Mounted Police Association of Ontario v. Canada (Attorney General)*, 2015 SCC 1. It remains to be seen what this has on bargaining levels. In the following week (in an otherwise favourable decision on the right to strike) the same court upheld very high thresholds to be met before a union is entitled to certification as a bargaining agent: *Saskatchewan Federation of Labour v. Saskatchewan*, 2015 SCC 4.
83. K.D. Ewing & J. Hendy QC, *Reconstruction after the Crisis – A Manifesto for Collective Bargaining* (Institute of Employment Rights 2013).

reform the bargaining system in a *less centralized* way, for instance by *removing* or *limiting* the 'favourability principle', or *introducing/extending* the possibility to derogate from higher level agreements or to negotiate firm-level agreements.

result in an overall *reduction* in the wage- setting power of trade unions.[84]

These proposals were no doubt highly controversial, which is perhaps why they come with a health warning that 'the taxonomy of reforms into 'employment-friendly' and 'other reforms' has no normative implications . . . and should not be understood as necessarily reflecting the recommendations of the European Commission in the field of employment and social policies'.[85]

There nevertheless appears to be a clear and expanding trajectory, as indicated in the following year's report from the same source:

> Efforts were stepped-up in 2012 to review the wage-setting mechanisms in a number of Member States, notably as part of the reform packages agreed in the framework of financial assistance programmes or in countries undergoing strong market pressure. This includes a drastic overhaul of the wage setting system in Greece, Portugal and Spain . . . , but also a move towards greater decentralisation of collective bargaining in Italy, as well as the reform of sectorial agreements in Ireland. The automatic extension of collective agreements after they expire was also eliminated in Estonia. *Limited progress was however made in countries with less urgent need for reforms, but where the functioning of certain wage setting and wage indexation systems has nevertheless been identified as a possible threat to competitiveness.*[86]

The changes are being driven by the new economic strategy and by the policies of austerity, with free trade likely to produce additional pressures. Many of the initiatives in the direction of deregulation and destruction of collective bargaining activity are likely to breach international labour standards, notably those relating to Romania and Greece, concerning which the ILO supervisory bodies have made the position fairly

84. European Commission, *Labour Market Developments in Europe 2012* (European Economy 5/2012), p. 104.
85. *Ibid.* Production of the report was coordinated by Alessandro Turrini (Head of Unit – Labour market reforms) and Alfonso Arpaia (Head of Sector – Labour market analysis). For comment, *see* Thorsten Schulten, 'The Troika and Multi-Employer Bargaining – European Pressure is Destroying National Collective Bargaining Systems', *Global Labour Column*, Number 139 (June 2013): 'The consequences of the strategy of radical decentralisation advocated by the Troika are already evident. Systems of collective bargaining that were once robust have been systematically eroded and destroyed. The collective agreement itself – as an instrument for collectively regulating wages and other employment conditions – is manifestly now at risk'. In a very short but lucid piece, Schulten provides an excellent analysis of the four strategies being used by the Troika to 'erode and destroy' collective bargaining arrangements: termination of national bargaining, derogation to firm level, restrictions on extension mechanisms, and the use of non-union 'bargaining' partners. *See also* Sharan Burrow, General Secretary, ITUC: 'The key objective ... is to slash labour costs by replacing multi-employer collective bargaining systems at industry or national level with enterprise level bargaining or to eliminate collective bargaining altogether. A retreat to enterprise-level bargaining is inequitable in all circumstances.' ITUC, *Frontlines Report Summary*, April 2013, p. 4. It is hard to argue with that.
86. European Commission, *Labour Market Developments in Europe 2013* (European Economy 6/2013), p. 56. Emphasis added. Unlike the 2012 Report, the 2013 Report is acknowledged to have 'benefited from useful comments and suggestions' from 'experts at the European Central Bank and International Monetary Fund'.

clear.[87] Spanish collective bargaining changes have also attracted the censure of the ILO supervisory bodies.[88]

The position is not so clear in relation to all the changes, including some of the most egregious such as the decentralisation from sector to firm, and the removal of extension mechanisms. This is not to say that the latter should not be contested along with the former, though we should be aware that the ILO supervisory bodies allow flexibility as to bargaining level and extension mechanisms.[89] However, as the supervisory bodies have indicated, that flexibility must accord with the wishes of the parties, and ought not to be imposed unilaterally by the State.[90] But even taking the most generous view possible of the recent conduct in relation to collective bargaining by the EU and by selected Member States, there is nevertheless a lengthy charge sheet that can be drawn up against the EU institutions and a number of national governments. The ECJ has gone AWOL,[91] leaving the IMF, the Commission and the European Central Bank to do pretty much what they like,[92] hiding behind the empty rhetoric of obligations that must be carried out consistently with ILO obligations, while simultaneously giving directions almost certainly in breach.[93]

One lesson for lawyers from the crisis is that social democratic legal instruments are no defence against neo-liberal economics, and that to win the campaign for social rights it is necessary to win the campaign for progressive economics. To reflect on an earlier era, Keynesian solutions led to social democratic institutions.[94] But social democratic institutions cannot command Keynesian solutions. At the moment, human rights and economics are in conflict. The latter will prevail, in a matter over which electors have no control, unless there is greater resistance and leadership from Europe's institutional labour movement than has so far been displayed. Our contribution as lawyers is to ensure that all EU institutions and all Member States live up to the commitment to the rule of law enshrined in TEU, Article 2.[95] Law serves no purpose if

---

87. It should also be noted that both the United Kingdom and Sweden have encountered problems in relation to compliance with ILO obligations as a result of the earlier decisions in *Viking* and *Laval, supra*. *See* respectively ILO, 99th Session, *Report of the Committee of Experts on the Application of Conventions and Recommendations* (2010), and ILO, 100th Session, *Report of the Committee of Experts on the Application of Conventions and Recommendations* (2011) (United Kingdom), and ILO, 102nd Session, *Report of the Committee of Experts on the Application of Conventions and Recommendations* (2013) (Sweden). *See also LO and TCO v. Sweden*, European Committee of Social Rights, Case No 85/2012 (European Social Charter, Article 6(2)).
88. ILO Committee on Freedom of Association, *Case No. 2947* (Spain), *supra*.
89. *See* Gernigon, Odero & Guido, *supra*.
90. *Ibid*. Extension mechanisms are not compulsory, but equally they do not violate the principle of voluntary collective bargaining: ILO Committee of Experts, *Giving Globalisation a Human Face* (2012), paragraph 245.
91. *Case 370/12, Pringle v. Ireland* [2012] ECR I-756.
92. We should not overlook the role of the OECD, which has also made a series of recommendations to members to decentralise or otherwise 'reform' wage bargaining arrangements, in relation specifically to Belgium, Italy, Slovenia and Spain: OECD, *Economic Policy Reforms* (2012). The latter report also highlights that by 2010 (the most recent data at the time), collective bargaining coverage had declined significantly in Estonia, Ireland, Portugal, and Spain (p. 146).
93. As in the case of Romania, discussed above.
94. Ewing and Hendy, *Reconstruction after the Crisis, supra*.
95. *See also* the powerful critique in S. Sciarra, 'Social Law in the Wake of the Crisis', Centre for the Study of European Labour Law, University of Catania, Working Paper (2014): 'The state of

courts have neither the courage nor the will to enforce it. As Delors had the wisdom to realise, without enforceable rights workers in some countries may rightly feel that they have no reason to support continuing membership of the EU. If Draghi is right that Social Europe is dead, then so too is the EU, a message that progressive lawyers need to express more loudly and clearly.[96]

emergency cannot justify renouncing the rule of law'. Professor Sciarra also raises equally important questions about the democratic legitimacy of the foregoing developments. On the rule of law dimension, *see further*, KD Ewing, 'Austerity and the Importance of the ILO and the ECHR for the Progressive Development of European Labour Law: A Case Study from Greece', in W. Daubler & R. Zimmer (eds), *Arbeitsvolkerrecht: Festschrift fur Klaus Lorcher* (Nomos, 2013), p. 361.

96. *This paper is part of an on-going programme of work with my colleague, John Hendy QC. Earlier versions were given in London on 9 May 2014 (Europe day), Dublin on 18 September 2014, and Paris on 15 November 2014.*

CHAPTER 14

The United Kingdom without the Charter of Fundamental Rights of the European Union: Putting Down the Dog That Did Not Bark?

Kieron Beale QC

§14.01 INTRODUCTION

In 1848, many of the countries of continental Europe were in the grips of revolutionary fervour. Established orders were being set aside, governments replaced. On 10 April 1848, around 150,000 people[1] attended a mass protest on Kennington Common in London. They were seeking support from the Government of the day for the principles laid out in the People's Charter, first developed a decade earlier in 1838. The requests were, by modern tastes, modest. 'Chartists' sought universal suffrage for every man (*sic*) over the age of 21. No property requirement for members of Parliament. A salary for members of Parliament to enable the poor to stand for election. Equally sized constituencies. They had dropped the controversial suggestion of a secret ballot.[2] The most radical suggestion was for Parliamentary elections to take place annually. This is not the stuff of revolutions. Nor was it to prove so. The Chartist leaders presented a petition of several million signatures to Parliament and went home. The large crowd dispersed. The entire event passed off peacefully. Parliament ignored the petition.

Moving forward 160 years, the English people received the benefit of a different Charter, also containing important constitutional rights which, to modern tastes, may seem relatively modest. This is the Charter of Fundamental Rights of the European Union ('the Charter'). The Charter was 'solemnly proclaimed' by the European

1. David Goodway, *London Chartism* (1982), pp. 129–42, cited in the *Wikipedia* entry for Chartism.
2. Asa Briggs, *The Age of Improvement 1873-1867* (1959, republished 2014) p. 262.

Parliament, the Council of Ministers and the European Commission at Nice on 18 December 2000.[3] The Cologne European Council meeting in June 1999 had set out the main objective for a Charter, which was that, 'the fundamental rights applicable at Union level should be consolidated in a Charter and thereby made more evident'.[4]

The Preamble to the Charter refers to the need to 'strengthen the protection of fundamental rights' by making them 'more visible'. However, the Charter project was not mere window dressing. It had a deeper constitutional significance. In a Commission paper published during the drafting process, the Commission described the Charter as 'an indispensable instrument of political and moral legitimacy, both for the citizens of Europe in relation to politicians, administrations and national powers and for economic and social operators. It is an expression of the common values that are at the very core of our democratic societies'.[5]

Yet despite its relatively modest ambit; the fact that it simply codified many of the pre-existing principles readily found under existing European Union law as reflecting the 'common constitutional traditions' of the Member States; and the decision of the United Kingdom as a Member State to adopt it as part of its agreement to the Lisbon Treaty, the political reception of the Charter has been unkind. Even before its formal adoption, its potential impact was being dismissed. In October 2000, the then Minister for Europe Keith Vaz MP famously attempted to dampen fears in the UK that the newly proclaimed EU Charter of Fundamental Rights was a 'litigator's charter'. He claimed that it had no more legal effect than a copy of the Beano.[6] The UK Government has also sought to disclaim its partial paternity of the Charter. At a European Council meeting in June 2007, the then Prime Minister claimed he had secured a legally binding 'opt-out' from the EU Charter in the 'Reform Treaty',[7] through a joint UK and Polish Protocol to the Treaties.[8] Mr. Blair MP stated that: 'It is absolutely clear that we have an opt-out from ... the charter.'[9] The Lisbon Treaty was subsequently signed by the Member States in Lisbon on 13 December 2007.[10] Article 6(1) of the Treaty on European Union

3. OJ [2000] C No. 364, 18 Dec. 2000, p. 1. *See generally* K. Beal & T. Hickman, *Beano no more: The EU Charter of Rights after Lisbon*, [2011] JR 113.
4. Presidency Conclusions of the Cologne European Council, 3–4 Jun. 1999, Doc 150/99 REV 1, paragraph 44 and Annex IV; COM (2000) 559 Commission Communication on the Charter of Fundamental Rights of the European Union, paragraph 7; *See also* Parliamentary Questions 23 Jan. 2001 P-3997/2000; OJ C 174E; Answer given by Mr Vitorino on behalf of the Commission.
5. *Ibid.* paragraph 8.
6. 'European summit Charter on rights "no more binding than the Beano"', *The Telegraph*, 14 Oct. 2000.
7. This was to become the Lisbon Treaty which now includes the Treaty on European Union ('TEU') and the Treaty on the Functioning of the European Union ('TFEU').
8. For press reporting see e.g., 'Historic EU Deal, but at What Price?' *Daily Mail*, 23 Jun. 2007: 'Mr Blair's final appearance on the European stage produced a clear negotiating success as Britain won a legally binding opt-out from the controversial charter.'
9. Hansard, 25 Jun. 2007 HC, cols 37and 39. In his initial statement to Parliament the Prime Minister appeared to be more guarded in his comments than he was in response to questions from the floor of the House, simply referring to a legally binding protocol that would make clear that there could be no expansion of EU law: see cols 21 and 27.
10. The Charter was found at OJ 2000 C 364, p. 8 in its original form. The version of the Charter considered as part of the ratification of the Lisbon Treaty is at OJ 2007 C 303, p. 1. The final, published version of the Charter in the Official Journal is at OJ 2010 C 83, pp. 389–403.

('TEU') conferred on the Charter the same legal value as any other article of the Treaties.

The UK's claimed opt out from the Charter continues to cause adverse political comment to surface in the media. Thrown into the gently simmering pot of rising Euro-scepticism has been the judgment of Mostyn J in *R (AB) v. Secretary of State for the Home Department*.[11] There a claim against the Government by a third country national involved a claim based on Article 7 of the Charter. Mostyn J held at paragraph 12 that it was 'clear that the contracting parties agreed that the Charter did not create one single further justiciable right in our domestic courts'. However, he went on to observe at paragraph 13 that this view was not shared by the Court of Justice of the European Union ('ECJ') in its judgment in Joined Cases C-411/10 and C-493/10 *SSDH v. NS and ME*.[12] It is worth citing at this stage paragraph 14 of the judgment:

> The constitutional significance of this decision can hardly be overstated. The Human Rights Act 1998 incorporated into our domestic law large parts, but by no means all, of the European Convention on Human Rights. Some parts were deliberately missed out by Parliament. The Charter of Fundamental Rights of the European Union contains, I believe, all of those missing parts and a great deal more. Notwithstanding the endeavours of our political representatives at Lisbon it would seem that the much wider Charter of Rights is now part of our domestic law. Moreover, that much wider Charter of Rights would remain part of our domestic law even if the Human Rights Act were repealed.

The learned Judge seemed particularly concerned that the claimant should assert a right to protection of his personal data. Notwithstanding that the rights found in Article 8 of the Charter do no more than codify the rights that have been recognised by the Data Protection Directive since October 1995.[13] That Directive was incorporated into UK law by the Data Protection Act 1998, without drawing significant, adverse comment.[14]

The Judge's observations prompted some caustic comments in the press. *The Times* reported as follows:[15]

> 'The prospect of a host of new human rights having been smuggled into the UK without anyone noticing – and contrary to what ministers believed to be the case – has caused a political storm.
>
> Moreover, the claim came from the judiciary – always viewed with suspicion where human rights are concerned.' It was a High Court judge, Mr Justice Mostyn, who said last week that recent European rulings relating to the charter suggested that it was now incorporated by proxy into UK law.

11. [2013] EWHC 3452 (Admin).
12. [2011] ECR I-13905, ECJ at paragraph 120.
13. Indeed, the terms of Articles 7 and 8 of the Charter were recently preyed in aid by the complainants in *Google Inc v. Vidal-Hall* [2015] EWCA Civ 311, CA.
14. The Court might have benefitted from a clearer exposition of how the issues in question fell within the scope of EU law. Mostyn J. was willing to apply, albeit *obiter*, the terms of Article 47 of the Charter in family proceedings in *MG and others* [2015] EWHC 564 (Fam) at [10] when concluding that the lack of availability of legal aid for private, children's proceedings might give rise to an inequality of arms, in breach of that Article. The learned Judge expressed the concern that 'the principle of individual justice has had to be sacrificed on the altar of public debt'.
15. 'Political row erupts over EU Rights', *The Times*, 20 Nov. 2013: Frances Gibb.

> His comments caused an outcry among Tory Euro-sceptics: a withdrawal from the EU was the only way, several said, to guard against 'mission creep' from European institutions. One, Julian Brazier, MP, said that if the charter had effect in the UK, we were 'at a point of no return' in relations with the EU.

The Secretary of State for Justice's reaction was also reported in the newspapers. It was purportedly in the following terms:[16]

> Last night, Mr Grayling said: 'Labour duped us when it signed the Lisbon Treaty and promised this kind of ruling wouldn't happen. We cannot go on seeing crucial decisions about our society and our system of justice and government being taken by unaccountable European courts. That's why we need to renegotiate our membership of the EU and have a proper in-out referendum.'
>
> The Charter, which contains a bewildering 54 new 'rights', including the right to strike, a 'right to marry and found a family', a 'right to collective bargaining' and a 'right to fair working conditions'. It was attached to the EU's Lisbon Treaty which was signed in 2007 and Tony Blair told MPs that it was 'absolutely clear that we have an opt-out'.

It is, perhaps, somewhat surprising that the media should take objection to the right to strike. The UK is a country which produced both the Tolpuddle martyrs and the outcry which followed; recognised trade unions with effect from the Trade Union Act 1871; and decriminalised picketing by Unions under the Conspiracy and Protection of Property Act 1875 (enacted during a Disraeli government). Similarly, the right to marry and found a family does not attract particular controversy. Yet when the Prime Minister recently wished to support a right for Members of Parliament to conduct a secret ballot in the selection of the Speaker, it was to the People's Charter of 1838 that he turned for support, not the Charter of Fundamental Rights of 2007.[17]

In this Chapter, I hope to show that the Charter has been unfairly demonised. The application of fundamental rights covered by the Charter in the UK is nothing new. With few exceptions, it broadly reflects the tenor of rights previously available to British citizens. These were either conferred by the common law; enshrined within the European Convention on Human Rights ('ECHR'); or already established by general principles of EU law prior to the adoption of the Charter. English Judges have been protecting fundamental rights, as one would expect, in accordance with EU law for some time. Indeed, English Court decisions have occasionally preceded equivalent rulings from the ECJ on the scope of application of EU law.

This Chapter will then move on to explore the extent to which the Charter has actually been used in English courts to a meaningful effect. Contrary to the fears expressed above, the Charter has not sparked an alien invasion of rights unknown to the common law. EU law as a whole may have flowed up our estuaries and rivers.[18] But the Charter has not become the legal equivalent of Japanese knotweed. It has not

16. 'Dozens of EU human rights are smuggled into the UK: Grayling attacks Brussels after claims by top judge', *The Daily Mail*, 12 Nov. 2013: Jason Groves.
17. *The Daily Telegraph* on 26 Mar. 2015 reported the Prime Minister as stating 'Secret ballots are very important. Remember the Chartists.' *See* 'Sour end to Parliament for Tories as "plot" against Bercow is routed', 26 Mar. 2015, Matthew Holehouse et al.
18. *Bulmer v. Bollinger Ltd* [1974] Ch 401, CA per Lord Denning MR at p. 418.

affected house prices. The evidence suggests that outside the fields of immigration, taxation and privacy, the provisions of the Charter have not been widely deployed by litigants. It has, however, been used to fill the gaps left by the suite of remedies available under the Human Rights Act 1998 ('HRA 1998'). The loss of the Charter – in the eventuality of a British exit from the European Union – would remove a practically beneficial source of human rights protection for British citizens. While it is undoubtedly true that the Charter, in its capacity as a guard dog of civil liberties, has not barked as often as its HRA 1998 counterpart, its bite has been more powerful.

§14.02 THE SCOPE OF EU FUNDAMENTAL RIGHTS PROTECTION IN THE UK PRIOR TO THE ADOPTION OF THE CHARTER

There are three separate facets to an analysis of the nature and extent of EU fundamental rights protection in the UK prior to the adoption of the Charter. First, the nature and extent of the fundamental rights recognised as general principles of EU law. Secondly, the extent to which domestic Courts were required to apply those principles to disputes before them. This turns primarily on the question of 'the scope of application of EU law'. Thirdly, the extent to which domestic Courts themselves recognised that they were obliged to apply fundamental rights protection to cases before them which fell within the scope of EU law. These areas will now be considered in turn. I shall also address some brief observations on the role the common law plays in the protection of fundamental rights.

[A] The Protection of Fundamental Rights through General Principles of EU Law

The notion of protecting human rights was not contained in the founding treaties of the European Communities.[19] The protection of fundamental rights was seemingly discussed by the drafters, but the idea of including provisions for the purpose was rejected.[20] It was believed that the Council of Europe would guard against violations of fundamental rights. The Council of Europe had only recently undertaken the task of drafting the ECHR and establishing the European Court of Human Rights in Strasbourg

19. These were: (i) the Treaty of Paris, signed in April 1951 establishing the European Coal and Steel Community ('ECSC' Treaty); (ii) the Treaty of Rome, signed in March 1957 establishing the European Economic Community ('EEC' Treaty); and (iii) the Treaty of Rome, signed in March 1957 establishing the European Atomic Energy Community ('EAEC' or 'EURATOM' Treaty). These Treaties have been amended and modified by the Single European Act 1986; the Treaty on European Union, signed at Maastricht in Feb. 1992; the Treaty of Amsterdam, which entered into force on 1 May 1999; and finally by the Lisbon Treaty with effect from 1 Dec. 2009. The Lisbon Treaty confirms that the Treaties applied at Union level are now the Treaty on European Union ('TEU'); and the Treaty on the Functioning of the European Union ('TFEU').
20. *See* Betten & Grief, *EU Law and Human Rights* 53 (1t ed, Longman 1998).

('ECtHR'). Moreover, it may have been thought that the development of the Communities based on a process of economic integration did not involve the risk of infringements of fundamental rights.[21]

The ECJ was keen from the start to protect the rights of individuals,[22] but anxious not to overstep the boundaries of its competence or risk the application of purely domestic law to areas properly subject to EU law. In some of the early cases before it, the ECJ rejected any suggestion that the protection of fundamental rights formed part of a Community 'common law'.[23] Indeed, in the case of *Geitling v. High Authority* the Court went so far as to state that 'Community law does not contain any general principle, express or otherwise, guaranteeing the maintenance of vested rights'.[24]

Nonetheless, with the emergence of the twin concepts of the supremacy[25] of Community law and its direct effect[26] in the national legal orders of Member States, the case for the recognition of core, fundamental rights became more pressing.[27] Direct effect and supremacy transferred permanently a degree of constitutional power from the Member States to what is now the European Union. These principles were well-established by the time that the UK acceded to the Treaties through the Act of Accession 1972. But other founding Member States had no forewarning of these judicial developments. The constitutional courts of certain Member States, such as Germany and Italy, were reluctant to accept the twin principles of supremacy and direct effect without an assurance that human rights would be protected at an EU level.[28] Their Courts would not willingly accept the principle of supremacy without some confirmation that there would be constitutional protection of basic human rights.[29] German and Italian appellants before the ECJ challenged decisions of Union

21. *See* G.F. Mancini, *The Making of a Constitution for Europe*, (1989) C.M.L. Rev. pp. 595–614 at p. 609.
22. *See*, for example, Case 6/60 *Humblet v. Belgium* [1960] E.C.R. 559 at p. 572, where the ECJ held that a provision establishing guarantees for the protection of individual's rights cannot be interpreted in a restrictive manner to the detriment of the individual.
23. *See* Case 1/58 *Stork v. High Authority* [1959] E.C.R. 17 at paragraph 4(a), which stated that the High Authority's decisions were not open to challenge on the grounds of breach of a Member State's constitutional law; Joined Cases 36-38 and 40/59 *Geitling v. High Authority* [1960] E.C.R. 423 at p. 439; and Case 40/64 *Sgarlata v. Commission* [1965] E.C.R. 215 at p. 227, in which the ECJ would not look to the 'fundamental principles governing all the Member States' when construing the Treaty.
24. *Ibid.* at pp. 438–439.
25. In Case 26/62 *Van Gend en* Loos [1963] E.C.R. 1 at pp. 12–13, the ECJ rejected the suggestion that the existence of infringement procedures initiated by either the Commission or Member States (under what is now Articles 263 and 265 TFEU) meant that the Treaty conferred no direct rights on individuals. The Court found that if rights of recourse were so restricted, it would 'remove all direct legal protection of the individual rights of their nationals'.
26. Case 6/64 *Costa v. ENEL* [1964] E.C.R. 585 at p. 593.
27. *See Van Gend en Loos supra* n. 25 at p. 13.
28. *See* J.H.H. Weiler, *Fundamental Rights and Fundamental Boundaries*, in *The Constitution of Europe* 107–108 (Cambridge 1999).
29. *See generally* A. Clapham, *Human Rights and the European Community: A Critical* Overview, Nomos: Baden-Baden, 1991; and, for one example, the Order of the *Bundesgerichtshof* dated 18 Oct. 1967, BverGE, 1967 at 223. That reticence persists today. As Advocate General Cruz-Villalón pointed out in his Opinion dated 14 Jan. 2015 in Case C-62/14 *Gauweiler and Others*, the Bundesverfassungsgericht (Germany's Federal Constitutional Court) made its first ever reference to the ECJ under Article 267 TFEU only in 2014. The reference was made in the context of

institutions on the grounds that they were in conflict with fundamental rights guaranteed by their respective constitutions.[30]

The opportunity for the ECJ to respond came first in the case of *Stauder*.[31] In addressing the conditions necessary to ensure the legality of coupons issued for reduced butter, the Court considered, albeit by way of obiter dicta, that 'interpreted in this way the provision at issue contains nothing capable of prejudicing the fundamental human rights enshrined in the general principles of Community law and protected by the Court'.[32] The ECJ next called upon the 'general principles of Community law' the following year in the seminal case of *Internationale Handelsgesellschaft*.[33] The ECJ ruled that it was not open to the national court to question the validity of measures adopted by Community institutions by reference to legal rules or concepts of national law.[34] They could only be judged in the light of EU law. Otherwise the uniformity and efficacy of EU law would be jeopardised. By way of quid pro quo, the ECJ nonetheless went on to examine whether 'an analogous guarantee inherent in Community law' had been disregarded by the contested Regulation in that case. The ECJ ascertained whether the system of deposits infringed 'rights of a fundamental nature, respect for which must be ensured in the Community legal system'.[35] This obligation arose because: 'In fact, respect for fundamental rights forms an integral part of the general principles of law protected by the Court of Justice. The protection of such rights, whilst inspired by the constitutional traditions common to the Member States, must be ensured within the framework of the structure and objectives of the Community.'

This open recognition of respect for fundamental rights within EU law represented a dramatic change of tack for the ECJ. The ruling in *IHG* paved the way for the Court in *Hauer*[36] to reject expressly the suggestion that Union law was capable of being challenged by constitutional requirements of domestic law. Nonetheless, the suggestion that the ECJ was exclusively or principally motivated by a desire to protect the supremacy of Union law[37] perhaps overlooks the Court's concern for the rights of the

a challenge before the German courts to the powers of the European Central Bank to engage in 'Outright Monetary Transactions'. That is, buying Government bonds from Euro-area Member States to shore up the monetary stability of the Eurozone. The Constitutional Court had already ruled in principle that the monetary support programme was unlawful under German and EU law. But it decided to refer the matter to the ECJ for confirmation. The Advocate General formed a different view. The Court has yet to rule on the matter.

30. In the words of a former Judge of the ECJ, these objections were 'a brutal blow, a blow jeopardizing not only the supremacy but the very independence of Community law. Something had to be done and the Court did it, both for fear that its hard-won conquests might vanish and because of its own growing awareness that a 'democratic deficit' had become apparent in the management of the Community': G.F. Mancini, *supra* n. 21, at pp. 609–610.
31. Case 29/69 *Erich Stauder v. City of Ulm* [1969] E.C.R. 419.
32. *Ibid.* at paragraph 7.
33. Case 11/70 *Internationale Handelsgesellschaft mbH v. Einfuhr- und Vorratsstelle für Getriede und Futtermittel* [1970] E.C.R. 1125, often known more simply as the 'IHG' case.
34. *Ibid.* at paragraph 3 of the judgment.
35. *Ibid.* at paragraph 4 of the judgment.
36. Case 44/79 *Liselotte Hauer v. Länd Rheinland-Pfalz* [1979] E.C.R. 3727 at paragraph 14.
37. *See* Jason Coppel & Aidan O'Neill *The European Court of Justice: Taking Rights Seriously?* (1992) 29 C.M.L. Rev. 669–692, at p. 669. The authors' contentions were subjected to unusually

individual. Such a concern was already latent in the existing case law.[38] Regardless of the motivation for the adoption of the terminology of 'fundamental rights', the practical effect was to enable the ECJ to develop 'general principles of law' along common law lines. While this level of 'creative jurisprudence' has been questioned,[39] as Professor Tridimas has validly pointed out, which Member State would have ratified a Treaty that was capable of violating the fundamental rights protected by its own constitution?[40]

The Court continued its development of a fundamental rights doctrine in subsequent cases. In *Nold*[41] the ECJ made its first express reference to the ECHR. The applicant alleged that a Commission decision interfered with his right to conduct a business activity, as protected not only by the German Constitution but also by 'various international treaties, including in particular the Convention for the Protection of Human Rights and Fundamental Freedoms of 4 November 1950 and the Protocol to that Convention of 20 March 1952'. The ECJ reiterated that fundamental rights formed an integral part of the general principles of law. It also developed its reference to the 'common constitutional traditions' as a source of inspiration and concluded that the Court was thereby precluded from upholding measures which were incompatible with fundamental rights recognised and protected by the Constitutions of the Member States. The ECJ was, however, prepared to go further and hold that:

> international treaties for the protection of human rights on which the Member States have collaborated or of which they are signatories, can supply guidelines which should be followed within the framework of Community law.

The ECJ expressly considered the actual content of the ECHR for the first time in *Rutili*.[42] The ECJ noted that limitations placed on Member States in respect of the control of aliens were 'a specific manifestation of the more general principle, enshrined

---

detailed scrutiny in Professor J.H.H. Weiler & N.J.S. Lockhart, '*Taking Rights Seriously' Seriously: The European Court of Justice and its Fundamental Rights Jurisprudence* (1995) C.M.L. 32 Rev. 51 and 579.

38. It is also somewhat ironic that, if it were the rationale, it did not have the desired, defensive effect. The constitutional courts of Germany, Italy and France continued to proclaim for some years that EU law that fell foul of their respective constitutions would not necessarily be accorded supremacy. *See* the judgments of the German Federal Constitutional Court in *Internationale Handelsgesellschaft (Solange I)* [1974] 2 C.M.L.R. 540; the Italian Constitutional Court in *Costa v. ENEL* [1964] C.M.L.R. 425, *Frontini v. Ministero delle Finanze* [1974] 2 C.M.L.R. 372 and, more recently in *SpA Fragd v. Amministrazione delle Finanze*, Decision no. 232 of 21 Apr. 1989; and the Conseil d'Etat in *Semoules* [1970] C.M.L.R. 395. The area has been revisited by the German Federal Constitutional Court more recently in its judgment of 12 Oct. 1993 on the Maastricht Treaty [1993] 1 C.M.L.R. 57, where it reserved to itself the right to declare EU acts inapplicable if they breached fundamental norms of the German Constitution. *See* Professor J.H.H. Weiler, 'Does Europe need a Constitution? Demos, Telos and the German Maastricht Decision' (1995) 1 E.L.J. 219.
39. Charges of 'naked law-making' have been periodically levelled against the ECJ in this area. For a summary of such accusations and a response, *see* Professor T. Tridimas, *The European Court of Justice and Judicial Activism*, (1996) 21 E.L. Rev. 199.
40. *See* Professor T. Tridimas, *The General Principles of EC Law*, First Edition, Oxford University Press, 1999 at p. 206.
41. Case 4/73 *J. Nold v. Commission of the European Communities* [1974] E.C.R. 491 at paragraphs 12 and 13.
42. Case 36/75 *Rutili v. Minister for the Interior* [1975] E.C.R. 1219 at paragraph 32.

in Articles 8, 9, 10 and 11 of the [Convention] ... that no restrictions in the interests of national security or public safety shall be placed on the rights secured by the above-quoted articles other than such as are necessary for the protection of those interests "in a democratic society"'.

It was precisely because the ECJ refused simply to apply ECHR rights or principles in the context of EU law – because the two sets of rights were not co-extensive[43] – that there was scope for the fundamental rights recognised by EU law to go beyond those 'human rights' afforded protection under the ECHR. Indeed, the EU Courts were also able to take into account the terms of other multilateral conventions concluded by the Member States, such as the European Social Charter of 18 November 1961; Convention No. 111 of the International Labour Organisation of 25 June 1958 concerning discrimination in respect of employment and occupation;[44] and the International Covenant on Civil and Political Rights of 19 December 1966.[45]

This potential for a broader interpretation, and its application to Member States, was first recognised in *Watson and Belmann.*[46] The ECJ was asked on a preliminary reference from the Pretura di Milano whether the prohibition of discrimination between nationals of Member States constituted a 'fundamental principle which the Court will enforce?' The case concerned the compatibility with EU law of an Italian law requirement for visiting foreigners to register with the authorities. The Pretura di Milano raised questions relating to Article 8 ECHR (the right to privacy) and whether, in the event of conflict, fundamental principles of EU law prevailed over national laws. The ECJ found that it was able, on the facts, to give judgment on the issues raised without specifically answering the above questions. Its answer related to the prohibition of discrimination on the grounds of nationality.[47] The ECJ did not address the question (raised by the UK Government in its observations) as to the extent to which EU law guaranteed fundamental rights not recognised by the Convention.[48] Nonetheless, the issue was dealt with by the Advocate General. He noted that:

> without impinging upon the jurisdiction of other courts, this Court too, can look into an infringement of a fundamental right by a State body if not to the same extent to which it could do so in reviewing the validity of Community acts, at least to the extent to which the fundamental right alleged to have been infringed may

43. Indeed, in other respects the protection afforded by EU law has been less extensive than that offered by domestic law. *See*, for example, Case C-550/07 P *Akzo Nobel Chemicals Ltd and Akcros Chemicals Limited v. European Commission* [2010] ECR I-8301, ECJ.
44. Case 149/77 *Defrenne v. Sabena (III)* [1978] E.C.R. 1365 at paragraph 28.
45. *United Nations Treaty Series*, vol. 999, p. 171 cited with approval in Case 374/87 *Orkem v. Commission* [1989] E.C.R. 3283 at paragraph 18, ECJ. *See also* Case C-249/96 *Grant v. South West Trains* [1998] E.C.R. I-621 at paragraph 44.
46. Case 118/75 *Lynne Watson and Allessandro Belmann* [1976] E.C.R. 1185 at p. 1187.
47. *Ibid.* at paragraph 9 of the judgment. The establishment of non-discrimination as a fundamental principle of Community law was confirmed in Case 63/83 *Kirk* [1984] E.C.R. 2689 at paragraph 14.
48. Interestingly, the other arguments raised by the UK Government in its observations (summarised at pp. 1190 to 1191 of the judgment) foreshadow many of the subsequent issues raised in the development of the fundamental rights doctrine in EU law. Examples include the jurisdictional interplay of the ECHR and EU institutions and the scope of application of EU fundamental rights to domestic law.

involve the protection of an economic right which is among the specific objects of the Treaty.[49]

Other examples of the ECJ recognising non-ECHR rights quickly arose. In *Defrenne*, the Court had no doubt that the elimination of discrimination based on sex formed part of the fundamental personal human rights recognised under Community law.[50] This perhaps represents a broader statement of principle than is to be found in Article 14 ECHR. In *Pinna* the Court stated that the principle of equal treatment prohibited not only overt discrimination on grounds of nationality but also 'all covert forms of discrimination which, by applying other distinguishing criteria, in fact achieve the same result'.[51] This prohibition of discrimination has been said to be merely a specific enunciation of the general principle of equality, itself one of the fundamental principles of Community law.[52] The Court has also recognised that the fundamental right to pursue an economic activity (if appropriate through a company) is derived from the Treaty freedoms.[53]

Long before the Charter, the ECJ's case law came to recognise a range of fundamental rights which were to be protected by EU law. As the Court increasingly came to apply human rights principles derived either from the ECHR or from the common constitutional concepts of Member States, so cross-fertilisation of Convention principles became more apparent. In *Testa*,[54] for example, the Court recognised that the competent services and institutions of the Member State might 'enjoy a wide discretion' in the national implementation of EU measures, subject to the obligation to take into account the general principle of proportionality. Indeed, it has been suggested that the 'margin of appreciation' recognised by Strasbourg case law is analogous to the ECHR principle of proportionality.[55] Moreover, in assessing the proportionality of measures affecting fundamental rights, EU law will naturally take into account the case law of the ECtHR on the issue.[56]

The position was thus reached, several years before the adoption of the Charter in 2000, that a corpus of jurisprudence had evolved conferring protection for the fundamental rights of EU citizens when they were able to invoke EU rights. As the ECJ noted in *ERT*,[57] it did not have the power to examine (for compatibility with the ECtHR)

---

49. *Watson and Belmann supra* n. 46, per Advocate General Trabucchi at p. 1207. The Advocate General went on to note (at p. 1208) that the principle of proportionality, for example, was a general principle applied to public authorities, EU or national, within the EU legal order.
50. Case 149/77 *Defrenne v. Sabena (III) supra* n. 44 at paragraphs 26 and 27.
51. Case 41/84 *Pinna v. Caisse d'allocations familiales de la Savoie* [1986] E.C.R. 1, at paragraph 23.
52. Joined Cases 201 and 202/85 *Klensch v. Secrétaire d'État à l'Agriculture et à la Viticulture* [1986] E.C.R. 3477 at paragraph 9.
53. Case 246/89 R *Commission v. United Kingdom* [1989] E.C.R. 3125 at paragraph 30.
54. Joined Cases 41, 121 and 796/79 *Testa, Maggio and Vitale v. Bundesanstalt für Arbeit* [1980] E.C.R. 1979 at paragraph 21.
55. Case C-159/90 *Society for the Protection of Unborn Children Ireland Ltd. v. Grogan and others* [1991] E.C.R. I-4685 per Advocate General Van Gerven at p. 4726. *See also Hauer supra* n. 36 at paragraph 22; and the express reference to 'margin of appreciation' at paragraph 22 of the ECJ's judgment in Case 5/88 *Wachauf v. Germany* [1989] E.C.R. 2609.
56. *See* p. 4726 of the Advocate General's Opinion in *Grogan ibid.*
57. Case C-260/89 *Elliniki Radiophonia Tileorassi AE v. Dimotiki Etairia Pliroforissis and Sotirios Kouvelas* [1991] E.C.R. I-2925 at paragraphs 42 and 43.

national rules that did not fall within the scope of EU law. Nonetheless, where such rules did fall within the scope of EU law, the Court was obliged on a reference for a preliminary ruling to 'provide all the criteria of interpretation needed by the national courts to determine whether those rules [were] compatible with the fundamental rights' recognised in EU law. More significantly, the Court held that the justification of any restriction on the freedom to provide services had to interpreted in the light of general principles of law. Member States could rely on the derogations provided by Articles 52 and 62 TFEU only if their national rules were compatible with the fundamental rights developed by the ECJ. It was for the national court to assess whether or not its national rules complied with the rules of EU law, 'including freedom of expression, as embodied in Article 10 of the [ECHR]'.[58]

[B] The Scope of Application of EU General Principles of Law: The ECJ Jurisprudence

The *ERT* judgment makes clear that one of the key issues that arose with the protection of fundamental rights at EU level was whether they could be preyed in aid by a litigant at all. This came to turn on the question of whether or not the issues in the dispute referred to the ECJ fell within the scope of EU law.

The current state of play is as follows. General principles of law can only be relied upon where EU law is engaged. But the question whether EU law is engaged is a difficult one to answer in abstract. The case law is still developing. In *Wachauf v. Germany*,[59] the ECJ held that the fundamental rights recognised by the Court were binding on the Member States when they *implement* EU rules. In contrast, a domestic law or practice that deals with a 'purely internal situation' does not give rise to enforceable EU law rights. Similarly, a purely hypothetical prospect of exercising an EU right does not establish a sufficient connection with EU law to justify the application of EU provisions.[60]

However there are well-known examples where fundamental rights have been held to be engaged even where a Member State is not implementing EU law in the strict sense. In the *ERT* case,[61] the ECJ stated that national rules 'fall within the scope of Community law' where a Member State is relying upon a derogation from the fundamental EU freedoms based on a public policy justification. In *Phil Collins*,[62] the

58. *Ibid.* at paragraph 45.
59. Case 5/88 *Wachauf v. Germany* [1989] E.C.R. 2609, ECJ, but see the conclusion of the ECJ in Case C-2/92 *R. v. Ministry of Agriculture, Fisheries and Food ex p. Dennis Clifford Bostock* [1994] E.C.R. I-955, ECJ, which is not easy to reconcile with *Wachauf* in all respects.
60. *See* Case C-309/96 *Daniele Annibaldi v. Sindaco del Comune di Guidonia and Presidente Regione Lazio* [1997] E.C.R. I-7493, ECJ at [24] (refusal of permission to plant a commercial orchard was outside community law although it affected the organisation of agriculture market); and Case C-299/95 *Kremzow* [1997] ECR I-2629, ECJ at [16]-[18] (unlawful term of imprisonment was not within field of application of EU law although would have hypothetically impeded freedom of movement between Member States).
61. Case C-260/89 *ERT* [1991] ECR I-2925, ECJ at [42].
62. Joined Cases C-92/92 and C-326/92 *Phil Collins v. Imtrat Handelsgesellschaft mbH and others* [1993] ECR I-5145, ECJ at [27].

ECJ held that the principle of non-discrimination on grounds of nationality[63] applied to German copyright law, even though that domestic law was not implementing any EU law. In the more recent case of *Carpenter*,[64] the ECJ held that the deportation of the wife of a British citizen whose business involved travel between Member States would be 'detrimental ... to the conditions under which Mr Carpenter exercises a fundamental freedom' and thus had to be consistent with Article 8 ECHR as given effect through the prism of EU law.

In an important recent Opinion in the case of *Zambrano*,[65] Advocate General Sharpston has proposed that the case law should be further developed. She has suggested that 'in the long run', the clearest rule would be one that made the availability of EU fundamental rights protection dependent neither on whether a Treaty provision was directly applicable nor on whether a right of free movement had been exercised, but rather on the existence and scope of a material EU competence. She has suggested that the rule would be that, provided that the EU had competence (whether exclusive or shared) in a particular area of law, EU fundamental rights should protect the citizen of the EU even if such competence has not yet been exercised. The ECJ did not address the issue in its judgment. The current position is therefore that EU general principles of law apply when a Member State is implementing EU law rules,[66] but the concept of 'implementation' may be a broad one.

[C] The Scope of Application of EU General Principles of Law: The Response of the UK Courts

The question of whether or not a national provision falls within the 'scope of EU law' has also given rise to a line of domestic authority. In *ex parte Hamble Fisheries*[67] the measure under consideration was a licensing policy adopted by the Ministry for Agriculture, Fisheries and Food ('MAFF') in relation to the fishing quota system adopted under the common fisheries policy of the Community. The claimant argued that a change in that policy had frustrated its legitimate expectations and caused it loss. The Government argued that the relevant law was entirely domestic. Sedley J rejected that submission as 'unreal'. He added: 'The availability of eventual recourse to the Court of Justice from and against all the Member States in relation to the carrying out of the common agricultural policy must require domestic courts to have full regard to the jurisprudence of the Court of Justice.'

63. Then contained in Article 7 EEC; now Article 18 TFEU.
64. Case C-60/00 *Carpenter v. Secretary of State for the Home Department* [2003] QB 416, ECJ at [39].
65. Case C 34/09 *Gerardo Ruiz Zambrano v. Office national de l'emploi (ONEM)*, [2011] ECR I-1177, at [163] and [177].
66. *See* Joined Cases C-20/00 and C-64/00 *Booker Aquaculture* [2003] ECR I-7411, ECJ at [46], [64] to [67], [88].
67. *R v. Ministry of Agriculture, Fisheries and Food* ex parte *Hamble Fisheries* [1995] 2 All E.R. 714 at pp. 724 to 725.

A narrower approach was adopted in *First City Trading Ltd.*[68] The domestic measure in issue was a MAFF aid package for beef exporters who were also slaughterers or cutters adopted in the aftermath of BSE crisis and the Commission's ban on the export of beef from the UK. Exporters who were not slaughterers or cutters challenged their exclusion from the aid on the basis that it was contrary to the EU law principle of equal treatment. The issue for the Court was whether such general principles of EU law fell to be applied. Laws J drew a distinction between two different types of situation, which would determine whether general principles of EU law were applicable:[69]

> On the one hand, a Member State may take measures solely by virtue of its domestic law. On the other a Community institution or Member State may take measures which it is authorised or obliged to take by force of the law of the Community. In the former situation I contemplate a measure which is neither required of the Member State nor permitted to it by virtue of Community Treaty provisions. It is purely a domestic measure. Even so, it may affect the operation of the Common Market and accordingly be held to be 'within the scope of application' of the Treaty. This was the *Phil Collins* case. It is of the first importance to notice that its falling within the Treaty's scope is by no means the same thing as it being done under powers or duties conferred or imposed by Community law. The second situation primarily includes (so far as Member States are concerned) measures which Community law requires, such as, for example, law which is made to give effect to a Directive. It includes also an act or decision done or taken by a Member State in reliance on a derogation or permission granted by Community law: as where for instance a restriction on imports or exports is sought to be justified by reference to Article 36 of the Treaty. In the first situation, the measure is in no sense a function of the law of Europe, although its legality may be constrained by it. In the second, the measure is necessarily a creature of the law of Europe. Community law alone either demands it, or permits it.

Laws J reasoned that even on the assumption that the scheme in question fell within the State Aid provisions of the Treaty (it had been notified to the Commission as a State Aid but was cleared) the situation was within the first category. Laws J distinguished the *Phil Collins* case by drawing a distinction between Treaty obligations such as the prohibition on nationality discrimination at issue in that case and judge-made law. He reasoned that the EU fundamental rights jurisprudence was a form of 'common law'[70] and could not be applied to action taken by Member States that is not authorised or required by EU law: 'The power of the ECJ, as it seems to me, to apply ...principles of public law which it had itself evolved cannot be deployed in a case where the measure in question, taken by a Member State, is not a function of Community law at all.'[71]

68. *R. v. Ministry of Agriculture, Fisheries and Food,* ex parte *First City Trading Limited* [1997] 1 C.M.L.R. 250, QBD.
69. *Ibid.* at paragraph 39.
70. The reliance on the distinction between judge-made law and Treaty law given by the learned Judge will now need to be reconsidered in the light of the adoption of the Charter.
71. *First City Trading supra* n. 68 at paragraph 42.

The approach in *First City Trading* was approved by the Divisional Court in *Lunn Poly*, a challenge to the imposition of a domestic tax – insurance premium tax.[72] Counsel for the applicants identified four circumstances where national measures might be examined for compatibility with EU fundamental rights: (1) where national authorities implement EU law by fulfilling an obligation to act, for example, implementing a Directive; (2) where national authorities implement EU law by acting within the scope of an EU enabling provision or authorisation; (3) where national authorities rely upon an EU derogation to justify a measure which restricts one of the fundamental freedoms protected by the TFEU; (4) where there is otherwise a sufficient Union context for the general principles to apply. Maurice Kay J considered the judgment of Laws J in *First City Trading*. He concluded with approval that Laws J. had accepted categories (1), (2) and (3), eliding (2) and (3) but rejected category (4). On the facts, the applicants failed to show any specific enabling provision of EU law upon which the insurance premium tax had been based. They consequently failed to come within categories (1) to (3). He also rejected an attempt to apply fundamental rights under category (4). That, in his judgment, would be 'a wholly unwarranted encroachment on sovereign powers'. There was accordingly no basis for applying the prohibition of non-discrimination to the facts of the case.

That, however, is not the end of the story. In *British Pig*,[73] a further challenge was mounted to certain financial assistance given in an agricultural sector governed in part by a common organisation of the market ('COM'). BSE support measures had been granted to the beef and sheep industries and pig farmers claimed that they had not received equal treatment by comparison. The applicants contended that the State Aid granted in the present case fell within the second situation envisaged by Laws J in *First City Trading*. That argument was rejected on the facts. Richards J nonetheless proceeded on the assumption that a challenge based on fundamental rights could theoretically have been lodged against Community support measures specifically adopted under the relevant COMs.[74] He went on to find that the COM context was as relevant in the *First City Trading* case as it was here, so that it could not simply be distinguished. Richards J accepted that the distinction between the two situations described by Laws J was not an easy one to apply. The Court held that a State Aid notified to the Commission had features of both situations. Any State Aid was prohibited by EU law unless it was notified to and approved by the Commission. Its validity was therefore ultimately dependent upon a specific permission under EU law. Richards J expressed 'real doubts'[75] about the correctness of *First City Trading* and *Lunn Poly* and concluded that:

72. *R. v. H.M. Customs and Excise* ex parte *Lunn Poly* [1998] Eu.L.R. 438 at pp. 444 to 446. The case went on appeal to the Court of Appeal on the State Aid ground only. *See* [1999] 1 C.M.L.R. 1357, CA.
73. *R. v. Ministry of Agriculture, Fisheries and Food ex parte British Pig Industry Support Group and Ward* [2000] Eu. L.R. 724 at pp. 745H – 747E.
74. *Ibid.* at paragraph 61.
75. Rather than ordering a reference on the point to the ECJ, his Lordship went on to examine the claimants' case on the facts, assuming in their favour that the principle of non-discrimination could be applied. Since he found against the claimants on the facts, the issue was not finally determined.

> Thus, although the grant of state aid cannot in my view be said to amount to 'implementation' of the COM or to be done 'pursuant' to Community law, I think it is well arguable that the grant of aid by a Member State falls within the scope of Community law to the extent that the fundamental principles of Community law apply to it. I also see some substance in Miss Sharpston's challenge to the validity of the distinction drawn in *First City Trading* between Treaty law and the fundamental principles of Community law as developed in the case law of the ECJ.

The most recent case in this line is *Zagorski*,[76] a challenge to the export of a drug used for lethal injections to the United States. The case actually concerned the scope of application of the Charter, rather than general principles of EU law. But the principles set out above were considered. The Government sought to distinguish the *ERT* case on the ground that no export ban had been imposed and therefore there was no derogation from, or interference with, free movement of goods. Lloyd Jones J held that the 'field in question' namely the imposition of export restrictions is 'occupied' by EU law and that it would be 'surprising if the answer to the question whether the Defendant was acting within the material scope of EU law depended on which was his decision went'. His Lordship held that in deciding whether to exercise a derogation from EU rights the Secretary of State was acting within the scope of EU law.[77] Nonetheless, it is clear that a search for a bright line test of whether a particular case falls within the scope of EU law may be a futile one.

[D] The Common Law Protection of Fundamental Rights

When addressing fundamental rights protection before the adoption of the Charter, mention should also be made of the common law protections. These have been available to the UK citizenry since at least the days of Magna Carta. The common law has been developed by judges in the absence of any written bill of human rights in the UK.[78] Thus, even in the dark days of the Star Chamber, the common law recognised that the prohibition on the use of torture was absolute. It was thus to the common law – and not EU law or the ECHR – that Lord Bingham turned in *A and others v. Secretary of State for the Home Department*.[79] As he noted at paragraph 12, '[b]y the common lawyers torture was regarded as ... 'totally repugnant to the fundamental principles of English law' and 'repugnant to reason, justice, and humanity'. One of the first acts of the Long Parliament in 1640 was, accordingly, to abolish the Court of Star Chamber,

76. *R (Zagorski & Baze) v. Secretary of State for Business, Innovation and Skills* [2010] EWHC 3110 (Admin), paragraph 70.
77. *Ibid.* at paragraph 70.
78. Many of the rights so recognised are of ancient vintage. Recent re-statements include *R v. Secretary of State for the Home Department ex p. Pierson* [1998] AC 539, HL; *R v. Secretary of State for the Home Department ex p. Simms* [2000] 2 AC 115, HL; *R (Daly) v. Secretary of State for the Home Department* [2001] 2 AC 532, HL. For discussion see J. Beatson, S. Grosz, T. Hickman & R. Singh, *Human Rights: Judicial Protection in the United Kingdom* [1-11] to [1-63], pp. 6–30 (Sweet & Maxwell, 2008).
79. *A v. Secretary of State for the Home Department* [2005] UKHL 71; [2006] 2 A.C. 221, HL per Lord Bingham at paragraphs 11 to 13.

where torture evidence had been received, and in that year the last torture warrant in our history was issued.'

Lord Justice Laws, speaking extra-judicially in the Third Hamlyn Law Lecture in November 2013,[80] recognised that an hostility to European law intruding on national sovereignty presented certain threats to the common law tradition. He warned that the 'catholicity' of the common law – its ability to draw inspiration from many sources, including European law principles – might be threatened by diminishing public confidence in laws emanating from Europe. He said this:

> Now, I have come to think that the political controversies and resentments concerning Europe, in which of course I have no voice and claim none, may undermine the confidence which thinking people ought to have in the common law's catholicity: in its use of principles which were born or have flourished in Luxembourg and in Strasbourg.

Lord Justice Laws was, with respect, quite right to point to the cross-fertilisation of the common law and EU law protection of fundamental rights. Common law protections have long infused the recognition of equivalent rights at an EU level.[81] Equally the common law has drawn on the comparative jurisprudence from Strasbourg and Luxembourg.[82] In the recent decision of the Supreme Court concerning the disclosure of letters from HRH the Prince of Wales in response to a Freedom of Information Act request,[83] it is possible to discern a greater reliance by the national courts on common law rights. The Executive's certificate confirming the refusal to disclose the relevant correspondence was challenged both on public law grounds and on the basis of the incompatibility of the decision with the Environmental Information Directive and Article 47 of the Charter. The majority of the Supreme Court disposed of the Attorney General's appeal by reference to common law, constitutional principles. Only the dissenting speech of Lord Wilson made a brief reference to Article 47 of the Charter.

The position reached prior to the adoption of the Charter was accordingly as follows:

- General principles of EU law had for many years been recognised by the EU Courts.
- These general principles largely echoed the protections afforded by the ECHR. Those protections were, of course, put on a separate, domestic statutory footing under the Human Rights Act 1998.
- The domestic Courts in the UK, pursuant to sections 2 and 3 of the European Communities Act 1972, had applied those principles to cases before it which properly fell within the scope of EU law.

80. Available at http://www.globalgovernancewatch.org/docLib/20140213_laws-lj-speech-hamlyn-lecture-2013.pdf.
81. *See* Case 155/79 *AM & S Europe v. Commission* [1982] ECR 1575, ECJ at paragraphs 19 to 21.
82. Lord Justice Laws concluded that the impact of European law principles could continue beneficially to influence the common law even if a political decision were taken by the UK to leave the EU.
83. *R (oao Evans) v. The Attorney General* [2015] UKSC 21, SC.

- Fundamental rights protection was also a recognised feature of the common law. The common law traditions had, in some cases, influenced the nature and extent of the fundamental rights recognised as a matter of EU law.
- There was accordingly a welcome degree of cross-fertilisation between three discrete, but inter-related, regimes of human rights protection: (1) the general principles of EU law; (2) Convention rights recognised by the ECHR and HRA 1998; and (3) the common law.

§14.03 THE ADOPTION OF THE CHARTER

It must therefore be doubted whether the adoption of the Charter really did create a seismic shift in the regime for human rights protection in the UK. The Charter was originally proclaimed as a political declaration. It had no direct legal effect, although it had been drafted explicitly with an eye to future incorporation in the Treaties.[84] Opposition from certain Member States prevented its initial incorporation, but it was anticipated that the Charter would inform the ECJ's fundamental rights jurisprudence from the outset. It did not take long for Advocates General,[85] the General Court of the European Union ('GCEU'),[86] and later the ECJ itself[87] to start referring to rights recognised by the Charter. The Court even began to answer questions on the interpretation of the Charter referred to it by the national courts of the Member States.[88]

The Charter became Part II of the Constitutional Treaty agreed between Member States in June 2003.[89] The status of the Charter was re-considered at the Brussels European Council in June 2007.[90] This led to it being recast in the way now adopted, prior to the signing of the Lisbon Treaty on 13 December 2007. Article 6(1) TEU now provides that the Charter has the 'same legal value as the Treaties'. The second sub-paragraph of Article 6(1) makes clear that the provisions of the Charter shall not, however, 'extend in any way the competences of the Union as defined in the Treaties'.

84. The so-called as if doctrine: COM (2000) 559, paragraphs 32–37 and COM (2000) 644 Communication from the Commission on the Legal nature of the Charter of Fundamental Rights of the European Union, paragraphs 7, 9 and 11.
85. Case C-173/99 *BECTU v. Secretary of State for Trade and Industry* [2001] ECR I4881, ECJ, per Advocate General Tizzano at paragraphs 27–28.
86. Case T-54/99 *Max.mobil Telekommunikation Service GmbH v. Commission*, [2002] ECR II-313, GCEU at paragraphs 48 and 57.
87. *See*, for example, Case C-232/02 P(R) *Commission of the European Communities v. Technische Glaswerke Llmenau GmbH* [2002] ECR I-8977, ECJ; and Case C-540/03 *European Parliament v. Council* [2006] ECR I-5769, ECJ at paragraph 38.
88. *See*, for example, Case C-275/06 *Productores de Música España (Promusicae)* [2008] ECR I-271, ECJ.
89. The Laeken Declaration in 2001 relating to the process of agreeing an EU Constitution stated that thought would have to be given to whether the Charter of Fundamental Rights should be included in the Constitution. This was something of a subsidiary issue compared to the other Constitutional issues that were identified to be considered but for many Member States the Charter was and remained important in making clear that the Union is not exclusively interested in economic matters. *See* The Laeken declaration (Annexes to the Presidency conclusions – Laeken, 14 and 15 Dec. 2001), SN 300/1/01 Rev 1, p. 24 and Jean-Claude Piris, The Lisbon Treaty – A Legal and Political Analysis (CUP 2010), p. 150.
90. *See* Paul Craig, *The Lisbon Treaty* 199 (OUP 2010).

Article 51(2) of the Charter similarly confirms that it does not extend the 'field of application of Union law beyond the powers of the Union or establish any new power or task for the Union, or modify powers and tasks as defined in the Treaties'.[91]

The express legal effect given to the Charter and the recognition given to the general principles of law is of practical significance. First, the provisions give a clear and direct route to EU human rights principles, without the need for citation of the ECJ's case law in support. Secondly, there is a more solid and legitimate legal basis for invoking such rights.[92] Thirdly, all of the rights set out in the Charter are afforded equivalent constitutional status, regardless of their provenance or nature. Finally, the Lisbon Treaty (building on the Treaty of Nice) has expressly endorsed the development of the Court's case law. It has removed the criticism that the development lacks democratic legitimacy (at least from the viewpoint of EU law).

Article 6(2) TEU provides further that the Union shall accede to the ECHR. This may take some time to achieve. Article 6(3) TEU now states that:

> Fundamental rights, as guaranteed by the European Convention for the Protection of Human Rights and Fundamental Freedoms and as they result from the constitutional traditions common to the Member States, shall constitute general principles of the Union's law.

This provides a firm and continuing legal basis for the ECJ's fundamental rights jurisprudence, in particular that drawing on the ECHR, running in parallel to the operation of the Charter. It is an approach broadly reminiscent of the survival of the common law protection of fundamental rights alongside the HRA 1998.

The Charter must be read in the light of the Explanations. These were originally drafted by the Praesidium of the Convention which drafted the Charter. The Explanations state that they do not have the status of law but are a 'valuable tool of interpretation'. In fact, both the Charter and the TEU require 'due regard' to be had to the Explanations in interpreting the Charter.[93] The Explanations set out not only the source of the rights in the Charter but, in some cases, other legal provisions relevant to their interpretation. The Explanations were updated and published prior to the conclusion of the Lisbon Treaty.[94]

---

91. The point is re-emphasised in the 'Declaration Concerning the Charter of Fundamental Rights of the European Union' attached to the Lisbon Treaty. The Declaration states: 'The Charter of Fundamental Rights of the European Union, which has legally binding force, confirms the fundamental rights guaranteed by the European Convention for the Protection of Human Rights and Fundamental Freedoms and as they result from the constitutional traditions common to the Member States. The Charter does not extend the field of application of Union law beyond the powers of the Union or establish any new power or task for the Union, or modify powers and tasks as defined by the Treaties.'
92. The contents of the rights themselves are, for the most part, unexceptionable and derived from pre-existing constitutional norms. With the exception perhaps of some of the solidarity provisions, the core rights are not dissimilar from those which would be derived from the 'thought experiment' of the 'original position' advocated by John Rawls in *A Theory of Justice*, 1971.
93. Article 6(1) of the TEU; and the Preamble to and Article 52(7) of the Charter.
94. The Explanations Relating to the Charter of Fundamental Rights (2007/C 303/02) can be found at OJ [2007] C No. 303 p. 17.

§14.04 THE SCOPE OF APPLICATION OF THE CHARTER

Article 51 makes clear that the field of application of the Charter is also limited. It states that the provisions of the Charter are addressed to the institutions, bodies offices and agencies of the Union with due regard to the principle of subsidiarity 'and to Member States only when they are implementing Union law'. This provision limits the scope of the Charter to the acts and omissions of Member States in circumstances which are arguably narrower on their face than the definition of 'scope of EU law' recognised in the case law cited above. The Explanations are particularly important here. They indicate that no such divergence with the case law of the ECJ is intended. The expression 'implementing' is used in a broad sense to mean 'within the scope of EU law'. The Explanations state:[95]

> As regards the [application of the Charter to] Member States, it follows unambiguously from the case-law of the Court of Justice that the requirement to respect fundamental rights defined in the context of the Union is only binding on the Member States when they act in the scope of Union law (judgment of 13 July 1989, Case 5/88 *Wachauf* [1989] ECR 2609; judgment of 18 June 1991, Case C-260/89 *ERT* [1991] ECR I-2925; judgment of 18 December 1997, Case C-309/96 *Annibaldi* [1997] ECR I-7493). The Court of Justice confirmed this case-law in the following terms: 'In addition, it should be remembered that the requirements flowing from the protection of fundamental rights in the Community legal order are also binding on Member States when they implement Community rules ...' (judgment of 13 April 2000, Case C-292/97 [2000] ECR I-2737, paragraph 37 of the grounds). Of course this rule, as enshrined in this Charter, applies to the central authorities as well as to regional or local bodies, and to public organisations, when they are implementing Union law.

The fact that 'the scope of EU law' may be broader than a strict implementation into domestic law of an EU measure has been recognised by the ECJ. In *Robert Pfleger*,[96] the ECJ adopted the same approach to construing the scope of application of the Charter as was adopted in relation to general principles of EU law in *ERT* and other cases. Advocate General Sharpston at paragraphs 37–42 observed that the expression 'within the scope' was broader than mere implementation through a positive domestic act to give effect to an EU law obligation. The Charter therefore applies when Member States implement national law relying on a public interest derogation from EU law rules.

But as with the case law on the scope of application of the general principles, the search for a bright line test is elusive. In *Fransson*,[97] the Charter was applied to a regime of VAT penalties adopted under purely domestic law, but which were nonetheless part of the implementation of the VAT system more generally. Implementation was treated as being equivalent to the expression 'within the scope of EU law'. At paragraph 21, the

---

95. The provisions of the Charter should be construed in accordance with the Explanations: Case C-206/13 *Siragusa* [2014] ECLI:EU:C:126, ECJ at paragraph 22; and Case C279/09 *DEB* [2010] ECR I13849, ECJ paragraph 32.
96. Case C-390/12 *Robert Pfleger* [2014] ECLI:EU:C:2014:281 at paragraphs 31 to 36; and per Advocate General Sharpston at paragraphs 41–46.
97. Case C-617/10 *Fransson* [2013] CLI:EU:C:2013:105 at paragraphs 19–23.

ECJ recognised that 'the applicability of EU law entails the applicability of fundamental rights guaranteed by the Charter'. VAT, of course, is an EU law tax. It contributes to EU 'own resources'. In *MG and NR*,[98] rights of the defence were found to be available in respect of the detention of a third country asylum seeker, since the domestic procedure came within the scope of Directive 2008/115/EC on the common standards and procedures in Member States for the return of illegal third country nationals.

But just as with the English Court's experience of the issue in *First City Trading* and *ex p. British Pig*, it is possible to cite other cases which retrench from an overly broad view of the 'scope of application' of the Charter. In *Siragusa*,[99] the ECJ found that a litigant could not rely on the Charter to challenge a decision by a planning inspectorate to require restoration of a modified building in a special conservation zone. The law protecting the landscape did not implement EU law and EU law had no specific provisions protecting the landscape which might bring the domestic legislation within scope. The ECJ acknowledged that it had no power to examine the compatibility with the Charter of national legislation falling outside the scope of EU law.[100] The Court found that the concept of 'implementing Union law' requires a 'certain degree of connection above and beyond the matters covered being closely related or one of those matters having an indirect impact on the other'.[101] At paragraph 25, the following guidance was given on the issue:

> In order to determine whether national legislation involves the implementation of EU law for the purposes of Article 51 of the Charter, some of the points to be determined are whether that legislation is intended to implement a provision of EU law; the nature of that legislation and whether it pursues objectives other than those covered by EU law, even if it is capable of indirectly affecting EU law; and also whether there are specific rules of EU law on the matter or capable of affecting it.

Two more recent judgments show that the dividing line in the jurisprudence may be thin. In *Sánchez Morcillo*,[102] the ECJ was asked by a Spanish Court to give guidance on the compatibility of domestic law with Article 47 of the Charter. The national dispute arose in the context of repossession proceedings brought by a bank against two mortgagors. Spanish law permitted a creditor a right of appeal in circumstances where an equivalent right of appeal was denied to a debtor. At paragraph 43, the ECJ found that the truncated nature of the Spanish procedure might mean that a consumer's ability effectively to rely upon Council Directive 93/13/EEC of 5 April 1993 on unfair terms in consumer contracts might be constrained. This was found to be a sufficient connection with EU law to enable the debtors to rely upon the equality of arms principles found in Article 47 of the Charter. In contrast in *Dano*,[103] an economically inactive migrant EU citizen could not claim the benefit of a non-contributory social security benefit by asserting rights under the Charter. Member States were not

98. Case C-383/13 PPU *MG and NR* [2013] ECLI:EU:C:2013:533 at paragraph 35.
99. Case C-206/13 *Siragusa* [2014] ECLI:EU:C:126, ECJ at paragraphs 24–34.
100. *Ibid*. paragraph 21.
101. *Ibid*. at paragraph 24.
102. Case C-169/14 *Sánchez Morcillo* [2014] ECLI:EU:2014:1388 at paragraphs 48–51.
103. Case C-333/13 *Dano* [2014] ECLI:EU:C:2014:2358, ECJ at paragraphs 88–91.

implementing EU law when defining the non-contributory benefits available under their domestic regimes. The Charter was not therefore applicable even in favour of a former worker who had exercised the right of free movement.

In terms of the position under English law, the meaning of the expression 'only when they are implementing Union law' was considered by Lloyd Jones J in *Zagorski*.[104] He held that the Charter applied to a decision not to impose an export ban because 'the Defendant is implementing EU law in the sense of applying it or giving effect to it'. The learned Judge refused to draw a distinction between the application of the Charter and the application of fundamental rights principles developed by the ECJ.[105] It is respectfully submitted that in accordance with the case law above, this is the right approach. The Lisbon Treaty has endorsed the ECJ's fundamental rights' jurisprudence without restricting its application. The approach of Lloyd Jones J has been sanctioned by the Supreme Court in *The Rugby Football Union v. Consolidated Information Services Ltd (formerly Viagogo)*.[106]

§14.05 THE DIVERSION OF THE SO-CALLED OPT OUT FOR THE UNITED KINGDOM

It appears that the comments from the Prime Minister (cited in paragraph Yet despite its relatively modest ambit; the fact that it simply codified many of the pre-existing principles readily found under existing European Union law as reflecting the 'common constitutional traditions' of the Member States; and the decision of the United Kingdom as a Member State to adopt it as part of its agreement to the Lisbon Treaty, the political reception of the Charter has been unkind. Even before its formal adoption, its potential impact was being dismissed. In October 2000, the then Minister for Europe Keith Vaz MP famously attempted to dampen fears in the UK that the newly proclaimed EU Charter of Fundamental Rights was a 'litigator's charter'. He claimed that it had no more legal effect than a copy of the Beano. The UK Government has also sought to disclaim its partial paternity of the Charter. At a European Council meeting in June 2007, the then Prime Minister claimed he had secured a legally binding 'opt-out' from the EU Charter in the 'Reform Treaty', through a joint UK and Polish Protocol to the Treaties. Mr. Blair MP stated that: 'It is absolutely clear that we have an opt-out from ... the charter.' The Lisbon Treaty was subsequently signed by the Member States in Lisbon on 13 December 2007. Article 6(1) of the Treaty on European Union ('TEU') conferred on the Charter the same legal value as any other article of the Treaties. above) may have prompted a number of domestic courts (and probably many lawyers more generally) to consider that the Charter simply did not apply to the United Kingdom. This myth has now been exposed. But it required a significant diversion to

104. *R (Zagorski & Baze) v. Secretary of State for Business, Innovation and Skills* [2010] EWHC 3110 (Admin), at [70].
105. *Ibid.* at [70].
106. [2012] UKSC 55, [2012] 1 WLR 3333, SC per Lord Kerr at paragraph 28. *See also Golden Eye (International) Ltd v. Telefónica UK Ltd* [2012] EWCA Civ 1740, CA per Patten LJ at paragraphs 17–21. See *Secretary of State for the Home Department v D Davis* [2015] EWCA Civ 1185 paras 91-92.

do so. There has long been a consensus from a reasonable body of professionals that the so-called opt-out from the Charter was no such thing.[107] But it was only with the entry into force of the TEU and TFEU on 1 December 2009 that the point became a live one. Shortly thereafter, in *Saeedi*,[108] Cranston J held that, given the wording of 'the Polish and United Kingdom Protocol',[109] the Charter 'cannot be directly relied on as against the United Kingdom, although it is an indirect influence as an aid to interpretation'. On appeal, the Secretary of State no longer sought to support such a finding. The Secretary of State's Respondent's Notice accepted that 'in principle, that fundamental rights set out in the Charter can be relied upon against the United Kingdom, and submits that the Judge erred in holding otherwise . . . The purpose of the Charter Protocol is not to prevent the Charter from applying to the United Kingdom, but to explain its effect'.[110] The Court of Appeal recorded the concession in a judgment but itself made no express finding on the point.[111]

There can no longer be any real doubt that the Charter has legal effect in UK law and that it can be relied upon by litigants here as a source of human rights' protection. In *NS v. Secretary of State for the Home Department*,[112] the ECJ at paragraph 119 held that Protocol (No 30) to the TFEU does not call into question the applicability of the Charter in the United Kingdom or in Poland. This was confirmed by the recitals in the preamble to that Protocol. The UK-Poland Protocol in no way exempted those countries from the full application of the Charter.[113] Furthermore, the national court was obliged to take into account the provisions of the Charter (in particular Article 4) when faced with an objection to the removal of a third country asylum seeker to another Member State for determination of his asylum claim.[114]

107. *See* for example the evidence given to the Parliamentary Committee on the EU in the House of Lords European Union Committee, 10th Report of Session 2007-08, 'The Treaty of Lisbon: an Impact Assessment', Vol I: Report, 13 Mar. 2008, HL Paper 62-I, summarised at paragraphs 5.88 to 5.111.
108. *R (Saeedi) v. Secretary of State for the Home Department* [2010] EWHC (Admin) 705 (31 Mar. 2010) (sub nom *R (NS) v. Secretary of State for the Home Department*), per Cranston J. at paragraph 155.
109. Protocol No. 30 on the Application of the Charter of Fundamental Rights of the European Union to Poland and to the United Kingdom.
110. [2010] EWCA Civ 990, per Lord Neuberger MR at paragraphs 6 and 7.
111. The appeal itself was stayed pending a reference to the ECJ on a number of questions including on effect of the Protocol: the reference led to judgment in C-411/10 *NS v. Secretary of State for the Home Department* [2011] ECR I-13905, ECJ.
112. C-411/10 *NS v. Secretary of State for the Home Department* [2011] ECR I-13905, ECJ.
113. *Ibid.* at paragraph 120.
114. At paragraph 106, the Court ruled that Member States could not compatibly with Article 4 transfer an asylum seeker to another Member State where 'they cannot be unaware that systemic deficiencies in the asylum procedure and in the reception conditions of asylum seekers in that Member State amount to substantial grounds for believing that the asylum seeker would face a real risk of being subjected to inhuman or degrading treatment within the meaning of that provision'.

§14.06 HAS THE CHARTER IN THE UK BEEN THE GUARD DOG WHICH DID NOT BARK?

Acknowledging that the Charter only became directly applicable in domestic Court proceedings with effect from 1 December 2009, it is nonetheless surprising how infrequently the terms of the Charter have been preyed in aid by British litigants since that time. With the exception of certain core areas of law, recourse is not routinely had to the Charter. Those core areas have principled involved tax cases, immigration cases and cases involving privacy rights. The first two areas can be readily explained. They are two areas of law where Strasbourg authority confirms that Article 6 ECHR rights are not engaged. The third core area represents perhaps the most significant area of the common law in which the cross-fertilisation of ECHR principles has produced a substantive change in the level of protection of fundamental rights. So it is understandable that practitioners have chosen to rely upon both Article 8 ECHR and Articles 7 and 8 of the Charter in tandem, in relation to the protection of privacy and data protection rights.

[A] Tax Cases

In *Ferazzini v. Italy*,[115] the ECtHR reviewed the established case law regarding the applicability of Article 6(1) to taxation matters and concluded that it was inapplicable. The case involved in part an assessment to stamp duty on the transfer of certain land. The ECtHR held that Article 6 ECHR was simply not engaged, even though pecuniary interests were involved.[116] The Court explained why tax involved separate considerations (regardless of the nature of the domestic legal system of the Contracting State).[117] The Court considered that tax matters still form part of the hard core of public-authority prerogatives, with the public nature of the relationship between the taxpayer and the community remaining. The ECtHR largely reiterated this reasoning in *Jussila v. Finland*[118] when dealing with a dispute concerning indirect taxation, namely value added tax.

Domestically, this line of case law has persuaded certain claimants to seek to rely upon Article 47 of the Charter in its stead. In *R (ToTel Ltd) v. FTT* [2011] EWHC 652 (Admin), it was conceded before Simon J that Article 6 rights were not engaged. But the taxpayer sought to invoke Article 47 of the Charter in order to overturn a procedural bar on bringing an appeal against a VAT assessment without first paying the disputed tax. Simon J held at paragraphs 136 and 137 that Article 47 should be applied co-extensively with Article 6, relying upon Article 52(3) of the Charter. The taxpayer had relied on the Explanations to the Charter as providing a reason for finding that the scope of Article 47 was expressly not limited to 'civil rights and obligations' as that term had been

115. [2001] STC 1314, ECtHR.
116. *Ibid.* at paragraphs 23–25.
117. *Ibid.* at paragraphs 27–29.
118. [2009] STC 29, ECtHR. *See also R (St Matthews West Ltd) v. HMRC* [2014] EWHC 1848 (Admin), per Andrews J at paragraph 91.

construed by the Strasbourg Court. Simon J found that to be a 'flimsy' basis for the contention. On appeal, however, the Commissioners accepted that Article 47 of the Charter could be relied upon in domestic VAT disputes.[119] The appeal was ultimately allowed on other grounds. The concession of the Commissioners is nonetheless recorded in the decision of the Upper Tribunal on the remitted appeal.[120]

In *LH Bishop Electric Co Ltd v. HMRC*,[121] the First Tier Tribunal (Tax Chamber) ('FTT') ruled that the compulsory requirement to file VAT returns online was unlawful for certain appellants, in that it breached Convention rights under Article 1 of the First Protocol read with Article 14 ECHR held by elderly and disabled persons, as well as those who lived in remote regions without internet access. The absence of exemptions for these three classes of person was therefore unlawful. The FTT nonetheless dismissed the appeal in respect of another appellant, on the basis that there was only a remote possibility of interception of the online communication by a third party and accordingly the right to privacy was not engaged on the facts of the case. The FTT accepted in principle that the Charter rights would apply to like extent,[122] but therefore dismissed the appeal on that ground for the same reasons.[123] Other Charter provisions were found not to be infringed on the facts of the case.[124] The FTT rightly recognised (at paragraph 825) that had Charter rights been engaged, the domestic Regulation requiring online filing of VAT returns could have been disapplied in favour of the appellant.

[B] Immigration Cases

The Strasbourg Court has repeatedly emphasised that immigration cases concerning the deportation or expulsion of aliens do not engage Article 6 ECHR.[125] As with tax cases, this has prompted those complaining of an infringement of a right to be heard or a right to a fair hearing to turn to Article 47, where the dispute falls within the scope of application of EU law. An example of this is to be found in C-411/10 *NS v. Secretary of*

119. *R (Totel Ltd) v. HMRC* [2012] EWCA Civ 1401, CA.
120. *Totel Ltd v. HMRC* [2014] UKUT 485 (TCC) per Nugee J at paragraph 91.
121. [2013] UKFTT 522 (TC), Judge Mosedale at paragraphs 803–811.
122. At paragraph 820, the learned Judge found that Article 6(2) TEU meant that an infringement of the ECHR would *ipso facto* give rise to a breach of EU law. This was said to be because 'the Convention is deemed to be part of European Law and Directives made under the Treaty must be interpreted consistently with the Convention because the Council of the European Union must act consistently with the Convention'. It is respectfully suggested that conclusion is right, but for slightly different reasons. Article 6(2) TEU protects general principles of EU law as if they were Treaty rights, including those derived from the Convention. But the EU does not apply the Convention. At all points prior to accession to the Convention, it has no jurisdiction to do so. Rather it applies the general principles of EU law as recognised now by Article 6(2) TEU. These general principles reflect the common constitutional traditions of the Member States (including most of the aspects of the ECHR) and protection is *de facto* achieved by that route. *See also R (Chester and another) v. Secretary of State for Justice* [2013] UKSC 63, [2014] AC 271, SC per Lord Mance at paragraphs 46 to 58.
123. *Ibid.* at paragraphs 825–829.
124. *Ibid.* at paragraphs 830–839.
125. *Maaouia v. France* (2001) 33 EHRR 42, ECtHR at paragraphs 37 and 38; and *Kaya v. Romania* (2010) 50 EHRR 14, ECtHR at paragraph 24.

State for the Home Department. The ECJ ruled that the UK courts had to apply Article 4 of the Charter (akin to Article 3 ECHR) when determining whether to transfer an asylum seeker to another Member State for his substantive asylum determination.

But an even more striking example of the part played by the Charter in domestic litigation can be found in *ZZ v. Secretary of State for the Home Department*.[126] The appellant, who was a dual Algerian and French national, was refused admission to the UK in 2006 on the grounds of national security. An exclusion order was made against him. His appeal to the Special Immigration Appeals Commission ('SIAC') was dismissed. Almost all of the case against him in SIAC was heard in 'closed' session. He was provided with very little explanation of the case against him in 'open'. Had the standards required under Article 6 ECHR by the House of Lords decision in *Secretary of State for the Home Department v. MB*[127] been met, he would have been provided with a sufficient gist of the case against him, or his appeal would have been allowed. But conversely, if domestic law applied without any consideration of Article 6 ECHR principles, then no gist need have been provided. Consequently, the absence of an Article 6 'hook' for ZZ was fatal to his case unless he could rely upon Article 47 of the Charter.

His appeal on domestic law grounds to the Court of Appeal was dismissed. But the Court of Appeal referred the question of whether he had received a fair hearing pursuant to Article 47 of the Charter to the ECJ. The ECJ in Case C-300/11 *ZZ*[128] held that if the judicial review guaranteed by Article 47 of the Charter is to be effective, the person concerned must be able to ascertain the reasons on which the decision taken in relation to him is based.[129] The Court acknowledged that it might be necessary not to disclose certain information to the person concerned, in the light of overriding considerations connected with state security.[130] Generally a party should have an opportunity to examine facts and documents relied upon by the other side, subject again to a derogation for national security.[131] But even in those cases where national security did preclude precise and full disclosure of the grounds and evidence, it was still necessary to inform the person affected of 'the essence of the grounds' on which the decision refusing entry was based. This was so even if the underlying documents in support of the grounds could not be disclosed.[132] It was for the national court to make this assessment.[133]

On the return of the reference to the Court of Appeal, the Court did just that. It concluded that even issues of national security could not justify the non-disclosure of

126. [2014] EWCA Civ 7, [2014] QB 820, CA.
127. [2007] UKHL 46, [2008] 1 AC 440, HL. That case concerned a non-derogating control order which restricted the controlled person's liberty, so Article 6 ECHR was engaged notwithstanding the immigration context in which the control order was imposed.
128. Case C-300/11 *ZZ v. Secretary of State for the Home Department* [2013] ECLI:EU:2013:363, ECJ at paragraphs 48–59.
129. *Ibid.* at paragraph 53.
130. *Ibid.* at paragraph 54.
131. *Ibid.* at paragraphs 56–57.
132. *Ibid.* at paragraphs 64–66.
133. *Ibid.* at paragraphs 67–68.

the essence of the grounds to the appellant.[134] This conclusion meant that ZZ had not been given the minimum level of disclosure which EU law required.[135] The matter was remitted to SIAC for a fresh determination in the light of the principles established by the ECJ's judgment.

In addition, Articles in the Charter (in particular Article 7, the right to private and family life) have frequently been deployed in immigration and asylum cases.[136] The relevant EU Directives governing the reception and treatment of asylum seekers have also been construed by reference to Charter rights.[137]

[C] Privacy Cases

The third area in which Charter provisions have been liberally cited in domestic case law concerns privacy and data protection cases. The impetus for this development seems to have come not so much as a result of the non-application of Convention principles, but because of the robust application of them. In *Campbell v. MGN Ltd (No 2)*,[138] the House of Lords recognised that the values found in Articles 8 and 10 ECHR were now part of the cause of action for breach of confidence. Lord Nicholls at paragraph 14 went so far as to recognise a species of tort categorised as 'misuse of private information'.[139] It is now uncontroversial that the tort of misuse of private information was specifically developed in order to bridge a gap in the common law and give protection to rights of privacy conferred by Article 8 ECHR.[140]

It did not take long for equivalent arguments concerning privacy and data protection rights to be made by reference to Articles 7 and 8 of the Charter. In *The Rugby Football Union v. Consolidated Information Services Ltd (formerly Viagogo)*,[141] the claimants sought *Norwich Pharmacal* relief requiring the defendant to disclose details of private vendors seeking to sell tickets for rugby matches in breach of the prohibition against resale of the ticket. Lord Kerr (for a unanimous Supreme Court) balanced competing rights found under the Charter before determining whether to grant the relief sought. At paragraph 28, Lord Kerr noted that the binding principles of the Charter (pursuant to Article 6(1) TEU) would only bind Member States when they

134. [2014] EWCA Civ 7, CA per Richards LJ at paragraph 26.
135. *Ibid.* at paragraph 35.
136. *See*, for example, *R (oao Efrem Medhanye) v. Secretary of State for the Home Department* [2011] EWHC 3012 (Admin) per Kenneth Parker J at paragraphs 41–44.
137. *R (Refugee Action) v. Secretary of State for the Home Department* [2014] EWHC 1033 (Admin) per Popplewell J at paragraphs 85–87.
138. [2004] UKHL 22, [2004] 2 AC 457, HL.
139. *See also HRH Prince of Wales v. Associated Newspapers Ltd* [2006] EWCA Civ 1776, [2008] Ch 57, CA per Lord Phillips at paragraphs 26–29; and *Murray v. Express Newspapers plc* [2008] EWCA Civ 446, [2009] Ch 481, CA per Sir Anthony Clarke MR at paragraphs 34–36. In *McKennitt v. Ash* [2008] 1 QB 73, CA, Buxton LJ at paragraph 8 recognised both that no tort of invasion of privacy existed, and that the existing tort of breach of confidence had to a certain extent been re-christened as 'misuse of personal information', so as to give effect to the UK's obligations under Articles 8 and 10 ECHR respectively.
140. *See Google Inc v. Judith Vidal-Hall* [2015] EWCA Civ 311, CA per Lord Dyson MR and Sharp LJ at paragraph 19.
141. [2012] UKSC 55, [2012] 1 WLR 3333, SC per Lord Kerr at paragraphs 45–46.

were implementing EU law. But that expression was to be construed broadly.[142] The domestic Courts have regularly conducted proportionality assessments in order to give effect to competing Charter rights when weighing up whether to grant *Norwich Pharmacal* or other interlocutory relief against internet service providers and others alleged to have been a conduit for copyright or trade mark infringements.[143]

More recently still, in *Google Inc v. Vidal-Hall*,[144] the Court of Appeal construed Article 23 of the Data Protection Directive (Directive 95/46/EC) as requiring compensation for both pecuniary and non-pecuniary loss to be available to victims of data protection breaches. This construction was mandated by a consideration of the purpose and aims of the Directive, read in conjunction with Article 8 of the Charter.[145] The Court also observed that the domestic transposition of Article 23 of the Directive failed to give effect to this construction. Section 13(2) of the Data Protection Act 1998 ('DPA 1998') wrongly limited the availability of damages to certain categories of person who had also suffered pecuniary loss and only in certain circumstances. The Court of Appeal acknowledged that section 13(2) could not be read conformably with Article 23 of the Directive on the standard *Marleasing* basis. It accordingly disapplied the provisions of section 13(2) DPA 1998, as it conflicted with the rights guaranteed by Articles 7 and 8 of the Charter.[146] This was needed also to permit a claim for full compensation to be brought, since no other solution would give full effect to the need to ensure an effective remedy for those whose EU rights have been infringed.[147] The reasons for doing so were set out at paragraph 98 and bear citation here in full:

> As this court stated in *Benkharbouche* at paras 69 to 85, (i) where there is a breach of a right afforded under EU law, Article 47 of the Charter is engaged; (ii) the right to an effective remedy for breach of EU law rights provided for by Article 47 embodies a general principle of EU law; (iii) (subject to exceptions which have no application in the present case) that general principle has horizontal effect; (iv) in so far as a provision of national law conflicts with the requirement for an effective remedy in Article 47, the domestic courts can and must disapply the conflicting provision; and (v) the only exception to (iv) is that the court may be required to apply a conflicting domestic provision where the court would otherwise have to redesign the fabric of the legislative scheme.

This remedy would simply not have been available to the complainants under the ECHR, as given effect to by the HRA 1998. The best which they could have hoped for was a declaration of incompatibility under section 4 HRA 1998. While Parliament may

142. His Lordship adopted with approval the observations of Lloyd-Jones J in *R (Zagorski & Baze) v. Secretary of State for Business, Innovation and Skills* [2010] EWHC 3110 (Admin), paragraphs 66–71.
143. *See*, for example, *Golden Eye (International) Ltd v. Telefónica UK Ltd* [2012] EWCA Civ 1740, CA per Patten LJ at paragraphs 17–21; *EMI Records and others v. British Sky Broadcasting Ltd* [2013] EWHC 379 (Ch) per Arnold J at paragraphs 94–100; and *The Football Association Premier League Ltd v. British Sky Broadcasting Ltd* [2013] EWHC 2058 (Ch) per Arnold J at paragraphs 53–59.
144. [2015] EWCA Civ 311, CA.
145. *Ibid.* per Lord Dyson MR and Sharp LJ at paragraphs 77 to 79. MacFarlane LJ agreed with the judgment at paragraph 142.
146. *Ibid.* at paragraph 95.
147. *Ibid.* at paragraph 105.

then have rectified the problem, it would not ordinarily have been retrospective in effect. The complainants would not themselves have been entitled to damages for non-pecuniary loss such as distress.

[D] Miscellaneous Cases

It is of course true that other litigants seeking to rely on the Charter have fared less well. In *R (Chester and another) v. Secretary of State for Justice*,[148] the claimants sought to challenge the well-known prohibition on UK prisoners' voting by reliance *inter alia* on the Charter. The prohibition has been subject to repeated decisions of the ECtHR finding a violation of the Convention.[149] The Supreme Court[150] declined simply to read the Strasbourg jurisprudence across to EU law and make comparable findings. It concluded that there was no warrant under EU law to do so. In addition, Lord Mance (at paragraph 59) rejected the suggestion that Articles 39 or 40 of the Charter conferred any rights on the individual litigants before the Court. Those Charter articles were intended to confer voting rights on those EU citizens who wished to vote in their Member State of residence where that was *different* to their Member State of nationality.[151]

But more recently, there has been growing evidence of Courts become increasingly receptive to arguments based on the Charter. In the Court of Appeal decision in *R (Evans) v. Attorney General and Information Commissioner*,[152] Lord Dyson MR at paragraph 57 recognised that Article 47 could be relied upon by a litigant whose EU law rights had been violated,[153] so as to require an effective remedy to be given. This was recognised as being equivalent to Article 6 ECHR. But it also meant that the certificate issued by the Secretary of State in that case fell to be quashed on the grounds of incompatibility with the Charter rights (at least in so far as it contained environmental information within the meaning of the Environmental Information Directive).

In *R (Teresa Gudanaviciene) v. The Director of Legal Aid Casework*,[154] the Court of Appeal held that the Director of Legal Aid Casework was obliged to grant civil legal aid under the Lord Chancellor's Exceptional Funding Guidance in any case where failure to do so would breach Article 6 ECHR or Article 47 of the Charter. These were to be applied co-extensively for that purpose. The test was not confined to 'exceptional

148. [2013] UKSC 63, [2014] AC 271, SC per Lord Mance (with whom Lords Hope, Hughes and Kerr agreed).
149. *See Hirst v. United Kingdom (No. 2)* (2005) 42 EHRR 849, ECtHR.
150. Per Lord Mance at paragraphs 46–58.
151. *See also* the speech of Lady Hale at paragraph 87 agreeing with the views of the majority on the EU law issues.
152. [2014] EWCA Civ 254, [2014] QB 855, CA. The Supreme Court dismissed the Attorney General's appeal on different grounds: *R (oao Evans) v. The Attorney General* [2015] UKSC 21, SC. Lord Dyson's reasoning was not disapproved, but the point was expressly left open to permit future consideration by the Supreme Court. *See* paragraph 107 of the speech of Lord Neuberger (with whom Lords Reed and Kerr agreed).
153. Lord Dyson MR found that the right comprised: (i) the right of access to a court or tribunal which can give decisions binding on all parties; (ii) the right to legal certainty and the finality of judgments; and (iii) the right to a fair hearing (including the right to equality of arms).
154. [2014] EWCA Civ 1622, CA.

circumstances'.[155] Rather the test to be applied was whether an unrepresented litigant was able to present his or her case effectively and without obvious unfairness. That required a consideration of all the circumstances of the case.[156] The Director's existing guidance was found to be unlawful, as being incompatible with both Article 6 ECHR and Article 47 of the Charter.[157]

The most striking example is the recent case of *Benkharbouche v. Embassy of the Republic of Sudan*.[158] This is the third in the hat-trick of cases in which the Master of the Rolls giving judgment in the Court of Appeal has struck down executive decisions and/or disapplied primary legislation so as to give effect to Charter rights. Arguably it is also of even further reach than *Google v. Vidal-Hall*, since it overrode a procedural immunity from suit granted by primary legislation (under section 16(1)(a) of the State Immunity Act 1978 ('SIA 1978'), rather than simply disapplying a restriction on the recoverability of damages.[159] Ms. Benkharbouche was a Moroccon national working as a cook at the Embassy of Sudan. She brought a claim against the Embassy for unfair dismissal and a failure to pay the minimum wage. The Embassy raised a defence based on sovereign immunity which was accepted before the Employment Tribunal, but overturned on appeal before the Employment Appeal Tribunal ('EAT'). The EAT found that the procedural immunity infringed Article 6 ECHR, could not be read down. Langstaff J in the EAT had no power to make a declaration of incompatibility under section 4 of the HRA 1998. But because the procedural immunity also infringed Article 47 of the Charter (the claim falling within the scope of application of EU law), the immunity from suit provisions in the SIA 1978 had to be disapplied.

The Court of Appeal upheld this result (and that in a joined appeal). It found that a rule of the breadth of section 16(1)(a) SIA 1978 was not required by international law. In its application to the claimants, it contravened Article 6 ECHR. Unlike the EAT, the Court of Appeal had jurisdiction to make a declaration of incompatibility – and did so. As indicated above, that would not, of course, have permitted Ms. Benkharbouche to bring her claim for unfair dismissal or recoup the minimum wage over her period of employment. It was common ground before the Court of Appeal that Article 47 of the Charter had a co-extensive ambit of application on the facts to that of Article 6 ECHR. The Court of Appeal also recognised that the EU law claim had potentially important consequences for the remedy.[160] The disapplication of sections 4(2)(b) and 16(1)(a) of the SIA 1978 would enable the claimants to obtain a substantial measure of justice. The Court of Appeal then proceeded to consider whether or not it could – and should –

155. *Ibid.* at paragraphs 31, 32, 45–46 and 58–59.
156. *Ibid.* at paragraph 56.
157. *Ibid.* at paragraph 181.
158. [2015] EWCA Civ 33, per Lord Dyson MR giving the judgment of the Court of Appeal consisting additionally of Arden and Lloyd-Jones LJJ.
159. The 'disapplication' in each case, however, involved the judicial exercise of declining to give effect to provisions of primary legislation which might otherwise have been relied upon by the opposing litigant. These were respectively the exception to the exclusion from immunity from suit conferred by section 16(1)(a) of the SIA 1978 (so that the exclusion under section 4 from the immunity from suit under section 1 SIA 1978 took effect); and the restriction on the recoverability of damages in section 13(2) of the DPA 1998.
160. *Ibid.* at paragraphs 71 and 72.

disapply sections 4 and 16 SIA 1978 so as to permit a remedy. The Court found that Article 47 enshrined a general principle of EU law which had horizontal direct effect.[161] It accordingly disapplied sections 4(2)(b) and 16(1)(a) SIA to those parts of the claims which fell within the scope of EU law.

§14.07 WILL WE MISS THE CHARTER IF IT GOES?

The fact that the Charter has been raised infrequently in domestic proceedings raises the natural question as to why that should be the case. If it truly is a guard dog of civil liberties, why has it not barked more often? The response cannot sensibly be that given in the Sherlock Holmes story, *Silver Blaze*. There the dog failed to bark because it recognised its owner as the guilty party. The UK Government is not the 'owner' of the Charter. Nor is it realistic to think that the various governmental bodies in their manifold forms have not infringed the fundamental rights of at least some citizens in the UK since December 2009. The number of decisions based on the HRA 1998 since that date belie that suggestion.

The availability of remedies under the HRA 1998 does, at least in part, explain the lack of popularity of the Charter among domestic complainants. It is not uncommon to be asked by a Judge what additional benefit reliance on the Charter will bring. If the answer is not much, the Judge (and the advocate, if sensible) is likely to concentrate on the more familiar principles and remedies available under the ECHR. The diversion of the 'opt out' issue also may account for the rather slow take up. But the recent domestic case law shows that the Charter is gaining prominence in the practitioner's toolkit. Litigants are increasingly aware of the practical benefits a claim based on the Charter can bring. These benefits also answer the charge that the abolition of the Charter would not cause any significant detriment to human rights protection in the UK, so long as the HRA 1998 was kept. Broadly these benefits fall into six categories.

First, the supremacy of EU law means that primary and subordinate national legislation which is declared incompatible with a directly effective Charter right, and therefore invalid, must be disapplied by national courts.[162] Many fundamental rights are likely to be directly effective. That encompasses horizontal direct effect as well.[163] Primary or subordinate domestic legislation that contravenes those rights protected by EU law must therefore be disapplied by national courts in respect of the person relying

161. *Ibid.* at paragraphs 77–81, applying Case C-144/04 *Mangold v. Helm* [2005] ECR I-9981, ECJ.
162. *See R v. Secretary of State for Employment* ex parte *Equal Opportunities Commission* [1995] 1 A.C. 1, HL at pp. 26E–27F. Also *R (D Davis) v Secretary of State for the Home Department* [2015] EWHC 2092 (Admin) but cf in the Court of Appeal [2015] EWCA Civ 1185.
163. In Case C-555/07 *Kücükdeveci* [2010] ECR I-365, the ECJ at paragraphs 22 and 23 recognised that the principle of protecting against age discrimination would apply if the domestic proceedings between an employee and an employer were within the scope of EU law. The ECJ upheld the principle that directly effective provisions of a Directive would not have direct effect horizontally, so as to be capable of being applied against individuals. But since the time for introduction of the Directive had expired, the domestic court had to apply the principle against age discrimination (as expressed in the Directive) and decline to apply any contrary provision of national law if it could not be interpreted in a manner consistent with the general principle. *See* paragraphs 53 and 54.

upon them.[164] By contrast, sections 3(2)(b) and (c) of the HRA 1998 provide that the validity, continuing operation or enforcement of primary legislation (and of subordinate legislation where primary legislation prevents the removal of the incompatibility), which cannot be read or given effect in a way which is compatible with the Convention, is not affected. Section 4 allows courts simply to make a declaration of the incompatibility of primary legislation with a Convention right, but this is of minimal practical use to the applicant.[165] The Strasbourg Court has held that it is not an effective remedy.[166] Indeed, defendants may attempt to defend claims by seeking refuge in a declaration of incompatibility.[167]

Secondly, there are also advantages to proceeding under EU law in terms of the *locus standi* of applicants. A challenge to a legislative or administrative act alleging infringement of Charter rights can often be brought by judicial review, providing a claimant has a sufficient interest in the matter.[168] An increasingly liberal approach to standing has been developed by the courts. Claims are often made by public interest groups established to campaign on particular issues or to represent specific interests.[169] By contrast, section 7(1) of the HRA establishes a narrower 'victim' test.

Thirdly, under EU law a complaint can be made about a failure to introduce primary legislation,[170] whereas this is expressly excluded under the HRA 1998 regime by section 6(6)(b).

Fourthly, the remedies available under EU law have more bite even where they do not have more teeth. Article 4(3) TEU obliges national courts to ensure the legal protection of rights which individuals derive from EU law.[171] Such protection by

164. In so far as that person is able to rely upon directly enforceable EU law rights. *See ICI v. Colmer (No 2)* [1999] 1 WLR 2035, HL; and *Gingi v. Secretary of State for Work and Pensions* [2001] EWCA Civ 1685, CA per Arden LJ at paragraph 44.
165. *See* section 4(6)(a)HRA 1998. An example of the potential advantage of relying on EU law in this respect is provided by the *Countryside Alliance* case in which the claimants argued that the ban on hunting with hounds engaged EU law in attempt to obtain a remedy that they could not obtain under the HRA, namely, the disapplication of the statute. *See R (Countryside Alliance) v. A-G* [2007] UKHL 52, [2008] 1 AC 719, HL.
166. *Burden & Burden v. United Kingdom* (2008) 47 EHRR 38, ECtHR, where the Court reiterated at paragraph 40 that a declaration of incompatibility did not provide an effective remedy (for the purposes of Article 35(1) and the requirement to exhaust domestic remedies) because it is not binding on the parties to the proceedings in which it is made and cannot form the basis of an award of monetary compensation.
167. *See*, for example, *Global Knafaim Leasing Ltd v. The Civil Aviation Authority* [2010] EWHC 1348 (Admin) where the Civil Aviation Authority argued that a declaration of incompatibility was the only available remedy, the effect of which would have been to defeat the restitutionary claim. Collins J dismissed the domestic and EU claims on the facts.
168. Senior Courts Act 1981, section 31(3).
169. *See* N. Plemming, 'The Contribution of Public Interest Litigation to the Jurisprudence of Judicial Review' [1998] J.R. 63; and the judgment of Maurice Kay J. in *R. v. Secretary of State for Trade and Industry* ex parte *Greenpeace Ltd (No. 2)* [2000] Eu.L.R. 196.
170. For example, in the context of a claim for *Francovich* damages. *See* Case C-48/93 *Factortame and Brasserie du Pêcheur* [1996] E.C.R. I-1029, ECJ.
171. This was already reflected in the case law. *See* Case 33/76 *Rewe v. Landwirtschaftskammer Saarland* [1976] E.C.R. 1989, ECJ at paragraph 5; Case C-2/88 *Zwartveld* [1990] E.C.R. I-3365, ECJ at paragraph 18; and Case C-312/93 *Peterbroeck v. Belgium* [1995] E.C.R. I-4599, ECJ at paragraph 12.

national courts in accordance with national procedural rules[172] is subject to two overriding principles. First, national rules that apply to EU law actions must not be discriminatory or less favourable than those governing analogous domestic actions (the principle of equivalence). Secondly, national rules must not make practically impossible the exercise of EU law rights which must be accorded effective protection (the principle of effective protection).

Fifthly, there is the related issue of damages. Under the *Francovich* test laid down by the ECJ and applied by the national courts, a claimant may claim damages against a Member State in respect of serious breaches of EU law.[173] Therefore, a claimant who has suffered damage as a result of the UK implementing EU legislation in a manner which is in breach of the Charter or general principles of EU law, may be able to sustain a damages claim, if the breach is sufficiently serious.[174] Damages awarded under EU law must constitute an effective remedy and provide adequate compensation. This is to be contrasted with the limited availability of damages under the HRA 1998. Under section 8, an award of damages is discretionary and, following the lead of the Strasbourg Court, exceptional. Where they are made, the amounts awarded are low.[175]

Sixthly, the coverage and the sources of the rights contained in the Charter is wider and more extensive than under the HRA 1998. The Charter draws not only on the ECHR as a source of fundamental rights but also on other international treaties for the protection of human rights of which the Member States are signatories or on which they have collaborated, in addition to the Treaties themselves.[176] The ECJ has referred to a number of international human rights instruments including the European Social Charter of 18 November 1961,[177] Convention No. 111 of the International Labour Organisation,[178] and the International Covenant on Civil and Political Rights of 19 December 1966.[179] This is reflected in the sources for the rights, freedoms and principles set out in the Charter.

It is also possible, particularly in the light of *Benkharbouche*, to anticipate future developments in the use of the Charter which would enable individuals to assert Charter freedoms in their dealings with corporations and not simply public bodies.

172. Joined Cases C-430/93 and C-431/93 *Van Schijndel v. SPF* [1995] E.C.R. I-4705 per the Opinion of Advocate General Jacobs at paragraph 29.
173. *See* Joined Cases C-6 and 9/90 *Francovich and Bonifaci v. Italy* [1991] E.C.R. I-5357, ECJ; Case C-392/93 *R. v. H.M. Treasury* ex parte *British Telecommunications plc* [1996] E.C.R. I-1631, at paragraph 38; and Case C-127/95 *Norbrook Laboratories v. Ministry of Agriculture, Fisheries and Food* [1998] ECR I-1531, at paragraphs 106 and 107.
174. *See Norbrook ibid.* at paragraph 109. The ECJ has held that a breach will be sufficiently serious where a Member State had manifestly and gravely disregarded the limits on its legislative powers. Furthermore, where a Member State was not called upon to make any legislative choices and had only a considerably reduced (or even no) discretion, the mere existence of an infringement of EU law may establish a sufficiently serious breach.
175. *See* Beatson, Grosz, Hickman, Singh, *supra* n. 78 at [7-129] to [7-190], pp. 669–697.
176. Case *Nold v. Commission* [1974] E.C.R. 491 ECJ at [12]-[14]; Case C-260/89 *ERT* [1991] I-2925 ECJ at paragraphs 41–45; Case 11/70 *Internationale Handelsgesellschaft v. Einfuhr- und Vorratsstelle Getreide* [1970] E.C.R. 1125, ECJ at paragraphs 3–4.
177. Case 149/77 *Defrenne v. Sabena* [1978] E.C.R. 1365, ECJ at paragraphs 25–28.
178. *Ibid.*
179. Case 374/87 *Orkem v. Commission* [1989] E.C.R. 3283, ECJ at paragraphs 18 and 31; Case C-168/91 *Konstantinidis* [1993] E.C.R. I-1191, per the Opinion of Advocate General Jacobs.

Recent 'soft law' has sought to apply human rights principles to large corporations. These are to be found in, for example, the United Nations Guiding Principles on Business and Human Rights ('the Ruggie Principles')[180] and the Organisation for Economic and Co-operation Development ('OECD') Guidelines for multinational enterprises.[181] But their application remains discretionary. The horizontal application of Charter principles to multinational corporations could achieve genuine protection of rights for citizens which would otherwise be incapable of enforcement. British exit from the EU would extinguish that possibility. The guard dog would be put down.

The ECJ in *AMS*[182] has recognised that the directly effective provisions of the Charter can be applied between private parties in domestic litigation. The questions referred raised expressly the issue of the horizontal implementation of the Charter between private parties. At paragraphs 36 and 37, the Court specifically found that the individual claimant could not rely upon the directly effective provisions of a Directive against a private individual. Nonetheless, it went on to consider whether application of Article 27 of the Charter would secure a different result. It held that the matter fell within the scope of EU law because the national legislation was adopted to implement a Directive. Provisions of the Charter could in principle be invoked by individuals to set aside inconsistent terms of national law. This would also apply to Charter articles if those articles were directly effective.[183] The Court explained that in *Kucukdeveci*, the principle of non-discrimination had been directly effective and therefore had conferred on an individual a right to set aside inconsistent domestic legislation in the context of proceedings between two individual parties.[184]

British exit from the European Union would damage the regime for human rights protection found in the United Kingdom. It would remove the ability of individuals to rely not only on the Charter, but on the general principles of EU law which have been applied domestically and at EU level for decades. Furthermore, the breach would not be filled by the HRA 1998, assuming that adherence to the Convention was maintained in the face of the UK's withdrawal from the Union. It is perhaps somewhat ironic that two of the great benefits of the Charter – its legitimisation of EU general principles and

---

180. The UN Guiding Principles were formulated by the UN's Special Representative, John Ruggie, as part of the UN's development of the 'Protect, Respect and Remedy' Framework. The Human Rights Council of the UN endorsed the Guiding Principles in Resolution 17/4 of 16 Jun. 2011. They do not purport to establish new international law obligations (and cannot create binding legal obligations in themselves).
181. The 2011 Edition of the OECD Guidelines for Multinational Enterprises contain a series of non-legally binding recommendations for responsible business conduct in a global context. They provide principles and standards of good practice consistent with applicable laws and internationally recognised standards (see paragraph I.1). Under paragraph II.A.2., enterprises should respect the internationally recognised human rights of those affected by their activities.
182. *See* Case C-176/12 *AMS* [2014] ECLI:EU:C:2014:2 at paragraphs 41–47.
183. However Article 27 was not intended to apply by itself but required a specific expression of its principles in other EU or domestic law. So on the facts, Article 27 of the Charter could not be used to set aside the national legislation.
184. Such provisions may thus be relied upon by individuals before the national courts, even if the case is brought against another individual and not against an emanation of the State. The doctrine of supremacy under EU law enables legislation, even primary legislation, to be overturned. *See ICI v. Colmer (No. 2)* [1999] 1 WLR 2035, HL per Lord Nolan at p. 2041.

its ability to confer protection even against primary legislation – will be the very focus of the opposition from those seeking UK withdrawal.

That would be a great shame, since the actual or potential impact of the Charter has been relatively modest. It has only been used to strike down primary legislation on two occasions. The general principles of EU law, over a much longer time-span, were never used to that effect. The beneficial effect of the Charter may, as intended, have been to raise the visibility of fundamental rights at an EU level. We can never know for sure, but the Charter may well have encouraged the very able drafters of primary legislation to bear in mind the fundamental rights under the Charter, given their potential deployment against statutory provisions. Such a persuasive impact on the quality of primary legislation is to be encouraged. In the event of a British exit from Europe, it may well be that the only practical course open to those complaining of infringements of fundamental rights by primary legislation or large companies will be political lobbying. Their slogan? Remember the Chartists.

CHAPTER 15

State Aid Control, Government Spending and the Virtue of Loyalty

Andrea Biondi

§15.01 INTRODUCTION

A recurring theme going through the various contributions in this volume is how to manage differentiation; exploring whether there are any constitutional or legal tools that can be employed in order to manage the different centrifugal forces that are at work in the constant evolution of the relationship between the United Kingdom and the European Union. The proverbial intolerance of this Member State against any excessive dirigisme from outside is also well documented in most of the chapters. My take is slightly different. I would like to argue that at least in some crucial sectors of EU policies, only a supranational model is able to deliver efficiency, transparency and equality of position between the different parties, in particular between the Member States and the EU institutions and between the Member States themselves. It could, surprisingly, also be conducive to the preservation of vital national interests and foster virtuous and fair economic policies. Further, it will be argued that a model of direct supranational *administration* does not need to equate to a model of full centralisation. Differentiation and delegation can, and actually should, exist and function within clearly pre-established parameters.

There are several areas which demonstrate and verify that it is sometimes worth *leaving it to the EU*. The chosen test case analysed here is the EU regulatory process on state aid control, an area extremely important for British economic policy. This chapter will be structured around two main themes. The first will try to sketch how the unique system of state aid control in Europe is providing an important tool to ensure a competitive level playing field between Member States and between undertakings; the second, is how such a system, properly employed, allows the development of coherent business and industrial policies. In particular, public spending channelled 'through EU levees' can be utilised to develop more responsible and eventually more socially useful economic practices. Needless to say, nothing is perfect. Thus a preliminary disclaimer might be necessary, as it is wise to acknowledge at the outset that there are deficiencies in the system and improvements and changes are of course always possible. Still the main contention remains unchanged: the machinery of control on anti-competitive public spending, as sketched by the EU Treaty, is one of the clearest reasons why European partnership is valuable for the United Kingdom to preserve.

§15.02 THE NUMBERS: GOVERNMENT SPENDING AND BUSINESS 'SUPPORT'

Despite some political rhetoric on the many virtues of the approach '*that government is best which governs least*', the public purse remains the main instrument for pursuing numerous policies. Even for those Member States, such as the UK, that are perceived as the champions of the free market and a reduced role for the state, the case remains compelling. The United Kingdom government's spending in the early 2000s was calculated at around 40% of national income. The vast amount was, and still is –despite a reduction in recent years – devoted to the performance of solidarity tasks such a social security, health, education, defence and public order.[1] Public spending in the UK cannot of course be dissociated from the vicissitudes of the financial crises. In 2009–2010, faced with the collapse of several banks, government spending shot up to 47% and in the financial year 2013–2014, the UK government spent GBP 714.2 billion, or 43.8% of the UK's national income.[2] The UK is also extremely active in its policies towards sustaining the private sector, either by direct intervention or through financial support. For instance, in recent years the sale of public assets such as the 3G and 4G spectrums and the transfer of Royal Mail's pension assets to the public sector, are examples of considerable commercial transactions. The government raised GBP 23.5 billion from the sale of the 3G spectrums in 2000–2001, and GBP 2.3 billion was raised from the sale of the 4G spectrum in 2012–2013. Royal Mail's pension assets were also transferred to the public sector in 2012–2013, to pave the way for postal service privatisation. This cost around GBP 28 billion. These operations were classified in the National Accounts as sales of a public asset, in other words, negative public sector investments.[3]

European Commission reports also contain some interesting data on more classic forms of financial support. The lion's share of UK public spending, unsurprisingly, is related to aid to financial institutions. A selection of examples are as follows. In relation to financial sector measures, between October 2008 and October 2014, the United Kingdom spending to support financial institutions peaks at EUR 191.5 billion (10.1%). In 2013, EUR 35.8 billion (1.9%) with another EUR 167.3 billion (8.8%) is spent on

1. http://www.ukpublicspending.co.uk/.
2. https://www.gov.uk/government/ PESA_2014. For a more digestible overview see S. Keynes & G. Tetlow, Survey of Public Spending in the UK, Institute for Fiscal Studies, 2014.
3. http://www.ons.gov.uk/ons/rel/naa1-rd/united-kingdom-national-accounts/index.html.

recapitalisation and other liquidity measures.[4] Even if one removes the aid to financial institutions and all the guarantees and other forms of support to ailing banks, which one could optimistically describe as a one in an hundred years episode, other sectors are also heavily subsidised.[5] Very well-known cases are Rolls- Royce, around GBP 34 million in 2010, or the GBP 28 million by the Welsh Assembly to Airbus in 2009, also Nissan, GBP 25 million between 2005 and 2010, or tech companies such Hewlett Packard, GBP 7.3 million in 2010, or Dell Corporation, awarded GBP 7.3 million in 2005.[6] Further recent research shows slightly more obscure but equally robust amounts of direct capital grants, corporate tax benefits, tax reductions or deductions estimated at around GBP 93 billion.[7] These transfers of course appear in different forms, such as: straight subsidies and grants, GBP 14.5 billion ranging from cash to the train operators to run services, subsidies to defence firms and pro investment grants to businesses. Corporate tax benefits are estimated at around a staggering GBP 44 billion. Insurance, advice and advocacy services to promote the state's insurance scheme for trading abroad – the export credit guarantee – GBP 406 million. The UK is of course not alone in the EU in using the public purse to support economic activities. However, the data shows that there are still huge differences in the level of public spending between Member States. The state aid scoreboard prepared by the European Commission is revealing:

EU Countries	*2013**
Belgium	1466.4
Bulgaria	120.7
Czech Republic	1658.1
Denmark	2526
Germany	12017.6
Estonia	63
Ireland	797.2
Greece	2919.7
Spain	2779.2
France	12988.8
Croatia	170.1
Italy	3520.4
Cyprus	104.2

4. http://ec.europa.eu/competition/state_aid/scoreboard/financial_economic_crisis_aid_en.html.
5. In a nicely performed budget make up, as most of the 'financial rescue' spending was considered only a temporary injection into the private sector (meaning that some money will be recouped) the Office for Budget Responsibility whose task is to monitor public spending, excluded these one-off changes.
6. See http://ec.europa.eu/competition/state_aid/register/msf_2013.pdf.
7. See K. Farnsworth database at http://www.corporate-welfare-watch.org.uk/Database/ as reported by A. Chakraborttty, 'Direct Aid, Subsidies and Tax Breaks, The Hidden Welfare Budget We Don't Debate', the Guardian, Wed 8 Jul. 2015, 12.

EU Countries	*2013**
Finland	2545.7
Latvia	373.6
Lithuania	205.3
Luxembourg	158.1
Hungary	1524
Malta	129.3
Netherlands	2006.7
Austria	1816.3
Poland	2671
Portugal	543
Romania	879.2
Slovenia	579.1
Slovakia	198.9
Sweden	3367.4
United Kingdom	4607.7
Total	62736.9

*Non-crisis state aid, excluding railways - million EUR, % of GDP.[8]

For instance in terms of percentage of GDP, the UK has spent less on aid over the last six years than all other countries except Luxembourg, and spends significantly less than comparable states such as Italy, France or Germany. It is also interesting to note that when the Commission published data in 2011, on how state aid spending by Member States was considered as a contribution to European common objectives collected under the umbrella of Europe 2020,[9] the UK came top in several categories.[10] For example, the UK was the largest spender on SMEs in Europe, its spending accounted for 14% of the EU total, with 70% of the total risk capital investments in SMEs in the EU. On broadband, UK spending amounted to 43% of the total EU spend. Therefore, the UK could be considered one of the most loyal Member States in term of EU objectives.

8. European Commission – DG Commission, 10 Jul. 2015, http://ec.europa.eu/eurostat/eurostat/tgm_comp/table.do?tab = table&init = 1&plugin = 1&language = en&pcode = comp_ncr_xrl_01 last (accessed 25 Jul. 2015).
9. These are encapsulated in the five, now famous, targets: (1) Employment, 75% of the 20–64 year-olds to be employed; (2) R&D 3% of the EU's GDP to be invested in R&. (3) Climate change and energy sustainability greenhouse gas emissions 20% (or even 30%, if the conditions are right) lower than 1990 20% of energy from renewables 20% increase in energy efficiency. (4) Education reducing the rates of early school leaving below 10% at least 40% of 30–34-year-olds completing third-level education. (5) Fighting poverty and social exclusion. See http://ec.europa.eu/europe2020/index_en.htm.
10. Report of the European Commission, State aid Scoreboard Report on State aid contribution to Europe 2020 Strategy – Spring 2011 Update – Brussels, 22 Jun. 2011 COM (2011) 356 final.

§15.03 CONSTITUTIONAL REFLECTIONS: THE RELATIONSHIPS BETWEEN THE EU AND ITS MEMBER STATES AND BETWEEN THE MEMBER STATES THEMSELVES

Loyalty, as one of the cornerstones of the European Union constitutional edifice, is the principle that each of the EU Member States has a duty of sincere cooperation with the EU institutions. This is imposed by the EU Treaty itself, which, in Article 4(3) TEU (formerly Article 10 TEU and Article 5 EC) so provides:

> *Pursuant to the principle of sincere cooperation, the Union and the Member States shall, in full mutual respect, assist each other in carrying out tasks which flow from the Treaties. The Member States shall take any appropriate measure, general or particular, to ensure fulfilment of the obligations arising out of the Treaties or resulting from the acts of the institutions of the Union. The Member States shall facilitate the achievement of the Union's tasks and refrain from any measure which could jeopardise the attainment of the Union's objectives.*

Despite some terminological differences, Article 4(3) TFEU can be considered as an approximate codification of forty years of consistent case law of the European Court of Justice. According to this *acquis*, the obligation imposed on Member States of cooperation is a '*principle inherent in the Community legal order*'[11] and it requires '*a duty of genuine cooperation and assistance which Member States owe the Community and which finds expression in the obligation laid down in Article 5 of the EEC Treaty (now Article 4(3) TFEU)*'.[12] As is well known, the principle of loyal collaboration is far from being an abstract moral commandment, but translates into very specific and demanding constraints on Member States, as they need to ensure that any provision of their legal system, any legislative, administrative measure or judicial practice which might impair the effectiveness of EU law, should not prevent European rules from having full force and effect.[13] The principle of loyal collaboration cannot however be merely equated to an obligation imposed by the Sovereign on its participating Member States.[14] As discussed in the literature, loyalty, in reality, performs several different functions, from guaranteeing the respective autonomy of the Member States and of the EU institutions, to managing the cooperation itself.[15] Thus, loyalty, on the one hand, serves to maintain unity with respect for independence, and on the other hand, ensures the effective application of EU policies. However, the idea of mutual collaboration has a further important objective; the mediation of conflicts, meaning primarily conflicts between a State and the EU, for which several different political and judicial procedures

11. Joined Cases C-46/93 and C-48/93 *Brasserie du Pêcheur SA v. Germany and The Queen v. Secretary of State for Transport, ex parte Factortame Ltd and Others* [1996] ECR I-1029, paragraph 95.
12. Case 44/84 *Derrick Guy Edmund Hurd v. Kenneth Jones* [1986] ECR 29.
13. Case 106/77 *Amministrazione delle Finanze dello Stato v. Simmenthal SpA* [1978] ECR 692, paragraphs 21–22.
14. M. Ross, '*Effectiveness in the European Legal Order(s): Beyond Supremacy to Constitutional Proportionality?*' (2006) 31 EL Rev 476; F.G. Snyder, 'The Effectiveness of European Community Law: Institutions, Processes, Tools and Techniques' (1993) 56 MLR 19, 40.
15. See the recent M. Klamert, *The Principle of Loyalty in EU Law*, OUP, 2014 and in particular A. Hatje, *Loyalität als Rechtsprinzip in der Europäischen Union*, Nomos, 2001.

are available. A secondary but equally relevant purpose is that by imposing on all participating states the same level of commitment, loyalty creates a locus for an unbiased and impartial resolution of the conflicting interests of the different Member States. Finally, it ensures that core EU law effectiveness should not be undermined by unilateral actions. Defection should therefore be effectively sanctioned and should not be considered as a viable option.

§15.04 LOYALTY AND DIRECT EXECUTION

The dynamics of Supranational – national loyalty are well documented. They are mainly *institutional* through Member States involvement in law making and in the implementation of EU rules both *substantive* and *procedural* through the necessity to comply with direct effect, supremacy, liability in damages and the armoury of EU law core principles. They are also *administrative* in nature, as national authorities need to comply with the European regulatory process. As for the latter, a full discussion of the entire EU administrative structure is beyond the scope of this chapter. For the sake of brevity and at the risk of oversimplification, I suggest we adopt Chiti's classification:[16] this is mainly based on the following models: *indirect execution*, EU policies are carried out by relying on national machinery; *bottom up mechanisms* of administration, EU objectives are carried out by all Member States in different shapes and forms; *bottom down* mechanisms, where the EU institutions instigate processes of administrative integration. In relation to the latter, the most well known is the creation of a European system of EU and national independent authorities. Under this model the administrative tasks are organised and distributed from an EU source to all national designated authorities. Finally, *direct execution*, which is correctly described by Chiti, not as the mere conferral to the executive branch – the European Commission – of certain administrative tasks, but '*that the functional prominence of the European Commission is required by the Treaty itself: the supranational component has not only a particularly strong role in the process of execution of the European Union regulation but it is also subject to 'constitutional' protection*'.[17] As previously mentioned, provided that the constitutional Treaty based guarantee and the prerogatives of the body entrusted to fulfil it are respected, the direct execution model can then display its effects in various shapes, and does afford a certain degree of delegation. In my view, state aid policy exactly fits the direct execution model.

§15.05 STATE AID CONTROL AS A DIRECT EXECUTION MODEL

The constitutional guarantee offered by the Treaty in the area of State aid law could not be stronger. The drafting of the relevant provision is itself revealing: it starts with a bang as Article 107(1) introduces a straight prohibition on any state intervention in the

16. E. Chiti *The Administrative Implementation of European Union Law: A Taxonomy and Its Implications*, in *Legal Challenges in EU Administrative Law: Towards an Integrated Administration* 9 (H.C.H. Hoffman & A. Turk eds, Edward Elgar Publishing 2009).
17. *Ibid.* at p. 26.

economy that could have the effect of favouring certain undertakings and thus produce a distortive effect and an obstacle to the free flow of trade. Such a blow is softened by centralising control over those measures and by simultaneously conferring on the European Commission a discretionary power to 'forgive' the States and make the aid in question compatible with EU objectives and policies. Article 107 provides for two kinds of compatibility: Article 107(2) covers aids which, as a matter of law, *are compatible* with the internal market, provided they meet certain conditions, and which the Commission *must* therefore approve; Article 107(3) concerns aids which *can be declared compatible* with the internal market, thus giving, unlike in (a) above, the Commission a wide measure of discretion in approving them, and in so doing weighing different interests. The effectiveness of the Commission's direct execution is guaranteed by an ad hoc procedure provided by Article 108 TFEU that requires a compulsory prior notification of all new aid measures. This mechanism is reinforced by the so called stand-still clause under which Member States are prevented from granting the proposed aid before the Commission has made its assessment. The constitutional elevation made by the founding Treaty of rules aimed at ensuring control over public spending is easily explained: a straight prohibition on financial assistance made sense in the context of a progressive abolition of regulatory measures which could have the effect of preventing free movement for economic actors.[18] From a European integration perspective, the abolition of internal borders would have been somewhat ineffective if a state was still allowed to create a de facto barrier by pouring money into a domestic undertaking. Historically, there were also concerns to avoid distortions of competition between companies and subsidies' races between Member States trying to attract companies to their territories.[19] Finally, national governments gained credibility in showing commitment to the new European enterprise.[20]

As with many other EU policies, state aid has been through different phases and came alive only after the initiation of the single market project with stronger Commission action backed by robust ECJ judgments.[21] Whatever the historical developments, it is clear that state aid is now one of the 'core EU policies'. As recently empathically reaffirmed by the European Court of Justice Grand Chamber in *Commission v. Spain*, State aid control rules are '*the expression of one of the essential tasks with which the European Union is entrusted under Article 2 EC, namely the establishment of a common market, and under Article 3(1) (g) EC which provides that the activities of the Community are to include a system ensuring that competition in the internal market is not distorted*'.[22] The functioning of the rather sophisticated mechanism laid down in the Treaty is however complicated and risky. Complicated as state aid control is a tool

18. Intergovernmental Committee on European Integration. The Brussels Report on the General Common Market (the Spaak Report), June 1956, Title II, Chapter 2.
19. W. Mederer, *Evolution of State Aid Control*, in *EU Competition Law – Vol. II State Aid*, Chapter 2 (W. Mederer, Nicola Pesaresi, Mark Van Hoff ed, 2008).
20. M.P. Smith, *Autonomy by the Rules: The European Commission and the Development of State Aid Policy*' 36 J. Com. Mkt. Stud. 55, at 60.
21. W. Mederer 'Evolution of State aid control' *supra*.
22. Case C184/11 *Commission v. Spain* [2014] ECLI-316, paragraph 70. See also Case C-126/97 *Eco Swiss China Time Ltd* v. *Benetton International NV* [1999] ECR I-305 5.that the objective of pursuing undistorted competition is essential for the accomplishment of the tasks entrusted to

for the fulfilment of the internal market but at the same time touches on traditional national interests such as industrial policy and employment. Risky because for national governments strictly applied state aid rules can signify a loss of their political power and autonomy. Therefore, the success of the EU model has to be earned. This can be done in at least three ways: *firstly* the sanctity of the role of the supranational arbiter, the Commission,[23] always needs to be protected; *secondly* the willingness of ALL the Member States to cooperate must be ensured and consequently adequate remedies for dealing with the recalcitrant ones should be provided; and *thirdly* a degree of discretion for the supranational actor to allow it to incorporate and develop legitimate national policy goals so as to avoid defection should be allowed and actually encouraged.

[A] The (Legal) Sanctity of the European Commission's Role

The European Court of Justice consistently emphasises that Article 4(3) TFEU imposes a duty of genuine cooperation on the Member States and the EU institutions when applying EU State aid law. The privileged position of *super partes* arbiter between Member States[24] is preserved in reality through a full transfer of competence. Together with very few other areas, the Commission competence in the area of state aid control cannot be regarded as anything but *pre-emptive* of any residual Member State powers as any kind of national unilateral action would endanger the uniformity and effectiveness of the EU constitutional regime.[25] Such 'field-pre-emption ' in the area of state aid therefore implies that Member States do not have any appreciable discretion when acting within the remit of the supranational arbiter – the Commission – as the Treaty operated a full transfer of competence. In its case law, the European Court of Justice repeated over and over its mantra that *'the assessment of the compatibility of aid measures with the common market falls within the exclusive competence of the Commission, subject to review by the Courts of the European Union'*.[26] This approach is exemplified by the case law of the Court where it did not hesitate in alienating some of its more trusted allies, the national courts, so as to preserve the Commission's role.

the EU, and that the functioning of the internal market is to be considered as an *orde public* rule that has to be applied fully by all national institutions.

23. *See* Case C-404/97 *Commission v. Portugal* [2000] ECR I-4897, paragraph 40.See also Case C-499/99 *Commission v. Spain* [2002] ECR I-6031, paragraph 24; Case C-278/00 *Greece v. Commission* [2004] ECR I-3997, paragraph 114; Case C-261/99 *Commission v. France* [2001] ECR 2001 I-2537, paragraph 24; Case C-378/98 *Commission v. Belgium* [2001] ECR I-5107, paragraph 31; Case 52/84 *Commission v. Belgium* [1986] ECR 89, paragraph 16.
24. No one is so naïve to suggest that the Commission is totally waterproof from political influence or in some cases politically biased. As in any form of government, independence and transparency although obvious, are not always easy to achieve. However, in all fairness DC Competition which is in charge of state aid policy is a well-respected segment of the European Commission, with officials of outstanding expertise. See further M.P. Smith, *How Adaptable is the European Commission? The Case of State Aid Regulation* 21 J. Pub. Pol. 219.
25. R. Schutze, *Supremacy without Preemption? The Very Slowly Emergence Doctrine of Community Pre-emption* 43 Com. Mkt L. Rev. (2006), 1036, at 1040.
26. Case C-39/94 *SFEI and Others* [1996] ECR I-3547, paragraph 42; Joined Cases C-261/01 and C-262/01 *van Calster and Others* [2003] ECR I-12249, paragraph 75, and Case C-368/04 *Transalpine Ölleitung in Österreich* [2006] ECR I-9957, paragraphs 37–38.

National courts have been denied their more powerful weapon -direct effect- to get instead a sort of ancillary role as a 'temporary' guarantor of state aid control before the Commission's final and decisive intervention.[27] For instance in the recent *Deutsche Lufthansa* ruling, the Court reaffirmed that if the Commission has already started the formal examination procedure of a possible aid measure then courts must refrain from taking decisions which conflict with a decision of the Commission, even if it is provisional.[28] The most striking example however, is the *Lucchini* judgment.[29] In that case the CJEU found that Italian provisions ensuring the principle of res judicata must not be applied in so far as their application prevented the exercise of an EU right, the recovery of State aid granted in breach of EU law. The Court held that '*the assessment of the compatibility of aid measures or of an aid scheme with the common market falls within the exclusive competence of the Commission, subject to review by the Community Courts. That rule applies within the national legal order as a result of the principle of the primacy of Community law.*'[30] As State aid is an area of centralised competence, it was logical that the Court, despite being confronted with a question dealing with an extremely relevant principle of national law – the finality of judgments – expressed in the strongest of terms the supremacy of the EU legal order over the domestic one.[31]

The pre-emptive effect of state aid constitutional supremacy is expressed by Advocate General Cruz Villaon, when referring to *Lucchini*, that in a context '*procedurally national but functionally and substantively Community proceedings, it was, therefore, possible for a judgment to be given which, from the point of view of national law, was without doubt final but which, in the context of the, substantively speaking, Community proceedings, was deprived of all legal effect*'.[32] In *Köbler* - the first case where liability for breaching EU law on account of judicial acts of courts of final resort was first raised, the United Kingdom submitted an extremely powerful argument maintaining that the liability of a Member State cannot be incurred in the case of a breach of EU law attributable to a court.[33] It relied on arguments based on res judicata, the principle of legal certainty, the independence of the judiciary, the judiciary's place in the Community legal order and so on. No such challenge was mounted in *Lucchini* as this latter judgment was conducive to the preservation of the impartiality/market efficiency role of the Commission. The Court itself made it clear that the supremacy/pre-emption *rationale* used in *Lucchini* cannot be automatically transplanted from state aid control to other areas of EU law or to any other situation. It consistently held that '*European Union law does not in all circumstances require a national court to disapply domestic rules of procedure conferring the force of* res judicata *on a judgment, even if to do so would make it possible to remedy an infringement of*

27. Case C-199/06 *CELF and Ministre de la Culture v. SIDE* [2008] ECR I-469, paragraph 38.
28. Case C-284/12 *Deutsche Lufthansa* ECLI:EU:C:2013:755, paragraphs 34–35.
29. Case C-119/05 *Ministero dell'Industria, del Commercio e dell'Artigianato v. Lucchini SpA, formerly Lucchini Siderurgica SpA* [2007] ECR I-6199.
30. *Ibid.* paragraphs 61–62.
31. A. Biondi, *The Lucchini Judgment* 45 Com. Mkt L. Rev. 1459 (2008).
32. Opinion of AG Cruz Villalon in Case C-507/08 *Commission v. Slovakia* [2010] ECR I-13489, paragraph 49.
33. Case C-224/01 *Köbler* [2003] ECR I-10239.

European Union law by the judgment in question'.[34] However, the robust stance exemplified in *Lucchini* will bite anytime the constitutional protection afforded to state aid control via specific administrative tasks entrusted to the Commission could be endangered.

[B] All Member States Must Cooperate: The Stick

A model of direct administration works only and in so far as all the interested parties collaborate equally and fairly. Thus it is remarkable to note that state aid control is even *procedurally* and *remedially* an area where EU law pre-empts Member State discretion. Let us take the sanction par excellence in the instance of a Member State's failure to cooperate: the action for recovery.[35] In the case of unlawful State aid, that is to say when the aid measure has not been notified, the Commission can decide that the Member State must take all necessary measures to recover the aid from the beneficiary in accordance with its national procedures. As the Court has repeatedly held, recovery of unlawful aid is the logical consequence of the finding that it is unlawful.[36] Consequently, the Member State obligation lies in the actual recovery of the sums owed in order to eliminate the distortion of competition caused by the competitive advantage procured by the unlawful aid.[37] Therefore, the action for recovery has as its only aim the achievement of a very specific outcome. In several instances, Member States have actually attempted to argue that the key consideration is not whether recovery is actually achieved, but whether the measures taken have the capacity *in abstracto* to ensure compliance. The case law does not support such a contention. Recovery presupposes an *obligation de résultat précis,* not one *de moyens.*[38] The Court always draws a clear distinction between means, the choice of which is with the Member State (which is the addressee of a recovery decision) to make in accordance with its own

34. Case C-234/04 *Kampferer* [2006] ECR I-258 and Case C-2/08 *Fallimento Olimpiclub* [2009] ECR I-7501.Even in the area of state aid, if the national court decision became final before the Commission decision, *Lucchini* rationale does not apply. C-507/08 *Commission v. Slovakia supra.*
35. See Sir J. Lever, *Some Procedural Conundrums in State Aid Law,* in A. Biondi, P. Eechout & J. Flynn, *The Law of State aid in the EU,* Chapter 16 (OUP 2004) and in general Righini, *Godot is Here: Recovery as an Effective State Aid Remedy,* in Liber amicorum Francisco Santaolalla Gadea, *EC State Aid Law,* Kluwer Law International, 2008, 200.
36. Case C-75/97 *Belgium v. Commission* [1999] ECR I-3671, paragraph 83.
37. With regard to the specific rules on the action for recovery, these are now contained in Article 14(1) of the Procedural Regulation Procedural Regulation of 2013 [OJ L 204 of 31.07.2013, p. 15 amending Council Regulation (EC) No. 659/1999,1]. Article 14(3) of the Procedural Regulation in particular provides that: '*Without prejudice to any order of the Court of Justice of the European Communities pursuant to Article 201 TFEU of the Treaty, recovery shall be effected without delay and in accordance with the procedures under the national law of the Member State concerned, provided that they allow the immediate and effective execution of the Commission's decision. To this effect and in the event of a procedure before national courts, the Member States concerned shall take all necessary steps which are available in their respective legal systems, including provisional measures, without prejudice to Community law*'.
38. Case C-527/12 *Commission v. Germany* [2014]. ECLI: EU: C: 2014:2193.

internal rules,[39] and the result, that is ensuring the effectiveness of EU law.[40] Thus the '*measures taken by the Member State must lead to the actual recovery of the sums owed*'.[41] The case law provides that recovery should be executed according to rules available in national law. However, such a *renvoi* to the domestic legal system should not be understood as softening the need to ensure a full and complete recovery. The objective character of the recovery action is also demonstrated by the fact that the discretionary choice that is in theory vested in Member States – that is to say the choice to decide which procedure the Member State should apply to execute a recovery decision – is in reality very limited. The Court requires only that in so far as the procedure laid down by national law is applicable to the recovery of an illegal aid, the relevant provisions of national law must be applied in such a way that the recovery required by EU law is not rendered practically impossible and the interests of the EU are taken fully into consideration.[42] However, this is not just an apparent minimum guarantee of justiciability, a possibility of ensuring that EU rights can '*be meaningful in practice*.[43] The case law in reality sketches an almost fully EU centralised procedure of recovery. For instance, in the celebrated *Alcan* case[44] the Court held that where the national authorities seek the recovery of State aid found by the Commission to be incompatible with the common market, the recipient cannot rely on the expiry of national time limits to resist an action for repayment. The effect of that judgment was to introduce a procedural norm that time limits are not applicable to an action of recovery, save for the limit established at supranational level. As suggested by Dougan, the CJEU acquis on recovery aid is an example of a line of cases that signals an attempt by the Court to support a highly centralised system of enforcement.[45] Such a long detour to simply state that a uniform 'centralised' recovery remedy is a guarantee for all parties involved.

There is also abundant evidence that action to remedy breaches is being actively taken. For example, since 2000, the Commission has ordered the recovery of illegal State aid in 202 cases across all Member States.[46]

---

39. Case C-549/09 *Commission v. France* [2011] ECR I-155, paragraph 29; and Case C-344/12 *Commission v. Italy* ECLI: EU: C: 2013:667, paragraph 40.
40. Case C-209/00 *Commission v. Germany* [2002] ECR I-11695, paragraph 34; and Case C-507/08 *Commission v. Slovakia* [2010] ECR I-13489, paragraph 51.
41. Case C-207/05 *Commission v. Italy* [2006] ECR I-70, paragraphs 36–37; and Case C-331/09 *Commission v. Poland* [2011] ECR I-2933, paragraph 5.
42. Case 94/87 *Commission v. Germany* [1989] ECR I-175, paragraph 12; Case 5/89 *Commission v. Germany* [1990] ECR I-3437, paragraph 12.
43. Joined Cases C-222-225/05 *Van der Weerd and Others v. Minister van Landbouw, Natuur en Voedselkwaliteit* [2007] ECR I-4233, Opinion of AG Maduro, paragraph 29.
44. Case C-24/95 *Land Rheinland-Pfalz v. Alcan Deutschland GmbH* [1997] ECR I-1591, paragraphs 34-37.
45. M. Dougan, *National Remedies before the Court of Justice: Issues of Harmonisation and Differentiation* (Hart Publishing 2004), pp. 349.
46. http://ec.europa.eu/competition/state_aid/studies_reports/recovery.html.

Time series on the number of recovery decisions (aid to industry and services) adopted and the situation (until 30/06/2014) on the recovery of the aid.

	2000	*2001*	*2002*	*2003*	*2004*	*2005*	*2006*	*2007*	*2008*	*2009*	*2010*	*2011*	*2012*	*2013*	*2014*
No. of decisions adopted	15	19	26	10	24	13	8	10	13	8	6	12	12	8	3
No. of decisions closed	15	13	25	9	23	11	6	7	10	4	4	7	4	1	0
(A): Total aid to be recovered	357.5	1508.6	2130.6	1126.7	4993.5	428.2	249.2	166.9	3449.5	609.3	148.9	305.2	2776.9	812.1	168.5
(B): Amounts recovered (excl. intrests) of which:	357.5	1501.5	2078.8	1003.5	4990.0	484.7	235.3	88.3	1202.3	574.4	9.5	144.9	1221.0	38.3	0
(a) Principal reimbursed/ or in blocked account	142.5	1412.6	2010.8	957.0	4118.9	484.7	199.6	84.3	1076.1	574.4	9.5	144.9	1221.0	38.3	0
(b) Aid lost in bankruptcy	215.0	88.9	68.0	46.5	871.1	0.0	35.8	4.0	126.3	0.0	0.0	55.9	647.0	0.0	0
(A)-(B): Amount outstanding	0.0	7.1	51.8	123.2	3.5	–56.5	13.8	78.7	2247.2	34.8	139.5	160.3	1555.9	773.8	168.5

Time series on the number of recovery decisions (aid to industry and services) adopted and the situation (until 30/06/2014) on the recovery of the aid.

	2000	*2001*	*2002*	*2003*	*2004*	*2005*	*2006*	*2007*	*2008*	*2009*	*2010*	*2011*	*2012*	*2013*	*2014*
% still pending to be recovered	0%	0%	2%	11%	0%	0%	6%	47%	65%	6%	94%	53%	56%	95%	100%
Aid amounts incl. interests registered in bankruptcy	0	10.9	2.9	3.0	0.3	7.9	0	100.6	418.5	15	29.54	91.47	23.8.8	0	0
Recovery interests	9.3	267.7	374.1	359.8	1446.8	94.8	50.7	20.2	331.5	7.5	1.7	14.6	75.8	12.9	0

Of those, only four were UK measures. This compares with a total of nine in Belgium, twenty in France, fifty in Germany, forty-one in Italy, nine in the Netherlands, and twenty-seven in Spain. To strengthen the recovery procedure even further, an almost de facto automatic fine attached to the failure to recover unlawful aid also increases the effective application of state aid rules. In the case of a failure to recover the sum, the Commission can routinely bring an action against the defaulting Member State under Articles 258 and 259 TFEU. In the instance of a total failure to comply with a Court ruling finding that the state had to recover the aid, Article 260(2) TFEU provides that the Commission can bring a second action asking for the imposition of a *lump sum or penalty payment to be paid by the Member State concerned which it considers appropriate in the circumstances.*[47] There have been several cases dealing with failure to recover unlawful aid and in all of them the Court decided in favour of the imposition of sanctions on the defaulting Member States.[48]

Once again the system is as far from perfect as it is laborious, sometimes heavily dependent on the vagaries of national procedural law and other forms of redress, such as actions in damages by competitors might be more effective.[49] Nonetheless, the action for recovery is one of the very few examples of an EU uniform procedural system acting as a deterrent for defecting states and a rather reassuring guarantee for the loyal ones.

§15.06 DIRECT ADMINISTRATION AND FLEXIBILITY: THE CARROT

It would be wrong to characterise state aid rules only in terms of 'sticks' when there is a 'carrot' dimension as well, which is gradually becoming more important. As argued elsewhere, state aid rules have been constantly evolving in response to the geographical, social and economic transformation of Europe.[50] In recent years the Commission has fully embraced a more flexible approach so as to ensure that if certain 'worthy' objectives are pursued by the state measure, state aid rules are not be used to block such virtuous intentions. The last decade has therefore seen a robust process of the

47. Despite Article 260(2) TFEU providing the Commission with the right to specify the amount of the lump sum or penalty payment, the Court has consistently stated that the Commission indication is merely a guide, which will not bind the Court. Therefore, both the quantification and the modalities of the payment can be decided entirely by the Court and secondly, the Court reserves for itself the authority to decide whether to condemn the Member State to payment of a financial penalty and/or a lump sum. The two financial sanctions are considered by the CJEU as performing a different function: the penalty payment is an instrument to coerce the State to comply as soon as possible; whilst the imposition of a lump sum is due to the consideration of the effect that a prolonged breach might have on private and public interests. The imposition of both, according to the Court, is necessary when the breach of the obligation to comply has continued for a long time and tends to persist. Case C-304/02 *Commission v. France* [2005] ECR I-6263.
48. See Case C-369/07, *Commission v. Greece,* [ECR] 2009 I-5703 and Case C-496/09 *Commission v. Italy,* [ECR] 2011 I-11483; and Case C-529/09 *Commission v. Spain ECLI*: EU: C: 2013:31; and Case C184/11 *Commission v. Spain* [2014] ECLI: EU: C: 2014:316.
49. J. Temple Lang, *EU State Aid Rules – The Need for Substantive Reform* Eur. St. Aid L. Q. (2014) 440.
50. A. Biondi & E. Righini, *An Evolutionary Theory of State Aid Control*, in *The Oxford Handbook of European Law,* Chapter 12 (A. Arnull & D. Chalmers OUP 2015).

replacement of individual ad hoc state aid decisions with general criteria codified in a varied list of soft law instruments such as guidelines, notices, etc. This has created a general framework that attempts to foster good business practice and competiveness whilst allowing Member States the flexibility to pursue such policies.[51] The recent European Commission modernisation plan of State aid control[52] and its implementation is particularly revealing. It speaks of targeting its policies at making Europe 'a smart, sustainable and inclusive economy with the objective of enabling the EU and its Member States to deliver high levels of employment, productivity and social cohesion'. It advocates that public spending should become more efficient, effective and targeted at growth-promoting policies that fulfil common European objectives. By putting an emphasis on the quality and the efficiency of public support, State aid should therefore be conceived as an instrument able to help strengthen budgetary discipline and to improve the quality of public finances, thereby reconciling the role of targeted public spending in generating growth with the need to bring budgets under control. To the Commission's credit, it has translated its rhetoric into practice in a relatively short period of time, revising many of the areas of state intervention; from research, development and innovation, to risk capital, broadband, regional aid, aviation, energy and environment.[53] The Commission has also proposed the revision of the Enabling Regulation, approved by the Council in 2013, on the basis of which the Commission has adopted an enlarged General Block Exemption Regulation (GBER)[54] whose scope now extends to block exemptions of certain categories of aid that are 'good' a priori as they are considered conducive to achieve the aims listed above. For instance, these categories include aid for innovation, culture, natural disasters, sport, certain broadband infrastructure, social aid for transport to remote regions and aid for certain agriculture, forestry and fisheries issues.

It could of course be argued that eventually the Commission's strategy simply means extending its control over many new areas. Devolving powers to Member States could instead reflect an attempt to ensure a viable partnership between the Commission and Member States. It seems that the UK government has often made good use of such a cooperative relationship. First, it played by the rules by fully complying with the duty to notify to the Commission of any potential state aid measures. Actually, in a perhaps well-calculated strategy, the number of 'British' notifications has steadily increased over the years. State aid approval requests from the UK to the Commission rose from twenty-nine in 2013 to forty-one in 2014. In 2010, only thirteen applications

51. See further O. Ştefan, *Hybridity before the Court: A Hard Look at Soft Law in the EU Competition and State Aid Case Law* 37 Eur. L. Rev. 49 (2012) and M. Blauberger, *Of 'Good' and 'Bad' Subsidies: European State Aid Control through Soft and Hard Law*, 32 W. Eur. Pol. 719 (2009).
52. Communication from the Commission to the European Parliament, the Council, the European Economic and Social Committee and the Committee of the Regions, COM (2012) 209 Final, 8 May 2012.
53. For a list of the measures adopted see www.ec.europa.eu/competition/state_aid/modernisation/index_en.html.
54. Commission Regulation (EU) No. 651/2014 of 17 Jun. 2014 declaring certain categories of aid compatible with the internal market in application of Articles 107 and 108 TFEU, OJ L 187, 26 Jun. 2014, pp. 1–78.

were made.[55] Of course such an increase can be due to economic difficulties as the UK government feels that financial support is needed now more than ever.[56] In my view, it shows a capability of using EU rules cleverly and in a manner that is also conducive to innovative and socially responsible economic policies. As for the clever usage, a rapid survey of recent UK - Commission state aid dealings shows clearly that in the vast majority of cases, the UK managed to have its state aid measures approved or classified as non-aid.

As for the subject matter of the measures notified, UK policies are mostly in line with EU policy on state aid rules, carefully matching the Commission orientations. For instance, in authorising state aid control, the Commission uses a two part test: firstly, it considers whether the aid is aimed at a well-defined object of common interest, and secondly, it performs a balancing exercise as to whether the proposed aid is a 'well designed instrument' which will deliver the objective of common interest. Such a discretionary assessment is obviously guided by consideration of the rationales that have driven the Member State in question to adopt a certain measure. These are usually efficiency rationales (correcting market failures) i.e., in certain circumstances free markets do not result in an efficient (or welfare maximising) outcome leading to a 'market failure'. State intervention then needs to be appropriate in order to correct the market failure.[57] The second can be branded equity rationale (redistribution/cohesion) – the outcome of the market process is efficient, but may not be socially acceptable. State intervention may then be appropriate for redistributive purposes.[58] Let us now confront these general orientations with two recent UK measures. The first concerned support of up to GBP 400 million to be provided by the United Kingdom for the creation of a social investment company called Big Society Capital (BSC). The object of BSC was to invest in social companies, so called Social Investment Finance Intermediaries (SIFIs) that had difficulties in procuring affordable funding from the markets. The UK authorities never denied in their notification the presence of several aid elements: the capitalisation of BSC through public monies and other advantages for the investees, mainly SIFIs, and finally at the level of the social end recipients of the investment. However, in an extremely well documented notification, the UK demonstrated how the measures were going to be necessary to fill the gap in a sector where the market did not provide adequate support for social activities. Relying on clear evidence showing how this sector was plagued by capital shortage and misperception of the risk/return relationship (meaning basically that banks were not likely to invest and that applications for funding were always rejected) the UK managed to persuade the Commission of the necessity of granting extra financial support.

55. According to Thomson Reuters legal business, which requested the data under the Freedom of Information Act as reported in The Global Legal Post, 17 Mar. 2015.
56. L. Hancher interviewed for S. Gordon, 'Sharp Rise in State Aid Approval Requests, study shows' in the Financial Times of 15 Mar. 2014.
57. D. Neven, & V. Verouden, *Towards a More Refined Economic Approach in State Aid Control*, in W. Mederer, N. Pesaresi & M. Van Hoof, *supra* and in general H.W. Friederiszick, L.-H. Roeller & V. Verouden (2007). *European State Aid Control: An Economic Framework, Handbook of Antitrust Economics. Massachusetts: MIT Press.*
58. T. Kleiner & A. Alexis, 'Politique des aides d Etat: une analyse economique plus fine au service de l interet commun, 4 *Concurrences*, 2005, 45.

As far as the necessity to pursue a common interest, an economic sector always singled out by the Commission as worthy of protection is aid for SMEs 'the backbone of the EU economy'.[59] Not only does the Block Exemption Regulation exempt aid granted in favour of SMEs from the obligation to notify but also the Commission has adopted a series of positive measures to incentivise this specific category of business. For instance, it adopted new rules on risk finance rules aimed at enhancing the incentives of private sector investors - including institutional ones – to invest and increase their funding activities in the area of SME financing.[60] The second example therefore can be drawn from a UK notification dealing with the British Business Bank (BBB), an integrated entity for managing SME access to finance programmes in the UK.[61] This structure was split in three parts: the Mandated Arm, Service Arm and Commercial Arm, providing distinct services. It is also planned that certain already existing programmes supporting SMEs will be integrated within the respective arms of the BBB. The BBB was also to manage new SME access to finance programmes. The UK considered that the whole scheme would have ensured a more effective deployment of programmes to support SMEs in their growth and thereby contribute to economic development and job creation. The Commission approved the measure and allowed the Mandated Arm of BBB to receive up to GBP 6 billion funding from the UK on a non-commercial basis for a certain period of years. Specific focus was devoted in the notification to the fact that the Mandated Arm was entitled to use these funds, within an approved remit, to provide SMEs with access to finance where a market failure was demonstrated, either on commercial terms (through so-called 'market conform schemes' in other words conditions that a private market operator could have accepted) or even on subsidised but non-market terms where that was necessary to ensure general social considerations. The dialogue with the Commission was also conducive to establishing certain conditions and safeguards to avoid any possible distortive effects. For instance, the public financing did not crowd out private finance providers. The Mandated Arm was also allowed to operate subsidised schemes involving state aid measures when that was in conformity with EU common objectives, such as the ones provided by the Commission's General Block Exemption Regulation or those representing participation in EU financial instruments, such as Horizon 2020.[62]

There are of course several controversial cases and decisions. Great media attention has been devoted for instance to the Hinkley Point decision.[63] Under the UK scheme notified to the Commission, the nuclear plant located in Somerset was going to receive stable revenues for a period of thirty-five years. The operator was also going to benefit from a State guarantee covering any debt, which the operator will seek to obtain

59. Communication from the Commission to the Council, the European Parliament, the European Economic and Social Committee and the Committee of the Regions 'Think Small First' A 'Small Business Act' for Europe, COM (2008) 394 Final, 25 Jun. 2008.
60. Guidelines on State aid to promote risk finance investments (2014/C 19/04).
61. SA 36061, JOCE C/460/2014.
62. The Commission also concluded that neither the activities of the Service Arm (which will only provide advice and services to the UK Government) nor those of the Commercial Arm (which will be funded on a commercial basis and will only carry out market conform interventions) involve any state aid, and are therefore not caught by EU state aid control.
63. SA34947, JOCE C/69/2014.

from financial markets to fund the construction of the plant. The Commission found that during the investigation, the UK authorities demonstrated that the support would address a genuine market failure. In particular, the promoters of the project showed, according to the Commission, that they would not have been able to obtain the necessary financing due to the unprecedented nature and scale of the project. The decision caused some concern for its impact on the environment and its inherent unqualified support for nuclear energy.[64] Paradoxically, the Hinckley Point controversy proves this chapter's argument. Energy is certainly one of the most underdeveloped of EU common objectives. In particular the EU rules on state aid in energy markets have for many years been confusing and contradictory. Only recently has the Commission managed to come up with some new guidelines in this sector and their effectiveness is still to be tested. Most importantly, whist renewable energy sources are now subject to at least some form of regulation, nuclear power generation is not.[65] The lack of 'direct administration command' has thus created a gap in supranational control that frees the Member States' selfish interests and increases the pressure on the Commission. However, the solidity of the constitutional framework is confirmed in a very unusual move; Austria has challenged the Commission's decision before the General Court.[66] The power to challenge a positive decision of the Commission has been very rarely exercised[67] and certainly to my knowledge an action brought by a Member State against another Member State measure via a Commission decision is almost unprecedented. The cumulation of the possible defection of a Member State, the alleged lack of scrutiny exercised by the Commission, and possibly the defence of the Austrian green energy market have now demanded judicial adjudication. That is loyalty in practice for you.

§15.07 CONCLUSIONS: STICK AND CARROT

The analysis of state aid control dispels the myth that aid, business and economic developments can exist without the state, it shows that public spending can be used in a rational way and that external control is useful and virtuous. This chapter has perhaps glossed over many problematic aspects: the length of proceedings, the excessive bi-focal dimension of the Commission versus the Member States, the limitation of control mechanisms, the politicisation of the process, the possible negative impact of such a strict regime in terms of global competiveness, etc. It could also be argued, and I agree, that more has to be done. It is clear in the case of the UK

64. Greenpeace defined the Commission decisions as a 'world record sell-out' to the nuclear industry at the expense of taxpayers and the environment. The Guardian, 8th of Oct. 2014.
65. Guidelines on State aid for environmental protection and energy 2014–2020. OJ C 200, 28 Jun. 2014, pp. 1–55. See further A. Wiesbrock, *Sustainable State Aid: A Full Integration of Environmental Protection in State Aid Rules*, in *Greening of European Business under EU Law: Taking Article 11 TFEU Seriously*, 74 (B. Sjåfjell, A. Wiesbrockhe eds, Routdlege 2014).
66. www.world-nuclear-news.org/NN-Austria-files-legal-action-against-Hinkley-Point-project-0607201502.html. An Association of green producers, municipalities and NGOs, also brought a second challenge.
67. See for instance C-279/08P *Netherlands v. Commission* [2011] ECR I-07671.

that a wide range of state policies towards corporate business largely goes undetected and the benefits for consumers and the businesses themselves are far from certain. In the field of taxation especially, the discrepancies between policies to support business welfare and general social welfare are particularly strident.[68] The recent investigations started by the Commission on private tax rulings – sometimes known as 'comfort letters' – that Luxembourg and other Member States signed with corporations allegedly granting favourable tax treatment is a step forward at least making these mechanisms more transparent and accountable.[69] Alleging that those measures had to be classified a state aids – whatever the outcome of the Commission enquiries, succeeded in starting an EU wide debate on aggressive tax practices and generally on public trust in the fairness of national tax systems.[70]

In conclusion, whatever its shortcomings, the supranational system of state aid rules as acknowledged by the unanimity of UK stakeholders themselves, is ultimately a fundamental guarantee to the ability of UK business to take advantage of EU membership to the UK's benefit.[71] Thus to paraphrase Mark Twain it could be concluded from a very UK viewpoint '*Loyalty to the country always. Loyalty to the (EU) government when it deserves it*'.[72]

---

68. See the comments and the statistics contained in K. Farnsworth, Public Policies for private corporations: the British Corporate welfare state, in Renewal, vol. 21, 51.
69. Ireland for Apple Sales International and of Apple Operations Europe; the Netherlands for manufacturing activities of Starbucks Manufacturing EMEA BV Luxembourg for the financing activities of Fiat Finance and Trade Luxembourg for the activities of Amazon, at http://europa.eu/rapid/press-release_IP-14-663_en.htm.
70. See for instance the works of TAXE the new Special Committee of the European Parliament on Tax Rulings and Other Measures Similar in Nature or Effect (TAXE). Its tasks is to 'look into tax ruling practices [...], but will also review the way the European Commission treats state aid in member states and the extent to which they are transparent about their tax rulings'. http://www.europarl.europa.eu/committees/en/taxe/home.html.
71. HM Government, Review of the Balance of Competences between the United Kingdom and the European Union Competition and Consumer Policy Report, 22 Jul. 2014.
72. M. Twain, *The Czar's Soliloquy* North American Review, 1905, 321, p. 324.

CHAPTER 16

Differentiated Integration and the Single Supervisory Mechanism: Which Way Forward for the European Banking Authority?

Pierre Schammo

§16.01 INTRODUCTION

The year 2014 will be remembered as a year of considerable change in the banking field. It saw the coming into force of the Single Supervisory Mechanism (SSM) – the EU's 'first step towards a banking union'.[1] The SSM will place the European Central Bank (ECB) at the heart of a new system of banking supervision.[2] It will bring about a higher level of integration in bank supervision. Crucially, however, it will not cover the whole of the EU. It will be limited to Eurozone countries and (non-euro) Member States that decide to join the SSM.

1. Recital (12) Council Regulation (EU) No. 1024/2013 of 15 Oct. 2013 conferring specific tasks on the European Central Bank concerning policies relating to the prudential supervision of credit institutions [2013] OJ L 287/63. *See also* recital (2) Regulation (EU) No. 1022/2013 of the European Parliament and of the Council of 22 Oct. 2013 amending Regulation (EU) No. 1093/2010 establishing a European Supervisory Authority (European Banking Authority) as regards the conferral of specific tasks on the European Central Bank pursuant to Council Regulation (EU) No. 1024/2013 [2013] OJ L 287/5 (hereinafter, 'EBA Amending Regulation').
2. For first contributions on the SSM, *see* E. Ferran & V. Babis, *The European Single Supervisory Mechanism*, 13 J. Corp. L. Stud. 255 (2013); R. Lastra, *Banking Union and Single Market: Conflict or Companionship* 36 Fordham Intl L. J. 1190 (2013); E. Wymeersch, *The Single Supervisory Mechanism or 'SSM', Part One of the Banking Union* (ECGI Law Working Paper No. 240/2014, February 2014); G. Ferrarini & L. Chiarella, *Common Banking Supervision in the Eurozone: Strengths and Weaknesses* (ECGI Law Working Paper No. 223/2013, August 2013); T. Tröger, *The Single Supervisory Mechanism – Panacea or Quack Banking Regulation?* (SAFE Working Paper Series No. 27, Oct. 2013).

Because of its limited scope, the SSM is an example of differentiated integration. A term of many meanings,[3] it describes the basic idea of variation among states which pursue integration: some deciding to join in initiatives advancing integration of which others decide to abstain. In the context of the SSM, these latter Member States (non-participating Member States or NoPS) – most prominently the UK – will not be part of the SSM. Nevertheless, NoPS will interact closely with Member States which are part of the SSM: for instance within the European System of Financial Supervision (ESFS) which covers the whole of the EU. Interactions will be especially close within the European Banking Authority (EBA) which is part of the ESFS and which, unlike the SSM, brings together competent authorities from all of the twenty-eight Member States. The point about these interactions is worth noting. They prompted the EU legislature to review the regulation governing EBA (the EBA Regulation) and amend the voting arrangements governing decision-making within EBA substantially.[4] The aim of this chapter is to reflect on these changes. They are indeed open to criticism. They are short sighted and, crucially, fail to give sufficient consideration to the functioning of EBA. This chapter therefore evaluates alternative approaches, by focussing in particular on the governance of EBA. The aim is to find a better balance between the interests of Member States, whose competent authorities are the main decision-makers in EBA, and the objective of ensuring that EBA functions properly. Specifically, this chapter will argue that the way forward is to rethink EBA's governance more fundamentally. It will set out the basic requirements of such an approach.

Underpinning much of the discussion that follows are a number of observations. The adoption by the EU legislature of changes to EBA's decision-making arrangements during the negotiations of the SSM was widely hailed as a significant political achievement for the UK government. The UK not only feared externalities from closer integration among Eurozone Member States. As a NoPS, it was also concerned about losing influence within EBA. Specifically, the UK feared the prospect of 'caucusing' among members of the SSM. Given that a majority of EBA members originate from SSM Member States, the UK felt that its interests in EBA were at risk. From the UK's standpoint, substantial changes to EBA's decision-making arrangements were necessary, a view which was ultimately accepted by the EU legislature. The adoption of these changes can therefore be described as an illustration of what the UK can achieve politically as a Member State which decides to *remain* within the EU, but prefers to stay clear of further integration. As far as the general narrative of the present book is concerned, the situation which I examine hereinafter is thus one that is closer to a 'partial withdrawal' or a 'partial exit' than a 'total exit' by the UK from the EU. However, like total exit, such a situation has implications and consequences: not only for the UK (or for that matter, any other NoPS) but also for the EU and in my case for EU decision-making bodies such as EBA which ultimately depend for their functioning

3. E.g., A. Stubb, *A Categorization of Differentiated Integration*, 34 J. Com. Mkt Stud. 283 (1996).
4. Regulation (EU) No. 1093/2010 of the European Parliament and of the Council of 24 Nov. 2010 establishing a European Supervisory Authority (European Banking Authority), amending Decision No. 716/2009/EC and repealing Commission Decision 2009/78/EC [2010] OJ L331/12, as amended.

on NoPS *and* SSM members. These consequences must not be forgotten. They must be examined and they must be subject to a proper debate.

The chapter proceeds as follows. Section 2 begins by presenting the SSM and the ESFS. It focuses in particular on the role of the ECB under the SSM and the role of EBA under the ESFS. Section 3 goes on to examine the way in which the EU legislature dealt with the concerns of NoPS. Given the importance of EBA as a place of interaction between NoPS and SSM members, it will mostly focus on the changes that were made to the EBA Regulation. Section 4 discusses alternative solutions for dealing with the SSM problematic within EBA. Section 5 concludes.

§16.02 THE SINGLE SUPERVISORY MECHANISM AND THE EUROPEAN SYSTEM OF FINANCIAL SUPERVISION: INTRODUCING THE ECB AND EBA

The aim of this section is to present the SSM and the ESFS, and more specifically the role of the ECB under the former **(A)**, and the role of EBA under the latter **(B)**. Both actors are active in the banking field. But even though they have different roles under the SSM and the ESFS respectively, the establishment of the SSM will bring them into close contact **(C)**.

[A] The SSM and the ECB

The establishment of the SSM must be seen in light of the EU's efforts to stabilise the Eurozone following the 2007–2008 financial crisis and the subsequent sovereign debt crisis. In June 2012, Eurozone leaders called for the establishment of the SSM in order to achieve a greater level of integration in banking supervision, but also as a condition for a possible direct recapitalisation of troubled banks by the European Stability Mechanism.[5] The SSM brings together competent authorities of participating Member States. The latter are Member States of the Eurozone. However, non-euro zone Member States are also allowed to join, provided that they enter into a close cooperation arrangement with the ECB.[6] The ECB is at the heart of the SSM. It is not only responsible 'for the effective and consistent functioning of the SSM',[7] but it is also a day-to-day supervisor which was vested with prudential supervisory tasks. The latter are specified in Council Regulation No. 1024/2013.[8] Overall, the SSM supervisory model can be described as based on an 'uploading' and 'unloading' of supervisory tasks: 'uploading' because the ECB will directly supervise credit institutions as a result of the establishment of the SSM;[9] 'unloading' because the ECB in its role as prudential

5. Euro Area Summit Statement (29 Jun. 2012) http://www.consilium.europa.eu/uedocs/cms_data/docs/pressdata/en/ec/131359.pdf.
6. Article 7, Council Regulation No. 1024/2013.
7. Article 6(1).
8. *Supra* n. 1.
9. For a description of the ECB's tasks, *see* Articles 4 and 5. Note that I use the term 'credit institution' or 'bank' hereinafter for convenience purposes. The more accurate concept is

supervisor will need to rely on the expertise and work of national authorities (e.g., to carry out day-to-day verifications)[10] and because the ECB will only directly supervise a fraction of credit institutions, i.e., those that are considered to be sufficiently significant. 'Less significant' institutions will as a general rule be supervised by the authorities of participating Member States.[11] The 'significance' of a credit institution is determined according to criteria set out in Council Regulation No. 1024/2013 which are further specified in an ECB framework regulation.[12] Council Regulation No 1024/2013 makes it plain that a bank should generally 'not be considered less significant' – and hence *be* subject to direct supervision by the ECB – in one of the following scenarios: the total value of its assets is more than EUR 30 billion; the ratio of its total assets over the GDP of the participating Member State represents more than 20% 'unless the total value of its assets is below EUR 5 billion'; or where a national competent authority notifies the ECB that it considers an institution to be of significant domestic economic relevance and the ECB, after evaluation, confirms its significance.[13] An institution must also be considered significant where public financial assistance has been requested or received 'directly from the ESFS or the ESM'.[14] The regulation also provides for the ECB to consider of its own initiative an institution to be significant in case where the latter operates across the border by way of subsidiaries in at least one participating Member States and where its cross-border assets or liabilities 'represent a significant part of its total assets or liabilities'.[15] Finally, the regulation requires the ECB to carry out its supervisory tasks in relation to the 'three most significant credit institutions' in each participating Member State 'unless justified by particular circumstances'.[16]

As noted above, banks that are not subject to the ECB's direct supervision will continue being supervised by the authorities of participating Member States. But even in this case, the ECB will solely be competent to: (i) authorise or withdraw the authorisation of a credit institution, and (ii) assess the notifications of the acquisition and disposal of holdings in credit institutions.[17] In addition, even where direct supervision rests with the authorities of participating Member States, the latter are subject to the authority of the ECB, which has also an oversight role to play.[18] Indeed, the regulation goes as far as providing for a sort of ad hoc 'uploading' of oversight

'supervised entity' which is defined in Regulation (EU) No 468/2014 of the European Central Bank of 16 April 2014 establishing the framework for cooperation within the Single Supervisory Mechanism between the European Central Bank and national competent authorities and with national designated authorities [2014] OJ L141/1, Article 2(20) (the 'SSM Framework Regulation').

10. Recital (37).
11. Article 6(4). *See also* recital (38).
12. Council Regulation No. 1024/2013 refers to size, importance for the economy, or significance of cross-border activities (*see* Article 6(4) sub-paragraph 1). Significance is established on an individual or consolidated basis. Note that a branch opened in a participating Member State by a credit institution established in a NoPS will also be subject to assessment as a supervised entity under the criteria set out in Article 6(4).
13. Article 6(4) sub-paragraph 2, point (i)-(iii).
14. Article 6(4), sub-paragraph 4.
15. Article 6(4) sub-paragraph 3.
16. Article 6(4) sub-paragraph 5.
17. Article 6(4).
18. Article 6(5)(c).

powers when allowing the ECB to take over the supervision of a credit institution which would otherwise be subject to national supervision.[19]

[B] The ESFS and EBA

The ESFS was created in 2010 as a response to the financial crisis and the recommendations of the *de Larosière* group, a group of experts set up by the Commission in 2008 in order to look into financial supervision.[20] Its main aim is to make sure that EU rules in the financial sector are properly implemented.[21] To meet its objectives, the ESFS brings together different actors: at macro-prudential level, the European Systemic Risk Board (ESRB) was established, a body without legal personality, which deals with macro-prudential oversight of the financial system.[22] At micro-prudential level, new European supervisory authorities (ESA) were established: the European Securities and Markets Authority (ESMA), the European Insurance and Occupational Pensions Authority (EIOPA) and of course the European Banking Authority (EBA).[23] The latter is the ESA that is active in the banking field. Its membership reflects the fact that unlike the SSM, the ESFS covers the whole of the EU. Thus, the main decision-makers within EBA are competent authorities from the twenty-eight Member States. They are the voting members of EBA's Board of Supervisors, the main forum of decision-making.[24]

Turning to EBA's role under the ESFS, the first point to note is that EBA has an important role to play in rule making. It participates in the creation of a so-called single rulebook.[25] For this purpose, it is vested with the power to develop draft technical standards, which are formally adopted by the Commission.[26] EBA is also responsible for developing a so-called European supervisory handbook;[27] it is supposed to monitor and assess market developments[28] and it has an increasingly important role to play in relation to bank resolution and recovery.[29] Crucially however EBA is not a day-to-day supervisor. In contrast to the ECB, the EBA model is not currently based on an 'uploading' of day-to-day supervisory tasks. Instead of a fully fledged transfer of competences, the EBA 'supervisory'[30] model is based on possible ad hoc interventions. These interventions are supposed to take place vis-à-vis competent authorities and possibly market actors in the case of: (i) disagreements between competent authorities; (ii) breaches of EU law; (iii) emergency situations; or (iv) if it is necessary to

19. Article 6(5)(b).
20. The high-level group on financial supervision in the EU, Report (2009), http://ec.europa.eu/internal_market/finances/docs/de_larosiere_report_en.pdf.
21. Article 2(1), EBA Regulation.
22. Article 2(2).
23. *Ibid.*
24. Article 40(1).
25. As called for by the European Council, 18/19 Jun. 2009 (11225/2/09 Rev 2, 10 Jul. 2009), paragraph 20, http://www.consilium.europa.eu/uedocs/cms_data/docs/pressdata/en/ec/108622.pdf.
26. Articles 10–15, EBA Regulation.
27. Article 8(1)(aa). The ECB on the other hand will develop a so-called supervisory manual.
28. Article 8(1)(f).
29. Article 8(1)(i).
30. I am using the term 'supervision' loosely.

temporarily ban or limit financial activities.[31] The thrust of these intervention powers is that they are binding and allow EBA to intervene in the relationship between competent authorities, or more exceptionally, in the relationship between competent authorities and market actors. However, the possibility of ad hoc interventions is nevertheless limited. The provisions are carefully worded and EBA's intervention will be subject to various conditions and requirements which are specified in the EBA Regulation and in sectoral legislation.[32]

[C] Interactions between EBA and the ECB following the Establishment of the SSM

The fact that the ECB and EBA are different actors with different roles does not mean that they do not interact. For one thing, both are active in the banking field and it is expected that EBA's activities in the area of a single rulebook, a supervisory handbook and stress testing will bring them in close contact.[33] There might also be a need to coordinate their activities at the international level.[34] Moreover, recall that Member States which participate in the SSM also participate in the ESFS, a point to which I will return hereinafter. Crucially as far as the ECB is concerned, the EBA Regulation now lists the ECB as among actors that are part of the ESFS[35] and includes it within the definition of competent authorities.[36] As a result, the ECB will be subject to the authority of EBA. The latter will be able to carry out its tasks (for instance, its power to settle disagreements or to act in emergency situations) with respect to the ECB 'as in relation to the other competent authorities'.[37] The ECB will also be subject to the technical standards which EBA drafts.[38] Likewise, it will be subject to EBA's

31. Articles 19, 17, 18 and 9(5), EBA Regulation.
32. For example, under the provisions on settling disagreements, breaches of EU law and emergency situations, EBA's power to intervene in the relationship between a market actor and a competent authority is not envisaged as a first line of response. Rather any such intervention is only possible if the relevant competent authority fails to comply with an EBA decision or, in the case of breaches of EU law, a formal Commission opinion (*see* Articles 17(6), 19(4), 18(4)). The EBA Regulation also enacts a safeguard clause under Article 38. The latter applies in case where EBA takes a decision vis-à-vis a competent authority under its provisions on the settlement of disagreements or emergency situations. Article 38 allows a Member State, which believes that its fiscal responsibilities are affected by this decision, to bring the matter in front of the Council. The latter may then decide the fate of EBA's decision. It is also worth noting that the ambiguous wording of some of these provisions may also limit their usefulness (*see* e.g., in relation to Article 19, A Enria 'The Single Market after the Banking Union' (Speech, Brussels, 18 Nov. 2013) https://www.eba.europa.eu/documents/10180/490003/2013 + 11 + 18 + - + AFME + - + EBF + - + Brussels + - + A + Enria.
33. V. Constâncio, Implications of the SSM on the ESFS (Public Hearing on Financial Supervision in the EU, Brussels, 24 May 2013) http://www.ecb.europa.eu/press/key/date/2013/html/sp1305 24.en.html.
34. *See* in this context Article 8, Council Regulation No. 1024/2013.
35. Article 2(2)(f), EBA Regulation.
36. Article 4(2)(i).
37. Recital (12), EBA Amending Regulation.
38. Article 4(3) ECB Regulation.

guidelines and recommendations and to the provisions of the EBA Regulation on the EU supervisory handbook.[39]

§16.03 THE ESTABLISHMENT OF THE SSM: THE APPROACH TO NOPS

Section 2 introduced the ECB's and EBA's role under the SSM and the ESFS respectively. This section turns to the core issues which this chapter examines: that is, the concerns which NoPS raised about the establishment of the SSM and the changes which the EU legislature made to the EBA Regulation in order to respond to these concerns. Recall that while NoPS do not participate in the SSM, they interact closely with members of the SSM in EBA whose membership extends to the whole of the EU. I will begin by examining the concerns which NoPS raised **(A)**, after which I will examine the safeguards which the legislature put in place in favour of NoPS **(B)**.

[A] The SSM Conundrum: The Concerns of NoPS

As noted earlier, NoPS such as the UK, were concerned about the impact which the SSM would have on EBA and on decision-making within EBA.[40] Specifically, they were concerned about the prospect of SSM members increasingly sharing common interests within EBA and NoPS losing influence as a result of 'caucusing' among SSM members.[41] Underpinning these concerns was the view that NoPS and SSM members might in the future have conflicting preferences for different courses of action within EBA: for instance on draft technical standards or on the use of EBA's intervention powers. For NoPS, the issue was especially concerning because the establishment of the SSM results in a membership asymmetry within EBA. Even if the ECB has neither a vote in EBA nor is tasked with expressing a common position among SSM members,[42] EBA's Board of Supervisors – EBA's main decision-making organ – will, following the establishment of the SSM, comprise *voting* members both from within and from outside the SSM. Furthermore, while the SSM will initially be made of the current nineteen Eurozone Member States, the membership of the SSM will increase over time: either because non-euro Member States decide to join the SSM voluntarily; or because they meet the euro entry requirements and are therefore required to join the euro.[43] In terms of EBA's membership this means that the constellation of SSM members and NoPS is

39. *Ibid.*
40. *See* e.g., House of Commons (Foreign Affairs Committee), *The Future of the European Union: UK Government Policy* (Volume I, 11 Jun. 2013), http://www.publications.parliament.uk/pa/cm201314/cmselect/cmfaff/87/87.pdf, 45 noting that the SSM 'raised questions about the rights of non-Eurozone states in the European Banking Authority (EBA)'.
41. Evidence of these concerns can be found in various reports: *see ibid.* at 7, 42, 46, 47; HM Government, *Review of the Balance of Competences between the United Kingdom and the European Union – The Single Market: Financial Services and the Free Movement of Capital* (2014) https://www.gov.uk/government/uploads/system/uploads/attachment_data/file/332874/2902400_BoC_FreedomOfCapital_acc.pdf, 108.
42. As in the past, an ECB representative will sit on the Board of Supervisors of EBA (Article 40(1)(d) EBA Regulation).
43. The only Member States which benefit from an 'opt-out' are the UK and Denmark.

asymmetrical in the Board of Supervisors and will become increasingly so in the future – hence the concern over caucusing among SSM members.

Admittedly, some might argue that the concerns of NoPS were misplaced. They might note – rightly so – that the precise impact which the SSM will have on the behaviour of EBA's members is yet unknown.[44] They might also argue that at any rate agency members have incentives to cooperate sincerely with one another. This is because – as members of a network – they are concerned about maintaining their reputation vis-à-vis their peers.[45] However, one should caution against overgeneralising such claims. Even though there is a large body of scholarship on EU agencies,[46] actual decision-making dynamics within EU agencies have attracted relatively little attention.[47] At any rate, any view or theory, which is too deterministic of the decision-making dynamics in agencies, is unlikely to capture the full picture. There is much variation among agencies. They operate in a variety of fields, including in fields where there has traditionally been a degree of competition between States. Even matters that are described as technical can have salience at Member State level. As far as EBA and its sister agencies are concerned, recall also that decision-making is firmly in the hands of national authorities: i.e., competent authorities.[48] Whilst the latter are meant to act in the public interest, they have nevertheless distinct organisational objectives and separate self-interest. Even if they are meant to act at arm's length from national governments, they are accountable for their actions at Member State level (e.g., in front of national Parliaments).[49] Hence, because of their national origins and their national accountability lines, it would be wrong to assume that competent authorities have necessarily the right incentives to genuinely cooperate when making

44. Admittedly, concerns over caucusing among Eurozone countries are by no means shared by all. *See*, e.g., the evidence given by Sir Jon Cunliffe, Permanent Representative of the UK to the EU in front of the Foreign Affairs Committee in February 2013 (House of Commons (Foreign Affairs Committee), *The Future of the European Union: UK Government Policy* (Volume II, 11 Jun. 2013), 43–44, http://www.publications.parliament.uk/pa/cm201314/cmselect/cmfaff/87/87ii.pdf).
45. This view is associated with G. Majone, *Dilemmas of European Integration – The Ambiguities & Pitfalls of Integration by Stealth* (OUP 2009) 101. *See also* B. Eberlein & E. Grande, *Beyond Delegation: Transnational Regulatory Regimes and the EU Regulatory State* 12 J. Eur. Pub. Pol. 89, 101 (2005), noting that networks transform national representatives 'from "locals" into "cosmopolitans"' (reference omitted).
46. *See* e.g., the special issue of the J. Eur. Pub. Pol. in 2011 (issue 6). *See also* the early work of R. Dehousse, *Regulation by Networks in the European Community: the Role of European Agencies* 4 J. Eur. Pub. Pol. 246 (1997); G. Majone, *The New European Agencies: Regulation by Information* 4 J. Eur. Pub. Pol. 262 (1997).
47. M. Egeberg & J. Trondal, *EU-level Agencies: New Executive Centre Formation or Vehicles for National Control?* 18 J. Eur. Pub. Pol. 868, 870 (2011).
48. Admittedly, the Commission is also likely to exert influence within agencies (*see ibid*). In relation to the ESA, *see* also F. Demarigny, J. McMahon & N. Robert, *Review of the New European System of Financial Supervision (ESFS) – Part 1*, http://www.europarl.europa.eu/RegData/etudes/etudes/join/2013/507446/IPOL-ECON_ET(2013)507446_EN.pdf, 34, noting that '[i]n practice, discussions and decisions have been heavily influenced by the major NCAs [national competent authorities] and the European Commission'.
49. E.g., P. Schammo, *EU Prospectus Law – New Perspectives on Regulatory Competition in Securities Markets* (CUP 2011) 23-4; Demarigny, McMahon & Robert, *supra* n. 48 at 34.

decisions within the ESAs, especially when salient issues are involved. A number of recent reports lend support to these observations.[50]

To be sure, only time will tell whether NoPS's concerns were justified. In any event, hereinafter, I will adopt assumptions similar to those which underpinned the legislative changes: i.e., that there is room for conflict between NoPS and SSM members and that the prospect of caucusing among SSM members, and the resultant marginalisation of NoPS, was a valid one. I feel free to take this approach because the aim of this chapter is not to question NoPS's assumptions about the decision-making dynamics in EBA following the establishment of the SSM, but instead to assess what ought to be done if these assumptions prove to be accurate. I will begin by examining in more detail the way in which the legislature sought to protect the (minority) interests of NoPS.

[B] The EU Legislature's Approach to NoPS

I will first examine how the EU legislature sought to protect the minority interests of NoPS **(1)**, after which I will examine the relevant provisions critically **(2)**. Given our interest in EBA, I will focus on the safeguards that are found in the EBA Regulation.[51]

50. While it is generally accepted that the ESAs have performed well (e.g., European Commission, *Report from the Commission to the European Parliament and the Council on the operation of the European Supervisory Authorities (ESAs) and the European System of Financial Supervision (ESFS)*, (COM(2014) 509 final) 2), the fact that national interests do matter and that the ESAs are not always places of genuine cooperation has been highlighted in a number of reports. The IMF for instance noted in 2013 that 'national interests may still influence decisions' in EBA (*see* IMF, *European Union: Publication of Financial Sector Assessment Program Documentation – Technical Note on European Banking Authority* (March 2013, IMF Country Report No. 13/74) 7 http://www.imf.org/external/pubs/ft/scr/2013/cr1374.pdf). More recently, the European Parliament noted in its resolution on the review of the European System of Financial Supervision that 'it has been difficult for national representatives to separate their role of head of a national competent authority and European decision-making challenging their ability to genuinely adhere to the requirement to act independently and objectively in the sole interest of the Union as a whole in accordance with Article 42 of the ESA regulations' (*see* European Parliament resolution of 11 Mar. 2014 with recommendations to the Commission on the European System of Financial Supervision (ESFS) Review (A7-0133/2014). In a similar fashion, ESMA's Securities and Markets Stakeholder Group noted that the ESA's governance represented the 'main threat' to the ESA's efficiency and that the composition of the boards of supervisors and management boards 'embed[ded] the interests of national authorities' (*see* ESMA Securities and Markets Stakeholder Group, *SMSG contribution to the ESFS consultation*, (18 Jul. 2013, SMSG/2013/013). 7.
51. A number of 'safeguard' provisions were also added to Council Regulation No. 1024/2013. Article 1 of Council Regulation No. 1024/2013 provides that: 'No action, proposal or policy of the ECB shall, directly or indirectly, discriminate against any Member State or group of Member States as a venue for the provision of banking or financial services in any currency'. The regulation also underlines the importance of maintaining the integrity or unity of the internal market (Article 1; recital (10); recital (30)), in accordance with the conclusions of the European Council (e.g., European Council Conclusions 18/19 Oct. 2012 (EUCO156/12, 19 Oct. 2012), http://www.consilium.europa.eu/uedocs/cms_data/docs/pressdata/en/ec/133004.pdf, paragraphs 6 and 8)). Indeed, the regulation goes as far as saying that the ECB has a 'duty of care for the unity and integrity of the internal market ...' (Article 1).

[1] Safeguards

The EU legislature sought to address the concerns of NoPS over the establishment of the SSM by amending or adding a number of provisions to the EBA Regulation. What they have in common is that they are supposed to protect the interests of NoPS as members of the EU and as members of EBA. The recitals of the EBA Amending Regulation set the tone by highlighting the importance of maintaining the unity or integrity of the internal market, the cohesion of the Union and the need to prevent discrimination.[52] The concerns of NoPS were also addressed in the legally binding text of the EBA Regulation. Thus, following amendment, the EBA Regulation states that EBA must act 'independently, objectively and in a non-discriminatory manner, in the interests of the Union as a whole'.[53] In an attempt to ensure 'unbiased' decision-making, amendments were also made to the provisions on the use of internal panels within EBA.[54] Specifically, the mandatory use of panels was extended. Thus, EBA must now convene a panel when it seeks to use its powers to police breaches of EU law.[55] The purpose of the panel is to propose a decision to the Board of Supervisors. Before amendment, the EBA Regulation already provided for the Board of Supervisors to rely on panels. But a panel had only to be convened when EBA used its powers to settle disagreements.[56]

However, the most noteworthy change in the EBA Regulation concerns the voting rules which apply in EBA's Board of Supervisors. These changes aim to ensure that NoPS continue to have an effective voice in EBA. Recall that the voting members in EBA's Board of Supervisors are competent (national) authorities. Simple majority voting continues to be the basic voting rule in EBA, with each voting member having one vote.[57] As in the past, this basic rule is modified in a number of cases. These cases were reviewed following the establishment of the SSM. Thus, decisions concerning the adoption of draft technical standards, as well as guidelines and recommendations continue to be adopted by a qualified majority, but this qualified majority must now include at least: (i) a simple majority of board members representing competent authorities of Member States which participate in the SSM; and (ii) a simple majority of board members representing competent authorities that are not among these Member States – NoPS in other words.[58] The same rule applies in case where EBA adopts measures under Chapter VI (dealing with budgetary matters) or under the third sub-paragraph of Article 9(5) which applies where EBA temporarily prohibits or

52. Recital (1); recital (10); recital (22), EBA Amending Regulation.
53. Article 1(5) EBA Regulation.
54. Article 41.
55. Article 41(1a).
56. For panels which intervene in the settlement of a disagreement, the regulation adds that the Board of Supervisors shall 'strive for consensus' when deciding on the composition of the panel (Article 44(1)). If no consensus can be found, the Board of Supervisors will be required to take decisions 'by a majority of three quarters of its voting members' (*ibid.*).
57. Article 44(1).
58. *Ibid.*

restricts certain financial activities and a Member State asks EBA to reconsider its decision.[59]

Decisions concerning: (i) breaches of EU law; (ii) the settlement of disagreements between competent authorities; and (iii) actions in emergency situations will be adopted by the Board of Supervisors on the basis of a simple majority of the voting members. However, this majority must now include: (i) a simple majority of board members representing competent authorities of Member States which participate in the SSM; and (ii) a simple majority of board members representing competent authorities that are not among these Member States.[60] As far as EBA's power to settle disagreements or to address breaches of EU law is concerned, the EU legislature added another requirement which will come to affect the voting modalities once the constellation of SSM members and NoPS becomes highly asymmetrical: i.e., in case where the number of NoPS drops to four or less. In this case the double-majority rule will cease to apply. Instead decisions will be taken by a simple majority 'which shall include at least one vote from members from competent authorities of non-participating Member States'.[61] A new review clause was also added to the EBA Regulation.[62] According to the latter, the Commission is required to review and report on the EBA voting arrangements, including those that apply to EBA panels, once the number of NoPS falls to four. To complicate matters further, the EU legislature added a 'soft' consensus principle, according to which the Board of Supervisors 'shall strive for consensus' when making decisions.[63] Finally, the composition of the Management Board now also reflects the new realities of closer integration among SSM members. EBA's Management Board ensures *inter alia* that EBA carries out its mission and its tasks.[64] It is made of the Chairperson and six *voting* members – hence six national authorities – of the Board of Supervisors.[65] Following amendment, the EBA Regulation now states that among the members of the Management Board at least two should be representatives from NoPS.[66]

[2] The Legislature's Approach: An Ill-considered Approach

My aim here is to reflect on the above changes. I will argue that the EU legislature's amendments to the EBA Regulation are open to criticism on at least two grounds: first, because they failed to take account of the lessons of the past; and second, because the EU legislature failed to differentiate meaningfully between the interests of Member States and the proper functioning of EBA.

59. *Ibid.*
60. *Ibid.*
61. Article 44(1) sub-paragraph 4.
62. Article 81a.
63. Article 44(4a).
64. Article 47(1).
65. Article 45(1).
66. Article 45(1).

– Failure to take account of the lessons of the past

In order to examine how the legislature failed to give proper consideration to past lessons, I will begin with the ESAs' predecessors – the so-called Level 3 supervisory committees: the Committee of European Securities Regulators (CESR), the Committee of European Banking Supervisors (CEBS), and the Committee of European Insurance and Occupational Pensions Supervisors (CEIOPS). The Level 3 committees were collective actors.[67] They had no independent, overriding choice over their preferences, but depended on the preferences of national authorities.[68] This could complicate effective decision-making, not least because decisions were initially taken by consensus.[69] Unsurprisingly the consensus principle was modified in 2009. To address the threat of deadlocks or decisions at the lowest common denominator, new arrangements provided for decisions to be taken by qualified majority, but only where no consensus could be reached.[70]

Turning to the ESAs, the first point to note is that at least in one important respect the ESAs are like their predecessors: competent authorities, as voting members of the Board of Supervisors or as members of the Management Board, are the main decision-makers within the ESAs. However there are important differences in terms of decision-making. In particular, when establishing the ESAs, the EU legislature adopted different voting requirements: decisions were as a rule to be adopted by a simple majority. Qualified majority voting was only applicable in specific cases and by way of derogation from the simple majority rule. These changes reflected the lessons of the past. Whilst not abandoning the collective nature of decision-making by competent authorities (as voting members of the ESAs), they reflected attempts to facilitate decision-making in the face of divisions between voting members. The changes proved useful. Especially the new voting requirements made a positive contribution to the functioning of the ESAs.[71]

As we have seen in the previous sub-section, the establishment of the SSM led to a rethink of the voting arrangements in EBA. These arrangements departed significantly from those that the Commission had initially proposed. Indeed in its proposal, the Commission sought to rely more on sub-delegation. It proposed to strengthen the role of independent panels.[72] Panels would be required to propose decisions to the Board of Supervisors not only for the purposes of settling disagreements under Article 19, but also in relation to breaches of EU law under Article 17.[73] As before, the panels would be made of the (full-time) EBA Chairperson and two (voting) members of the

67. Schammo, *supra* n. 49, at 23 (in relation to CESR).
68. On the meaning of collective actors, *see* F. Scharpf, *Games Real Actors Play – Actor-Centered Institutionalism in Policy Research* (Westview Press 1997) 54–55.
69. *See* European Commission, *Public consultation paper on amendments to Commission Decisions establishing CESR, CEBS & CEIOPS*, (23 May 2008), http://ec.europa.eu/internal_market/finances/docs/committees/consultation_en.pdf, 9.
70. E.g., Commission Decision of 23 Jan. 2009 establishing the Committee of European Banking Supervisors [2009] L25/23, Article 14.
71. Demarigny, McMahon & Robert, *supra* n. 48 at 34.
72. *See* European Commission, *Proposal for a Regulation of the European Parliament and of the Council amending Regulation (EU) No 1093/2010 …*, (COM(2012) 512 final, (September 2012).
73. Article 41(2) (as proposed).

Board of Supervisors.[74] Given that EBA's Chairperson is a member of the panel ex officio, members of the Board of Supervisors were left with only two members to appoint to the panel. Under the Commission proposals, at least one of them was supposed to be from a NoPS.[75] Significantly, the Commission proposed that panel decisions be adopted by EBA unless *rejected* by the Board of Supervisors by way of a simple majority. This majority had to include at least three votes from members of States participating in the SSM and three votes from NoPS.[76] It is plain that this 'reverse voting mechanism' would have weakened the influence of the Board of Supervisors over the decisions taken by the independent panel since panel decisions could only be blocked if voting members from within and outside the SSM had a shared interest in doing so.

The EU legislature rejected the Commission's approach. Its response to the establishment of the SSM was to reaffirm the say of board members over EBA's decisions and to cement more forcefully the division between SSM members and NoPS in the voting structure of EBA's Board of Supervisors: we saw the voting arrangements earlier. Thus, the legislature rejected the idea of a reverse voting mechanism and extended the double-majority system. It also strengthened the influence of the Board of Supervisors over the panels. As amended, panels will be made of the Chairperson and six other EBA members who are, according to recital (15) of EBA's Amending Regulation, *voting* members of the Board of Supervisors – hence national authorities. Panel decisions are adopted 'where at least four members vote in favour'.[77] As Ferran and Babis note, the thinking was that by broadening the participation of Member States, the position of the panel would be strengthened.[78] However, by widening participation, these amendments also effectively lessened the influence of the only full-time independent EBA representative: that is EBA's Chairperson. The EU legislature also introduced a general 'soft' consensus principle for decisions taken by the Board of Supervisors. As noted above, the Board of Supervisors must now 'strive for consensus' when making decisions.[79] Although the requirement to strive for consensus is meant to be without prejudice 'to the effectiveness of the Authority's decision-making procedures',[80] for a supposedly technocratic body such as a EBA whose decisions ought to be argument- or evidence based, the merit of the consensus principle is nevertheless questionable – not least because it will make it more complicated to impose decisions in the face of differences between competent authorities.

Hence, in short, the Commission's proposed response to closer integration among Eurozone members was to put greater emphasis on a 'sub-delegation' and to weaken the influence of EBA's Board of Supervisors in the process. However, the Commission failed to deal comprehensively with the issues raised by closer integration when proposing revisions to the voting arrangements. For the EU legislature, closer

74. *Ibid.*
75. *Ibid.*
76. Article 44(1) (as proposed).
77. Article 41(1a) and (2), EBA Regulation.
78. Ferran and Babis, *supra* n. 2, at 280.
79. Article 44(4a), EBA Regulation.
80. *Ibid.*

integration meant that national influences over EBA had to be maintained if not strengthened. As a result, the EU legislature reaffirmed the influence of EBA's Board of Supervisors over EBA. In conclusion, it can be suggested that closer integration among SSM members has brought about a change of thinking: whilst in the past the EU legislature was concerned about putting in place modalities for ensuring that the ESAs could make decisions in the face of divisions between their members (e.g., simple majority voting, no consensus requirement), the more recent changes suggest that the EU legislature now considers that divisions in EBA are an inevitable outcome of closer integration among SSM members and that protecting the interests of Member States, especially the minority interests of NoPS, justifies the potential costs associated with new, more burdensome, decision-making arrangements (double majority system; soft consensus requirement).

– *Failure to differentiate meaningfully between the interests of Member States and the proper functioning of EBA*

It is plain that from an EU point of view, the legislature's concern with Member State interests is not unproblematic. The new decision-making arrangements might well be at the expense of the effective functioning of an EU body (EBA). However for the EU legislature, it was no cause for concern. From its perspective, the point was simply that EBA would no longer function properly if the voice of NoPS were at risk of being marginalised in EBA.[81] Thus: (i) the need to protect the interests of Member States – especially the interests of NoPS – and (ii) the need to ensure the proper functioning of EBA required one and the same solution: that is changing the voting modalities. This thinking is reflected in Recital (14) of the EBA Amending Regulation which states that the amendments to the decision-making arrangements in the Board of Supervisors were necessary in order to 'ensure that the interests of all Member States are adequately taken into account and to allow for the proper functioning of EBA ... '. Yet, this approach, which does not meaningfully differentiate between these two objectives, is open to criticism. In contrast to an intergovernmental 'club' such as the Council, EBA is (normatively speaking) not a forum for defending and promoting Member States' interests.[82] Agencies are generally established for their technical and scientific know-how: '[t]he independence of their technical and/or scientific assessments is ... their real raison d'être' according to the Commission.[83] Hence, while it is plain that the proper functioning of an institution such as the Council must be seen as closely linked to the issue of protecting the interests of Member States, the same is not true for an EU agency such as EBA. To be sure, protecting the interests of Member

81. *See also* the European Parliament's reading of the changes in its resolutions of 11 Mar. 2014, *supra* n. 50 at paragraph BF, noting that '... the changes in the original voting system of EBA ... were a concession to some Member States and made the decision making procedures in the Board of Supervisors more onerous and cumbersome'.
82. Admittedly, in actual fact, decision-making in EBA is more complicated. As noted earlier, national interest considerations are not necessarily absent when competent authorities make decisions in EBA.
83. European Commission, *The Operating Framework for the European Regulatory Agencies*, (COM(2002) 718 final, 11 Dec. 2002) 5.

States – i.e., Member States' interests in ensuring that the voice of their competent authorities cannot systematically be marginalised in EBA – is a legitimate aim given the pivotal role which competent authorities play as decision-makers in EBA. But the question of whether EBA functions properly cannot simply be reduced to the issue of whether the interests of Member States are taken account of. Instead of amalgamating the above objectives, it is suggested that an answer to the question of whether EBA functions properly must be found in EBA's founding regulation. EBA depends for its operation on the rules that are set out therein; it owes its existence to it. Among other things, the regulation defines requirements and rules which EBA must observe when exercising its statutory tasks and in doing so sets constraints on the choices that competent authorities, as voting members of EBA, can make when exercising their decision-making powers. Article 1(5) lays down the basic requirements which EBA must satisfy. Pursuant to this provision, EBA is meant to act independently, objectively and in a non-discriminatory manner when exercising its tasks. Importantly, it must also act 'in the interests of the Union as a whole'. Hence, the question of whether EBA functions properly should be assessed in light of the requirements of Article 1(5). They essentially establish a baseline for assessing acceptable EBA behaviour and in doing so allow determining whether EBA functions properly. Moreover, these requirements are by no means trivial. Principles such as independence, objectivity, or indeed the requirement to act in the EU interest are not unique to EBA. They reflect more deep-rooted expectations about the behaviour of agencies or other EU bodies.[84] Given their importance, they are unlikely to be called into question by the EU legislature.

However, once we accept that the proper functioning of EBA should be determined along the above lines, the legislature's approach to decision-making in EBA suffers from a serious weakness: it is difficult to resolve successfully the conundrum of giving proper consideration to the interests of Member States (especially, the minority interests of NoPS) whilst ensuring that EBA can function properly. This is because the new voting arrangements will complicate, if not obstruct, decision-making in EBA.[85] Moreover, the voting arrangements will become especially problematic once the constellation of NoPS and SSM members becomes highly asymmetrical in the Board of Supervisors.[86] This is because it will give any remaining NoPS a disproportionate say over EBA's activities and indeed ultimately the last remaining NoPS, a veto power.[87]

84. Principles such as independence and objectivity are strongly linked to agency governance. Principles such as to act in the EU's interest are found elsewhere as well: e.g., in the founding regulation of EBA's sister agencies, but also in provisions dealing with other bodies (e.g., Article 309 TFEU on the European Investment Bank).
85. *See also* e.g., Enria, *supra* n. 32, noting in relation to the new voting modalities that '[i]n order to protect national interests, we risk not being able to decide at the European level when this is most needed'; Demarigny, McMahon & Robert, *supra* n. 48 at 33, noting with regard to the double-majority requirement that it 'does not contribute to a more independent and EU interest orientated vote by members'.
86. Recall that the number of NoPS is expected to diminish over time, as Member States join the euro or decide to join the SSM voluntarily.
87. Admittedly, this did not escape the attention of the legislature. *See* the review clause in Article 81a EBA Regulation.

Such a voting system is not in the interest of the Union as a whole and will therefore not contribute to the proper functioning of EBA.

§16.04 ALTERNATIVE APPROACHES

It is useful to begin by summarising our argument so far. The previous section examined the changes which the EU legislature made to the EBA Regulation in order to protect Member States' interests, especially the minority interests of NoPS. I criticised the legislature for failing to differentiate meaningfully between two objectives: taking account of Member States' interests (especially, protecting the minority interests of NoPS against the majority interests of the SSM) *and* ensuring that EBA can function properly. In this context, I submitted that the safeguards which the legislature adopted (i.e., a double-majority system and a 'soft' consensus principle) did not help to draw a proper balance between these two objectives. I concluded by noting that the new decision-making arrangements in EBA (at best) complicated decision-making. I also argued that if the number of NoPS continued to fall, the voting arrangements would increasingly be unfit for purpose. None of this is in the interest of the Union as a whole and as such does not contribute to the proper functioning of EBA. This section evaluates alternative ways for dealing with the above objectives. The aim is to find a better balance between them.

I will consider two types of strategies: fitting EBA's functions to its governance (hence varying its functions) **(A)** or, fitting its governance to its functions (hence varying its governance structure) **(B)**. I will argue that the main weakness of the first strategy is that it is inadequate for addressing relevant issues or that it simply concedes that the ESA model has failed. The main weakness of the second strategy is that it demands significant concessions from Member States which might prove a step too far for NoPS in particular.

[A] Varying EBA's Functions: Fitting Functions to Governance

Under this first approach, the current EBA governance model, which vests overwhelmingly decision-making powers in national authorities, is maintained. However, instead of relying on cumbersome voting arrangements such as the double-majority system, EBA's functions are reassessed following the establishment of the SSM. This re-assessment also extends to the requirements which EBA members ought to satisfy when carrying out these functions. I will start with these requirements, which I will call 'rules of conduct'.

[1] Setting 'Rules of Conduct'?

Establishing 'rules of conduct' that EBA members must respect when taking decisions in EBA might be considered a first line of response to closer integration among SSM members.[88] Rules of conduct are defined here as *ex ante* requirements which target the behaviour of competent authorities. Their purpose is to deal with potential spillovers affecting decision-making within EBA: e.g., the prospect of 'caucusing' among SSM members in EBA which might leave NoPS without an effective voice within EBA. Moreover, by targeting the behaviour of EBA's members (competent authorities), these rules could arguably also improve EBA's functioning. However, it is questionable whether such a strategy would have much to offer. Spillovers that affect decision-making can be difficult to address. Take the example of 'caucusing' among SSM members. There is in itself nothing illegitimate about SSM members sharing common preferences for courses of actions within EBA. If caucusing occurs, it will reflect converging interests among SSM members which is ultimately the consequence of all Member States having agreed to establish the SSM.

There are other problems with rules of conduct. For one thing, they must be properly monitored and enforced. This may well prove problematic. Consider in this context Article 42 of the EBA Regulation which requires (*inter alia*) that voting members of EBA's Board of Supervisors act 'in the sole interest of the Union as a whole'. Recall also that following amendment, the EBA Regulation states that the Board of Supervisors should 'strive for consensus when taking its decisions'.[89] Both provisions target the behaviour of competent authorities; both can be described as rules of conduct. However, as Wymeersch notes, it is hard to see how the requirement to act in the EU's interest could effectively be enforced.[90] The same appears to be true of the requirement to 'strive for consensus'. It is questionable whether the Court of Justice of the European Union would consider itself able to carry out an extensive review of this requirement.[91]

[2] Allowing for Dissenting Views?

The EU legislature might also consider taking more drastic action. For example, it might allow competent authorities, which hold minority views, to adopt dissenting views within EBA: for instance, on draft technical standards.[92] Recall that EBA adopts these draft standards in order to contribute to a single rulebook. Allowing for dissenting views could be an effective means to deal with caucusing among SSM members. It

88. 'Rules of conduct' are highlighted as a strategy for dealing with differentiated integration in CEPR *Flexible Integration – Towards a More Effective and Democratic Europe*, (1995) 71.
89. Article 44(4a).
90. E. Wymeersch, *The European Financial Supervisory Authorities or ESAs*, in E. Wymeersch, K. Hopt & G. Ferrarini (eds), *Financial Regulation and Supervision: a Post-Crisis Analysis*, 232, 298.
91. *See* in this context the Court's approach to enhanced cooperation and especially its 'hands-off' approach to the requirement imposed on the Council to adopt a decision authorizing enhanced cooperation 'as a last resort'. *See* Joined cases C-274/11 and C-295/11 *Kingdom of Spain and Italian Republic v. Council of the European Union* [2013] ECR I-0000, paragraph 53.
92. *See also* the evidence given by K. Lannoo in front of the House of Lords, *European Banking Union: Key Issues and Challenges – Written Evidence*, http://www.parliament.uk/documents/lords-committees/eu-sub-com-a/EuropeanBankingUnion/BankingReformWEFINAL12.12.12.pdf, 147 referring to, but not elaborating on, the idea of 'dissenting opinions'.

might also contribute to resolving bottlenecks and hence allow decision-making to progress in all other matters in the interest of the Union as a whole.

However, here too, there are complications. First of all, dissenting views on draft standards would have no binding force unless the Commission would endorse them together with the draft technical standards to which they relate. Furthermore, it is plain that a system based on dissenting views would threaten to exacerbate differences between NoPS and SSM members. Crucially, such a system would risk undermining the so-called single rulebook, which as an objective, is closely associated with the establishment of the ESFS.[93] A fragmented rulebook would in turn be difficult to reconcile with a basic principle underpinning the SSM: that is, preserving the unity and integrity of the internal market. The latter is a principle that the UK sought to uphold during the negotiations, but which was also endorsed by the European Council in its conclusions[94] and given a legislative basis in Article 1 of Council Regulation No. 1024/2013.[95] Hence, a system based on dissenting views would not be in the interest of the Union as a whole and would therefore not contribute to the proper functioning of EBA.

[3] Abolishing Some of EBA's Functions?

An even more drastic change would be to abolish some of EBA's functions: for example, some or all of EBA's intervention powers. It would arguably be a pragmatic response to closer integration among SSM members, especially if the constellation of NoPS and SSM members becomes highly asymmetrical in EBA's Board of Supervisors. It would recognise that EBA is not a supranational actor and that it faces limitations when using its intervention powers in a post-SSM world where its members are either within or outside the SSM. Take for example the case where EBA would attempt to use its dispute settlement powers in a disagreement between two powerful institutions such as the Bank of England and the ECB: the former being the central bank of possibly the only Member State which might not be part of the SSM in the future; the latter being at the heart of the SSM and as such at the heart of the concerns of its members.[96] The point is that EBA will find it difficult to act independently, objectively and in the interest of the Union as a whole if its intervention powers are targeted at those that decide over them.[97]

Hence, abolishing some or all of EBA's functions might help to resolve this conundrum. However, it would not be an attractive solution, especially as far as EBA's

93. Recital (5) EBA Regulation.
94. European Council 28/29 Jun. 2012, Conclusions, (EUCO 76/12, 29 Jun. 2012), paragraph 4 http://www.consilium.europa.eu/uedocs/cms_data/docs/pressdata/en/ec/131388.pdf; European Council conclusions 18/19 Oct. 2012, *supra* n. 51, paragraph 6.
95. *See also* rec (30), Council Regulation (EU) No. 1024/2013.
96. *See also* Lannoo's evidence in front of the House of Lords (*supra* n. 92), 146 noting that 'EBA's mediation power will no longer have any importance once ECB is in place'.
97. EBA will thus find it difficult to satisfy the expectations of those who *see* it as a future mediator between different blocs of Member States. See e.g., FT 'UK opposes Mario Draghi role at watchdog' (27 Jan. 2014) referring to comments by J De Larosière.

intervention powers are concerned. This is because these powers were among the main innovations introduced under the ESFS. Abandoning them would in many ways leave the ESFS toothless. Meanwhile, the issues which they were meant to address – e.g., a lack of cooperation between competent authorities or a lack of consistency in a crisis situation – and which the establishment of the SSM might come to exacerbate would remain unaddressed.

[B] *Varying EBA's Governance: Fitting Governance to Functions*

In the preceding part, I found fault with all of the contemplated strategies. This section considers a different approach to the post-SSM conundrum. Under this approach, EBA's functions are maintained but its governance model is reassessed. Specifically the proposal is to add a group of appointed members – I will refer to them as trustees – to the Board of Supervisors. Like EBA's Chairperson and Executive Director, these members would be full-time independent professionals.

The idea of rethinking the membership of the ESAs' Boards of Supervisors has gained currency in recent years. For example, ESMA's Securities and Markets Stakeholder Group suggested in relation to the ESAs, that each Supervisory Board should include six independent members which should also be members of the respective ESA Management Boards.[98] Likewise, a report commissioned by the European Parliament concluded that the Supervisory Boards of the ESAs should include a number of full-time members.[99] Following this report, the European Parliament in its March 2014 resolution on the ESFS recommended that the ESA Management Boards should be staffed by professionals who should become voting members of the ESA Supervisory Boards.[100]

Hereinafter, I will examine whether the basic idea of reorganising the Board of Supervisors and relying on appointed members has anything to offer in the context of closer integration among SSM members.[101] I will begin by considering the rationale for relying on independent appointees (or 'trustees') **(1)**, after which I will specify their tasks **(2)**.

[1] Independent Appointees as Trustees

The idea of relying on independent full-time appointed members or 'trustees' is examined here as a way to improve the balance between the two objectives identified earlier: i.e., to take account of the interests of Member States in a post-SSM world (especially, NoPS' interests not to be marginalised by a majority of SSM members in

98. ESMA Securities and Markets Stakeholder Group, *supra* n. 50 at 8.
99. Demarigny, McMahon & Robert, *supra* n. 48 at 117.
100. *See* Annex to the European Parliament resolution of 11 Mar. 2014, *supra* n. 50.
101. I will not discuss the role of EBA's Management Board. Suffice it to say that I have argued in the past that the role of the Management Board should be reconsidered in favour of a stronger Office of Executive Director as a counterweight to the Board of Supervisors. *See* Schammo, *supra* n. 49, at 347 (in relation to ESMA).

EBA) *and* ensuring that EBA can function properly. The notion of 'trustee' is borrowed from Majone who looked at the concept when attempting to explain the thinking behind different forms of delegation.[102] For the present purposes, the analogy with the concept of trust has some usefulness, for it allows highlighting the basic characteristics of appointed members. Translated into the present context, the point is that the new EBA Board Members would be appointed in order to act independently and in the best interest of their sole beneficiary: that is the Union *as a whole*.

Hence, as trustees, appointed members would act independently of national interests. That is not to say that trustees would necessarily be inimical to Member States' interests. For one thing, there is no reason to think that the Union's interests and Member States' interests are necessarily exclusive of each other. Also, by defining the role of trustees in the above manner (i.e., to act independently and solely in the interest of the Union *as a whole*), it is possible to give consideration to both objectives. Thus, by acting independently and in the interest of the Union as a whole, trustees would seek to ensure that EBA functions properly. Moroever, by acting in this manner, they would also, within the limits of their powers, aim to make sure that EBA does not act in the interests of a group of Member States only: SSM members or NoPS for that matter. However, admittedly, trustees are not agents of individual Member State interests and the need to improve the balance of interests might well require a line to be drawn. Thus, whilst protecting NoPS from being systematically marginalised is a legitimate objective, ultimately any measure aimed at achieving this objective must not conflict with the proper functioning of EBA.

To be sure, a strategy that relies on independent trustees might be open to criticism on a number of grounds. Some might argue that I place too much 'trust' in full-time, independent appointees and that they might not necessarily act in the EU's interest. In this context, these critics might also point out that the objective of acting in the 'interest of the Union as a whole' does not allow prescribing in advance a single specific course of action.[103] The critique is beside the point. I use the notion of trustees precisely because appointees must be capable of making independent choices. Moreover, the point about independent full-time appointees is not that they are meant to be perfectly benevolent actors but that in comparison to actors which are embedded in a national context, independent appointees (whose self-interest is moreover closely intertwined with the fate of EBA) are comparatively more likely to identify themselves with EBA's objectives and thus give them due consideration when deciding over different courses of action.

Others might object to the idea of reserving the role of trustees to full-time appointed members only. They might argue that currently EBA's Board of Supervisors is mainly made of heads of independent administrative authorities who are already subject to a statutory duty to act in the interest of the Union as a whole.[104] There is

102. E.g., G. Majone, *Two Logics of Delegation – Agency and Fiduciary Relations in EU Governance*, 2 *European Union Politics* 103 (2001).
103. *See generally* F. Scharpf, *Games Real Actors Play – Actor-Centered Institutionalism in Policy Research* (Westview Press 1997) 65 discussing normative role orientations.
104. Article 42 EBA Regulation.

however a crucial difference between full-time appointed members and heads of national authorities. The 'primary institutional affiliation'[105] of the latter is to institutions at national level: i.e., competent authorities. They are accountable for their actions/inactions to national actors (e.g., national parliaments) who have national interests in mind. Not only is the self-interest of heads of agencies intertwined with the fate of the authorities which they head, but they are also likely to identify themselves strongly with the separate organisational objectives of these agencies. Indeed, one can expect them to have a particularly strong sense of affiliation.[106] On the other hand, full-time, independent appointees would have no affiliation to institutions at Member State level. Their sole affiliation would be to EBA. The assumption is that by insulating them in this manner, they would be better placed to act independently of national interests and in accordance with the requirements of EBA's founding regulation and Article 1(5) in particular.[107]

[2] Tasks of Trustees

So far, I considered the basic rationale for appointing independent 'trustees' to EBA's Board of Supervisors. Ultimately, however, the merit of this approach depends on the powers which trustees are vested with. Hereinafter, I will consider the merit of a two-stage approach. The basic thinking behind this approach is that the issues which the current voting arrangements raise will become more severe as the membership asymmetry between SSM members and NoPS in EBA's Board of Supervisors increases.

– *First stage*

As noted, initially, we assume that the membership asymmetry between NoPS and SSM members in EBA is not too great. The current voting arrangements would

105. I borrow the phrase from M. Egeberg, *Experiments in Supranational Institution-Building: the European Commission as a Laboratory*, 19 J. Eur. Pub. Pol. 939, 939 (2102).

106. *See also* European Parliament resolution of 11 Mar. 2014 *supra* n. 50, noting that 'it has been difficult for national representatives to separate their role of head of a national competent authority and European decision-making challenging their ability to genuinely adhere to the requirement to act independently and objectively in the sole interest of the Union as a whole in accordance with Article 42 of the ESA regulations'.

107. Admittedly, even in the absence of a national institutional affiliation, appointees still have national (Member State) origins. These origins might still be seen as having an impact on the issue of independence. It is worth noting in this context that if appointees are supposed to be judged on the basis of their independence, integrity and competence, there is no reason why they should not be third-country nationals. This is all the more so for a body such as EBA which is not a policy-making body. There is some literature which examines the impact of nationality in the context of the European Commission. Egeberg differentiates between Commission officials and Commissioners (Egeberg, *supra* n. 105). After reviewing various studies, he notes with respect to Commission officials that even though nationality is not unimportant in all respects, 'nationality clearly plays a minor role' (*ibid.* 947). With regard to Commissioners, he concludes that nationality probably matters more, but 'nationality is only one of several parts of their compound role, and not necessarily the part most frequently evoked' (*ibid.*). At any rate, he notes that in comparison to politicians with a 'secondary affiliation to a purely territorially arranged structure' – he points to the European Council – the behaviour of Commissioners is still markedly different (*ibid.*).

therefore remain in place. Competent authorities, especially those originating from NoPS, would continue benefiting from the double-majority voting system. However, in order to improve the balance between the two objectives mentioned earlier, trustees would be appointed to the Board of Supervisors. Initially, they would participate in a non-voting capacity and their tasks within the board would be limited to monitoring and offering opinions on all matters, including on draft standards.[108] This type of independent scrutiny appears necessary in order to address, *inter alia*, the prospect of draft technical standards being watered down in the Board of Supervisors. This is not an unlikely prospect. Recall that Board Members must now 'strive for consensus' when making decisions.

In addition to their role in the Board of Supervisors, trustees would be vested with one major task: to make sure that competent authorities 'play by the rules'. The rationale for this proposal has to do with the consequences of differentiated integration. Specifically, the point is that differentiated integration can give rise to important externalities.[109] In the case of the SSM, these externalities can *a priori* be imposed by SSM members or by NoPS (e.g., trade deflections as a result of differences in the application of common rules). It is therefore in the common interest of all the Member States that the power to deal with such externalities belongs to actors who are different from those that can impose them.[110] Two of EBA's intervention powers are closely related to this task: the power to participate in policing breaches of Union law under Article 17 and the power to settle disagreements under Article 19 of the EBA Regulation. Currently these powers are not administered independently: competent authorities, as voting members of EBA's Board of Supervisors, decide over their use. This state of affairs is unsatisfactory and will be even more so under EBA's new voting arrangements. As noted earlier, the latter will complicate, if not obstruct, decision-making. Hence in the presence of externalities it is in the interest of EBA and Member States that the power to settle disagreements and police breaches of EU law be vested in trustees. Trustees will be better placed to ensure that EBA can act independently and by doing so ensure that all competent authorities play by the rules.[111]

– Second stage

Further changes will be necessary if the constellation of NoPS and SSM members becomes highly asymmetrical in the Board of Supervisors.[112] This is because the

108. Opinions on draft technical standards would obviously be considered by the Commission.
109. *See generally*, *Flexible Integration*, *supra* n. 88.
110. *Ibid.* at 129–130.
111. It is worth noting that the European Parliament in its March 2014 resolution appears similarly to recommend that some intervention powers be removed from the hands of competent authorities. Thus, the Parliament recommended that the Board of Supervisors focus 'on giving strategic guidance to the ESAs work, adopting technical standards, general guidelines and recommendations and decisions on temporary interventions and other decisions are taken by the Management Board with, in certain cases a right for the Board of Supervisors to object to the Management Boards proposal' (European Parliament resolution of 11 Mar. 2014) (*supra* n. 49).
112. The fact that reforms to the voting arrangements might be necessary is also reflected in Article 81a EBA Regulation which provides that if the number of NoPS drops to four, the Commission needs to review the operation of EBA's voting arrangements.

current voting arrangements will increasingly be unfit for purpose in this case: as the number of NoPS continues to diminish, any remaining NoPS (indeed possibly only the UK) will be left with a disproportionate say over EBA's activities. As noted earlier, such a state of affairs is not in the interest of the Union as a whole and will not therefore contribute to the proper functioning of EBA. However, simply abandoning EBA's double-majority system with no further changes is not in the Union's interests either, as it would give the SSM an in-built majority in EBA.

To address this conundrum, it is suggested that the role of trustees be reassessed at this stage. A possible way forward is for them to become more actively involved in decision-making in the Board of Supervisors. Specifically, trustees should be given the right to vote alongside competent authorities. The guiding principle underpinning such a change was repeatedly mentioned: to find a better balance between (i) ensuring that EBA can function properly and (ii) making sure that the interests of Member States are taken into account. Whilst the first objective pleads against maintaining the current voting modalities once the composition of the board is highly asymmetrical, the second objective rules out a wholesale transfer of decision-making powers to trustees. Thus, to improve the balance of interests, it is suggested that the way forward is to maintain a double-majority requirement[113] between SSM members and NoPS, but to provide for trustees to act as a third group of voting members. The crux of this approach is that a decision would no longer necessarily require votes from both NoPS *and* SSM members. Under the proposed voting system, an EBA decision could be adopted with either the support of SSM members *or* NoPS, provided that a decision would also have the unanimous support of trustees. Such a system would arguably be superior for a number of reasons. For one thing, NoPS would continue benefiting from a double-majority requirement (or a similar arrangement which seeks to protect the say of NoPS by differentiating between them and SSM members for voting purposes)[114] in their interactions with SSM members. In particular, the requirement would continue protecting any remaining NoPS from the SSM's in-built majority in EBA. At the same time, however, the new voting system would allow mitigating the effects of an increasingly asymmetrical Board of Supervisors. Specifically, the new modalities would contribute to preventing a very small number of NoPS from having a disproportionate say over EBA's actions. An EBA decision could thus be adopted with the support of SSM members, provided that such a decision would also benefit from the unanimous support of trustees.[115] Moreover, by allowing EBA to adopt a decision in this way, the proposed voting modalities would contribute to resolving any bottlenecks which may come to obstruct decision-making under the current voting system. Trustees would be held to decide unanimously in order to give their decisions greater legitimacy. Moreover, their duty to act in the sole interest of the Union as a whole

113. Or a similar arrangement which seeks to protect the say of NoPS by differentiating between them and SSM members for voting purposes. Recall that the number of NoPS may well fall to one.
114. *See supra* n. 113.
115. Equally, of course, a decision could be adopted if it had the support of NoPS and the unanimous support of trustees.

would rule out any action or decision which would be bluntly in favour of either the SSM or NoPS.

It is important to stress that a more active involvement of trustees would not prevent NoPS and SSM members from reaching common decisions without the support of trustees. Moreover, trustees would have no power to make decisions unilaterally, except as far as dispute settlement and breaches of EU law are concerned. As argued earlier, it is in the interests of all the Member States that these powers be administered independently.

§16.05 CONCLUSION

The aim of this chapter was to consider ways in which EBA could move forward in the wake of the establishment of the SSM. I focused on defining the basic principles of an approach which seeks to rely on independent, full-time, appointed members. Admittedly, this approach would require further elaboration. Questions such as the appointment procedure of trustees, their term of office, and their accountability procedures are just a few questions which I have left open. Moreover, it is plain that implementing this approach would require concessions from Member States which some might be unwilling to make. Political feasibility therefore remains an issue. In this chapter, I have nevertheless resisted taking the path of least (political) resistance. Instead, I have put forward ambitious proposals in an effort to open a necessary debate on the future governance of EBA following the establishment of the SSM. I rejected the idea that EBA's interest is simply the sum of the interests of Member State authorities. From the perspective that I adopted, the point was that EBA's current voting arrangements were unlikely to offer a lasting solution. They will ultimately need to be reassessed if the number of NoPS falls over time.

That said, in order to improve the odds of the proposals, a range of strategies could *a priori* be envisaged. Aspects such as those left open could be subject to negotiation as long as they do not undermine the basic principles outlined above. Safeguards could be put in place or simply re-affirmed. For instance, transferring day-to-day supervisory powers to the ESAs should be ruled out. As far as Article 19 of the EBA Regulation is concerned (dealing with dispute settlement), it is also important to stress that conciliation would continue to be a first line of response. Thus competent authorities would remain free to reach an agreement on their own during an initial conciliation phase. Moreover, as far as Article 17 is concerned (dealing with breaches of EU law), the Commission, as the guardian of the Treaties, would obviously continue playing a pivotal role under this provision. The role of trustees would as a result be limited.

Before drawing this chapter to a close, it is worth considering one final point with respect to the UK. In this chapter, I was interested in the choices which the EU and thus the UK might come to face with regard to EBA if the UK stays in the EU as a NoPS: that is, as a State which is not, and does not intend to be, part of the SSM or the Banking Union for that matter. Hence, I was not primarily interested in assessing the consequences of a *total* exit by the UK of the EU. It is plain that if the UK were to leave the

EU, it would no longer be a NoPS. It would no longer be a voting member of EBA either. That is not to say, however, that the UK would necessarily be shielded from closer integration among SSM members. Externalities, for example, can be imposed on third countries just as they can be imposed on NoPS. In the highly unlikely event of the UK deciding to join the SSM, the UK would no longer be a NoPS either. Under the SSM, it would be treated as a non-euro participating Member State. It would continue to be part of EBA, but it would also be subject to the authority of the ECB in its role as prudential supervisor. In both cases (total exit or participation), the problematic which is discussed above would find a simple resolution, provided of course that all other (non-euro) Member States were ready to join the SSM. There would no longer be a need for complicated voting arrangements in EBA.

Index

EUROPEAN MONOGRAPH SERIES

1. Lammy Betten (ed.), *The Future of European Social Policy,* 1991 (ISBN 90-654-4585-4).
2. Annemarie Loman, Kamiel Mortelmans, Harry H.G. Post & Stewart Watson, *Culture and Common Law: Before and After Maastricht,* 1992 (ISBN 90-654-4638-9).
3. John A.E. Vervaele, *Fraud against the Community: The Need for European Fraud Legislation,* 1994 (ISBN 90-654-4634-6).
4. Philip Raworth, *The Legislative Process in the European Community,* 1993 (ISBN 90-654-4690-7).
5. Jules Stuyck, *Financial and Monetary Integration in the European Economic Community,* 1993 (ISBN 90-654-4718-0).
6. Jules Stuyck & A.J. Vossestein (eds), *State Entrepreneurship, National Monopolies and European Community Law,* 1993 (ISBN 90-654-4773-3).
7. Jules Stuyck & A. Looijestijn-Clearie (eds), *The European Economic Area EC-EFTA,* 1994 (ISBN 90-654-4815-2).
8. Rosita B. Bouterse, *Competition and Integration: What Goals Count?,* 1995 (ISBN 90-654-4816-0).
9. René Barents, *The Agricultural Law of the EC: An Inquiry into the Administrative Law,* 1994 (ISBN 90-654-4867-5).
10. Nicholas Emiliou, *Principles of Proportionality in European Law: A Comparative Study,* 1996 (ISBN 90-411-0866-1).
11. Eivind Smith, *National Parliaments as Cornerstones of European Integration,* 1996 (ISBN 90-411-0898-X).
12. Jan H. Jans, *European Environmental Law,* 1996 (ISBN 90-411-0877-7).
13. Síofra O'Leary, *The Evolving Concept of Community Citizenship: From the Free Movement of Persons to Union Citizenship,* 1997 (ISBN 90-411-0878-5).
14. Laurence W. Gormley (ed.), *Current and Future Perspectives on EC Competition Law,* 1983 (ISBN 90-411-0691-X).
15. Simone White, *Protection of the Financial Interests of the European Communities: The Fight against Fraud and Corruption,* 1998 (ISBN 90-411-9647-1).
16. Morten P. Broberg, *Broberg on the European Commission's Jurisdiction to Scrutinise Mergers*, 4th Edition, 2013 (ISBN 978-90-411-3339-7).
17. Doris Hildebrand, *The Role of Economic Analysis in the EC Competition Rules: The European School,* 2nd Edition, 2002 (ISBN 90-411-1706-7).
18. Christof R.A. Swaak, *European Community Law and the Automobile Industry,* 1999 (ISBN 90-411-1140-9).

19. Dorthe Dahlgaard Dingel, *Public Procurement: A Harmonization of the National Judicial Review of the Application of European Community Law,* 1999 (ISBN 90-411-1161-1).
20. John A.E. Vervaele (ed.), *Compliance and Enforcement of European Community Law,* 1999 (ISBN 90-411-1151-4).
21. Martin Trybus, *European Defence Procurement Law: International and National Procurement Systems as Models for a Liberalized Defence Procurement Market in Europe,* 1999 (ISBN 90-411-1167-0).
22. Helen Staples, *The Legal Status of Third Country Nationals Resident in the European Union,* 1999 (ISBN 90-411-1277-4).
23. Damien Geradin (ed.), *The Liberalization of State Monopolies in the European Union and Beyond,* 1999 (ISBN 90-411-1264-2).
24. Katja Heede, *European Ombudsman: Redress and Control at Union Level,* 2000 (ISBN 90-411-1413-0).
25. Ulf Bernitz & Joakim Nergelius (eds), *General Principles of European Community Law,* 2000 (ISBN 90-411-1402-5).
26. Michaela Drahos, *Convergence of Competition Laws and Policies in the European Community,* 2002 (ISBN 90-411-1562-5).
27. Damien Geradin (ed.), *The Liberalization of Electricity and Natural Gas in the European Union,* 2001 (ISBN 90-411-1560-9).
28. Gisella Gori, *Towards an EU Right to Education,* 2001 (ISBN 90-411-1670-2).
29. Brendan P.G. Smith, *Constitution Building in the European Union,* 2001 (ISBN 90-411-1695-8).
30. Friedl Weiss & Frank Wooldridge, *Free Movement of Persons within the European Community,* 2nd Edition, 2007 (ISBN 978-90-411-2545-3).
31. Ingrid Boccardi, *Europe and Refugees: Towards an EU Asylum Policy,* 2002 (ISBN 90-411-1709-1).
32. John A.E. Vervaele & André Klip (eds), *European Cooperation Between Tax, Customs and Judicial Authorities,* 2001 (ISBN 90-411-1747-4).
33. Wouter P.J. Wils, *The Optimal Enforcement of EC Antitrust Law: Essays in Law and Economics,* 2002 (ISBN 90-411-1757-1).
34. Damien Geradin (ed.), *The Liberalization of Postal Services in the European Union,* 2002 (ISBN 90-411-1780-6).
35. Nick Bernard, *Multilevel Governance in the European Union,* 2002 (ISBN 90-411-1812-8).
36. Jill Wakefield, *Judicial Protection through the Use of Article 288(2) EC,* 2002 (ISBN 90-411-1823-3).
37. Sebastiaan Princen, *EU Regulation and Transatlantic Trade,* 2002 (ISBN 90-411-1871-3).

38. Amaryllis Verhoeven, *The European Union in Search of a Democratic and Constitutional Theory,* 2002 (ISBN 90-411-1872-1).
39. Paul L.C. Torremans, *Cross Border Insolvencies in EU, English and Belgian Law,* 2002 (ISBN 90-411-1888-8).
40. Malcolm Anderson & Joanna Apap (eds), *Police and Justice Cooperation and the New European Borders,* 2002 (ISBN 90-411-1893-4).
41. Christin M. Forstinger, *Takeover Law in EU and USA: A Comparative Analysis,* 2002 (ISBN 90-411-1919-1).
42. Antonio Bavasso, *Communications in EU Antitrust Law: Market Power and Public Interest,* 2003 (ISBN 90-411-1974-4).
43. Fiona G. Wishlade, *Regional State Aid and Competition Policy in the European Union,* 2003 (ISBN 90-411-1975-2).
44. Gareth Davies, *Nationality Discrimination in the European Internal Market,* 2003 (ISBN 90-411-1998-1).
45. René Barents, *The Autonomy of Community Law,* 2003 (ISBN 90-411-2251-6).
46. Gerhard Dannecker & Oswald Jansen (eds), *Competition Law Sanctioning in the European Union,* 2004 (ISBN 90-411-2100-5).
47. Nauta Dutilh (ed.), *Dealing with Dominance: The Experience of National Competition Authorities,* 2004 (ISBN 90-411-2211-7).
48. Stefaan van den Bogaert, *Practical Regulation of the Mobility of Sportsmen in the EU Post Bosman,* 2005 (ISBN 90-411-2327-X).
49. Katalin Judit Cseres, *Competition Law and Consumer Protection,* 2005 (ISBN 90-411-2380-6).
50. Philipp Kiiver, *The National Parliaments in the European Union: A Critical View on EU Constitution Building,* 2006 (ISBN 978-90-411-2452-4).
51. Alexander Turk, *The Concept of Legislation in European Community Law,* 2006 (ISBN 978-90-411-2472-2).
52. Dimitrios Sinaniotis, *The Interim Protection of Individuals before the European and National Courts,* 2006 (ISBN 978-90-411-2498-2).
53. M. Holoubek & D. Damjanovic, M. Traimer (eds), *Regulating Content: The European Regulatory Framework for the Media and Related Creative Sectors,* 2006 (ISBN 978-90-411-2597-2).
54. Anneli Albi & Jacques Ziller (eds), *The European Constitution and National Constitutions: Ratification and Beyond,* 2006 (ISBN 978-90-411-2524-8).
55. Gustavo E. Luengo, *Regulation of Subsidies and State Aids in WTO and EC Law: Conflicts in International Trade Law,* 2007 (ISBN 978-90-411-2547-7).
56. Eniko Horvath, *Mandating Identity: Citizenship, Kinship Laws and Plural Nationality in the European Union,* 2007 (ISBN 978-90-411-2662-7).

57. Rass Holdgaard, *External Relations Law of the European Community: Legal Reasoning and Legal Discourses,* 2007 (ISBN 978-90-411-2604-7).
58. Jill Wakefield, *The Right to Good Administration,* 2007 (ISBN 978-90-411-2697-9).
59. Dimitry Kochenov, *EU Enlargement and the Failure of Conditionality: Pre- accession Conditionality in the Fields of Democracy and the Rule of Law,* 2008 (ISBN 978-90-411-2696-2).
60. Despina Mavromati, *The Law of Payment Services in the EU: The EC Directive on Payment Services in the Internal Market,* 2008 (ISBN 978-90-411-2700-6).
61. Anne Meuwese, *Impact Assessment in EU Lawmaking,* 2008 (ISBN 978-90-411-2720-4).
62. Ulf Bernitz, Joakim Nergelius & Cecilia Cardner (eds), *General Principles of EC Law in a Process of Development,* 2008 (ISBN 978-90-411-2705-1).
63. Johan van de Gronden (ed.), *The EU and WTO Law on Services: Limits to the Realisation of General Interest Policies within the Services Markets?,* 2008 (ISBN 978-90-411-2809-6).
64. Alina Tryfonidou, *Reverse Discrimination in EC Law,* 2009 (ISBN 978-90-411-2751-8).
65. Mikael Berglund, *Cross-Border Enforcement of Claims in the EU: History Present Time and Future,* 2014 (ISBN 978-90-411-4564-2).
66. Theodore Konstadinides, *Division of Powers in European Union Law: The Delimitation of Internal Competence between the EU and the Member States,* 2009 (ISBN 978-90-411-2615-3).
67. Mattias Derlén, *Multilingual Interpretation of European Union Law,* 2009 (ISBN 978-90-411-2853-9).
68. René Barents, *Directory of EU Case Law on the Preliminary Ruling Procedure,* 2009 (ISBN 978-90-411-3150-8).
69. Yan Luo, *Anti-dumping in the WTO, the EU and China: The Rise of Legalization in the Trade Regime and its Consequences,* 2010 (ISBN 978-90-411-3207-9).
70. Patrick Birkinshaw & Mike Varney (eds), *The European Union Legal Order after Lisbon,* 2010 (ISBN 978-90-411-3152-2).
71. Thomas Gr. Papadopoulos, *EU Law and Harmonization of Takeovers in the Internal Market,* 2010 (ISBN 978-90-411-3340-3).
72. Bas van Bockel, *The* Ne Bis In Idem *Principle in EU Law,* 2010 (ISBN 978-90-411-3156-0).
73. Veljko Milutinović, *The 'Right to Damages' under EU Competition Law: From* Courage v. Crehan *to the White Paper and Beyond,* 2010 (ISBN 978-90-411-3235-2).

74. Amandine Garde, *EU Law and Obesity Prevention*, 2010 (ISBN 978-90-411-2706-8).
75. Leonard Besselink, Frans Pennings & Sacha Prechal (eds), *The Eclipse of the Legality Principle in the European Union*, 2011 (ISBN 978-90-411-3262-8).
76. Sacha Garben, *EU Higher Education Law: The Bologna Process and Harmonization by Stealth*, 2011 (ISBN 978-90-411-3365-6).
77. Dimitry Kochenov (ed.), *EU Law of the Overseas: Outermost Regions, Associated Overseas Countries and Territories, Territories Sui Generis*, 2011 (ISBN 978-90-411-3445-5).
78. Pablo Ibáñez Colomo, *European Communications Law and Technological Convergence: Deregulation, Re-regulation and Regulatory Convergence in Television and Telecommunications*, 2012 (ISBN 978-90-411-3829-3).
79. Elise Muir, *EU Regulation of Access to Labour Markets: A Case Study of EU Constraints on Member State Competences*, 2012 (ISBN 978-90-411-3823-1).
80. Tim Corthaut, *EU Ordre Public*, 2012 (ISBN 978-90-411-3232-1).
81. Oana Ştefan, *Soft Law in Court: Competition Law, State Aid and the Court of Justice of the European Union*, 2013 (ISBN 978-90-411-3997-9).
82. Francesco Rossi dal Pozzo, *Citizenship Rights and Freedom of Movement in the European Union*, 2013 (ISBN 978-90-411-4660-1).
83. Jens Hartig Danielsen, *EU Agricultural Law*, 2013 (ISBN 978-90-411-3280-2).
84. Ulf Bernitz, Xavier Groussot & Felix Schulyok (eds), *General Principles of EU Law and European Private Law*, 2013 (ISBN 978-90-411-4683-0).
85. Michelle Everson, Cosimo Monda & Ellen Vos (eds), *European Agencies in between Institutions and Member States*, 2014 (ISBN 978-90-411-2843-0).
86. Stefan Leible & Matthias Lehmann (eds), *European Contract Law and German Law*, 2014 (ISBN 978-90-411-2588-0).
87. Piero Leanza & Ondrej Pridal, *The Right to a Fair Trial: Article 6 of the European Convention on Human Rights*, 2014 (ISBN 978-90-411-4855-1).
88. Patrick J. Birkinshaw, *European Public Law: The Achievement and the Challenge*, 2014 (ISBN 978-90-411-4744-8).
89. George Cumming, *Expert Evidence Deficiencies in the Judgments of the Courts of the European Union and the European Court of Human Rights*, 2014 (ISBN 978-90-411-4123-1).
90. Vesna Rijavec, Tomaž Keresteš & Tjaša Ivanc (eds), *Simplification of Debt Collection in the EU*, 2014 (ISBN 978-90-411-4854-4).
91. Nina Półtorak, *European Union Rights in National Courts*, 2015 (ISBN 978-90-411-5863-5).
92. Kyriaki-Korina Raptopoulou, *EU Law and Healthcare Services: Normative Approaches to Public Health Systems*, 2015 (ISBN 978-90-411-5013-4).
93. Torsten Frank Koschinka & Piero Leanza, *Preliminary Injunctions: Germany, England/Wales, Italy and France*, 2015 (ISBN 978-90-411-5833-8).

94. Vesna Rijavec, Tomaž Keresteš & Tjaša Ivanc (eds), *Dimensions of Evidence in European Civil Procedure*, 2016 (ISBN 978-90-411-6662-3).
95. Stefan Leible (ed.), *General Principles of European Private International Law*, 2016 (ISBN 978-90-411-5955-7).
96. Patrick J. Birkinshaw & Andrea Biondi (eds), *Britain Alone!: The Implications and Consequences of United Kingdom Exit from the EU*, 2016 (ISBN 978-90-411-5832-1).